Re-thinking Dionysius the Areopagite

T0366878

Re-thinking Dionysius the Areopagite

Edited by
Sarah Coakley and Charles M. Stang

WILEY-BLACKWELL

A John Wiley & Sons, Ltd., Publication

Library of Congress Cataloging-in-Publication Data

Re-thinking Dionysius the Areopagite / edited by Sarah Coakley and Charles M. Stang.
    p. cm.—(Directions in modern theology)
  Originally published as: Modern theology, v. 16, issue 1, 2000.
  Includes bibliographical references and index.
  ISBN 978-1-4051-8089-4 (pbk. : alk. paper)
  1. Pseudo-Dionysius, the Areopagite. I. Coakley, Sarah, 1951– II. Stang, Charles M., 1974–
  BR65.D66R4 2009
  230′.14092—dc22

                                                                                                    2008051437

A catalogue record for this book is available from the British Library.

Set in 10/12pt Palatino by SNP Best-set Typesetter Ltd, Hong Kong

01   2009

CONTENTS

INTRODUCTION—RE-THINKING DIONYSIUS THE AREOPAGITE

SARAH COAKLEY

Introduction: Dionysian Studies in Transition

The remarkable recent upsurge of interest in the mysterious early sixth-century[1] author, "Dionysius the Areopagite", has undeniably been a by-product of the post-modern "apophatic rage" (as one scholar has termed the current post-Heideggerian turn in continental philosophy and theology).[2] But "rages" are not always tempered by scholarly caution or philosophical precision; and "apophatic" ones are arguably the more dangerous for being, by definition, hard to define. "Loose talk costs lives"—even "apophatic" talk of the intoxicating Derridean variety.[3] The immediate spur for the production of this new collection of chapters on Dionysius and his interpreters is thus an urgent contemporary one. It aims first to provide a scholarly, but accessible, account of the reasons for the current Dionysian revival, and at least an attempted analysis thereby of the various ways that the *Corpus Dionysiacum* (henceforth *CD*) is being received today.

But therein of course lies the rub. For since the identity of the mysterious author of the *CD*, who styled himself as Paul's first convert in Athens (see Acts 17. 22–34), remains unknown, and his original provenance and context contested, there are no straightforward ways to assess the relation of his intentions to his later interpreters. As Paul Rorem has well put it, "The Pseudo-Dionysian style and message may both perplex and enchant. . . . [But] a perplexed reader is in good company, for the history of Christian doctrine and spirituality teems with commentators and general readers who have found the Areopagite's meaning obscure, and yet his mysterious appeal irresistible".[4]

Sarah Coakley
The Divinity Faculty, The University of Cambridge, West Road, Cambridge, CB3 9BS, UK
norris-hulse@divinity.cam.ac.uk

It is not the undertaking of this volume to provide an introductory account of that "irresistible" *contents* of the CD:[5] its unique blend of neo-Platonism and Christianity; its ontology of an ecstatic intermingling of divine and human "eros"; its vision of a "hierarchical" cosmos conjoining the angelic as well as the human; its ecclesiastical anchoring in acts of liturgical praise; and its alluring invitation to an unspeakable "union" with the divine by means of "mystical contemplation". That initial allure of the text should be allowed its own impact on the reader; there is no substitute for a close engagement with the primary source. But unfortunately we then have to ask forthwith: which "primary source", and for what community was it intended? For these are the immediate, and next, difficulties for the interpreter. And so the second—and necessary—task of this volume is to give some account of the most recent scholarly hypotheses about the CD's origins, intentions, and initial *milieu*. The CD as we now have it may not be in its original textual form; and the reasons for the adoption of the Dionysian *persona* by the author also remain debated. The first chapters in this collection are therefore devoted to discussing these intriguing problems. But when we set out (first) from the contemporary post-modern interest in Dionysius, and then return (second) to the riddle of his original context, we find ourselves inexorably drawn into the fascinating cycles of later interpretation which arose in quest of his meaning. It is thus the third, and indeed most substantial, undertaking of this volume to provide the reader with a kind of systematic road-map for negotiating the rich variety of historic receptions of Dionysius, in both Eastern and Western Christian traditions. If we cannot get at the "historical Dionysius" with any sure confidence, what we can and should do is to provide a discerning account of the different refractions of light shed from his "dark ray".

In the last decade or so there have been a number of important new scholarly advances in this task of tracing the Dionysian *Rezeptionsgeschichte*;[6] and two recent volumes from continental Europe, in particular, have already blazed the trail in providing collections of learned essays on the interpretation of the CD at different times.[7] But for the student, or systematic or philosophical theologian, who may not be *au courant* with these specialized historical studies, there seems to be a pressing need for the sort of English-language survey we provide here. Whilst we have regrettably not been able to commission chapters on all the strands of reception that we might have liked to see treated,[8] we believe that this collection gives a balanced and judicious taste of the major—and often passionately competing—lines of influence in the reception of the CD, both East and West.

It has long been a commonplace to divide the reception of Dionysius (in the West) into the so-called "intellectual" and "affective" readings of the CD: in the former, the "unknowing" "beyond the mind"[9] of which the *Mystical Theology* (MT) speaks, continues to be construed as relating to the intellect (howsoever conceived); in the latter, the will compensates for the intellect's incapacity by means of love. One of the major lessons that should emerge from a close reading of this volume, however, is that this binary taxonomy, whilst still not without some remaining heuristic worth, is far too blunt a tool to account for the historic variety of Dionysian influences down the centuries. Not only is it an essentially Western taxonomy (*eros* and *nous* being closely entwined in the Platonic tradition, and in the Eastern Christian thought following it, in a way different from the Augustinian carving of the mind into *intellectus, voluntas/affectus* [and *memoria*][10]); but the subdivisions *within* the so-called "intellectual" and "affective" interpretations of Dionysius in the West, and the capacity of many authors creatively to combine them, are as noteworthy as is the tendency to a disjunction.[11] Moreover, at least as important as this binary categorization in terms of a key hermeneutical problem in the *MT*, is the prior issue of how the *MT* is variously read in relation to the rest of the *CD* in the first place. It is a notable feature of a certain phase of the medieval reception in the West—although not the earliest one, as Paul Rorem shows[12]—that the *MT* became a supreme focus of interest, thereby sundering it from its liturgical and ecclesiastical moorings in the *Celestial Hierarchy* (*CH*) and the *Ecclesiastical Hierarchy* (*EH*). Such a sundering, as this volume will indicate, has rarely, if at all, been the tendency of Eastern interpretations of the *CD*; and indeed, one of the more intriguing, even perplexing, features of the early Syriac reception (insofar as we can accurately reconstruct it) is precisely its *lack* of interest in the *MT*, *tout court*.[13] As one Orthodox scholar writing on Dionysius has recently and trenchantly argued, then, a theory about the order in which the *CD* was composed, and the importance thereby given to the prioritizing of one text over another, can deliver a vastly different theological impact from some other alternative reading.[14] *Caveat lector*: there are no short cuts in the business of Dionysian reception. Not only must the *CD* as a whole be read,[15] but the varieties of reception here traced cannot be constrained into simple categories of opposition. That is not to say that certain "schools" of interpretation cannot usefully and revealingly be identified, which is what this collection of chapters, taken together, aims to provide.

Thematic Constellations

I should like to take the rest of this short *Introduction* to draw attention to a number of key, constellating, themes which run through the chapters as a whole. While each chapter may profitably be read on its own, there are some significant theses which conjoin the arguments of more than one contributor, and together they might be said to constitute something of the "re-thinking" that this little volume aims to engender. I have chosen here to alert the reader to aspects of the discussion which have potential contemporary *systematic* import, as well as having historical interest *per se*.

The first theme may be discerned by reading the last three chapters in this collection together. It involves a question about the causes and contexts of the

"Dionysian renewal" in the twentieth century in the West, and it provides the immediate backdrop to the current (post-modern) interest in "apophaticism". What the chapters by Gavrilyuk and Jones jointly reveal, first, is that there was already a remarkable Dionysian renewal in the early/mid-twentieth-century in France, a sort of ecumenical "pincer-movement" which produced, on the one hand, a regeneration of Dionysian studies amongst the gifted Jesuits of de Lubac's *ressourcement* movement (von Balthasar, *par excellence*), and almost simultaneously a polemical reinterpretation of Dionysius by Vladimir Lossky, precisely in aid of an *assault* on Western "scholasticism". We cannot read this double development, I would suggest, without an understanding both of the Roman Catholic context of the mandated neo-scholasticism of *Aeterni Patris* (and the subsequent revolt of the followers of *la nouvelle théologie*), and of the underlying philosophical travails of post-Kantianism and of Heidegger's assault on "ontotheology".[16] The return to Dionysius, in other words, could be seen both as a rescue from the rigidity of certain forms of neo-scholastic readings of Thomas Aquinas, and simultaneously as the means of an end-run around Kant's ban on speculative metaphysics. That such a context could produce a new East/West *disjunction* (à la Lossky), rather than an ecumenical meeting of Dionysian minds, is an irony that will not be lost on readers of this volume. Suffice it to say that a shared commitment to "apophaticism" by no means brings a necessary ecclesiastical accord in its wake.

But it is—indirectly—against this particular philosophical and theological backcloth that the later Derridean project of *différance* was then to emerge in France. As Rubenstein so ably demonstrates in this volume, Derrida is as anxious as Dionysius is about what can, and cannot, be properly "said" theologically; and Derrida's own project is often misread if one fails to see that his later *political* interests have something intrinsic to do with the linguistic issue of "unsaying". But there is an enormous "difference" of another sort between original Dionysianism and the Derridean project, which Rubenstein helps us highlight. The former *assumes* revelatory divine authority; the latter baulks at any such. The former enjoins us to "contemplative" practice (ultimately to an *ekstasis* of "union" which courts prior divine activity); the latter resists any such submission, although not without a bold commitment to transgressive political transformation.[17] Read through the lens of "Dionysian reception", then, the contrasting figures of Derrida and Jean-Luc Marion are also seen, here in this volume, in a rather new light.[18] Whereas Derrida stresses "unsaying" to the point of stammering nescience, Marion seems equally haunted by Kant until he realizes that the Dionysian corrective need not *disallow* authority of a particular sort. Although Marion's early work smuggled back such authority rather artlessly in the person of the bishop,[19] and accused even Aquinas of "ontotheology", his more recent writing acknowledges that one may read Thomas quite without such danger once his own Dionysian strand is properly understood.[20]

This reflection on the profound Dionysian influence on contemporary theological developments leads us back to the second thematic issue that this book addresses cumulatively, through various inputs from its contributors. It is this: what are we to make of the original context of the Dionysian corpus, given that there are some reasons for suspecting that our Greek *textus receptus* had had to be massaged towards "orthodox" acceptability?[21] To be sure, this was an "acceptability" in any case right at the edge of what might have been expected as doctrinally normative, even in the late fifth and early sixth century; and Louth's account of the history of Eastern reception up to the time of Gregory Palamas shows how artfully the *CD* became blended into "orthodoxy" by a variety of creative re-readings in the Byzantine period, a story which has no exact counterpart in the West. But the *CD*'s particular blend of (Proclean) neo-Platonism and Christianity was doomed to become freshly controversial, and for different reasons, in a modern era of Protestant German historiography bent on dividing the Christian "kernel" from its Hellenistic "husk";[22] and modern scholarship has thus struggled mightily— and still does—in the agonistic debate about whether Platonism or Christianity finally triumphs in the *CD*.[23] If there is a lesson that now emerges from our joint reconsideration of these issues in this volume, however, it is that any attempt to *disjoin* "Platonic" and "Christian" influences upon the *CD*, or to adjudicate its "orthodoxy" accordingly, is strangely misled—indeed remarkably fruitless, both intellectually and spiritually. For a start, as Stang argues in his input to this volume, such a disjunctive choice fails to register the extent to which the author of the *CD* immerses himself intentionally in the thought-world of Paul, and in the precise context of Acts 17. The modern quest for Dionysian "authenticity" (Platonism *versus* Christianity) has bracketed the possibility of such a natural convergence of the "unknown God" with Pauline Christianity, even as the New Testament itself quite happily entertains it. Further, Perczel's chapter on the earliest Syriac reception of the *CD* (speculative as it must necessarily remain), adds the important insight that the *CD* may well have originated in "Origenistic" circles, and thus will have fallen foul, early on, of the suspicion against Platonist—and especially monastic— élitism already abroad by the very end of the fourth century. The smooth alignment of *agape* and *eros* in Origen, and the convergence of desert wisdom and Platonic speculation in the work of his disciple Evagrius, could indeed have supplied a fertile ground for the cultivation of Dionysian ideas, even though this hypothesis about the context of the production of the *CD* must inevitably remain conjectural. It could also, however, account for an early resistance to the Dionysian writings and reasons for a suspicious critique. In neither case—Origenism nor Evagrian monasticism—was Platonism seen as an enemy to Christianity, of course; on the contrary it was its natural ally and philosophical sustainer.

What follows from this second point is an accompanying reflection on how human selfhood might now be re-construed from a Dionysian perspective, given that—arguably—we need no longer drive the problematic wedge between "Platonic" and "Christian" heritages, nor force a disjunction, "beyond the mind", between intellect and will. It has been pointed out by a number of recent secondary commentators[24] that it might be appropriate to talk of an "apophatic anthropology" in the Dionysian mode, to complement—albeit mysteriously—what is equally "apophatic" about God in his system. This touches on an issue, however, which was part of Lossky's original "Dionysian" polemic against Western scholasticism. Lossky's claim was that the West posited the "apophatic" merely as a *complement* to the "kataphatic", and thus failed to acknowledge the radicality of the Dionysian move beyond that "dialectic" to a moment of "experiential" union in darkness.[25] Rowan Williams has surmised that Lossky himself was probably affected, in the mode of this claim, by a certain Western existentialism regnant at the time of his writing;[26] and new swords have been drawn more recently about whether contact with Dionysian "darkness" should be construed in *any* sense as an "experience".[27] What the contributors to this current volume add, however, to this already-conflicted and somewhat tortuous debate, is the insight that selfhood in Dionysius is essentially *porous*. If Dionysius's insistence on the Pauline dictate about "No longer I" (Gal. 2. 20) is to be taken seriously, then the old nervousness about "experiences" *versus* "philosophical dialectic" seems rather beside the point, and unnecessarily mired in modernistic presumptions about categories of selfhood that are individualistic. Not for the first time, a post-modern access to pre-modern texts has allowed the reconsideration of a lost, transformative, option in anthropology.

The third, and last, major area in which this collection tracks a somewhat new path is in its consideration of some aspects of the early modern reception of Dionysius in the West. In an intriguing and novel chapter, Malysz probes beneath the overt, and renowned, rejection of Dionysian "mystical" thought by Martin Luther, and enquires whether the influence of the CD—mediated doubtless most strongly through the Rhineland mystics—does not actually continue to haunt Luther's whole vision of justification by faith. The *exitus/ reditus* scheme is still ontologically infused within it, Malysz suggests, leaving the main point of difference between Luther and his "mystical" forebear the centrality granted by Luther to a theology of the cross. Yet even there, given a full and close reading of the CD, the disjunction is not as extreme as might be supposed:[28] the relative absence of christological reference in the MT is well compensated for in the other writings (as Golitzin and Perl have also stressed in their recent studies[29]).

Doubtless Malysz's thesis will be controversial. But his chapter stands interestingly alongside a new consideration, by Girón-Negrón, of the huge debt to the Dionysian heritage in both of the great sixteenth-century Carmelites, Teresa of Ávila and John of the Cross. Not for the first time are certain ironic parallelisms between John of the Cross and Luther thus revealed: the forms of "darkness" with which they struggle may not be strictly *egal*, but both inherit the tradition of *noetic* darkness from Dionysius and add their own distinctive variations and nuances.[30] Moreover, Girón-Negrón's astute reading of Teresa allows him completely to forestall the old-established adage that Teresa is merely a "female" mystic, unschooled in the "male" intellectual Dionysianism which John of the Cross champions.[31] Nothing, in a way, could be further from the truth, since Teresa shows in a number of passages in her writings that she is fully cognizant of the main themes of the *MT* as received via such writers as Hugh of Balma, Osuna and Laredo, and mediated to her through her more learned confessors and spiritual advisors. Questions of "mystical theology" and gender are not so easily carved up according to an expected binary as earlier generations of scholarship presumed.

A writer as gnomic, intriguing and profound as Dionysius the Areopagite will never lack new interpreters. If this volume helps readers to re-think his historic significance amidst the crowd of contemporary "apophatic" imitators, it will have served its modest purpose. If in addition it succeeds in drawing readers more deeply into the contemplative *practices* that Dionysius enjoins on his readership, its effect on contemporary discussion will be the more profound.[32]

NOTES

1 For the problem of the dating of the *CD* (for which the available evidence suggests either a late fifth- or early sixth-century placing), see Paul Rorem and J.C. Lamoreaux, *John of Scythopolis and the Dionysian Corpus: Annotating the Areopagite* (Oxford: Clarendon Press, 1998), pp. 9–15, and the chapters by Louth and Perczel, below. Perczel's theory about what might be concluded from the earliest Syriac reception causes him to hypothesize a dating closer to the mid-5th century, but this is not the standard scholarly consensus.

2 The phrase is that of Martin Laird, OSA, " 'Whereof we speak': Gregory of Nyssa, Jean-Luc Marion and the Current Apophatic Rage", *Heythrop Journal* 42 (2001), pp. 1–12. Other commentators have suggested a combination of reasons for the contemporary Western "apophatic turn": see the editorial introduction to Oliver Davies and Denys Turner (eds), *Silence and the Word* (Cambridge: Cambridge University Press, 2002), where it is proposed that there are three main reasons for the renewed fascination with pre-modern forms of "apophaticism": 1. a prevalent cultural religious scepticism; 2. a philosophical engagement with radical "difference"; and 3. a new turn to "experience": the "privatisation and internalisation of religion" (*ibid.*, pp. 1–2).

3 If this remark sounds somewhat jaded, it is merely the result of years of grading student essays written in sometimes unconstrained "post-modernese". The genuineness of the editors' appreciation of Derrida's contribution to contemporary theology will emerge later in this Introduction, as well as in Rubenstein's chapter commissioned for this volume.

4 Colm Luibheid (trans), *Pseudo-Dionysius: The Complete Works* Classics of Western Spirituality (New York, NY: Paulist Press, 1987), p. 3.

5 In the English-language treatments, what we may call the three principals in the recent resurgence of scholarly interest in the *CD* have each produced judicious introductions to the text and context of the corpus: see Andrew Louth, *Denys the Areopagite* (London: G. Chapman, 1989); Paul Rorem, *Pseudo-Dionysius: A Commentary on the Texts and an Introduction to their Influence* (New York and Oxford: Oxford University Press, 1993); and Alexander Golitzin, *Et introibo ad altare dei: The Mystagogy of Dionysius the Areopagite* (Thessalonika: Patriarchikon Idruma Paterikôn Meletôn, 1994). Luibheid's translation for the Classics of Western Spirituality series has made the *CD* available to a wide English reader-

ship. Finally, the two-volume critical edition of the Greek text has superseded the often-troubled Migne text: Beate Regina Suchla (ed), *Corpus Dionysiacum I [DN]* (Berlin: de Gruyter, 1990); Günter Heil and Adolf Martin Ritter (eds), *Corpus Dionysiacum II [CH, EH, MT, Ep.]* (Berlin: de Gruyter, 1991).

6 Apart from the useful introductory essays about Dionysian reception in Luibheid (trans), *Pseudo-Dionysius: The Complete Works* (1987), see, since then, Rorem and Lamoreaux, *John of Scythopolis and the Dionysian Corpus: Annotating the Areopagite* (1998); James McEvoy, *Mystical Theology: The Glosses by Thomas Gallus and the Commentary of Robert Grosseteste on De Mystica Theologia* (Paris: Peeters, 2003); L. Michael Harrington, *A Thirteenth-Century Textbook of Mystical Theology at the University of Paris* (Paris: Peeters, 2004); Paul Rorem, *Eriugena's Commentary on the Dionysian Celestial Hierarchy* (Toronto: Pontifical Institute of Mediaeval Studies, 2005); Isabel de Andia, *Denys L'Aréopagite: Tradition et Métamorphoses* (Paris: J. Vrin, 2006).

7 See Isabel de Andia (ed), *Denys l'Aréopagite et sa postérité en orient et en occident* (Paris: Institute d'études augustiniennes, 1997); T. Boiadjiev, G. Kapriev and A. Speer (eds), *Die Dionysius-Rezeption im Mittelalter* (Turnhout: Brepols, 2000).

8 For instance, the Eastern *Rezeptionsgeschichte* includes the Armenian and the Arabic (and thence Islamic) receptions (see the recent work of S. La Porta and A. Treiger, respectively); or the English/Welsh line of reception moves from *The Cloud of Unknowing* to Augustine Baker and Serenus Cressy (see the work of Justin McCann, OSB, Gerard Sitwell, OSB, Placid Spearritt, OSB); or the full—and complex—story of the assimilation of, or repulsion from, Dionysianism as found in the varieties of Western Thomism from *Aeterni Patris* to the present day (see the recent work of Wayne Hankey).

9 *MT* 1.3 1001A.

10 The important work of John M. Rist, on both sides of this East/West divide, should be noted in this regard: see, *inter alia*, his "A Note on Eros and Agape in Pseudo-Dionysius," *Vigiliae Christianae* 20 (1966), pp. 235–243; and *ibid.*, *Augustine: Ancient Thought Baptized* (Cambridge: Cambridge University Press, 1994), esp. chaps. 3–5.

11 Here Bernard McGinn's survey article ("Love, Knowledge, and Mystical Union in Western Christianity: Twelfth to Sixteenth Centuries", *Church History* 56:1 [1987], pp. 7–24) remains a particularly helpful introduction to this issue in Western mystical theology.

12 In his chapter in this volume and, in greater detail, in his book, *Eriugena's Commentary on the Dionysian Celestial Hierarchy*.

13 See István Perczel's chapter in this volume, especially note 34.

14 See Alexander Golitzin's objections to the order of the Classics of Western Spirituality edition of the *CD* in "Dionysius Areopagita: A Christian Mysticism?" *Pro Ecclesia* XII/2 (2003), pp. 161–212. This may be the point at which also to mention Golitzin's most recent work: a brilliant, collective enterprise by him and some of his former students which endeavours to demonstrate that the *CD*, and indeed the whole of Eastern Christian spirituality, emerges from the "matrix" of Second Temple Judaism. See Basil Lourié and Andrei Orlov (eds), *The Theophaneia School: Jewish Roots of Eastern Christian Mysticism* (Saint-Pétersbourg: Byzantinorossica, 2007), especially Golitzin's two introductory essays: "Theophaneia: Forum on the Jewish Roots of Orthodox Spirituality" (pp. xvii–xx) and "Christian Mysticism Over Two Millenia" (pp. xxi–xxxiii). A critical discussion of this hypothesis unfortunately lies outside the remit of this volume.

15 One must also mention the issue: what constitutes the "whole" *CD*? The author alludes to several other works which have not come down to us. While many scholars regard these "lost" works as fictitious, in this volume Perczel offers a different, and daring, explanation of their fate.

16 For the history of this neo-scholasticism, see Gerald A. McCool, *The Neo-Thomists* (Milwaukee, WI: Marquette University Press, 1994). The touchpoint text for the critique of "ontotheology" is of course Martin Heidegger's "The Onto-theo-logical Constitution of Metaphysics", in idem, *Identity and Difference* (Chicago, IL: University of Chicago Press, 2002), pp. 42–74.

17 On these points of comparison see Mary-Jane Rubenstein, "Unknow Thyself: Apophaticism, Deconstruction, and Theology after Ontotheology", *Modern Theology* 19/3 (July, 2003), pp. 387–417, in addition to her contribution to this volume.

18 Here compare the contributions of Rubenstein and Jones, below.

19 Jean-Luc Marion, *God Without Being: hors-texte* (Chicago, IL: University of Chicago Press, 1991), esp. 153–154, a passage for which Marion received much criticism.
20 For this recantation see Jean-Luc Marion, "Thomas Aquinas and Onto-theo-logy", in Michael Kessler and Christian Shepherd (eds), *Mystics: Presence and Aporia* (Chicago, IL: University of Chicago, 2003), pp. 38–74.
21 As Perczel argues in his chapter in this volume.
22 *À la* Adolf von Harnack.
23 Thankfully, some contemporary scholars are no longer keen, as many of their predecessors were, to fault the author of the *CD* for his obvious debt to late Neoplatonism. For an heroic analysis already along these lines, see Placid Spearritt, OSB, *A Philosophical Enquiry Into Dionysian Mysticism* (PhD thesis: Fribourg, 1968), and more recently: Christian Schäfer, *The Philosophy of Dionysius the Areopagite* (Leiden: E. J. Brill, 2006); Eric Perl, *Theophany: The Neoplatonic Philosophy of Dionysius the Areopagite* (Albany, NY: State University of New York, 2007); Sarah Klitenic Wear and John Dillon, *Dionysius the Areopagite and the Neoplatonist Tradition: Despoiling the Hellenes* (Aldershot: Ashgate, 2007).
24 See Bernard McGinn, *The Growth of Mysticism* (New York, NY: Crossroads, 1994), pp. 105–106; see also Denys Turner, *The Darkness of God: Negativity in Christian Mysticism* (New York and Cambridge: Cambridge University Press, 1995), p. 6.
25 See Vladimir Lossky, *The Mystical Theology of the Eastern Church* (London: J. Clarke, 1957), pp. 215–216 and 229–230, and Rowan Williams's critical discussion of this point in Lossky in *Wrestling with Angels: Conversations in Modern Theology*, edited by Mike Higton (London: S.C.M. Press, 2007), pp. 1–24, esp. p. 12. As Jones discusses in her chapter in this volume, below, von Balthasar also appeals to a "third" moment in Dionysius *beyond* the "kataphatic" and the "apophatic".
26 See again Williams, in *Wrestling with Angels*, pp. 1–12.
27 The claim that "darkness" states in Western "mystical" texts should *not* be read as "experiences" in any sense has been put forcefully by Turner, in *The Darkness of God*. For an astute critical assessment of this thesis, see Bernard McGinn's review of *The Darkness of God* in *The Journal of Religion* 77 (1997), pp. 309–311. It should be noted that Dionysius himself speaks just once of "experience": *DN* 2.9 (648B).
28 Only consider the importance for Dionysius of Gal. 2.20a, just discussed: "I have been *crucified* with Christ; it is no longer I who live, but Christ who lives in me . . ."
29 See Alexander Golitzin, " 'Suddenly, Christ': The Place of Negative Theology in the Mystagogy of Dionysius Areopagites", in Kessler and Shepherd (eds), *Mystics: Presence and Aporia*, pp. 8–37; Eric Perl, "Symbol, Sacrament, and Hierarchy in St. Dionysios the Areopagite", *Greek Orthodox Theological Review* 39 (1994), pp. 311–355.
30 It may not be inappropriate here to add a final note, in aid of a certain semantic hygiene, about the dangers of too easily conflating "apophaticism" of the Dionysian mode and "negative theology", with its variety of Western meanings. It is often presumed that these terms are interchangeable; but strictly speaking this is not so. The term *apophasis* (ἀπόφασις) literally means, in Greek, "saying no", or "saying negatively" (from the verb *apophemi* [ἀπόφημι]), making it ostensibly equivalent to the Latin *via negativa*; but the Greek noun *apophasis* can also convey the meaning of "revelation" (from the verb *apophaino* [ἀποφαίνω]), thus giving it richer overtones than the Latin. Apart from this initial point of comparison between Eastern and Western terms, we also need to distinguish between extra possible evocations of "negative theology"/"negativity" in the Western tradition beyond that of merely "speaking negatively" (or "unsaying"). Here I propose extending a three-fold typology of the meanings of "negative theology" provided by Bernard McGinn in "Three Forms of Negativity in Christian Mysticism", in ed John W. Bowker, *Sciences and Religions: Knowing the Unknowable about God and the Universe* (London: I. B. Taurus, forthcoming), thus: (1) *The theological practice of "unsaying" claims about God*, of negating the positive to express God's uniqueness and transcendence. (This is where "negative theology" *intersects* with Dionysian "apophasis", although it should be noted that the relation of the negating and the positive positing may be different in different writers: some see the two as dialectically related and mutually correcting; others—like Dionysius himself—insist that even the negative pole has to be negated as well); (2) *The ascetic practice of detachment of the human will/desire from false goals* (Eckhart is a prime example for McGinn of this type); (3) *The paradoxical theology of divine absence-as-divine-affliction* (Luther's theology of the cross and John of the

Cross's second "night of spirit" both fit this mould); and (4) (which I add to McGinn's typology) *The distinctively modern expression of radical divine absence* (Simone Weil, at least in some moods, and R. S. Thomas come to mind: here the "dazzling" nature of Dionysius's darkness seems suppressed, and modern atheism, as well as Kant's problematic *noumenal* darkness, hover in the background). It is a disputable question how Derrida's project of "deferral" fits into the above typology. It seems in continuity with (4), but also to involve a new, post-modern, reading of (1), (perpetual "unsaying"), but without the attendant ascetical practices of "contemplation", or the assumption of revelatory ballast, which are found in the pre-modern writings of Dionysius.

31   This well-established binary is unfortunately still imported into some contemporary *feminist* assessments of "mystical" writers: see, e.g., Grace M. Jantzen, *Power, Gender and Christian Mysticism* (Cambridge: Cambridge University Press, 1995).

32   The editors wish to thank Mark Scott for his careful formatting assistance, and Paul Rorem and Andrew Louth for invaluable editorial advice at an early stage in the project.

1

DIONYSIUS, PAUL AND THE SIGNIFICANCE OF THE PSEUDONYM

CHARLES M. STANG

This chapter advances a new approach to the *Corpus Dionysiacum*: I suggest that we interpret the *CD* through the lens of the pseudonym, Dionysius the Areopagite, and the corresponding influence of Paul.[1] We have known since the late nineteenth century, when Hugo Koch and Josef Stiglmayr published their independent demonstrations, that the author of the *CD* was substantially indebted to the writings of the fifth century Neoplatonist Proclus and therefore was no first century disciple of Paul but a late fifth- or early sixth-century pseudepigrapher.[2] Since this revelation, however, very few scholars have regarded the pseudonym and the corresponding influence of Paul as at all relevant, never mind crucial, to a proper understanding of this author and his perplexing corpus.[3] On the whole, scholars have tended to explain away the pseudonym as a convenient means either to win a wider readership for the *CD* or to safeguard the author from censorship and persecution in an age of anxious orthodoxies. Scholars have also tended to pass over the influence of Paul and have instead situated the *CD* against the backdrop of late Neoplatonism or late antique Eastern Christianity.

The influence of Paul by no means displaces the influence of late Neoplatonism or of late antique Eastern Christianity—both of which are, to my mind, undeniable. The pseudonym and the influence of Paul constitute the best interpretive lens for understanding the *CD* not because they push these influences to the margins, but precisely because they help us to organize, appreciate, and bring into better focus these influences. In this chapter, I will limit myself to three general points regarding Paul and the pseudonym. First, I will argue that the entire *CD* needs to be read against the backdrop of Paul's

Charles M. Stang
Harvard Divinity School, Harvard University, 45 Francis Avenue, Cambridge, MA 02138, USA
cstang@hds.harvard.edu

speech to the Areopagus, whereupon it becomes clear that the author writes under the name of Dionysius the Areopagite in order to suggest that, following Paul, he will effect a new rapprochement between the wisdom of pagan Athens and the revelation of God in Christ. Second, I will demonstrate how crucial Paul is for Dionysius' own "apophatic anthropology,"[4] in other words, his view of how the human self that would solicit union with the "unknown God" (Acts 17:23) must also become somehow "unknown." Third, having traced this apophatic anthropology and its attribution to Paul, I will hazard a final hypothesis regarding the significance of the pseudonym: that the practice of pseudonymous writing is itself an ecstatic devotional practice in the service of "unknowing" both God and self. This hypothesis will require a short detour through a modern theory of pseudonymous writing and evidence for that theory from the late antique Christian East.

Paul's Speech to the Areopagus

Apart from writing under the name of Paul's famous convert from Acts 17, Dionysius the Areopagite, the author of the *CD* quotes from and alludes to Paul's life and letters more than he does all the four gospels combined or the whole of the Johannine material.[5] It bears mentioning at the outset, however, that this author, along with most of his late antique peers, believed not only that Paul was the author of *all* the canonical letters (perhaps including Hebrews), but also that his words and deeds were reliably recorded in Acts and even in certain apocryphal texts. In what follows, then, "Paul" refers to this collective literary portrait, not to the modern *historical* Paul, author of only some of the canonical letters. The most obvious and relevant episode from the life of Paul is his missionary speech to the court of the Areopagus in Athens, as recorded in Acts 17, which begins:

> Athenians, I see how extremely religious you are in every way. For as I went through the city and looked carefully at the objects of your worship, I found among them an altar with the inscription, "To an unknown God." What therefore you worship as unknown, this I proclaim to you. (17:22–23).

Paul begins his speech with characteristic irony. The barb of his comment is more keenly felt in the Greek: the word δεισιδαιμονεστέρους can mean exceedingly "superstitious" or "bigoted" just as easily as "pious" or "religious."[6] Paul holds the attention of his audience with flattery so that he can deftly appropriate their own altar "to an unknown god": what had been established as a safety measure honoring foreign gods still unknown to the Hellenistic world is now transformed in Paul's hands into the sign of an incipient faith.[7] Throughout his speech, Paul appeals to this incipient faith by drawing on his audience's own literary, philosophical, and religious lexicon— even citing a famous poet to the effect that "we too are [God's] offspring"

(17:28). Paul concludes with a call to repentance and the promise of a day of judgment "by a man whom [God] has appointed, and of this [judgment] [God] has given assurance to all by raising him from the dead" (17:31). Paul thereby establishes a new order: the new dispensation absorbs and subordinates the incipient faith. The resurrected Christ stands with the unknown god at the zenith of this new order, which baptizes ancient wisdom into a new life.

Acts 17:34 says that "some of [the Athenians] joined [Paul] and became believers, including Dionysius the Areopagite." One would expect that the author who wrote under the name of this Athenian judge would make much of his conversion, and yet nowhere in the *CD* does Dionysius *seem* to mention this event or quote from Paul's rousing speech. Why does he choose to write under the name of a man converted by precisely this speech?

Paul intends in his speech to enfold pagan wisdom into Christian revelation. But whereas Athens is for Paul both a place "full of idols" and home of the altar "to an unknown god," it is for our author the seat of Plato's Academy and its *diadochoi* or "successors," especially Proclus.[8] Might our author be turning to Paul—especially the Paul who speaks to the Areopagus—in order to provide a template for absorbing and subordinating pagan wisdom? Might our author, steeped in Neoplatonism as he surely is, be taking on the role of a convert of Paul precisely to make the point that the riches of Neoplatonism do not constitute "foreign divinities" (17:18) but rather an incipient faith?

This would certainly square with Paul's letter to the Romans, where he laments the fact that although all of the nations once knew God's "eternal power and divine nature" (1:20), all but the Jews fell away from this ancient faith and "became fools" (1:22). The gentiles "exchanged" (1:23, 25) their ancient faith in God for idolatrous images and human foolishness masquerading as wisdom. For our author, this is no less evident in his day than it was in Paul's. Just as for Paul the pagan literary, philosophical and religious traditions of Athens still bear the traces of their knowledge of God—preeminently the inscription to "an unknown god"—so too for our author the Neoplatonic tradition bears traces of that same ancient knowledge of God that was subsequently corrupted by human folly. This is corroborated by Dionysius' "Seventh Letter," in which he calls on Paul to help him rebut a certain sophist, Apollophanes, who has charged him with "patricide" for "making unholy use of things Greek to attack the Greeks."[9] Dionysius is said to be guilty of betraying his paternal tradition, subordinating Greek wisdom to his faith in Christ. Dionysius responds that it is the Greeks who are guilty, for it is they "who make unholy use of godly things to attack God."[10] God has given the Greeks "wisdom" and "divine reverence" which they have squandered. This gift was none other than the "knowledge of beings" or "philosophy."[11] Had they remained faithful to the true philosophy revealed to them by God in ancient times, "true philosophers [would have been] uplifted to him who is the Cause not only of all beings but also of the very knowledge which one can have of these beings."[12]

The pseudonym suggests that the entire *CD* needs to be understood against the backdrop of Paul's speech to the Areopagus, that is, as an attempt to enfold pagan wisdom into the new order and dispensation in Christ.[13] On this reading, the fact that the *CD* is shot through with Plotinus, Iamblichus, and Proclus should not be taken as evidence of corruption by alien wisdom, but rather as an effort to show that much within this philosophical tradition still bears the seal of God. If this is the case, Dionysius can sample widely and deeply from this tradition, as long as Christian revelation remedies the human folly that prevents this tradition from being truly uplifting.

By way of the pseudonym and the shadow of Paul, therefore, the author actually tells us how to interpret his own substantial debt to Neoplatonism. One result of this *interpretatio sui* is that many of the features that have struck modern scholars as manifestly Neoplatonic and therefore as obvious evidence of his true allegiance to pagan philosophy are, on this construal, better understood as features of the original philosophy revealed by God and marshaled by Paul to bring the wayward Greeks back into the fold. For example, the simultaneous divine operations of procession, rest and return (πρόοδος, μονή, and ἐπιστροφή), which form the backbone of Neoplatonic metaphysics, are, according to our author, technical terms derived from Paul, who says of God in his letter to the Romans (11:36) that "from him and through him and to him are all things" (ὅτι ἐξ αὐτοῦ καὶ δι' αὐτοῦ καὶ εἰς αὐτὸν τὰ πάντα).[14]

So too with Dionysius' widespread appeal to "theurgy" (θεουργία, a contraction of ἔργον θεοῦ = the "work of God"): modern scholars have either cited his appeal to theurgy as evidence of his true identity as a Neoplatonist or desperately sought to distance him from theurgy so as to safeguard his Christian identity.[15] The practice of theurgy or "god-work" became popular in the second century after the widespread circulation of a collection of oracular sayings, *The Chaldean Oracles*, which were composed—or channeled—by a father and son team, both named Julian.[16] According to the oracles, the heavens are teeming with gods and spirits. Between this busy heavenly realm and our own there exists a secret "sympathy," which, when understood, permits the theurgist, or "god-worker," to use the earthly to manipulate the heavenly, that is, to use special elements and words in rituals in order to compel the gods to do our bidding. In the late third and early fourth century, the philosopher Iamblichus, a student of Plotinus and rival of Porphyry, offered a philosophical defense of the practice of theurgy. His *On the Mysteries*, however, shifts the understanding of what is at work in theurgy and how.[17] For Iamblichus, we do not compel the gods to do our bidding, but rather we step into the stream of divine work and are thereby deified.

Dionysius borrows the language of "theurgy" directly from Iamblichus, and means by it much the same as the pagan philosopher did, namely that we step into the saving work of God and are thereby deified.[18] The difference between the two, of course, comes down to what each believes the preeminent work of God is and how we access it: for Iamblichus, we access the restorative work of the gods through ancient, revealed rites that we must recover from obscurity and now practice; for Dionysius, the work of God is none other than the Incarnate, crucified and resurrected Christ, to whom we have access through the liturgical and sacramental life of the Church, and who appears to us in baptism as light and love. Perhaps surprisingly, Dionysius can credit this understanding of theurgy to Paul, for while most of Paul's use of the word "work" (ἔργον) is reserved for the distinction between faith and works, he does mention the "work of God" in Rom 14:20. This single phrase allows Dionysius to infer that Paul was a theurgist, and was reminding the Greeks of the true meaning of theurgy, which they had no doubt forgotten or corrupted. For Dionysius, traces of the true meaning of theurgy are to be found in Iamblichus, but he has mistaken ancient pagan rituals for the liturgy of the Church, the work of the gods for the true work of God, who is none other than Christ.

Finally, it seems fairly obvious that Dionysius' insistence that God is ultimately "unknown" or "unknowable" is a self-conscious allusion to Paul's appropriation of the Athenians' altar "to an unknown God"—indeed the adjective "unknown" (ἀγνώστος) suffers a sort of lexical explosion in the CD. For instance, Dionysius insists that there exists a rarefied state of "unknowing" (ἀγνωσία)—not ignorance, but a sort of hyper-knowledge. We suffer this "unknowing" when we solicit the descent of the unknown God through contemplative practice. This notion of "unknowing" also comes from Dionysius' creative rereading of Paul, although you would not know it from the NRSV translation of Paul's crucial line from Acts 17:23, ὃ οὖν ἀγνοοῦντες εὐσεβεῖτε, τοῦτο ἐγὼ καταγγέλω ὑμῖν. The NRSV reads, "What therefore you worship as unknown, this I proclaim to you." A better translation, and one that you will find in many commentaries, reads, "What therefore you unknowingly [or ignorantly] worship, this I proclaim to you."[19] The thrust here is that Paul's proclamation of the risen Christ will dispel the ignorance with which the Athenians worship God. And yet the circumstantial participle ἀγνοοῦντες—which I have rendered adverbially as "unknowingly"—has tremendous elasticity in Greek. Dionysius can read this same line and legitimately understand it to mean, "What therefore you worship *through [your] unknowing*, this I proclaim to you"—or, to invert the order, "I proclaim to you that which you worship *through [your] unknowing*." Dionysius, therefore, creatively rereads this line from Paul's speech such that the apostle emerges as the authoritative witness to this peculiar hyper-knowledge of the divine, this rarefied ἀγνωσία or "unknowing."[20]

Paul and the "Apophatic Anthropology" of the CD[21]

Dionysius insists that the self that suffers this "unknowing," who is united to the unknown God, must also become unknown, that is, suffer "an absolute abandonment of [self] and everything, shedding all and freed from all."[22] Thus his apophatic theology assumes what I am calling an "apophatic anthropology," wherein the self is progressively unsaid, or, to use another favorite term of this author, "cleared away" (from ἀφαιρέω).[23] The way of negation is then a practice of transforming that self so that it can best solicit union with the unknown God. Apophasis is, for Dionysius, a sort of asceticism, an exercise of freeing the self as much as God from the names and categories that prevent it from being divine.[24] This may seem an obvious point, namely that the effort to suffer union with the unknown God will necessarily transform the human subject, conform him or her to the God beyond being. And yet modern scholars have been less interested in the theological anthropology implicit in this ascetic endeavor, often instead treating the affirmation and negation of the divine names as a sort of scholastic discourse that aims either to police speech about God or to solve problems that arise when creatures speak of the uncreated. To the contrary, our author draws attention to such insoluble problems precisely so that his readers might make *use* of the problems inherent in language in their efforts to invite the divine to break through language. According to Dionysius, then, making appropriate use of language—specifically the divine names—will change the user, and that change, that transformation of the contemplative, ascetic subject is what I am calling the "apophatic anthropology" of Dionysius.

The two most relevant places to turn for Dionysius' "apophatic anthropology" are Chapter 1 of the *Mystical Theology* and Chapter 4 of the *Divine Names*. Immediately following the opening prayer addressed to the "Trinity beyond being, being God, beyond good," Dionysius offers Timothy the following advice:

> Timothy, my friend, my advice to you as you look for a sight of the mysterious things, is to leave behind [ἀπόλειπε] you everything perceived and understood, everything perceptible and understandable, all that is not and all that is, and, with your understanding laid aside [ἀγνώστως, "unknowingly"], to strive upward as much as you can toward union with him who is beyond all being and knowledge. By an undivided and absolute abandonment [ἐκστάσει] of yourself and everything, shedding all and freed from all [πάντα ἀφελὼν καὶ ἐκ πάντων ἀπολυθείς], you will be uplifted to the ray of the divine shadow which is above everything that is.[25]

The effort to solicit union with the unknown God is here figured as a liturgical event: the "sight of the mysterious things (τὰ μυστικὰ)" is a clear reference to the mysteries of the Eucharist.[26] This liturgical event, however, asks quite a bit from the worshipper, namely that he or she "leave behind" his or her perception and intellection, as well as the distinction between being and non-being—"shedding all and freed from all." We divest ourselves of our dearest faculties and categories in hopes of "being uplifted to the ray of the divine shadow." But this ascent to the luminous, divine darkness also requires that we stand outside ourselves, that we suffer ecstasy (τῇ . . . ἑαυτοῦ . . . ἐκστάσει).

The model for this liturgical ascent is none other than "the blessed Moses," who leaves all his impure fellows behind as he scales Sinai. At the summit, alone, Moses

> . . . plunges into the truly mysterious darkness of unknowing. Here, renouncing all that the mind may conceive, wrapped entirely in the intangible and the invisible, he belongs completely to him who is beyond everything. Here, being neither oneself nor someone else [οὔτε ἑαυτοῦ οὔτε ἑτέρου], one is supremely united to the completely unknown by an inactivity of all knowledge, and knows beyond the mind by knowing nothing.[27]

This description of Moses in the "cloud of unknowing" repeats the advice Dionysius gave Timothy in the opening of the *MT*. Here, an effort of radical renunciation prompts the self to suffer ecstasy, to stand outside itself: "being neither oneself nor someone else." This ecstasy invites someone else, namely he "who is beyond everything," to take possession of this split self, and to unite itself—"the completely unknown"—to this ecstatic self. From the vantage of this self who is no longer entirely itself, union hinges on the "cessation of all knowledge," or rather, "knowing nothing."

In Chapter 4 of the *Divine Names*, Dionysius offers a much fuller account of apophatic anthropology, and one in which the exemplar is not Moses, but the apostle Paul. He describes there how God's love for the world is best understood as ἔρως: God creates because God is "beguiled by goodness, by love [ἀγαθότητι], and by yearning [ἔρωτι] and is enticed away from his transcendent dwelling place and comes to abide within all things, and he does so by virtue of his supernatural and ecstatic capacity to remain, nevertheless, within himself."[28] Dionysius acknowledges that someone might think that this elision between *agape* and *eros* "runs counter to scripture," since 1 John 4:16 calls God *agape*, not *eros*.[29] Be that as it may, he goes on to insist that just as the ecstatic God once stood outside itself to create, so now that same God graciously stands outside itself calling us to answer with our own ecstatic yearning. Ecstasy must answer ecstasy, according to Dionysius.[30] Thus the self that would suffer union with God must learn how to yearn to such an extent that it suffers ecstasy, becomes literally beside itself for God.

The model for this pursuit is none other than "the great Paul," who was, according to Dionysius,

> . . . swept along by his yearning for God and seized of its ecstatic power, [and] had this inspired word to say: "It is no longer I who live, but Christ who lives in me." Paul was truly a lover and, as he says, he was beside himself for God, possessing not his own life but the life of the One for who he yearned, as exceptionally beloved.[31]

According to Dionysius, Paul so yearned for God that he was carried outside of himself. Paul, of course, never appeals to *eros* in his letters. But Dionysius quotes 2 Corinthians 5:13, where Paul famously asserts: "if we are beside ourselves [ἐξέστημεν]—it is for God; if we are in our right mind, it is for you [Corinthians]." Because, for Dionysius, *eros* and *agape* have the same meaning and because *eros* delivers ecstasy, he infers that Paul must "truly [have been] a lover (ἐραστής)." Paul emerges then as the model of the ecstatic lover of the divine beloved. And lest we suppose that this single mention of ecstasy was an isolated indiscretion for the apostle, Dionysius also cites Gal 2:20: "It is no longer I who live, but Christ who lives in me."[32] Paul is "possessed" by his yearning and "participates" in its ecstatic power, such that he comes to live the life of his beloved. By Paul's own confession, then, he has been ecstatically displaced to the point where, to paraphrase the *MT*, he is "neither [entirely] himself nor [entirely] someone else." For while Paul says "no longer I," he also says "Christ . . . lives *in me*." In short, Dionysius attributes this apophatic anthropology to the apostle, whom he regards as having yearned for God so zealously that he stretched himself to the point of splitting and thereby opened himself to the indwelling of Christ.

The Significance of the Pseudonym—A Hypothesis

We have already charted two senses of the pseudonym. First and foremost, the author of the *CD* writes under the name of Dionysius the Areopagite in order to suggest that, following Paul in his speech to the court of the Areopagus, he will effect a new rapprochement between the incipient faith of pagan Athens and the supervening revelation of God in Christ. Second, the author of the *CD* attributes his own apophatic anthropology to the apostle, whom he figures as the exemplary ecstatic lover of the divine beloved, whose love splits him down the middle and thereby opens him to Christ. I wish to offer a third and final interpretation of the sense and significance of the pseudonym. What drives my hypothesis is a suspicion that the very practice of writing under a pseudonym may be integral to the ascetic and mystical enterprise described in the *CD*, the unknowing of both God and self.

In order to lay the groundwork for this final hypothesis, we must broaden our inquiry into pseudonymity. There is a wealth of pseudonymous writing (or pseudepigrapha) from the ancient and late ancient worlds—Jewish, Christian, and other (notably Pythagorean). By and large, modern scholarship has focused on the pseudepigrapha from the biblical periods, especially those pseudonymous writings that are included in the Jewish and Christian canons. The practice of pseudonymous writing, however, continued well into the late antique period. Although the *CD* is one of the more remarkable instances of pseudonymous writing from late antiquity, scholars have by and large neglected to investigate this prominent literary conceit. To redress this oversight, I have looked to scholarship on earlier pseudepigraphical traditions in order to see whether it provides models for understanding the pseudonymity of the *CD*.

I will highlight one: D. S. Russell, in *The Method and Message of Jewish Apocalyptic: 200 BC–100 AD*,[33] ventures an explanation for the pseudonymous quality of Jewish apocalyptic writing. Apart from the obvious mercenary motives many ancient writers may have had when writing under false names, he argues that there are other motives at play in the Jewish apocalyptic tradition, where authors write under the names of ancient visionary authorities (such as Enoch). In this pseudonymous tradition, he argues, the authors believe that the distance between past and present can be collapsed such that the ancient authorities come to inhabit them and speak in their stead. On this construal, the pseudonymous author would come to understand himself as an "extension" of the personality of the ancient authority.[34] In other words, historical time would collapse into "contemporaneity" and the voice of the ancient authority and the present author would merge in the very act of writing.[35]

But how might Russell's theory square with the understanding of time and writing in the late antique Christian East? In the imagination of late antique Christians, the apostolic period was not past; the present was always porous to the past. A host of scholars have remarked on this peculiar understanding of time and its manifestations, chiefly the manner in which the apostolic saints are understood as traversing time, haunting the late antique world, working miracles for edification.[36] The scholarly consensus here is that in the late antique Christian imagination the distance between the historical past and present can be collapsed or "telescoped," such that the apostolic (and sub-apostolic) age and the contemporary world may be fully present to one another.[37] This presence, however, has to be achieved, and so there developed a resurgence of devotion to the apostolic period, an intense effort to study the literary remains from that period, on the conviction that these texts and traditions contain within them the means to effect this all-important encounter with that past.

In his recent book, *Writing and Holiness*,[38] Derek Kreuger argues that the late antique Christian East witnesses the emergence of a new understanding of the practice of writing. In Krueger's words, writing was "not so much a proprietary claim over literary output as a performative act, a bodily practice . . . [that was] figured as an extension of the authors' virtuous ascetic practice . . . [and] . . . exemplified emerging Christian practices of asceticism, devotion, pilgrimage, prayer, oblation, liturgy, and sacrifice."[39] Krueger argues that for these late antique authors writing becomes a form of devotion itself, whose aim—as is the case with any *askesis*—is a "reconstituted self."[40]

Take, for instance, the *Life and Miracles of Saint Thekla* [*LM*], a fifth century anonymous collection of stories regarding Thekla—an early disciple of Paul—that narrates how, after a life devoted to preaching and teaching the gospel, she descended into the earth, still living, and now continues to wander her native Selefkia working miracles. Scott Fitzgerald Johnson has recently produced a study of this collection and highlights an episode that demands our attention.[41] In the thirty-first miracle in the collection, Thekla appears to the anonymous author in a waking vision, just at the moment when he is trying to write down another one of her miracles.[42] She takes the notebook from his hand and recites back to him what he has written, indicating with a smile and a glance that she is pleased. The visitation from the saint and her intervention in his writing prompt in the author both fear and a renewed desire to write, and he commits himself to the task in which he had been flagging. With her encouragement and the promise of such visitations, the very practice of writing her life and miracles becomes part of the author's devotion to the living saint. In other words, the practice of writing the *LM* is for our author a devotional exercise with which he summons Thekla, and thereby refashions himself as a disciple of a living saint.

Hagiography is not the only genre in which we witness both this peculiar understanding of time coupled with a practice of writing that aims to collapse historical time. In her study of John Chrysostom's homilies on Paul, Margaret M. Mitchell shows how Chrysostom, in his reading, writing and preaching, worked to summon Paul into the present both for himself, privately, and for his audience, publicly.[43] If Cyril Mango is right that late antique Christians understood the saints as the "living dead," then Mitchell has warrant to characterize Chrysostom's homiletics as an "inherently necromantic art."[44] Of course Paul was not really dead at all: Chrysostom goes so far as to say that Paul's decayed limbs in Rome are in fact more alive now than they were when he was on earth.[45] Paul may be absent, but by reading, writing and preaching we may summon him. Echoing the consensus examined above regarding the peculiar understanding of time in the late antique Christian East, Mitchell characterizes Chrysostom's efforts to summon the presence of Paul as a form of "time-travel": "not his own trek back in time but Paul's movement forward . . . creates [Chrysostom's] encounter with the Paul he knows."[46] Just as the anonymous author of the *LM* does with Thekla, Chrysostom also asks that Paul travel forward in time so that he and his audience might bask in his presence. Witnesses claim to have seen Paul leaning over John's shoulder as he wrote, whispering in his ear.[47] And sometimes Paul would appear without warning and seize control of the moment: John speaks of how Paul would "take possession" of him as he wrote, such that their voices would merge.[48] In a pair of homilies on Ephesians he confesses that he "cannot bear to resist" such a possession, that he could no better stop speaking about Paul as a drunk could stop drinking.[49] And he even invites his audience into his own possession: "What is happening to me? I wish to be silent, but I am not able."[50]

I suggest that we interpret the *CD* in light of both Russell's theory of pseudonymity and the peculiar understanding of time and writing in the late antique Christian East. In other words, we should understand this pseudonymous endeavor as resting on the conviction that historical time can be collapsed such that the apostolic past and the present enjoy "contemporane-ity," and that writing is a means by which to collapse that distance, such that the author in the present comes to understand himself as an "extension" of the personality of the ancient authority. One difference between the two cases briefly treated here and the *CD* is that both Chrysostom and the author of the *LM* summon their saints into the present, that is, they ask Paul and Thekla to travel forward in time; whereas the author of the *CD*, on the other hand, transports himself into the past, that is, he asks the apostles and their dis-ciples to receive him into their communion. Another difference is that while Chrysostom invites *Paul* to take up residence in himself, the anonymous author of the *LM* and the pseudonymous author of the *CD* invite not Paul but one of his disciples: Thekla and Dionysius the Areopagite respectively. But these differences are relatively superficial, for if the present and the past are porous and can be collapsed, then both directions of time travel are warranted. And if Paul has Christ in him (Gal 2:20), and admonishes his disciples to "be imitators of me, just as I am of Christ" (Gal 4:16), then when Chrysostom invites Paul to inhabit his own self, or when the author of the *LM* becomes a disciple of Thekla, or when our author makes of himself an extension of Dionysius the Areopagite, what they are all ultimately soliciting is the indwelling of Christ himself. In other words, the fact that Christ broke into the "I" of Paul guarantees the chain of *imitatio Christi*, guarantees that what we are imitating in Paul or his disciples is in fact Christ himself. The result is what D. S. Russell would call a "corporate personality," a sort of chain of possession at the end of which is Christ.

The author of the *CD* literally assumes the identity of Dionysius the Areopagite. He addresses his works to other apostles and disciples; he trans-ports himself into this apostolic community, to the point that he is present at the Dormition of Mary;[51] he counsels John the Evangelist in exile on Patmos.[52] And yet all the while the author is also in the fifth century: quoting—sometimes at great length and with little cover—from Proclus' works,[53] treading dangerously close to contemporary Christological controversies,[54] describing the ceremonials of Byzantine churches rather than the humbler home churches of the New Testament. The author is, in words borrowed from his description of Moses, "neither himself nor someone else," neither the contemplative from Syria who scholars assume him to be nor the Athenian judge under whose name he writes. Like the ecstatic God with whom he seeks to suffer union, as a writer he simultaneously remains where he is and stretches outside himself.

Although the *MT* is but one (and indeed, the shortest) treatise in the *CD*, one should understand the entire *CD* as a single, coherent "mystical theology," the aim of which is "unknowing." To "unknow" the unknown God, one must contravene the Greek sages and "unknow oneself."[55] The *CD* spells out two inseparable paths of unknowing God and self. The first is through the hierar-chies, specifically "our hierarchy," the Church, wherein we assent in baptism to be ecstatically displaced by the light and love of Christ, consenting to have that light and love move through us and rest in us—this Dionysius calls "cooperation" (συνεργία) with the work of God (θεουργία). Within the ecclesiastical hierarchy that mediates this light and love, Dionysius offers a further contemplative practice: the perpetual saying and unsaying of the divine names of scripture and the symbols of the liturgy, a prayerful meditation that follows divine procession and return, transcendence and immanence, all with the hope of soliciting the descent of an "unknowing union" with the unknown God. To conduct the divine light, to become a "co-worker with God" (συνεργὸς θεοῦ)—this is the path to "unknowing" that the *CH* and *EH* commend. To say (κατάφασις) and unsay (απόφασις) the divine names, in perpetuity, in order to solicit union with the unknown God—this is the path to "unknowing" that the *DN* and *MT* commend (often called "apophatic" although it is no less "kataphatic"). The two paths form a sort of double helix that together govern our loving movements in pursuit of the God who was first moved by love for us. Lest the reader think that I am driving a wedge between the "hierarchies" (*CH* and *EH*) and the "theology" (*DN* and *MT*) of the *CD*,[56] I wish to insist that the entire enterprise, the double helix, is ineluctably hierarchical and theological: the hierarchies are no less theological than the theology, and the theology no less hierarchical than the hierarchies. What binds the two together to form a double helix is the logic of ecstasy, whereby we are called to contemplate the visible to the point that it leads us upward (ἀναγογία) to the invisible, yearn for the divine beloved to the point that we split, stretch language to the breaking point, and thereby render ourselves open to the indwelling of God as Christ, with Paul in the lead.

I have come then to my final hypothesis regarding the sense and significance of the pseudonym. I suggest that the very practice of writing pseudonymously is itself a third path of unknowing God and self. I submit that for Dionysius writing under a pseudonym is no mere ploy for sub-apostolic authority and thereby a wider readership, but is in fact itself an ecstatic devotional practice in the service of an apophatic anthropology, and thereby of soliciting deifying union with the unknown God. Pseudonymous writing renders the self "neither [entirely] oneself nor [entirely] someone else," that is to say, somehow both oneself and someone else. In the case of the author of the *CD*, he is both himself, an anonymous writer from the late fifth or early sixth century, and also someone else, Dionysius the Areopagite. Pseudonymous writing is for our author a practice that stretches the self to the point that it splits, renders the self unsaid, that is, unseated from its knowing center, unknown to itself and so better placed, because displaced, to suffer union with "him who has made the shadows his hiding place."[57] But this is no arbitrary doubling; the other with whom the self must now share its space is a disciple of Paul, Dionysius the Areopagite, a disciple who follows Paul's mimetic imperative: "be imitators of me, just as I am of Christ" (Gal. 4:16). And Paul, by his own admission in Gal. 2:20, is already doubled: he is both Paul *and* Christ. Only through the apophasis of the single self—what Paul calls the "I"—only through unknowing oneself, can one clear (ἀφαιρέω) space in the self for the indwelling of the other. In short, our pseudonymous author offers an account of what it is to be properly human in relation to God—namely, no longer an "I," neither yourself nor someone else, because you are now both yourself *and* Christ. And, *in the very telling*, he performs an exercise aiming to render his own self cleft open, split, doubled and thereby deified.

NOTES

1 This chapter is a distillation of my dissertation, entitled "'No Longer I': Dionysius the Areopagite, Paul and the Apophasis of the Self" (ThD diss., Harvard Divinity School, 2008). I would like to thank those who have read previous drafts of this chapter, including Sarah Coakley, Benjamin Dunning, Amy Hollywood, Sarabinh Levy-Brightman, Paul Rorem, and Mark Scott.

2 Hugo Koch, "Proklos als Quelle des Pseudo-Dionysius Areopagita in der Lehre vom Bösen", *Philologus*, 54 (1895), pp. 438–454; Josef Stiglmayr, "Der Neuplatoniker Proklos als Vorlage des sogenannten Dionysius Areopagita in der Lehre von Übel", *Historisches Jahrbuch*, 16 (1895), pp. 253–273 and 721–748.

3 There are some important exceptions to this trend. Alexander Golitzin argues that the author chose a sub-apostolic pseudonym in order to rebut wayward monastic movements in fifth-century Syria, who traced their own roots back to apostolic times through the apocryphal Thomas literature (Alexander Golitzin, "Dionysius Areopagita: A Christian Mysticism?" *Pro Ecclesia*, 12/2 [2003], pp. 161–212). Andrew Louth argues that the pseudonym situates the author squarely in Athens and thereby suggests a synthesis between Christian revelation and pagan philosophy (Andrew Louth, *Denys the Areopagite* [London: G. Chapman, 1989], especially pp. 10–11). Following Louth, Christian Schäfer argues that the author of the *CD* takes on the name of Paul's convert from Athens precisely in order to "baptize" pagan wisdom into a new life in Christ (Christian Schäfer, *The Philosophy of Dionysius the Areopagite* [Leiden: E. J. Brill, 2006], especially pp. 7, 170–171). Most intriguing, if cryptic, is von Balthasar's suggestion that the pseudonymous enterprise is based on a "mystical relationship" between the author and Dionysius (Hans Urs von Balthasar, "Denys", in id., *The Glory of the Lord: A Theological Aesthetics*, vol. 2 [New York: Crossroad, 1983–84], p. 151).

4 I am borrowing this phrase from Bernard McGinn and Denys Turner, both of whom discern an "apophatic anthropology" at work in many of Dionysius' heirs. See Bernard McGinn, *The Growth of Mysticism* (New York, NY: Crossroads, 1994), pp. 105–106; idem., "The Negative Element in the Anthropology of John the Scot", in René Roques (ed), *Jean Scot Érigène et l'histoire de la philosophie. Actes du II Colloque international Jean Scot Erigène* (Paris: Éditions du Centre national de la recherche scientifique, 1977), pp. 315–325; idem., *The Mystical Thought of Meister Eckhart* (New York, NY: Crossroads, 2001), p. 48; see also Denys Turner, *The Darkness of God: Negativity in Christian Mysticism* (New York and Cambridge: Cambridge University Press, 1995), p. 6.

5 See the approximate and conservative tabulations of the total quotations from the New Testament compiled in Paul Rorem, *Biblical and Liturgical Symbols Within the Pseudo-Dionysian Synthesis* (Toronto: Pontifical Institute of Mediaeval Studies, 1984), p. 14 n.8.

6 H. G. Liddell and R. Scott, *Greek-English Lexicon* (Oxford: Oxford University Press, 1980), p. 375; Joseph A. Fitzmyer, *The Acts of the Apostles* (New York, NY: Doubleday, 1998), p. 606.

7 Fitzmyer, *The Acts of the Apostles*, p. 607.

8 See Louth, *Denys the Areopagite*, pp. 10–11.

9 *Ep.* 7.2 1080B; *CD* II, 166.7–9.

10 *Ibid.*; 166.9–10.

11 *Ibid.*; 166.14–15.

12 *Ibid.*; 167.1–2.

24   Charles M. Stang

13   See Schäfer, *The Philosophy of Dionysius the Areopagite*, especially pp. 7, 25, 164–166, 170–171. Although I read his book late in my own efforts, I am pleased to acknowledge my substantial agreement with him on this point.
14   Nowhere is this clearer than in *DN* 4.10 708A (*CD* I, 155.5–7), where Dionysius concludes a long discussion of these three operations by quoting Romans 11:36.
15   See Paul Rorem, "Iamblichus and the Anagogical Method in Pseudo-Dionysius' Liturgical Theology", *Studia Patristica*, 18 (1979), p. 456; idem., *Biblical and Liturgical Symbols within the Pseudo-Dionysian Synthesis* (Toronto: Pontifical Institute of Mediaeval Studies, 1984), pp. 14–15; idem., *Pseudo-Dionysius: A Commentary on the Texts and an Introduction to their Influence* (New York, NY: Oxford University Press, 1993), p. 120. Rorem suggests that Iamblichus understands theurgy as an *objective* genitive, that is, as our work *on* the gods, while Dionysius understands theurgy as a *subjective* genitive, that is, God's own work. Louth takes up Rorem's distinction between genitives so as to guard readers from being "so hasty as to suppose that [Dionysius] means by [theurgy] just what the Neoplatonists did" (Louth, *Denys the Areopagite*, pp. 73–74).
16   See Ruth Majercik, *The Chaldean Oracles: Text, Translation and Commentary* (Leiden and New York: E. J. Brill, 1989).
17   See Iamblichus, *On the Mysteries*, translated with Introduction and Notes by Emma C. Clarke, John M. Dillon, and Jackson P. Hershbell (Atlanta, GA: Society of Biblical Literature, 2003).
18   See Gregory Shaw, "Neoplatonic Theurgy and Dionysius the Areopagite", *Journal of Early Christian Studies*, 7/4 (1999), pp. 573–599. I am inclined to agree with Shaw that Rorem's distinction between genitives (and thereby his distinction between Iamblichean and Dionysian understandings of theurgy) does not hold up under scrutiny (see Note 14).
19   Martin Dibelius translates the line thus: "Now, I am going to tell you what you honor even without recognizing it" (*Studies in the Acts of the Apostles* [New York, NY: Scribner's, 1956], p. 37). Fitzmyer's translation is more elegant and just as accurate: "Now what you thus worship unknowingly I would proclaim to you" (*The Acts of the Apostles*, p. 607).
20   See *Ep.* 5 1073A–B; *CD* II, 162.11–163.5.
21   For an earlier attempt to trace the apophatic anthropology of the *CD*, see my " 'Neither Oneself Nor Someone Else': The Apophatic Anthropology of Dionysius the Areopagite", in Catherine Keller and Christopher Boesel (eds), *Apophatic Bodies: Infinity, Ethics, & Incarnation* (forthcoming from Fordham University Press).
22   *MT* 1.1 1000A; *CD* I, 142.9–11.
23   Αφαίρεσις(from ἀφαιρέω) is a sculptural term, made famous by Plotinus in *Enneads* I.6.9, where he bids us become sculptors of our selves.
24   Thomas Tomasic, "Negative Theology and Subjectivity: An Approach to the Tradition of the Pseudo-Dionysius", *International Philosophical Quarterly*, 9 (1969), p. 428: "[negative theology is] a purgation, an asceticism, indispensable for attaining . . . the radical, ontological 'otherness' of subjectivity over against what it is not."
25   *MT* 1.1 997B–1000A; *CD* II, 142.5–11.
26   See Rorem and Luibheid, *Pseudo-Dionysius: The Complete Works*, p. 70 n.131.
27   *MT* 1.3 1001A; *CD* II, 144.9–15.
28   *DN* 4.13 712A–B; *CD* I, 159.12–14.
29   1 John 4:16: ὁ θεὸς ἀγάπη ἐστίν. For ease, and following Rorem and Luibheid, I will generally translate *eros* as "yearning" and *agape* as "love."
30   What René Roques calls a "symmetry of ecstasies" ("Symbolisme et théologie negative chez le Pseudo-Denys", *Bulletin de l'Association de Guillaume Bude*, 1 [1957], p. 112).
31   *DN* 4.13, 712A; *CD* I, 159.3–8: Διὸ καὶ Παῦλος ὁ μέγας ἐν κατοχῇ τοῦ θείου γεγονὼς ἔρωτος καὶ τῆς ἐκστατικῆς αὐτοῦ δυνάμεως μετειληφὼς ἐνθέῳ στόματι"Ζῶ ἐγώ," φησίν, "οὐκ ἔτι, ζῇ δὲ ἐν ἐμοὶ Χριστός." Ὡς ἀληθὴς ἐραστὴς καὶ ἐξεστηκώς, ὡς αὐτός φησι, τῷ θεῷ καὶ οὐ τὴν ἑαυτοῦ ζῶν, ἀλλὰ τὴν τοῦ ἐραστοῦ ζωὴν ὡς σφόδρα ἀγαπητήν.
32   *DN* 4.13 712A; *CD* I, 159.5–6.
33   D. S. Russell, *The Method and Message of Jewish Apocalyptic: 200 BC–AD 100* (London: SCM Press, 1964).
34   *Ibid.*, p. 138.
35   *Ibid.*, p. 134. Behind Russell's views on time are the speculative work of Thorleif Boman (*Hebrew Thought Compared with Greek* [London: SCM Press, 1960]) and the more sober

scholarship of L. H. Brockington ("The Problem of Pseudonymity," *Journal of Theological Studies*, 4 [1953], pp. 15–22). Critics of Russell include James Barr, *Biblical Words for Time* (Naperville, IL: Allenson, 1962), especially pp. 96, 130–131, and David G. Meade, *Pseudonymity and Canon: An Investigation into the Relationship of Authorship and Authority in Jewish and Earliest Christian Tradition* (Tübingen: J. C. B. Mohr, 1986).

36 See Andrew Louth, *Denys the Areopagite* (London: G. Chapman, 1989), p. 10; see also Cyril Mango, "Saints" in Guiglielmo Cavallo (ed), *The Byzantines* (Chicago, IL: University of Chicago Press, 1997), p. 263; Nicholas Constas, " 'To Sleep, Perchance to Dream': The Middle State of Souls in Patristic and Byzantine Literature," *Dumbarton Oaks Papers*, 55 (2001), pp. 91–124; Claudia Rapp, "Byzantine Hagiographers as Antiquarians, Seventh to Tenth Centuries," *Byzantinische Forschungen*, 31 (1995), pp. 31–44; Scott Fitzgerald Johnson, *The Life and Miracles of Thekla: A Literary Study* (Washington, DC: Center for Hellenic Studies, 2006), pp. 104–109; idem., "Apocrypha and the Literary Past in Late Antiquity" (unpublished paper); idem., "Wandering with the Apostles: Apocryphal Tradition and Travel Literature in Late Antiquity" (unpublished paper).

37 When Louth claims that the "tendency to telescope the past . . . [is the] conviction that underlies the pseudonymity adopted by our author" (*Denys the Areopagite*, p. 10), he implicitly draws a connection between the pseudonymity of the author of the *CD* and earlier theories of pseudonymity. For, although he does not offer a citation, this phrase in fact derives from Brockington, who says that the "timelessness of Hebrew thought [was such that] centuries could be telescoped and generations spanned" (Brockington, "The Problem of Pseudonymity," p. 20).

38 Derek Krueger, *Writing and Holiness: The Practice of Authorship in the Early Christian East* (Philadelphia, PA: University of Pennsylvania Press, 2004).

39 *Ibid.*, pp. 10, 9.

40 *Ibid.*, p. 11.

41 Scott Fitzgerald Johnson, *The Life and Miracles of Thekla: A Literary Study* (Washington, DC: Center for Hellenic Studies, 2006).

42 *Ibid.*, pp. 118–119.

43 Margaret M. Mitchell, *The Heavenly Trumpet: John Chrysostom and the Art of Pauline Interpretation* (Tübingen: Mohr Siebeck, 2000).

44 Cyril Mango, "Saints," p. 263; Mitchell, *The Heavenly Trumpet*, p. xix.

45 *hom. in Rom.* 32.4 [60.680]; cited in Mitchell, *The Heavenly Trumpet*, p. 30.

46 Mitchell, *The Heavenly Trumpet*, p. 393.

47 *Vita Joh. Chrys.* chap. 27 (François Halkin, *Douze récits byzantins sur Saint Jean Chrysostome*, Subsidia hagiographica 60 [Brussels: Société des Bollandistes, 1977]), pp. 142–148; cited in Mitchell, *The Heavenly Trumpet*, p. 35.

48 *hom. in Is.* 45:7 3 [56.146]; cited in Mitchell, *The Heavenly Trumpet*, p. 69.

49 *hom. in Eph.* 9.1 [62.69]; cited in Mitchell, *The Heavenly Trumpet*, p. 69; *hom. in Eph.* 8.8 [62.66], cited in Mitchell, *The Heavenly Trumpet*, pp. 69 n.3, 184.

50 *hom. in Eph.* 8.8 [62.66]; cited in Mitchell, *The Heavenly Trumpet*, p. 184 n.267.

51 *DN* 3.2 681C-D; *CD* I, 141.4–17. For a very different interpretation of the passage, see István Perczel's chapter in this volume.

52 *Ep.* 10 1117A–1120A; *CD* II, 208.1–210.4.

53 Most infamously, *DN* 4.19–35 716B–736B (*CD* I, 163.7–180.7) is a paraphrase of Proclus' *On the Existence of Evils*.

54 In matters of Christology, Dionysius is ambiguous, seeming to speak in places as a Chalcedonian ("[Christ] . . . remaining unmixed," *EH* 3.13 444C [*CD* II, 93.16]), and in others as a Monophysite ("theandric activity," *Ep.* 4. 1072C [*CD* II, 161.9]).

55 I borrow this phrase from the title of Mary-Jane Rubenstein's excellent essay, "Unknow Thyself: Apophaticism, Deconstruction, and Theology after Ontotheology," *Modern Theology*, 19/3 (July, 2003), pp. 387–417.

56 As René Roques does in *L'univers dionysien: structure hiérarchique du monde selon le Pseudo-Denys* (Paris: Aubier, 1954). In *Le Mystère de Dieu* (Brussels: Desclée, De Brouwer, 1959), Vanneste divides the *CD* even more sharply than Roques; see also idem., "Is the Mysticism of Ps.-Dionysius genuine?" *International Philosophical Quarterly*, 3 (1963), pp. 286–306.

57 *MT* 1.2 1000A; *CD* II, 142.14–15.

2

THE EARLIEST SYRIAC RECEPTION OF DIONYSIUS[1]

ISTVÁN PERCZEL

In this chapter I trace the earliest Syriac reception of the *CD*, and hypothesize that this tradition allows us to move closer to the original text and context of the *CD* than does the parallel Greek reception centered around the figure of John of Scythopolis. In the first part of this chapter, I introduce some of the problems that we face with the edition of the *CD* that was completed in John's circle, specifically the fact that this edition, in all likelihood, introduced significant changes into an already complicated text tradition and that John's scholia provided for the *CD* an orthodox interpretation that sufficed for posterity. In the second and third parts of this chapter, I survey the earliest Syriac reception, which is comprised of three principal texts: Sergius of Reshaina's translation of the entire *CD* from Greek into Syriac; his lengthy Introduction to that translation; and a baffling treatise on mystical theology allegedly authored by Dionysius' own mysterious teacher, entitled *The Book of the Holy Hierotheus*. All three texts betray the influence of (what is often pejoratively labelled) "Origenism," a tradition or movement that, while long under suspicion and officially condemned in 553, survived and even flourished in sixth-century Syrian circles, especially among Syriac-speaking intellectuals. Despite its name, this movement owes much to Evagrius of Pontus, who developed a philosophically-founded spiritual doctrine out of Origen's speculations and a corresponding asceticism centered on the fight with evil thoughts. I argue that the early and enthusiastic reception of the *CD* among such Syriac-speaking Origenists as Sergius and the author of *The Book of Holy Hierotheus* suggests that the original author of the *CD*, whoever he was, also belonged to a similar, if not identical, milieu. One of the most important pieces of my argument is that we no longer have direct access to the original

István Perczel
Department of Medieval Studies, Central European University, H-1051 Budapest, Nádor u. 9, HUNGARY
perczeli@hotmail.com

text of the *CD*, but only to these two early receptions, the Greek and the Syriac. And although neither preserves the original text and context in all details, I hypothesize that the earliest Syriac reception—replete with Origenistic influences—is a much more faithful, if indirect, witness to that original text and context than the Greek reception, which seems to obscure the overt Origenism of the author. I conclude this chapter with some thoughts on how the original Origenism of the *CD* and its subsequent incorporation into orthodox tradition complicates our understanding of such categories as "orthodoxy" and "heresy" during this period.

The Earliest Greek Reception

In order to understand the importance of the earliest Syriac reception of the *CD*, we must briefly recall what we know about its Greek text tradition. Salvatore Lilla[2], Günther Heil[3], and Beate Regina Suchla[4] agree that all the known Greek manuscripts derive from a single *editio variorum*, that is to say, a kind of late antique critical edition, which, somewhat later, was provided with commentaries. This *editio variorum* was completed in the circle of John, the first Greek commentator on the *CD* and bishop of Scythopolis in Palestine between approximately 536 and 548.[5]

It was John of Scythopolis whose introduction to and commentaries on the *CD* provided it its standard interpretation. When faced with particularly vexing passages, John gave questionable glosses, which then became the standard view. The fiction that the author was Dionysius the Areopagite, the Athenian judge who converted to Christianity upon hearing Paul's famous speech from Acts 17, seems to be the cornerstone of the *CD*. This fiction, however, received in John's hand even further elaboration, destined to become the standard tradition. Consider for example the famous story from *DN* 3.2, which is allegedly the author's eyewitness account of the Dormition of Mary, the Mother of God, in Jerusalem.[6] The text, however, does not say anything like this. It only speaks about an event where "Dionysius," "Timothy" the addressee of his treatises, "many of their holy brethren," as well as "James the Brother-of-God" and "Peter, the coryphee and most venerable Head of the theologians," as well as the author's teacher, the "holy Hierotheus," all "gathered together to contemplate the Body that is Principle-of-Life and Receiver-of-God." After this contemplation, "it was judged just that all the high-priests celebrate, according to their capacities, the infinitely powerful Goodness of the weakness of the Principle-of-Divinity."[7] In his commentary on this passage, John hazards a guess: "perhaps he [Dionysius] calls 'Body that is Principle-of-Life and Receiver-of-God' that of the holy Mother-of-God at her Dormition."[8] From this hypothesis, however, grew the whole legend of Dionysius' and Hierotheus' presence at the Dormition, finally canonised in the service to Saint Dionysius on October 3 by Theophanes the Confessor.[9]

My reading of this text is that here "Dionysius" is not inventing a fictitious story but is encoding a real one; the gathering was that of bishops contemporary to "Dionysius," who are mentioned under pseudonyms, too, so that "James the Brother-of-God" should be the bishop of Jerusalem and "Peter," apparently adorned by the attributes of the "Apostolic See," the bishop of Rome,[10] while the contemplation of the Lifegiving and Godbearing Body is a concelebration of the Eucharist followed by the "celebration of the powerful Goodness of God's weakness," that is, a discussion on the Incarnation. So I believe that here Dionysius describes a council in which he took part, possibly the Council of Chalcedon.[11]

This example serves to illustrate how remote we are with John's edition from the original context of the *CD*. In fact, the Greek *editio variorium* from which all our manuscripts derive was already dealing with a scattered text tradition displaying an unrecoverably corrupt text.[12] If we take this evidence into account, we have to admit that when we speak about "Pseudo-Dionysius," or "Dionysius the Areopagite," or even the "*Corpus Dionysiacum*," we are not speaking about a person, who anyway eludes us, but about a relatively late reception of the original text, a reception that produced the *CD* as we know it and determined its interpretation, and that cannot be dated earlier than the mid-sixth century. We should also consider that we do not have any direct access to even this sixth-century reception of the Greek text. Our oldest Greek manuscripts of the *CD* were written in the ninth century during the second stage of the Iconoclast debate, when the "correct interpretation" of Dionysian theology was very much the order of the day.

The First Syriac Reception

There exist three translations of the *CD* into Syriac: (1) that of Sergius of Reshaina (see below); (2) a thorough revision of Sergius' translation by Phocas bar Sargis completed in 684/686, to which Phocas applied different principles of translation and used as the basis for his revision of the contemporary Greek text, namely the commented edition of John of Scythopolis;[13] (3) an anonymous translation of the *Mystical Theology* only, made on the basis of the Latin translation of Ambrogio Traversari contained in three manuscripts of Indian origin.[14] One might say that these three translations in four editions roughly represent four stages in the Syriac reception of the Corpus.

If we are to move closer to the original text and context of the *CD*, we have to leave the Greek-speaking world and turn our attention to the first stage, the earliest Syriac reception, for which the *terminus ante quem* is 536, the year the first translator into Syriac, Sergius of Reshaina, died in Constantinople. Sergius of Reshaina was a chief physician, Church politician, and translator of medical and philosophical texts. Besides the works of Dionysius, he translated several works of Galen, while some other translations, notably of Aristotle and Porphyry, are attributed to him without his authorship being proven.[15] Sergius' translation is available in only one manuscript, written most probably in the second half of the sixth century or, at the latest, in the beginning of the seventh. So it is *the* earliest extant manuscript containing the *CD*.[16] In addition to his translation, Sergius prefaced his translation with an Introduction, in which he gives a summary of Dionysius' doctrine.[17]

Sergius' Introduction to the CD

From the *Ecclesiastic History* of Pseudo-Zachariah of Mytilene, we learn that Sergius was a follower of Origen and belonged to the Origenist movement, which was very strong in the first half of the sixth century.[18] This is largely corroborated by Sergius' Introduction to the *CD*, which plainly identifies Dionysius' teaching with that of Evagrius of Pontus, the main authority of the Origenist movement, and interprets the former within the framework of the latter. Although Sergius, as he himself states, wrote the Introduction before starting the translation, he wrote it in good knowledge of Dionysius' writings, already using the vocabulary that he was going to employ in translating the Greek text.[19] In his Introduction Sergius first goes through the main stages of the spiritual life according to Evagrius. He describes the soul's original oneness in which it contemplates God and in which it exists as "pure mind,"[20] whence it falls and acquires the spirited and desiderative faculties of the soul, while its rational faculty is also darkened.[21] To heal the soul in its fallen state each one of its parts needs a remedy. The lower faculties, Sergius insists, should be purified by the "practice of the commandments,"[22] but the mind needs an ascending range of spiritual contemplations, which lead it back to its original state.[23] Sergius borrows the gnoseological structure of these contemplations from Evagrius.[24] They are:

(1) *"natural science"* or *"science of the virtues of the visible beings"*; this is the quadrivium of geometry, arithmetics, astronomy and music.
(2) whatever is above these sciences is called, "under a comprehensive name, spiritual contemplation or divine science"; this is the science of "the substances of the rational and intellectual[25] virtues." This higher contemplation consists of two parts:
(2a) "the one that concerns the states[26] that come from without through the free will and which extends to the rational beings"; this is called *second natural science.*
(2b) "the hidden and secret vision of the mind, which stretches itself up,[27] as far as it is capable and through a remote likeness received from these [rational beings], toward the ungraspable Ray[28] of the Substance ܐܝܬܘܬܐ (*ītūtō*)"; this is the vision that is "alone called *divine contemplation*".[29]

According to Sergius, this gnoseological structure determines the whole construction of the *CD*, which he presents in the following way:

All those things that are not permitted to communicate and all those that humans do not have the right to speak about, he [Dionysius] committed to his holy books in an elevated way and admirably, in one word, divinely. He exposed all the practice and fulfilment of the commandments and the immaculate purification of the soul in the treatise *On the interpretation of the mysteries of the Church*.[30] There he divinely taught how the mind is refined and purified and how it is clothed in all the power of virtue. In the treatise *On the symbolic expressions and on those that have been divinely composed from the visible natures* he wisely showed the exercise and investigation through the spiritual contemplation concerning the natural science, the one by which the mind begins contemplation. It is evident that in the treatise *On the hierarchy of the rational and intellectual powers*[31] he overtly taught about the spiritual contemplation and the science of the intelligible natures. Finally, in his *Compositions on theology* and in the treatise *On the interpretation of the divine names*[32] he divinely exposed the doctrine on the higher science and the lofty contemplation of the hidden Substance itself.[33]

This systematic ordering of the Dionysian treatises shows how consistently Sergius interpreted Dionysius in the light of Evagrian gnoseology. His exposition establishes the following connections between the Dionysian treatises and their Evagrian stages: *The Ecclesiastical Hierarchy* [*EH*]—*praktike*, ascetic and sacramental life; *The Symbolic Theology* [*ST*: lost]—natural science; *The Celestial Hierarchy* [*CH*]—second natural science, contemplation of the intelligibles; *The Theological Outlines* [*TO*: lost][34]; and *The Divine Names* [*DN*]—"substantial knowledge."

Apart from its Evagrian influence, one of the most remarkable features of Sergius' presentation of Dionysius' writings is that he does not distinguish between the "extant" treatises, those that comprise the *CD* as we now have it, and the so-called "lost" treatises, of which scattered mentions are made in the *CD* itself and which the majority of scholars consider to be purely fictitious.[35] For Sergius, however, these "lost" works constitute organic parts of the systematic doctrinal exposition that he credits to Dionysius. As Franz Mali has observed, it sounds as if Sergius were speaking in good knowledge of a much wider corpus, having indeed read the "lost" treatises too, although they were not included in the corpus that he translated into Syriac.[36] This might seem a far-fetched hypothesis, given that Sergius's descriptions of the "lost" works could derive from the scattered references to these works in the *CD* and not from his having had any direct access to them.[37] I do not know whether or not Sergius had indeed read these "lost" treatises; however, I do think that they were not "lost", but simply published under *different* pseudonyms. In fact, I believe that I have discovered one of these so-called "lost" works: the *De trinitate*, a long and odd theological treatise that Mingarelli erroneously attributed to Didymus the Blind, is in fact, as I have argued elsewhere, none other than the "lost" *Theological Outlines* of Dionysius.[38] I have collected further philological evidence for this identification, which I intend to publish soon.[39]

Sergius' Syriac Translation

Sergius' translation contains the Dionysian treatises in a unique order, not echoed by any manuscript in the Greek text tradition. This is DN-CH-MT-EH-Ep. This ordering seems to mirror Sergius' elaborate correspondences between the stages of the spiritual life and the Dionysian treatises, treated above. If we supplement it with the missing treatises that Sergius mentions in his Introduction to the *CD*, we get the following order: TO-DN-CH-ST-MT-EH-Ep.[40]

Sergius' translation of the *CD* permits us to come somewhat closer to the original text than if we rely only on the Greek text from the circle of John of Scythopolis. First of all, I contend that the Greek text was still intact when it reached Sergius, so that a careful philological study of Sergius' Syriac text will permit a critical reconstruction of the original Greek text. The kind of philological reconstruction I am proposing here is only possible, however, when the Syriac text is very close to our Greek text.[41] At other points the Syriac text seems to diverge substantially from our Greek text. While a certain number of such divergences can be attributed to Sergius' rather free translation method, other divergences are, I believe, due to the fact that Sergius translated another, earlier, redaction of the same text. This seems to be quite obvious in the case of the *Ecclesiastical Hierarchy*, whose chapter structure in the Syriac is entirely different from the Greek. The extant Greek version contains seven chapters (an introduction on the concept of hierarchy and six chapters treating six sacraments, each chapter being subdivided into a description of the administration of the given sacrament and its theoretical/spiritual interpretation); the Syriac contains eighteen chapters with a more linear, less complicated structure, wherein chapter endings often do not correspond to any subdivision in the Greek text of the *EH*. Likewise, in certain instances when the logic of the Greek text is broken, even perturbed, the Syriac offers a perfect logic, consistent with other parts of the *CD*.[42] So too the Syriac contains word-for-word or free citations from Proclus where there is either no citation or a different citation in the Greek. A particularly striking instance of this is the chapter titles, which, in both the Greek and the Syriac, are modelled on the chapter titles of Proclus' *Platonic Theology*. Although the Greek and Syriac chapters often differ, both sets of titles seem to go back independently to Proclus.[43] Where there are discernable traces of Origenist doctrines in the Greek, those influences are often much clearer in the Syriac.[44] All this gives the impression that the original Greek text, to which Sergius' translation bears witness, was more openly Origenist, but that John and his circle subsequently softened these references in order to make the *CD* more palatable to orthodox readers. The most astonishing feature of the Syriac, and one that suggests that it reflects an earlier version of the *CD*, is that, in contrast to the Greek, it is clear and comprehensible, an observation already noted by Sebastian Brock.[45]

The Book of the Holy Hierotheus

Another witness to the earliest Syriac reception of the *CD* is the *Book of the Holy Hierotheus* (henceforward *Hierotheus*),[46] probably written by Stephen Bar Sudhaili, a Syrian monk active at the beginning of the sixth century and (in)famous for his Origenism.[47] Whoever the author may have been, he writes under the name of Hierotheus, whom Dionysius at several points in the *CD* names as his teacher and initiator into the divine mysteries. A Syriac legend elaborates on the connection between these two figures and their writings: Dionysius in fact asked Hierotheus to write this book and then wrote the *CD* as a kind of exoteric commentary thereon: "And when the holy Dionysius had read in this book, it was as holy leaven in his heart; its mystery he concealed, (but) its glory and sublimity he revealed".[48]

Hierotheus offers a unique and radical mystical theology that describes the descent of the "divine Minds" from their original unity and their ascent to final union with God in the uncreated divine Substance, where all duality disappears. This spiritual internalisation of the "Origenist myth" is as complicated as it is bold, and is particularly challenging to any interpretative effort. *Hierotheus* is probably contemporary to Sergius' translation, and constitutes a radical rethinking of the *CD* in terms of Origenistic theology.

Whoever he was, the author of *Hierotheus* seems to have known Sergius' Syriac translation of the *CD*: he draws on Sergius' peculiar vocabulary throughout.[49] In my view, the only way to clarify the obscurities of *Hierotheus* and Sergius' translation of the *CD* would be to establish the precise correspondences between their theological lexicons and to interpret the former in light of the latter.[50] But this would be an enormous labor, prior to which we can hazard some hypotheses regarding the relationship between the two. It is possible that the author of *Hierotheus* was among the first to have read Sergius' translation and to use it in his own speculations.[51] It is also possible that both works emerge from one and the same milieu, perhaps a school of Syriac-speaking Origenists, and that their authors knew each other's work. If the author of *Hierotheus* is indeed Stephen Bar Sudhaili, as both ancient West Syrian and modern authors agree, it is entirely possible that the two contemporary Syrian Origenists might have known each other personally. There is an odd and intriguing reference in Sergius' Introduction:

As to our brother, Mor[52] Stephen, who was, from all his soul and all his will, a prompt attendant for the translation of this book, let Christ, the

King of the worlds, deem him worthy of the Ray of His Glory, so that he [Stephen], through the New Life, becomes one with It [the Ray] and remains without motion eternally![53]

This prayer is remarkable for several reasons, first and foremost for its concise Origenist doctrine. Christ is called here "the King of the worlds" (in plural), a favorite Christological title of Evagrius, who holds that after the first Motion of the rational beings Christ created variegated worlds for housing the fallen minds according to their estates.[54] The final bliss that Sergius requests for Stephen is defined as a unification, through the intermediary of the New Life—a standard expression in Syriac for the Resurrection—with the Ray of Christ's Glory, or the Substantial Ray, that is, His Divinity, and as an eternal return to the original motionless contemplation in the Unity. It seems that Sergius the Origenist is wishing for this apocatastatic state for the sake of a fellow-Origenist who, moreover, had been his helper in the translation of the CD. It is tempting to identify this Mor Stephen with Stephen Bar Sudhaili, whom many believe to have authored the *Book of the Holy Hierotheus*. This hypothesis would give a plausible explanation for the shared vocabulary between the Syriac CD and *Hierotheus*: the former could have been a joint work of Sergius and his (most probably younger) "attendant", whom I am tempted to identify as Stephen Bar Sudhaili.[55]

Conclusions

The earliest Syriac reception of the CD is comprised of three parts: (1) Sergius' translation of the CD from Greek to Syriac; (2) his Introduction to that translation; and (3) *The Book of Holy Hierotheus*, probably by Stephen bar Sudhaili, who seems to have known both (1) and (2), and perhaps even helped Sergius to prepare both. The earliest Syriac reception is significant not only because it parallels, but also *antedates* the Greek reception. Furthermore, as I have argued, the earliest Syriac readers and translators were using a different, earlier, redaction of the CD than the one issuing from the circle of John of Scythopolis. Through the earliest Syriac reception, then, we can have indirect access to an earlier version of the CD, prior to the *editio variorum* of John of Scythopolis and his glosses. At the very least, this fact should give us caution when we speak about "Dionysius" or "Pseudo-Dionysius," and imagine some monk sitting in a hidden monastery and writing under divine inspiration, or a disguised Neoplatonist philosopher clothing in a "Christian garb" his commitment to the pagan Proclus' philosophy. Of course there must have existed a real person who wrote the original version of the four treatises and ten letters, but we have no direct access either to this person, whose identity remains obscure, or to his original writings, whose original Greek text was apparently lost. The original author and his original work can still be perceived but, in a very Dionysian way, only through the "veils" of the different redactions, receptions and adaptations, which all have assimilated the original thought to their own milieus and times. I am convinced, however, that from all those veils the thinnest and the most transparent is precisely the first, that is, the earliest Syriac reception.

One of the most conspicuous features of the earliest Syriac reception of the *CD* is that the relevant characters were all dedicated to a specific tradition or movement that many of their contemporaries pejoratively labelled "Origenism" and regarded as a heresy. The most interesting question is whether this is a coincidence or whether it indicates the original provenance of the *CD* and its author. One way of addressing this question is to examine the extant Greek text for traces of Origenist doctrines. Another way is to compare Sergius' Syriac translation with the extant Greek at those places where the two substantially and meaningfully diverge and to hazard hypotheses as to how the putative text of the *first redaction* was altered in the *second redaction*. My research inclines me to believe that the abundant Origenism evident in Sergius' Introduction and translation is not entirely his own, but rather testifies to the fact that the author of the *CD*, whoever he was, must also have belonged to an Origenist milieu.

Furthermore, I believe that this explains why the *CD* was so enthusiastically received by Syriac-speaking Origenists in the sixth century: it did not have far to go. After its first condemnation in 400 in Alexandria and Rome and before its ecumenical condemnation in 553 in Constantinople, Origenism was a semi-clandestine underground movement, forbidden but widely tolerated,[56] a situation conducive to diverse writing techniques used to preserve the *disciplina arcani* and to avoid censorship. I am inclined to believe that the original *CD* was never meant to be widely read but was instead produced for a select, esoteric audience of Origenists. According to this reconstruction, it was John of Scythopolis and his circle who wished to produce an edition for a wider, exoteric readership, and so had to alter or simply explain away troublesome passages. In other words a new, second "veil" had to be put before the "light" of the Dionysian discourse, in addition to the first one constituted by the original Dionysian pseudonym. If intellectuals belonging to the Origenist movement, such as Sergius and the author of *Hierotheus* (presumably Stephen) had access to an earlier version of the *CD*, perhaps that was because they were insiders. And if the earliest Syriac reception reflects the original *CD* more accurately, this may be because Syriac itself served as a sort of veil, protecting the original from censorship, to which the Greek text was more exposed. Once again, one way to check this reconstruction is to examine the Greek reception of the *CD* and see whether there were persons who knew about an earlier version and commented upon it. It seems that there were such persons, the most important of whom is John of Schythopolis, who, living in the midst of the "Second Origenist Controversy", was perfectly aware of the possibility of an Origenist interpretation of certain passages, as evidenced in his scholia both by his careful denial of such an interpretation in some instances, and by his habit of reintroducing such an interpretation in other instances.

Be this as it may, the recognition of the Origenism of the *CD* is a puzzling fact, for here we have a "heretical" body of literature that has exerted a tremendous influence on "orthodox" tradition. With the Origenism of the *CD*, then, we are facing the borderlines of the categories of "orthodoxy" and "heresy." The *CD* is another instance in a mounting body of evidence that demonstrates how elements from this specific "heresy" survived—even flourished—in the "orthodox" fold.[57] Perhaps we need to shift our focus from figures (who was or was not a "heretic"?) to specific doctrines, and inquire which elements in the system disparagingly called "Origenism" were rejected and which were incorporated into the orthodox tradition. While the ecumenical condemnations focus on a mythical-metaphysical system labelled "Origenism" that was apparently in circulation in the sixth century, the "Origenists" whom we encounter, Sergius and Stephen included, are more concerned with the ascetic life and the inner contemplation of the soul. This spiritual element of "Origenism" was never condemned; instead, it was warmly welcomed and enthusiastically incorporated into orthodox tradition. The *CD*—in its second edition, to which generations of theologians appended the appropriate commentaries—was one of the main vehicles of this incorporation. "What God hath cleansed, that call not thou common" (Acts 10:15).

NOTES

1   I am grateful to Mr. Emiliano Fiori for his careful reading of and remarks on several drafts of the present chapter.
2   S. Lilla, "Ricerche sulla tradizione manoscritta del *De divinis nominibus* dello Pseudo Dionigi l'Areopagita", *Annali della Scuola Normale Superiore di Pisa [ASNSP]*, Serie II 34 (1965); idem, "Osservazioni sul testo del *De divinis nominibus* dello Ps. Dionigi l'Areopagita", *ASNSP*, Serie III 10 (1980). See also idem, "Zur neuen kritischen Ausgabe der Schrift *Über die Göttlichen Namen* von Ps. Dionysius Areopagita", *Augustinianum*, XXXI/2 (1991), pp. 424–426.
3   R. Roques, G. Heil, M. de Gandillac, *Denys l'Aréopagite*, Sources Chrétiennes 58, 58bis (Paris: Cerf, 1958¹, 1970²), here pp. 42–48.
4   B. R. Suchla, "Die sogenannten Maximus-Scholien des Corpus Dionysiacum Areopagiticum", *NAWG* (1980/3), pp. 31–66; idem., "Die Überlieferung des Prologs des Johannes von Skythopolis zum griechischen Corpus Dionysiacum Areopagiticum. Ein weiterer Beitrag zur Überlieferungsgeschichte des *CD*", *NAWG* (1984/4), pp. 177–188; idem., "Eine Redaktion des griechischen Corpus Dionysiacum Areopagiticum im Umkreis des Johannes von Skythopolis, des Verfassers von Prolog und Scholien. Ein dritter Beitrag zur Überlieferungsgeschichte des *CD*", *NAWG*, (1985/4) pp. 179–194; idem, "Die Überlieferung von Prolog und Scholien des Johannes von Scythopolis zum griechischen Corpus Dionysiacum Areopagiticum", in *Studia Patristica*, 18/2 (1989), pp. 79–83; idem (ed), *Corpus Dionysiacum I. Pseudo-Dionysius Areopagit: De divinis nominibus*, PTS 33 (Berlin-New York: Walter de Gruyter, 1990), pp. 36–64.
5   For John of Scythopolis' dates see B. Flusin, *Miracle et histoire dans l'oeuvre de Cyrille de Scythopolis* (Paris: Etudes Augustiniennes, 1983), pp. 20–21; P. Rorem and J. C. Lamoreaux, *John of Scythopolis and the Dionysian corpus: annotating the Areopagite* (Oxford: Clarendon Press, 1998), pp. 26–27.

6 *DN* 3.2, 681 CD, p. 141, ll. 4–14.

7 For understanding the Pauline allusions see 1 Cor. 15:43, 2 Cor. 12:9, 2 Cor. 13:4, Heb. 5:2—the weakness is that of the earthly body, the strength is that of the Divinity, so that the "weakness of the Principle-of-Divinity" is God's Incarnation. This precisely is also the interpretation given by John of Scythopolis, see his scholion *ad locum*: PG 4, 236 C-237 B.

8 PG 4, 236 BC.

9 For a vivid and accurate description of how Dionysius was handled by the Iconoclasts and the Iconodules and the circumstances of the composition of Theophanes' canon, see A. Louth, "Saint Denys the Areopagite and the Iconoclast Controversy" in Y. de Andia (ed), *Denys l'Aréopagite et sa postérité en Orient et en Occident. Actes du Colloque International; Paris, 21–24 septembre 1994* (Paris: Institut des Etudes Augustiniennes, 1997), pp. 329–339, especially 337–339.

10 Of course, Peter could also be the bishop of Antioch, but the vocabulary used indicates Rome, in my view.

11 If "Dionysius" was present in Chalcedon in the company of his bishop, "Hierotheus," this means that the Corpus could not have been written much later than twenty or thirty years after, that is, in the 470s, 480s. This slightly contradicts the triple *terminus a quo* established by previous scholarship (the death of Proclus in 485, the Henoticon of Zeno in 482, and the introduction of the Creed into the liturgy by Peter the Fuller in 474). As P. Rorem and J. C. Lamoreaux judiciously note, none of these time barriers can be firmly fixed (P. Rorem and J. C. Lamoreaux, *John of Scythopolis and the Dionysian Corpus*, pp. 9–10). If it is indeed Chalcedon, "Peter" was present speaking through the *Tome* of Pope Leo, as those present have acknowledged this in fact, and "James," that is, the Apostolic founder of the see of Jerusalem, in the person of Juvenalius.

12 B. R. Suchla, *Corpus Dionysiacum I*, pp. 55–57, 65–66; S. Lilla, "Osservazioni sul testo del *De divinis nominibus* dello Ps. Dionigi l'Areopagita", p. 196; idem, "Zur neuen kritischen Ausgabe der Schrift *Über die Göttlichen Namen* von Ps. Dionysius Areopagita", p. 438.

13 There is also a second edition of Phocas' translation, which combines the latter with the Introduction of Sergius of Reshaina and places John's scholia within the text—this was completed in 766/7 by Cyriacus bar Shamona in Mosul. On these translations see J.-M. Hornus, "Le Corpus dionysien en syriaque", *Parole de l'Orient*, 1 (1970), pp. 69–93; G. Wießner, "Zur Handschriftenüberlieferung der syrischen Fassung des Corpus Dionysiacum", *NAWG* (Göttingen: Vandenhoeck & Ruprecht, 1972) pp. 3–42.

14 *MS Ernakulam MAP 7*, ff. 508r–512r and *MS Cambridge Oo 1.29*, pp. 192–198. The fact that this translation is from Traversari's Latin has been established by Prof. Sebastian Brock (information in a personal letter of Prof. Brock to the author, dated October 21, 2004).

15 See S. Brock, *A Brief Outline of Syriac Literature* (Kottayam: St Ephrem Ecumenical Research Institute, 1997), p. 43, and also Henri Hugonnard-Roche, *La logique d'Aristote du grec au syriaque: études sur la transmission des textes de l'Organon et leur interprétation philosophique* (Paris: Vrin, 2004). Although A. Guillaumont put forward the hypothesis that the Syriac translation of the untampered Greek text of Evagrius of Pontus' *Kephalaia Gnostica* (S_2) is also by Sergius, a comparative analysis of the translation methods of Sergius and the author of S_2 does not confirm this hypothesis.

16 The main part of the manuscript is contained in *Sinai Syriacus 52*, from which the beginning of the first part of the Divine Names and Letters 6–10 are missing because of the truncation of the beginning and of the end. It was hypothetically identified as containing Sergius' translation by Dom P. Sherwood and Jean-Michel Hornus in P. Sherwood, "Sergius of Reshaina and the Syriac versions of the Pseudo-Denis", *Sacris Erudiri*, 4 (1952), pp. 174–183, and J.-M. Hornus, "Le Corpus dionysien en syriaque", *Parole de l'Orient*, 1 (1970), pp. 69–93. Some fragments from the damaged end of the manuscript were found in 1975 in the Monastery and were edited by Sebastian Brock in his *Catalogue of Syriac Fragments (New Finds) in the Library of the Monastery of Saint Catherine, Mount Sinai* (Athens: St Catherine's Monastery-Mount Sinai Foundation, 1995), pp. 101–105. More recently, Mathias Quaschning-Kirsch and myself, independently of each other, identified a part of a miscellaneous Paris manuscript *BN. Syriacus 378* (ff. 42–54) as containing part of the missing beginning of the Sinai manuscript. This fragment contains the second half of Sergius' Introduction and the missing beginning of DN I. See M. Quaschning-Kirsch, "Eine weiterer Textzeuge für die syrische Version des Corpus Dionysiacum Areopagiticum: Paris B.N. Syr.

378", *Le Muséon*, 113/1–2 (2000), pp. 115–124, and I. Perczel, "Sergius of Reshaina's Syriac Translation of the Dionysian Corpus: Some Preliminary Remarks', in C. Baffioni (ed), *La diffusione dell'eredità classica nell'età tardo-antica e medievale. Filologia, storia, dottrina* (Alessandria: Edizioni dell'Orso, 2000), pp. 79–94. This identification has also provided the definitive proof for the attribution of the text in the Sinai manuscript, confirming Sherwood's hypothesis. Finally, Paul Géhin found another separate leaf from the same manuscript in the Ambrosianum in Milano (*A 296 inf.* f. 86), belonging just before the beginning of the Paris MS. See P. Géhin, "Manuscrits synaïtiques dispersés I : les fragments syriaques et arabes de Paris", *Oriens Christianus*, 90, 2006, pp. 23–43.

17   The Introduction was published in P. Sherwood, "Mimro de Serge de Rešayna sur la vie spirituelle", *L'Orient Syrien*, 5 (1960), pp. 433–457 and 6 (1961), pp. 95–115, 121–156. The newly identified Paris manuscipt contains the second half of Sergius' Introduction, beginning with Chapter LXIV in the edition of Sherwood. My translations in what follows will often diverge from the French translation of Sherwood.

18   Ps.-Zachariah Rhetor, *Historia Ecclesiastica* 8.5, in F. J. Hamilton and E. W. Brooks (trans.), *The Chronicle known as that of Zachariah of Mytilene* (London: Methuen & Co., 1899), pp. 266–268.

19   It is noteworthy that Sergius' Evagrian interpretation of Dionysius' doctrine does not contain the so-called Origenist myth, namely a consistent cosmological myth about the pre-existence of the souls as incorporeal minds in a unique created substance and their final restoration into the same state, a doctrine that was going to be condemned at the Fifth Ecumenical Council in 553. While the interpretation that Sergius provides is perfectly compatible with the "myth", it contains none of the doctrines that were later condemned.

20   Sergius, Introduction, Chap. LXXII-LXXIII, Sherwood (1961), pp. 112–115, BN Syr. 384, f. 44r°: "[The soul in this state] is entirely mind and luminous intellect that receives, just as a pure mirror, the imprint of the character of its Maker."

21   *Ibid.*, One might say that this is Sergius' gnoseological interpretation of the so-called Origenist myth.

22   *Ibid.*, Chap. LXXV-LXXVI, Sherwood (1961), pp. 114–115, BN Syr. 384, f. 44v°.

23   *Ibid.*, Chap. LXXVI-LXXVIII, Sherwood (1961), pp. 122–123, BN Syr. 384, f. 44v°-45r°.

24   *Ibid.*, Chap. LXXXI, Sherwood (1961), pp. 124–125, BN Syr. 384, f. 45v°. In a study published in 1999, I proposed that the Evagrian gnoseological structure was to be considered the clue for Dionysius' doctrine (I. Perczel, "Une théologie de la lumière: Denys l'Aréopagite et Evagre le Pontique", *Revue des Etudes Augustiniennes*, 45/1 (1999), pp. 79–120. I wrote that study before reading Sergius' Introduction.

25   "Intellectual": in Syriac ܪܘܚܢܐ *rukhono*, meaning literally "spiritual". In Sergius' translation of Dionysius this is one of Sergius' standard translations for νοερός that is, "intellectual".

26   "States": in Syriac ܙܘܥܐ *zaw'e*, meaning literally "motions". This is Sergius' standard translation for ἕξεις, that is, "habits", "states". Sergius speaks here of the different ranks of the rational beings, namely angelic ranks, human and demonic states, which, according to the Origenist doctrine, are the consequences of the acts of free will of the rational creatures.

27   "Stretches itself up": in Syriac ܡܬܡܬܚ *metmatkho*. This is Sergius' standard translation for the Greek ἀνατείνω, "to tend toward something higher".

28   "Ray": in Syriac ܣܡܟܐ *semkho*. This is one of Sergius' standard translations for the Greek ἀκτίς.

29   It is worth noting that in Sergius' interpretation the *second natural science* relating to the actual states of the rational beings examines their present states, that is, their angelic, human and demoniac hierarchies, not as resulting from their original creation, but as resulting from their acts of free will preceding their incorporation in their present states. If one re-reads the *Hierarchies* in this light, even in their presently available Greek text, one may find out that, notwithstanding the present consensus, this is the real doctrine exposed therein. It is also noteworthy that the final unifying knowledge is obtained via an elevation going through the remote likenesses offered by the rational beings toward the Divine Ray—here called "the Ray of the Substance"—which is to be identified with Jesus in His divine nature, being the condescending manifestation of the Father, who is represented here and in the Corpus by the solar disc being the Source of the Ray (See Perczel, "Une théologie de la lumière", pp. 79–89). One may finally remark the positive, even "substantial" language replacing here the famous extreme Dionysian apophatism; in fact, on the one hand, Sergius is careful to establish the equivalence between the Dionysian "knowledge through ignorance" and the Evagrian "substantial knowledge" (Sergius, Introduc-

tion, Chap. LXXX, Sherwood (1961), pp. 124–125, BN Syr. 384, f. 45vᵒ) and, on the other hand, in Sergius' translation, instead of some apophatic expression or, simply, of "God" or "divine", many times one finds the terms "Substance", "substantial", either having no equivalent in the Greek Dionysius, or translating a number of terms, such as ὕπαρξις ("existence") or Χρῆμα ("reality").

30 This is, obviously, the *Ecclesiastical Hierarchy*. Finally, Sergius adopted a different, much more complicated, translation for the title of this treatise: "On the Order of High-Priesthood that is Followed in the Tradition of the Holy Church" (Sin Syr. 52, f. 80rᵒ).

31 This is the *Celestial Hierarchy*. Sergius' translation of the title in Dionysius' text is: "On the Heavenly High-Priesthood."

32 This is the *Divine Names*. Sergius' translation of the title in Dionysius' text is: "On the Divine Names" (BN 378, f. 53rᵒ).

33 *Ibid.*, Chap. CXVI-CXVII, Sherwood (1961), pp. 148–149, BN Syr. 384, f. 51vᵒ- 52rᵒ.

34 See BN 378, 53rᵒ, Syn. Syr. 52, 1rᵒ, 3vᵒ, 4vᵒ, 6vᵒ etc. In fact the Syriac expression for "Compositions on Theology" is precisely the way Sergius translates the Greek title *Theologikai hypotyposeis*. This has been observed by Emiliano Fiori both in his MA thesis and in a letter to the author, dated 21.01.2008.

35 There remains another odd feature of Sergius' presentation of the Dionysian system, namely that while he includes two of the "lost" treatises, he omits one of the extant treatises, namely the *Mystical Theology* (E. Fiori treated this question in his MA thesis). While it is difficult to give a compelling explanation for this striking omission, here I want to forward the hypothesis that this omission is due to the fact that the apophatic method endorsed by the *MT* did not fit into Sergius' system advocating positive theology, so that he was unable or unwilling to establish any correspondence between the *MT* and one of the stages of the contemplative life. As we shall see, the way he treated the *MT* within the Dionysian system and the manner he handled apophatic expressions in his translation confirm this hypothesis. This self-distancing from the Neoplatonist apophatic method seems to characterise other sixth-century Origenist works, too, such as the treatises of Leontius of Byzantium and the Pseudo-Caesarius. For Leontius and Dionysius see D. B. Evans, "Leontius of Byzantium and Dionysius the Areopagite", *Byzantine Studies/Etudes Byzantines*, 7 (1980), pp. 1–34, and I. Perczel, "Once Again on Dionysius the Areopagite and Leontius of Byzantium", in T. Boiadjiev, G. Kapriev and A. Speer (eds), *Die Dionysius-Rezeption im Mittelalter* (Turnhout: Brepols, 2000), pp. 41–85; on Pseudo-Caeasarius see idem, "Finding a Place for the *Erotapokriseis* of Pseudo-Caesarius: A New Document of Sixth-century Palestinian Origenism", in Shafiq Abuzayd (ed.), *Palestinian Christianity: Pilgrimages and Shrines*, ARAM Periodical 18–19 (2006–2007), pp. 49–83.

36 See Franz Mali, "Hat die Schrift *De symbolica theologia* von Dionysius Ps.-Areopagita gegeben? Anmerkungen zu den Nachrichten des Sergius von Rēš'ainā über Dionysius Ps.-Areopagita' in M. Tamcke", *Syriaca. Zur Geschichte, Theologie, Liturgie und Gegenwartslage der syrischen Kirche* 2. Deutsches Syrologen-Symposium (Juli 2000, Wittenberg) (Hamburg: Lit, 2002), pp. 213–224.

37 It is in this sense that Emiliano Fiori criticised Mali's conclusions in his MA thesis (cited above, n. 21).

38 See I. Perczel, "Denys l'Aréopagite, lecteur d'Origène", in W. A. Bienert and U. Kühneweg (eds), *Origeniana Septima. Origenes in den Auseinandersetzungen des 4. Jahrhunderts* (Leuven: Leuven University Press and Uitgeverij Peeters, 1999) pp. 673–710, here pp. 690–702.

39 The connection between the *CD* and the *De Trinitate/Theological Outlines* is most easily established by the fact that, often, both works draw on the same passages from the same works of Proclus, some of the very passages that early twentieth-century scholars used to prove the pseudonymous character of the *CD*.

40 The fact that Sergius inserted *MT* after the *Symbolic Theology* shows that he treated it as having no other organic part in the spiritual education than being a summary of the treatises on contemplation, which it indeed is according to the treatment of the theological method given in chapter 3 of the *MT*.

41 I have attempted such a reconstruction, combined with other methods, of a particular Dionysian text in I. Perczel, "The Christology of Pseudo-Dionysius the Areopagite: The *Fourth Letter* in its Indirect and Direct Text Traditions", *Le Muséon*, 117/3–4 (2004), pp. 409–446.

42   I have analysed one such passage, also trying to establish a valid methodology for studying Sergius' Syriac text in Perczel, "Sergius of Reshaina" Syriac Translation of the *Dionysian Corpus*', pp. 79–94. Whatever I published on Sergius' translation before that study displays a very imperfect methodology, which had led me to a number of errors, which I now regret. I believe, however, that with this study I was able to lay down a sound methodological basis for further investigations.

43   For such cases see I. Perczel, "Denys l"Aréopagite, lecteur d'Origène', pp. 687–689 and id., "Pseudo-Dionysius and the Platonic Theology", in A. Ph. Segonds and C. Steel (eds), *Proclus et la Théologie Platonicienne* (Leuven and Paris: Leuven University Press and «Les Belles Lettres», 2000), pp. 491–532, here (on the chapter titles), pp. 497–500.

44   For such cases see I. Perczel, "Denys l'Aréopagite, lecteur d'Origène", pp. 685–702, although with a number of regrettable philological errors, and, principally, id, "Pseudo-Dionysius and Palestinian Origenism", in Joseph Patrich (ed) *The Sabbaite Heritage in the Orthodox Church from the Fifth Century to the Present* (Leuven: Peeters, 2001), pp. 261–282; here pp. 267–270 and 276–279.

45   "Sergius' translation [. . .] is much more readily understandable than the difficult Greek original" (S. Brock, *Spirituality in Syriac Tradition* (Kottayam, Kerala: St Ephrem Ecumenical Research Institute, 1989), p. 30).

46   Fred Shipley Marsh (ed and trans), *The Book of the Holy Hierotheos, Ascribed to Stephen Bar-Sudhaile (c500 A.D.), with Extracts from the Prolegomena and Commentary of Theodosios of Antioch and from the "Book of Excerpts" and Other Works of Gregory Bar-Hebraeus*, Syriac Texts, Edited from Manuscripts in the British Museum and the Harvard Semitic Museum, Translated and Annotated, with an Introduction and Indexes (London: Text and Translation Society, 1927, reprint Amsterdam: Apa-Philo Press, 1979). For studying this work, its rootedness in and influence upon the Syriac tradition, the recent monograph of Karl Pinggéra, *All-Erlösung und All-Einheit: Studien zum "Buch des Heiligen Hierotheos" und seiner Rezeption in der syrisch-orthodoxen Theologie* (Wiesbaden: Reichert, 2002), is very useful.

47   Bar Sudhaili's authorship of "Hierotheus" is assumed by John of Dara and Gregory Bar Hebraeus. It is also rendered probable by many similarities between "Hierotheus'" text and the theses that Philoxenus of Mabbugh, who personally knew Bar Sudhaili, attributed to the latter. This identification was first proposed in modern scholarship by A. L. Frothingham Jr., *Stephen Bar Sudhaili, the Syrian Mystic (c500 A. D.) and "The Book of Hierotheos" on the Hidden Treasures of the Divinity* (Leyden 1886, reprint Amsterdam: Apa-Philo Press, 1981), pp. 63–68, and then by Marsh, *The Book of the Holy Hierotheos*, pp. 227–232. See also I. Hausherr, "L'influence du «Livre de saint Hiérothée»" in id, *De doctrina spirituali christianorum orientalium*, IV, *Orientalia Christiana*, 30 (1933), pp. 176–211, and A. Guillaumont, *Les "Képhalaia Gnostica' d'Évagre le Pontique et l'histoire de l'Origénisme chez les Grecs et chez les Syriens* (Paris: Seuil 1962), pp. 311–318. The most comprehensive modern discussion of this question can be found in Pinggéra, pp. 7–26.

48   Marsh, p. 135*–136* (Syriac text), p. 150 (translation). "The story of the Holy Hierotheus" is incorporated into the commentary upon "Hierotheus" written by Theodosius Romanus of Takrit, Syrian Orthodox Patriarch of Antioch (887–896), but, according to Marsh, is an earlier text.

49   A detailed demonstration of this relationship is yet to be published.

50   Some concrete examples for this method and its application can be found in I. Perczel, "A Philosophical Myth in the Service of Religious Apologetics: Manichees and Origenists in the Sixth Century", in Y. Schwartz and V. Krech (eds), *Religious Apologetics—Philosophical Argumentation* (Tübingen: Mohr Siebeck, 2004), pp. 205–236, here pp. 228–234.

51   The recent hypothesis of R. T. Arthur is that Bar Sudhaili's work would be primary to that of Dionysius, whose Corpus would be a reply to Bar Sudhaili—see R. T. Arthur,,"A Sixth-Century Origenist: Stephen bar Sudhaili and his Relationship with Ps-Dionysius", *Studia Patristica*, 35 (2001), pp. 368–373, and idem, *Pseudo-Dionysius as Polemicist: The Development and Purpose of the Angelic Hierarchy in Sixth Century Syria* (Aldershot: Ashgate, 2008). I cannot accept this view for a host of reasons, philological, doctrinal and chronological.

52   "Mor" is an honorific title before the names of saints or ecclesiastic authorities, most often of bishops. Here, however, Mor Stephen is called "our brother" and an "attendant" to the translation, which indicates that Mor Stephen fulfilled a lower ecclesiastic task than that of

a bishop. A scribe of Sergius' Introduction also gave the same title "Mor" to Sergius himself, who was a simple priest, in Chap. CXXIV, BN 378, f. 52v°.
53   Sergius, Introduction, Chap. CXXIII, Sherwood (1961), pp. 152–153, BN Syr. 384, f. 52v°.
54   See, for example, Evagrius of Pontus, KG II.2: "In the second natural contemplation we see the wisdom full of variety of Christ, which he used when he created the worlds; and in the science concerning the rational beings, He has taught us about Himself."
55   Once again, this hypothesis was originally proposed by Franz Mali in his study referred to above, in note 35.
56   I cannot give detailed references here; at present I am working on a monograph reconstructing (on the basis of the available documents) the history of semi-clandestine Origenism in the fifth-sixth centuries.
57   See the converging research done by Gabriel Bunge and others on Evagrius, David Evans on Leontius of Byzantium, Samuel Rubenson on Saint Antony, and György Heidl on Saint Augustine.

3

THE RECEPTION OF DIONYSIUS UP TO MAXIMUS THE CONFESSOR

ANDREW LOUTH

It is now well-nigh universally accepted that the works ascribed to the Athenian convert of the Apostle Paul, Dionysius, i.e., the *Corpus Areopagiticum* or *Corpus Dionysiacum*, are a much later fabrication. The story of the beginnings of their reception is little understood and tainted by a kind of scholarly distaste, as if, having discovered that these writings are inauthentic—bluntly, forgeries—scholarship is unwilling to forgive their author, and needs to find further grounds for recrimination.[1] His evident Neoplatonic leanings, or borrowings, are invoked to demonstrate that "Dionysius the Areopagite" (as I shall call him, for his mask of pseudonymity fits so closely that the efforts by scholars to prise off the mask and identify the person behind it have been completely fruitless) was not really a Christian at all, but a pagan Neoplatonist who sought to preserve in the harshly Christian empire of Justinian the Neoplatonic tradition—which that emperor had tried to destroy in closing the Platonic academy at Athens in 529—by draping it in the liturgical finery of Christianity.[2] Or his affinities with Syrian Christianity—one of the few secure results of the quest for the "real" author of the *CD*—are turned into an accusation that Dionysius was a Monophysite (after all, the first person to refer to him seems to have been the great Monophysite heresiarch, Severus of Antioch), and the story of his reception told in such a way that the "real" Dionysian doctrines are seen to have been in some way neutered by his Orthodox advocates, John of Scythopolis and especially Maximus the Confessor.[3] Or the profound significance for Dionysius of the Christian liturgy—another insight established by recent scholarship—is turned on its head, so that it is Dionysius who is blamed for turning the liturgical encounter of the people of God with the risen Christ in the Eucharistic liturgy gathered under

Andrew Louth
Department of Theology and Religion, Durham University, Abbey House, Palace Green, Durham, DH1 3RS, UK
andrew.louth@durham.ac.uk

the bishop into an elaborate dramatic performance, laden with complex symbolism, that demands an equally elaborate conceptual interpretation, furnished by an individual whose presence is that of a spectator.[4] The trouble with all these grudging ways of interpreting the reception of Dionysius in the sixth century is that they fail to explain why the Dionysian writings came to be interpreted at all, if in essence they are so rebarbative to authentic Christianity. The sixth century was by no means a period when Christianity was exceptionally gullible, and thus easily taken in by the outrageous act of forgery that, at one level, these works represent. The long-running contest between those who accepted and those who rejected Chalcedon had led to the sharpening of scholarly tools. A scholar like Leontius of Byzantium was perfectly capable of detecting Apollinarian forgeries, and it has long been observed that the need to convince opponents—or at least not to maintain what opponents could laugh-off as ridiculous—had an effect on the way the lives of the saints were presented, reining in over-enthusiastic claims, and introducing at least a measure of reserve.[5] And it was the sixth century that saw the high point of commentary on the works of Aristotle, mostly, perhaps entirely, conducted by Christian scholars in Alexandria.[6] It was, indeed, in an age of critical scholarship that the CD was received and interpreted—and interpreted with an enthusiasm that seems to have grown as the works became more widely known.

Let us first sketch the story of the emergence and reception of the CD. The received story goes something like this. The first references to Dionysius' works are found among the opponents of Chalcedon, called by their opponents "monophysites" (or "miaphysite", the barbarous construction favoured by modern scholarship), in particular (as already mentioned) the great monophysite theologian, Severus of Antioch. At the colloquy between the Chalcedonians and non-Chalcedonians, called in Constantinople in 532 by Justinian, the monophysites cited a passage from the CD in support of their case. The Orthodox bishop, Hypatius of Ephesus, protested against this recourse to "Dionysius", someone unknown to the great Fathers like Athanasius or Cyril. This is generally interpreted as an authentically Orthodox rejection of Dionysius, which, however (alas), was quickly overruled by the distinction of the pseudonym, so that soon Dionysius came to be accepted amongst the Orthodox, too. Nonetheless, this Orthodox reception was made possible, or palatable, by the rather strained commentary that came to accompany the CD, initiated by John of Scythopolis and continued by Maximus the Confessor, which masks his truly monophysite tendencies—which are, strangely enough, often interpreted as failure to be genuinely Christocentric (as if the "monophysites" dissolved the humanity of Christ in his godhead, as the Orthodox accused them of doing)—and renders him acceptable to the Orthodox. This received story has been completely overturned by Paul Rorem and John Lamoreaux in the first chapter of their book on John of Scythopolis,[7] where they point out that Hypatius' objection to the citation of the Areopagite concerns simply the fact that he had been hitherto unknown, even to Fathers like Athanasius and Cyril, not to what he said in the passage cited. Indeed, as Rorem and Lamoreaux point out, Hypatius' suggestion that, had Athanasius and Cyril known of the Dionysian passage cited (*DN* 1. 4, 113, 6–12),[8] they would have used it, requires that he found nothing unorthodox in the passage.[9] For the rest of the sixth century, although Dionysius was popular amongst monophysites, he was just as popular, if not more so, amongst the Orthodox. One should not however exaggerate his popularity in the sixth century; it was only a few bits of the *CD* that were cited (parts of the *Divine Names* and especially the letters, in particular the Christological *ep.* 4, with its fateful mention of Christ's "theandric activity"), though some of Dionysius' distinctive vocabulary quickly became fashionable: e.g., the use of ἱεραρχία and the prefix ὑπέρ. John of Scythopolis' comments on the *CD* had a much wider purpose than taming his Christology; indeed, in his comments on the crucial *ep.* 4, John does not give the impression that he felt Dionysius' language dangerously monophysite at all. Rather he is quite clear that Dionysius does not say that Christ is a θεανδρίτης (a god-man: neither god nor man), but that Christ's activity was sometimes θεανδρική, divine-human, as when he healed (a divine activity) by touch (a human activity).

Another aspect of Dionysius that it is claimed was neutered by John and the later scholiasts is his Neoplatonism, an aspect of Dionysius acknowledged by all strands of modern scholarship. Of course, it could hardly be claimed that John sought to disguise a dependence on Neoplatonism of which he was himself aware; that would take John to have colluded in Dionysius' pseudonymity in a way that would be simply incredible. Nevertheless, John is conscious of parallels with ancient philosophy—Dionysius' use of the Aristotelian notion of *nous*, for instance—and one of the most interesting aspects of his own use of Dionysian ideas is the way in which he seems to illustrate the Areopagite with ideas drawn from Plotinus. Quite how John viewed what we see as indebtedness to Greek philosophy, and especially Neoplatonic philosophy, is hard for us to judge. He will have accepted the general early Christian conviction that what we now regard as borrowings from Greek philosophy were, in fact, borrowings by the Greek philosophers themselves from the Old Testament, especially from Moses (whom they believed to be the author of the Pentateuch). What seems most likely is that John shared Dionysius' attitude to the wisdom of the Greek philosophers; it was not a problem, but a common attitude of mind that John developed in his own way.[10]

Nevertheless, it was certainly as a legacy from the apostolic age that these writings came to be treasured. This is probably the explanation for one of the most curious facts about the transmission of the *CD*, namely that, as Beate Suchla has demonstrated, all the existing Greek manuscripts of the *CD* derive from an edition made in the sixth century, barely a decade after the writings seem first to have become known, by John, Bishop of Scythopolis.[11] It is this to which we now have access: a carefully compiled edition, complete with variant readings, commentary (scholia) and prologue. All the manuscripts, all the translations, go back to this *editio princeps*, save the translation into Syriac, made some time before he died in 536 by Sergius of Reshaina, of which more later. The reason for this edition, then, is not, as is commonly suggested, that the *CD* was too dangerously monophysite (or Neoplatonic) to be let loose in the Byzantine world without careful commentary, neutralizing its heterodox tendencies, but precisely because it was regarded as a precious legacy from the apostolic age. It was too fascinating to escape for long the attention of scholars, the first of whom was John of Scythopolis. The web of scholarly commentary that surrounded the text, filling the margins of the manuscripts, was there to capture the least drop of honey from the Apostle Paul's convert and the friend and intimate of some of the revered names of the earliest days of the Church—Titus, Timothy, Bartholomew, Polycarp and, last but not least, the Apostle and Evangelist John—someone who, from as far away as Heliopolis (in Egypt, as John of Scythopolis clarifies),[12] had witnessed the darkening of the sky at the time of the Crucifixion and later been a witness of the last hours of the Virgin Mother of God and her assumption into heaven.

Whatever the reason for this edition of the *CD*, it meant, as Rorem and Lamoreaux have put it, that "subsequent generations did not read the Areopagite; they read the annotated Areopagite—and John had the early monopoly on those annotations. It is hard to overemphasize the significance of this literary phenomenon, this linkage of text and exegesis".[13] We do not know much about John. Patriarch Sophronius of Jerusalem cites him in the next century as a staunch defender of Chalcedonian orthodoxy. He seems to have been fairly prolific in his defence of Chalcedon, and was one of the first to identify as Apollinarian forgeries some of the works to which the monophysites appealed, but very little of his works has survived; we catch glimpses of them through references from other writers. At some point, he was bishop of Scythopolis, and Rorem and Lamoreaux argue that this was in the period between 537 and 548. It seems that it was towards the beginning of this period that he made his edition of the Areopagite and wrote his prologue and scholia.[14] As printed in Migne's *Patrologia Graeca* (in this following Balthasar Corderius' modern *editio princeps* of 1634, and the majority of the manuscripts), the scholia are ascribed to Maximus the Confessor. Hans Urs von Balthasar was the first to identify the earliest stratum of scholia and ascribe it to John of Scythopolis,[15] who emerged from the scholia as "a personality of significant dimensions ... a great scholar and no mediocre philosopher", writing in an "elegant style, limpid in comparison with Maximus", who "cites poets and historians, philosophers and theologians of pagan and Christian antiquity", who "everywhere arouses the impression of comprehensive, effortless, even playful learning".[16] Suchla's research attributes fewer scholia to John, who now appears somewhat less impressive.[17]

Much of John's commentary is what one would expect of a scholiast: he identifies sources, he draws parallels, he elucidates difficulties. So, for instance, when Dionysius speaks of sun, morning star, fire that illuminates without harm, living water and ointment as symbols of God (*CH* 2. 5, 15, 11–16), John identifies the biblical texts where such symbolism is found. More interestingly, perhaps, Neoplatonic-sounding terminology—such as offshoots, flowers and lights (*DN* 2. 5, 132, 1–3), theurgy (*CH* 4. 4, 23, 3), paradigms (5. 8, 188, 6)—is given a biblical source, though often enough John is only following the Areopagite's example in this. He is greatly interested in the Areopagite's descriptions of (supposedly) apostolic liturgical practice, and notes differences from what he is familiar with. He sometimes corrects the Areopagite: an example, influential perhaps because well-founded, is his reversal of the Dionysian order of the highest rank of celestial beings. For Dionysius, the highest rank consists of seraphim, cherubim and thrones in descending order, whereas for John the highest of these beings are the thrones, on which God, as it were, immediately rests, for which he cites Ezekiel.[18] Another change occurs with his treatment of the Dionysian notion of hierarchical order. As we shall see, the notion of rank and authority is relatively secondary in Dionysius' understanding of "hierarchy", whereas for John, Bishop of Scythopolis, it is the authority of the hierarch that is paramount.[19] Yet another interesting feature of John's commentary is his use of the Fathers. As Rorem and Lamoreaux comment, it is not quite what one would expect from a sixth-century Chalcedonian theologian. He seems especially interested in pre-Nicene theologians: Africanus, Aristo of Pella, Clement of Alexandria, Hermas, Hippolytus, Irenaeus, Justin, Methodius of Olympus, Origen, Papias, Polycarp, Symmachus, and the *Apostolic Constitutions* (not, of course, pre-Nicene, but John of Scythopolis would have thought them so).[20] An interesting footnote reveals that several of these pre-Nicene references are also found in Eusebius' *Church History*.[21] His post-Nicene references do not go much beyond the Cappadocian Fathers (he is especially keen on Basil). In particular, he does not cite Cyril of Alexandria, a common point of reference for both Chalcedonian and non-Chalcedonian, nor does he refer to any of the decrees of the synods of the Church. What are we to make of this? The interest in the pre-Nicene Church, largely as depicted by Eusebius, is something John shares with Dionysius; it is striking how much of the Areopagite's picture of the Church is drawn from Eusebius (something not sufficiently noted by scholars). One can relate this to the tendency that becomes more pronounced in the wake of the Nicene synod to present the belief and life of the Church as apostolic.[22] Indeed, one might wonder whether, as the divisions of the post-Chalcedonian Church became more and more deeply rooted, there may not have been a tendency to look back with a kind of nostalgia to an earlier age, and whether this nostalgia found nourishment in Eusebius' *Church History*. Some of the other features that Rorem and Lamoreaux remark on in John are not peculiar to him. Maximus, for instance, makes few references to synodical decrees (a fact somewhat disguised by the fashion of speaking of his "Chalcedonian logic").[23] Moreover, an interest in pre-Nicene theology is one of the striking features of the early seventh-century *Pandects* of Antiochus of the Monastery of Mar Saba and the *Hiera* (also known as the *Sacra Parallela*), ascribed, probably with justice, to John Damascene: two monuments to the learning of the Palestinian monks.[24] Perhaps the Scythopolite's predilections are not that surprising; maybe it is the way our view of post-Chalcedonian theology is over-determined by the Christological quarrels that makes John's interests seem unusual to us.

Indeed, although it is certainly the case that later generations read the annotated Areopagite, one begins to wonder whether this is as significant as Rorem and Lamoreaux make out. What exactly is it that is "hard to overemphasize" about this undoubted fact? There seems to me a much greater continuity between the concerns of the Areopagite and those of John of Scythopolis, as well as between the concerns of John of Scythopolis and those of later Byzantine theologians, for it to be at all clear in what way the presence of annotation affected the subsequent reading of the Areopagite. More work needs to be done on the reception of the "divine Denys" before this question can be satisfactorily answered. But what seems so obvious from the unusual circumstances of the textual tradition of the *CD* is perhaps less significant than it might appear at first sight.

Whatever reference John of Scythopolis makes to the Fathers, there is no question but that his own Christological position is Chalcedonian, and he is certainly aware of the fact that Dionysius was appealed to by those who rejected Chalcedon (though it is equally clear that he regards such an appeal as illegitimate: see above, for John's discussion of the Dionysian idea of a theandric activity in Christ). Another contemporary controversy of which John displays knowledge is that over "Origenism". The whole question of fourth-century Origenism is the subject of scholarly dispute.[25] What John attacks is the Origenist doctrine of a pre-cosmic fall, in the precise form that the angelic ranks are the result of injury (λώβη) that led to the fall.[26] As Rorem and Lamoreaux note, this is a doctrine that Dionysius himself specifically denies, referring to the angels as "uninjured", ἀλώβητοι.[27] John is not, then, guarding against a misreading of Dionysius; on the contrary, he enlists Dionysius as rejecting the Origenist doctrine in advance, as it were, from his sub-apostolic vantage point. Nonetheless, it is beyond question that Dionysius had himself read Origen: the sequence of ideas in his discussion of the words ἔρως and ἀγάπη and, in particular, the use of the quotation from Ignatius' *Epistle to the Romans*, "my love is crucified", in *DN* 4.12 are too close to Origen's discussion in the prologue to the commentary on the Song of Songs for it to be a coincidence; similarly his use of the expression πηγὴ τῆς θεότητος of the Father in *DN* 2.5 is most likely indebted to Origen (cf. *De Principiis* I.3.7; not to the Cappadocians, who do not use the expression, despite what some textbooks say).[28]

Though all later access to the Areopagite was mediated through John of Scythopolis, the first translation of the *CD* into Syriac, by the learned doctor Sergius of Reshaina, predates the Scythopolitan edition. This very early Syriac translation of the Areopagite underlines the Syrian affinities of the *CD*. There is also preserved in Syriac a unique attempt to supplement the *CD*: the work known as *The Book of the Holy Hierotheos*.[29] In this context, it is worth recalling that the *CD* presents itself as the surviving volumes of a somewhat larger corpus of writings to which references are made in the surviving works. Lost works are mentioned: there are frequent references to the *Theological Outlines* and the *Symbolic Theology*, and occasional references to *On angelic properties and orders*, *On the just and divine judgment*, *On intelligible and sensible beings*, and *On the soul*. There are also references to and quotations from two works by his "famous teacher", Hierotheos: *Elements of Theology* and *Hymns of Love*. Outside the *CD*, there is no trace of any of these; it is a natural thought that the mention of these works was intended to give the impression that the works that emerged in the sixth century were all that had survived from apostolic times of a larger corpus of works. The Syriac *Book of the Holy Hierotheos* seems to be a partial exception: it must be intended to supplement the existing Dionysian writings. It is not, however, one of the lost works mentioned by Dionysius, but another one, unknown to—or, at least, unmentioned by—him. Later writers—John of Dara, who wrote commentaries on Dionysius' works on the hierarchies, and Kyriakos, patriarch of Antioch, both eighth/ninth-century, and the thirteenth-century Bar Hebraeus—regarded the work as pseudonymous, and credited Stephen bar-Sudhaili with its composition. Philoxenus of Mabbug and Jacob of Sarug, both his contemporaries, give us colourful accounts of Stephen as an Origenist, who believed in the final restoration of all, ἀποκατάστασις παντῶν, in which the distinction between Father, Son and Spirit would be transcended, and was fond of strange interpretations of scriptural passages, into which he claimed to have had special, visionary insight. To some extent, the *Book of Hierotheos* fits this picture of Stephen bar-Sudhaili. The last of the five discourses is certainly concerned with the final consummation of all things, in which all distinctions will be obliterated, even the distinction within the Blessed Trinity, and everything will return to a primal unity. This last discourse also contains esoteric utterances, even a quotation from Heraclitus "the Obscure";[30] there is promise of further revelation—"we are not receivers of revelations but givers of revelation"[31]—in which the secret meaning of scriptural passages will be made known. This esotericism is found throughout the four earlier discourses, but their content is different. The first discourse is cosmological, giving an account of the origination of everything in the Good, which is dispersed in multiplicity through a Fall, the place in the scale of being of each entity or species being determined by the extent of its fall. The nine-fold division of heavenly beings found in Dionysius is the basis for a more elaborate set of divisions in which there are 243 (3^5) kinds of heavenly beings. These minds or intellects receive knowledge and impart purification. The picture presented in the first discourse is an elaboration of Origenist and Dionysian themes. The middle three discourses are concerned with the ascent of the mind or intellect. Five kinds of intellectual motion are distinguished: "natural", "after nature", "above nature", "below nature" and "beyond nature". Of these, the first is neutral, the second and third ascending, and the fourth and fifth descending. The "ascent of the intellect" described in these discourses is of the third kind, transcending nature, or supernatural. The detail of the account is complex, expressed in scriptural language, leading to the "firmament", and beyond that to the "mansions". Then follows a passage through Gethsemane—crucifixion—often repeated several times, resurrection—union with oneself—and finally transfiguration before the angels. Then, the intellect is plunged back into the "abyss of impurity", and emerges separated from it. A final purification takes place involving the "tree of evil", a passage through baptism to a heavenly Eucharist, which leads to paradise and eating of the "tree of life". The final stage involves judgment and a cosmic war, having passed through which the intellect learns the secret of life, descends into hell, and then emerges, having passed beyond Christ, and is now united as creator with the Good in a union of love.

The judgments of the first editor of the *Book of Hierotheos* on all this are curious: "the least tedious of extant Syriac mystical works".[32] Perhaps something has been learned in the course of the last century, with the discovery of such genuine spiritual giants as Isaac of Nineveh ("the Syrian"), John of Dalyatha, or Joseph Hazzaya. It is hard to think of someone confessing to such a judgment nowadays. Although the *Book of Hierotheos* draws on Origenist ideas, and to a lesser extent on Dionysius, it is hard to rid oneself of the impression that it belongs to a different world, much more frankly esoteric, with gnostic and Manichaean affinities.

There is something frustrating about this, admittedly brief, survey of the early reception of Dionysius. The Syriac evidence suggests that some aspects of the Dionysian vision found ready acceptance among some esoterics—as has perhaps always been the case, and certainly the case from the eighteenth century onwards, when the CD was eagerly read and interpreted amongst those who rebelled against the rationalism of the Enlightenment. The evidence of John of Scythopolis suggests something rather different: a figure who seems very much at home in some, at least, of the preoccupations of sixth-century theology, though not particularly those that have attracted the most scholarly attention. The technical Christology of that century has left little imprint on the Areopagite; indeed part of the reason for his pseudonymity may have been to escape that suffocating world. The gradual acceptance of Dionysius' works may well be regarded as shadowing another transition, a transition in which the language of imagery took over from the technical language of much sixth-century theology.[33]

For as the sixth century drew to a close, Dionysius comes into his own. His works gradually come to be known throughout the Byzantine world, even in Rome, where Pope Gregory the Great refers to him as an "ancient and venerable Father" in his homilies on the Gospels.[34] Their eventual popularity doubtless owed much to their "ancient and venerable" pseudonym, but the rather pedantic reception he received from John of Scythopolis suggests that this can hardly be the whole story. Rather it is the case that Dionysius, in his works, expressed in a novel and exciting way ideas already firmly established in the Byzantine Christian mind. His conviction of the mystery of God, a mystery communicated in the Incarnation and made palpable in the Divine Mysteries—the Eucharistic Liturgy—but nonetheless a mystery that remains unfathomable, not only to human minds but even to the angelic mind, so that angels are at once sureties that we are in communion with God and also witnesses to the utter unknowability of God, because the divine is veiled even from them; his sense of community, which turns the manifold variety of the created order from a "realm of unlikeness", in which we are cut off from one another and from God, into an infinitely sensitive manifestation of God so that all creatures, however divided or even depraved, can catch some glimpse of the Divine Beauty calling out to them and drawing them back into union with the divine—this sense of community expressed by his coinage, *hierarchia*, which for Dionysius meant "a sacred order, knowledge and activity, which is being assimilated to God as much as possible" (*CH* 3. 1, 17, 3–4), a rather different notion from what is nowadays meant by "hierarchy"; his use of the terms apophatic and kataphatic—negation and affirmation—of our language of God, a language better thought of as praise, than simply predication of attributes; and the implications for individual ascetic endeavour of the calling of creatures to union with God, expressed in his triad of purification, illumination and union, together with the sense that this individual asceticism had cosmic implications. All this—and more, a sense of the sacramental, the place of the monastic order within the life of the Church—was already the firm conviction of the Christian Church. The enthusiasm for the Dionysian writings as they gradually made their way in the Byzantine world is not hard to account for: in succinct and sometimes intoxicating language, Dionysius expressed convictions that were dear to the Byzantine Christian mind. This is not at all to deny that frequently what Dionysius contributes is something peculiar to himself, and often enough something that he imports into Christian theology from the Neoplatonic writings that he evidently so loved. The terminology of apophatic and kataphatic theology he borrows from Proclus, and his enthusiasm for liturgy, for heavenly beings, also has parallels with that great pagan philosopher. The distinction of purification–illumination–union, destined to leave such a mark on Christian "mystical" traditions, seems to be Dionysian in that form. The word "hierarchy" is his. But though there is much that is peculiar to Dionysius, the realities he is responsive to are already present in the Byzantine tradition. John Chrysostom, for instance, has the same mix of a sense of the mystery of God, expressed in "apophatic" language, the role of the angels in both preserving and disclosing this mystery, and the liturgy as the place, *par excellence*, where this mystery is acknowledged and celebrated.[35] The parallels with the liturgical practice of the Syrian East that we find in the CD further serve to demonstrate how Dionysius is embedded in the life of the Church. His enthusiasm for the monastic order is authentically sixth-century, and the sense of the cosmic significance of asceticism is well established in the traditions that emerge from the fourth-century Egyptian desert. It may be that Archimandrite Alexander Golitzin lets his enthusiasm run away with him, as he traces the foreshadowings of the CD, but his instinct is true. The way in which the concerns of Dionysius and his editor and scholiast John overlap is further evidence that Dionysius came, as it were, to a world that already knew him. If Dionysius—and not least his language and concepts—became a presence in the Byzantine world that is impossible to ignore, that was, at least in part, because he expressed so well its own fundamental convictions.

NOTES

1   See Hans Urs von Balthasar, *The Glory of the Lord: A Theological Aesthetics*, II: Studies in Theological Style: Clerical Styles (Edinburgh: T. & T. Clark, 1984), p. 144.
2   For example, Vanneste, Hathaway, Brons, and many other scholars.
3   For example, Meyendorff, and even Grillmeier.
4   Schmemann, and also Meyendorff.
5   See H. Delehaye, *L'Ancienne hagiographie byzantine: les sources, les premiers modèles, la formation des genres*, Subsidia Hagiographica 73 (Brussels: Société des Bollandistes, 1991).
6   See the later essays in *Aristotle Transformed. The Ancient Commentators and their Influence*, ed. Richard Sorabji (London: Duckworth, 1990).
7   Paul Rorem and John C. Lamoreaux, *John of Scythopolis and the Dionysian Corpus. Annotating the Areopagite* (Oxford: Clarendon Press, 1998), pp. 9–22. Because this book is ostensibly about John of Scythopolis, this chapter has perhaps escaped the attention of people writing on Dionysius: in A. Grillmeier's great work, *Jesus des Christus im Glauben der Kirche, vol. 2/3 Die Kirche von Jerusalem und Antiochien*, ed. Theresia Hainthaler, Rorem and Lamoreaux's book is only mentioned in the section on John of Scythopolis (pp. 163–167), and not in the section on Dionysius the Areopagite (pp. 309–356). For the reception of Dionysius, see also Theresia Hainthaler, "Bemerkungen zur Christologie des Ps.-Dionys und ihrer Nachwirkung im 6. Jahrhundert", in Ysabel de Andia (ed), *Denys l'Aréopagite et sa postérité en orient et en occident*, Collection des Études Augustiniennes, Série Antiquité 151 (Paris: Institut d'Études Augustiniennes, 1997), pp. 267–292.
8   Passages from the *Corpus Dionysiacum* are cited from the new critical edition (*Corpus Dionysiacum*, vol. 1, *De divinis nominibus*, Beate Suchla (ed), vol. 2, *De coelesti hierarchia, De ecclesiastica hierarchia, De mystica theologia, Epistulae*, Günter Heil and Adolf Martin Ritter (eds), Patristische Texte und Studien 33, 36 (Berlin: Walter de Gruyter, 1990–1), with the customary abbreviations [DN = *De divinis nominibus*; CH = *De coelesti hierarchia*; EH = *De ecclesiastica hierarchia*; MT = *De mystica theologia*; Ep. = *Epistula*], so DN 1. 4, 113, 6–12 = *De divinis nominibus* 1. 4, [*Corpus Dionysiacum* vol. 1], p. 113, lines 6–12).
9   Rorem-Lamoreaux, p. 18.
10 On this issue, see Rorem-Lamoreaux, pp. 106–137.
11 See Beate Suchla, *Corpus Dionysiacum*, vol. 1, pp. 54–57. The date of the edition is given as between 537 and 543 by Rorem-Lamoreaux: op. cit., pp. 38–39.
12 PG 2:541C.
13 Rorem-Lamoreaux, p. 2.

14   For all this, see Rorem-Lamoreaux, pp. 23–36.
15   Hans Urs von Balthasar, "Das Scholienwerk des Johannes von Skythopolis", which first appeared in *Scholastik*, 15 (1940), pp. 16–38, and was substantially reproduced in the second edition of *Kosmische Liturgie. Das Weltbild Maximus' der Bekenner* (Einsiedeln: Johannes-Verlag, 1961), pp. 644–672 (Eng. trans. by Brian Daley, *Cosmic Liturgy. The Universe according to Maximus the Confessor* (San Francisco, CA: Ignatius Press, 2003), pp. 359–387).
16   Balthasar, *Cosmic Liturgy*, p. 366.
17   See, Beate Regina Suchla, "Die sogenannten Maximus-Scholien des Corpus Dionysiacum Areopagiticum", *Nachrichten der Akademie der Wissenschaften in Göttingen: i. Philologisch-historische Klasse*, (1980) 3, pp. 31–66.
18   PG 2:64C; the Ezekiel reference is Ezek. 1:26. This interpretation of Dionysius is, however, supported in the recent book by Sarah Klitenic Wear and John Dillon, *Dionysius the Areopagite and the Neoplatonist Tradition. Despoiling the Hellenes* (Aldershot: Ashgate, 2007), p. 59.
19   All these examples are drawn from Rorem-Lamoreaux, Part I, chapter 3: Sources of the *Scholia* (pp. 46–65).
20   Rorem-Lamoreaux, p. 57.
21   Rorem-Lamoreaux, p. 55 n. 70.
22   See my brief comments in *Denys the Areopagite* (London: Geoffrey Chapman, 1989), pp. 7–8). Throughout that book, I noted parallels between the Areopagite's picture of the Apostolic Church and that found in Eusebius. I would be inclined to make much more of them now.
23   See, most recently, Melchisedec Törönen, *Union and Distinction in the Thought of St Maximus the Confessor* (Oxford: Oxford University Press, 2007), pp. 2–6 (who also notes Maximus' lack of reference to synodal decisions).
24   See Karl Holl, *Die Sacra Parallela des Johannes Damaskenos*, Texte und Untersuchungen 16 (1897).
25   For a reliable guide, see Brian Daley, 'What did "Origenism" mean in the Sixth Century?', in G. Dorival and A. Le Boulluec (eds), *Orieniana Sexta* (Leuven: University Press/Peeters, 1995), pp. 627–638.
26   PG 4.172C.
27   Rorem-Lamoreaux, p. 179, n. 24 (for: *CH*, read: *EH*).
28   See István Perczel, "Denys l'Aréopagite, lecteur d'Origène", in W. A. Bienert and U. Kühneweg (eds), *Origeniana Septima. Origenes in den Auseinandersetzungen des 4. Jahrhunderts* (Leuven: Leuven University Press/Peeters, 1999), pp. 673–710, and other articles by the same author.
29   *The Book of the Holy Hierotheos*, ed. and trans. by F. S. Marsh (London & Oxford: Williams and Norgate, 1927; Gregg Reprint, 1969).
30   "All from one and one from all": Marsh, *Book of Holy Hierotheos*, p. 140.
31   Marsh, *Book of Holy Hierotheos*, p. 131.
32   Marsh, *The Book of the Holy Hierotheos*, p. 247.
33   See my "From the Doctrine of Christ to the Icon of Christ: St Maximus the Confessor on the Transfiguration of Christ", in Peter W. Martens (ed), *In the Shadow of the Incarnation: Essays on Jesus Christ in the Early Church in Honor of Brian E. Daley, S.J.* (Notre Dame, IN: University of Notre Dame Press, 2008 [forthcoming]), pp. 260–275.
34   Gregory the Great, *In Evang. Hom.* 34. 12 (PL 76:1254), cited in Rorem, *Pseudo-Dionysius, a Commentary on the Texts and an Introduction to their Influence* (New York and Oxford: Oxford University Press, 1993), p. 75.
35   See my article, "Apophatic Theology: Before and after the Areopagite", *Bogoslovni Vestnik*, 56 (1996), pp. 297–310.

4

THE RECEPTION OF DIONYSIUS IN THE BYZANTINE WORLD: MAXIMUS TO PALAMAS

ANDREW LOUTH

Just as the story of the immediate reception of the Dionysian writings is hampered by the distaste of much modern scholarship, prejudiced by the galling success of his daring pseudonym, so it is with the story of his influence on the Byzantine world. Much scholarship seeks to diminish his influence and cast him as a "lonely meteorite" in the night sky of patristic (and Byzantine) thought.[1] As such Dionysius can be dismissed as untypical and someone who can safely be ignored.[2] The reasons for this and the contexts in which such neglect is valued have been sketched at the beginning of my earlier chapter. This keenness to downgrade Dionysius is not just character-istic of Protestant, and especially German, scholarship, where such an atti-tude might be expected, but of some influential Orthodox theologians, too. Other scholars are content, or even eager, to detect the influence of Diony-sius, to the extent of seeing Dionysius' influence as deep and pervasive in Byzantine theology. This is true of Vladimir Lossky, for instance, and also of Christos Yannaras, both of whom are happy to find in Dionysius the source of ideas they value in the Byzantine tradition of theology. It is also true of secular scholars who readily trace the aesthetic ideals of the Byzantines, or their hierarchical notions of political society, back to Dionysius, sometimes perhaps without sufficient discrimination.[3] Sergei Averintsev's remarkable book, *Poetika Rannevizantiyskoy Literatury* ["The Poetics of Early Byzantine Literature"], makes many references to "Pseudo-Dionysius" throughout the work.[4] In this chapter, I shall argue that the truth is, as ever, rarely pure, and never simple. Dionysius' influence is pervasive, though not all-pervasive. It is

Andrew Louth
Department of Theology and Religion, Durham University, Abbey House, Palace Green, Durham, DH1 3RS, UK
andrew.louth@durham.ac.uk

also uneven, both in the sense that some Byzantines seem more open to his influence than others, and also in the sense that there is a very generalized influence, alongside genuine attempts at engagement with his thought. I shall deal first with the general issues and then in more detail with the evidence of theological encounter with Dionysius.

It needs to be recognized that Byzantine theology itself is scarcely a uniform, undifferentiated phenomenon. The way in which *Wirkungsgeschichte* affects our perception of the past has some very specific consequences for our grasp of Byzantine theology. After the collapse of Byzantine civilization before the onslaught of the Turks and the indifference of the West, the values of that civilization were preserved by the monks; it was in the monasteries that the glories of the Byzantine liturgy and the subtleties of its thought were preserved. The worship of the modern Eastern Orthodox Church is fundamentally monastic, and the near hegemony of "philokalic" theological reflection in modern Orthodox thought—that is, an approach to theology inspired by the collection of fundamentally monastic ascetic and mystical texts published in 1782 as the *Philokalia*—only reinforces a sense of the centrality of monastic experience in modern Orthodoxy. I would argue that this is a strength, but I would also observe that it is different from the Byzantine religious culture that met its end in the fires of Constantinople in 1453. Alongside monastic theology there was also a strong lay interest in theology, a tradition that has been called "humanist"[5] or "lay".[6] As Sir Steven Runciman observed,

> Throughout the history of the Eastern Empire there was a large lay population that was as well educated as the clergy. The professors, the government servants, and even the soldiers were usually as cultured as the priests. Many of them were highly trained in theology, and almost all of them felt themselves perfectly competent to take part in theological discussions. No one in Byzantium thought that theology was the exclusive concern of the clergy.[7]

Prominent representatives of this humanistic tradition were the great ninth-century patriarch Photius and the eleventh-century "consul of the philosophers", Michael Psellus (the fact that the former became patriarch and the latter a monk only illustrates how difficult it is to draw lines of classification in Byzantine society). A first observation about the Areopagitical influence is that it is primarily manifest in the monastic, not the humanist, tradition.

It is surprising how little impact Dionysius seems to have made on the Byzantine humanist theological tradition. Photius does not include his works in his *Bibliotheca*, though this may be less significant than might appear, as we cannot be sure that the list of books treated in that work was intended to be exhaustive, but elsewhere in that work he only refers to Dionysius a handful of times, in every case because the writers he is reviewing have made reference to Dionysius (e.g., the mysterious sixth-century Job the monk, and the seventh-century defenders of Orthodoxy, Sophronius of Jerusalem and Maximus the Confessor). In his epistles and *Amphilochia*, where Photius demonstrates his theological prowess, there is scarcely a mention of Dionysius: one letter (*ep.* 249) and one of the *Amphilochia* (*amph.* 182) each have a couple of brief references (there are nearly 300 epistles and over 300 *Amphilochia*, though many of the epistles reappear as *Amphilochia*). The picture gained from the new critical edition of Michael Psellus' works is much the same: there are occasional references to Dionysius in his philosophical treatises, mostly con-cerned with the doctrine of participation, the three references in the poems (many of them theological) are to Dionysius' listing of the celestial beings (which Psellus does not follow at all strictly, anyway), and even in the theo-logical treatises more than two-thirds of the references (26 out of 37) come in a single treatise (*op.* 112 in the volume edited by Gautier)[8] which is a para-phrase of Dionysius on the doctrine of the heavenly beings. In the case of Photius, this neglect may be due to his doubts about the authenticity of the Areopagite. The very first book reviewed in the *Bibliotheca* is a work, now lost, by a priest called Theodore, defending the authenticity of the *Corpus Areopagiticum* against four objections: Why is Dionysius not quoted by later Fathers? Why is he unknown to Eusebius? Why does he describe later tradi-tions as contemporary with himself? Why does he, a contemporary of the apostles, quote from Ignatius, who came a generation later? Photius lists the objections, but simply comments on Theodore's refutations that "[t]hese are the four problems he makes an effort to resolve, confirming to the best of his ability that the book of the great Dionysius is genuine". As Nigel Wilson remarks, "the nuance of the Greek allows one to put forward the hypothesis that Photius is here expressing in a guarded and tactful way his own scepti-cism".[9] Michael Psellus' neglect of this (in part) disciple of the Neoplatonists may, too, be due to his own profound knowledge of the real thing, especially the "Lycian philosopher", Proclus. Nonetheless, it is striking that neither Photius nor Psellus makes much of Dionysius, and this may well be typical of the "lay tradition" of Byzantine theology (insofar as anything can be regarded as typical of a tradition mostly known to us through exceptional individuals).[10]

In those much better known traditions of theological reflection and cel-ebration influenced by the monastic tradition the presence of Dionysius is much more evident. This presence manifests itself, broadly speaking, in two ways. First of all, there is a general enthusiasm for the themes that Dionysius made his own: a sense of the mystery of God expressed by a delight in apophatic, or negative, language applied to God; the way in which this sense of the divine mystery is symbolized by the angelic realm that lies between humankind and God, both protecting God from the prying human intellect, but also communicating something of the divine to human kind; the role of the liturgical in the approach to God, both making central the language of praise and entreaty as the most typical *theological* language (in the sense of language that appropriately reaches out towards God) and also suggesting that it is only in an ecclesial encounter with God that we come to know Him at all; a sense that this ecclesial encounter with God is hierarchical, in which higher beings pass on to lower beings the fruits of their contemplation (though, as noted in the last chapter, the primary meaning of hierarchy for Dionysius is not subordination, but assimilation to the divine appropriate to each particular created being); a sense that this human encounter with God in not simply a matter of individual effort and endeavour, but something in which the whole cosmos is involved and in which humankind comes to fulfil a cosmic function; but combined with this, a sense that human engagement with God is costly, the purification of a deep longing of love, in which the human is drawn into the divine life, assimilated to God and finds fulfilment in deification (usually expressed in terms of a triad that came to have a vast influence: purification, illumination, union or perfection); and furthermore, and for the moment finally, that this combination of individual ascetic struggle and social and liturgical communion with other beings, reaching beyond the human to the cosmic, finds expression above all in the monastic life. In all of this, one finds a general Dionysian influence, though because, as we saw in an earlier chapter, Dionysius gives signal expression to tendencies already characteristic of the Byzantine tradition, it is often not clear how integral Dionysius is to this tradition; indeed, Dionysian influence is often only unmistakably betrayed by the use of characteristic language.

Whether this affinity with the monastic tradition is because, fundamentally, as Hieromonk Alexander Golitzin has claimed, Dionysius embraces an understanding of monastic experience as "interiorized apocalyptic", derived from Jewish apocalytic, seems to me less clear. Golitzin has identified some very striking parallels between the true Dionysian understanding of the function of hierarchy and the monastic understanding of monastic experience as passed on by the institution of elderhood (*starchestvo* in the later Russian tradition), and found striking parallels between the visionary core of Christian monastic experience and the Jewish apocalyptic notion of the "open heaven". But this does not necessarily mean that Dionysius derived his ideas directly from Jewish apocalyptic; it may simply be another, immensely fruitful, way of exploring the bonds of affinity that exist between the monastic tradition and Dionysius.

This generalized influence of the Areopagite within the Byzantine monastic tradition may be illustrated from a work that was to become the touchstone of Byzantine theology, and those other traditions, not least the Slavic, that flow from it: John Damascene's work in a hundred chapters—that is, properly speaking, a "century"—generally known in the West as *On the Orthodox Faith*, the title given it by the influential thirteenth-century translation into Latin.[11] John begins this work by emphasizing the incomprehensibility of God, so that God is only made known by God, through revelation, a revelation culminating in the Incarnation, witnessed by prophets and apostles, in which God is made known as fundamentally unknown (*exp. fid.* 1). John then goes on to invoke various distinctions made by theologians to protect the ultimate ineffability of the God thus revealed: the distinction between knowing God and knowing "about" him; the use of denial, *apophasis*, in our knowledge of God, who is thus revealed as "ineffable, incomprehensible, invisible, inconceivable, ever existing", as the Divine Liturgy of John Chrysostom puts it—all adjectives beginning with alpha, and therefore with negative force (so that even "ever", ἀεί, is made to seem like an alpha-privative); the distinction between *theologia* and *oikonomia* (the doctrine of God in Himself, and of God as manifest in creation); the distinction between God's unknowable essence and knowable energies (*exp. fid.* 2). John's ways of expressing the mystery of God go beyond what we find in Dionysius, but he gratefully and extensively draws on Dionysius and his sense of the fundamental character of apophatic theology; furthermore, his sense of tradition is deeply hierarchical, though he does not use the word. The Dionysian influence is palpable a little later on in the work, when John comes to treat of the angels (*exp. fid.* 17). For the rest one may say that we find the same emphases in John as in the Dionysian tradition—the liturgical, the cosmic, the ascetic/monastic—but generally without any specific reference to Dionysius, though in the liturgical poetry that John pioneered we find a "baroque" use of overloaded adjectives, headed with the prefix *hyper-* or the alpha privative, that owes much to Dionysius. Just how typical John is of the Byzantine tradition becomes more apparent when it is realized how deeply monastic John's theology is, not least in *On the Orthodox Faith*, a century of chapters, conforming to the monastic genre created, it would seem, by Evagrius Ponticus; not so much a systematic presentation of theology, as a series of points for meditation.[12] The influence of Dionysius is found in the presentation of theology of a similar complexion, even though in detail it is often expressed differently: the liturgical, the cosmic and the ascetic are all there in John, but he mostly draws on other traditions to give them expression. There is one point in John's theology, however, where arguably we find a deeper engagement with Dionysius, and one that lends Byzantine theology its distinctive character. This is found in the role and function of the image. John is well known as a defender of icons against Byzantine iconoclasm, something he did from the safety of his position as a subject of the Umayyad caliph, but the whole notion of image is fundamental to John's theology, and in his development of this, he makes his own a central dimension of the Dionysian vision. For both of them, images combine the material and the spiritual, enable a transition from the material to the spiritual by means of the material, and thus make the body and the bodily fundamental to their vision of God's dealing with the created order. For John, the notion of the image underlies the nature of creation, which functions as a theophany. The Incarnation is then something new, certainly—the "only new thing under the sun", as John puts it (*exp. fid.* 45)—but not unexpected, for it fits in with the duality John finds in a material creation that discloses the immaterial God, and the duality that is fundamental to the human, created as body and soul. In this John develops ideas that remain little more than hints in the Areopagite, and gives a curious twist to the angelology that owes so much to Dionysius, arguing that the very simplicity of angelic beings prevents them from the richness of communion with God offered to beings of body and soul, whose communion with God becomes palpable in the Eucharist.[13]

John's engagement with Dionysius is, however, glancing, compared with what we can find in other parts of the Byzantine tradition, before him and after. This we shall now pursue, looking at three figures: Maximus the Confessor, Nicetas Stethatos, and Gregory Palamas (and hesychasm and the hesychast controversy in general).

Maximus' receptiveness to the Dionysian tradition has been much discussed. The attribution of the scholia on the Dionysian writings to Maximus once made it seem that Maximus had been a close student of Dionysius. However, the recent discovery (first by Hans Urs von Balthasar, and now confirmed by the research of Beate Suchla) that most of the scholia were compiled by John of Scythopolis (as discussed above) has changed the terms of the debate. Initially many scholars tended to play down the influence of Dionysius, and this mood of scholarship came to serve the notion of Meyendorff that Maximus fundamentally disagreed with Dionysius and only accepted his ideas after subjecting them to a "Christological correction".[14] The influence of Dionysius on Maximus is, however, manifest, even if we discount the few scholia that may still belong to Maximus. Maximus acknowledges it explicitly in his *Mystagogia*, which is presented as a supplement to the *Ecclesiastical Hierarchy*,[15] and the use of apophatic theology and the other themes mentioned as part of the generalized influence of Dionysius are found throughout Maximus' writings. What we find, too, however, is an engagement with Dionysius' ideas that develops them in a novel way. I shall discuss three examples: first, the Christological use of apophatic and kataphatic theology; secondly, the way Maximus relates the cosmic and the ascetic in his *Mystagogia*; and thirdly, the Maximian doctrine of the *logoi*, or principles, of creation.

Maximus' Christological Use of Apophatic and Kataphatic Theology

As already mentioned, in Maximus we find the (by his time) traditional use of the categories of apophatic and kataphatic theology; in his treatment of the Transfiguration in several of his earlier works, we find a quite novel use of these categories.[16] Maximus discussed the Transfiguration three times in his early works.[17] In what is probably the second treatment, in *Quaestiones et Dubia* 191–2,[18] he remarks of the disciples' experience that

> The Word leads those who possess faith, hope and love up on to the mountain of theology and is transfigured before them, so that to call him

God is no longer to affirm that he is holy, king and suchlike, but to make denial of him according to the fact that he is beyond God and beyond holy and everything said of him transcendently (*QD* 191, 41–6).

This is a straightforward use of the categories of apophatic and kataphatic theology. What follows, however, is not. Maximus remarks that "the face of the Word, that shone like the sun, is the characteristic hiddenness of his being" (*QD* 191, 47–8). The Greek word for face, *prosopon*, is also the word for person. The divine person of Christ is apprehended by the disciples in an act of *apophasis*: the dazzling glory of the face discloses the hidden reality of the divine, which can only be apprehended in its hiddenness. Maximus gives a Christological twist to the categories of apophatic and kataphatic: the kataphatic affirms the created human reality of Christ, the apophatic points to the hidden mystery of the divine person Christ is. This interpretation is taken a stage further in the discussion of the Transfiguration in *Ambiguum* 10.[19] The brightness that transfigures Christ's body and garments is subject to a long development of something already mentioned briefly in the treatment in the *Quaestiones et dubia*, namely that diaphanous glory of Christ's body and garments symbolizes the clear message of the Scriptures and of creation, transparently clear to those with purified minds and hearts: this represents kataphatic theology, the affirmations we make of God in concepts and images. But the disciples are also "taught hiddenly that the all-blessed radiance that shone resplendently from his face, as it overpowered the sight of the eyes, was a symbol of His divinity, that transcends mind and sense and being and knowledge" (*Amb.* 10.17: 1128A). They were taught to see in one who was "without form or beauty" the "Word made flesh . . . fair with beauty beyond the sons of men". Explicitly Maximus asserts that it is "by a theological denial (ἀπόφασις) that praises Him as being completely uncontained, [that] they were led contemplatively to the glory as of the Only-begotten of the Father, full of grace and truth" (1128B). Later on in the *Ambiguum* he returns to the topic of the Transfiguration and asserts that "the light from the face of the Lord, therefore, conquers the human blessedness of the apostles by a hidden apophatic theology (τῆς κατ' ἀπόφασιν μυστικῆς θεολογίας)" (10. 31d: 1168A). What we find here is not just the influence of a Dionysian theme, but an engagement with it—a creative theological development. It is true that Maximus takes the notion of apophatic and kataphatic theology out of the realm of theology in general and gives it a Christological application, but we should not construe this as a "Christological corrective"; Maximus is not correcting Dionysius, rather he is redeploying one of the theological categories he introduced.

Maximus' Relation of the Cosmic and the Ascetic

The *Mystagogia*, as already mentioned, is presented by Maximus as a supplement to the *Ecclesiastical Hierarchy*.[20] The body of the text is an interpretation of the ceremonies of the Eucharistic liturgy, developing and extending what we already find in Dionysius' treatise. Several of these interpretative passages later found their way into the commentary on the liturgy called "Ecclesiastical History and Mystical Contemplation" (probably more intelligibly translated as "What happens in Church and its hidden meaning"), ascribed by many to Patriarch Germanus I of Constantinople (*c.*640–*c.*733), though attributed in the manuscripts most frequently to Basil the Great, which became the most influential interpretation of the Divine Liturgy in the Byzantine world.[21] The most striking feature of Dionysius' interpretation of the Divine Liturgy is perhaps his emphasis on movement, the movement of the hierarch out from the sanctuary, around the Church, and back again into the sanctuary, symbolizing the circular movement, expressed in the Neoplatonic language of rest, procession and return, that underlies the whole of reality. Maximus has the same sense of the liturgical or ecclesial space as a locus of meaning, but gives this a much richer significance than we find in Dionysius. He does this by prefacing his account of the Divine Liturgy by a series of chapters on the symbolism of the liturgical space itself.[22] The Church first of all symbolizes God, for as God embraces everything and draws it into unity, so too the Church embraces the whole of humankind and draws it into unity (*Myst.* 1). The parallelisms that follow are based on the church as a building, rather than a community—and therefore a liturgical space—divided into sanctuary and nave, and trace this division between sanctuary and nave in other "spaces": in the cosmos of invisible and visible reality, in the visible cosmos of heaven and earth, in the human form of soul and body, in the soul as comprising the intellectual and the living (*Myst.* 2–5). Two final chapters of this introduction suggest a parallelism between the human, comprising body and soul, and the Scriptures, comprising Old and New Testaments, or alternatively, patient of a literal and spiritual interpretation (*Myst.* 6), and between the human and the cosmos, so that the human may be regarded as a microcosm, a miniature cosmos, and the cosmos as the human writ large, a "makranthropos" (*Myst.* 7). This repeated parallelism, like a series of Chinese boxes, means that what happens in the church building has reverberations of interpretation that range from the cosmic to the innermost human soul. An example of how this functions may be seen in the following quotation:

The human is a mystical church, because through the nave which is his body he brightens by virtue the ascetic force of the soul by the observance of the commandments in moral wisdom. Through the sanctuary of his soul he conveys to God in natural contemplation through reason the principles of sense purely in spirit, cut off from matter. Finally, through the altar of the mind he summons the silence abounding in song in the innermost recesses of the unseen and unknown utterance of divinity by another silence, rich in speech and tone. And as far as is possible for humans, he dwells familiarly within mystical theology and becomes such as is fitting for one made worthy of his indwelling and he is marked by dazzling splendour (*Myst.* 4).

The theme of spiritual progress through purification, illumination and union, to use the Dionysian terms, is given a liturgical significance, and beyond that a cosmic significance, making explicit the interrelationships that in Dionysius' own writings are left more or less implicit.

The Maximian Doctrine of the Logoi

One of the most characteristic of Maximus' cosmic ideas is his doctrine of the *logoi* of creation, the principles in accordance with which the whole creation, and each created being, is fashioned, the way in which creation through the Word, or *Logos*, of God is spelled out in detail. In some of the passages already discussed this idea has been implicit: the radiant garments of Christ are said to disclose the *logoi* both of creation and Scripture (the *logoi* of Scripture being both the words of which it is composed and their meaning), and the way in which meaning is expressed through the juxtapositions implied by the parallelisms discussed in the introductory chapters of the *Mystagogia* sometimes makes mention of the *logoi*: "for the whole intelligible cosmos is imprinted in a hidden way on the whole sensible cosmos through the symbolic forms, while the whole sensible cosmos can be understood to be present to the intelligible cosmos through its principles (*logoi*) that reveal its simplicity to the intellect" (*Myst.* 2).

Maximus' doctrine of the *logoi* of creation could well be described as a "lonely meteorite"; its antecedents are scarce and its influence almost nil. It has however been rediscovered in modern times and is a feature of Maximus' cosmic theology that has attracted a good deal of attention.[23] Here is not the place to explore the meaning and ramifications of this doctrine, rather to point out that one of the authorities Maximus cites for the doctrine is a passage in Dionysius' *Divine Names*, where Dionysius says:

> We say that paradigms (παραδείγματα) are the principles (λόγους) that pre-exist as a unity in God and give being to what is, which the theologians call predeterminations (προορισμούς) and divine and good wills (θελήματα), that are definitive and creative of what is, in accordance with which [principles] the One beyond being predetermines and directs everything that is (*DN* 5. 8: 188. 6–10).

Maximus refers to this in justification of his doctrine of the *logoi* in *Ambiguum* 7 (1085A). Again what we find in Maximus is the making explicit and the development of an idea that remains largely implicit in Dionysius. What we find, too, in Maximus' doctrine of the *logoi* is the linking up of the doctrine of the *logoi* he finds in Dionysius with what he found in the Origenist tradition, especially, it would seem, in Evagrius Ponticus.

Nicetas Stethatos was an eleventh-century monk of the Stoudios monastery in Constantinople, who as a young man came to know Symeon the New Theologian in his latter years, and promoted his memory by, among other things, composing his life. He acquired his nickname, Stethatos ("courageous"), for his noisy opposition, quite in the Stoudite tradition, to the Emperor Constantine Monomachos' liaison with his mistress, Skleraina. He also attacked the use of unleavened bread in the Eucharist by the Armenians and the Latins. A number of his other works are polemical. Despite his connexion with Symeon the New Theologian, the differences between them are considerable and nowhere more so than in the question of their reception of Dionysius. Although there are several apparent points of contact between Dionysius and Symeon,[24] the evidence suggests rather that they belong to a common tradition, than that Symeon was drawing directly on Dionysius. With Nikitas the situation is quite different. He quoted Dionysius not infrequently (especially from his works on the hierarchies), and wrote two works where the influence of Dionysius is palpable: *On Hierarchy* and the three *Centuries*, the latter of which were included by Makarios of Corinth and Nikodimos the Agiorite in the *Philokalia*. *On Hierarchy*[25] is concerned to complete what appeared to Nikitas incomplete in the Dionysian works on the hierarchies. Whereas the *Celestial Hierarchy* gives an account of three triads of celestial beings—seraphim, cherubim, thrones; lordships, powers, authorities; principalities, archangels, angels—the *Ecclesiastical Hierarchy* speaks only of two triads of beings (plus a triad of mysteries)—hierarchs, priests, ministers; servers (or worshippers: *therapeutai*), contemplatives, catechumens (plus penitents and the possessed, i.e., those excluded from communion). Nikitas tidies this up in two ways. First of all, he makes the language more ecclesiastical. Dionysius had avoided the settled language of the Church; Nikitas brings it into line with ecclesiastical usage, so that Dionysius' two triads become: bishops, presbyters, deacons; subdeacons, readers, monks. Secondly, he provides a triad of the highest rank: patriarchs, metropolitans, archbishops (cf. *H* 22). The effect of these two changes is to identify the ecclesiastical hierarchy with the clerical hierarchy, thus undermining Dionysius' original understanding of "our hierarchy" (as he called it: "ecclesiastical hierarchy" only occurs in the, possibly editorial, title). Hierarchy becomes less the way in which the divine theophany reaches out into multiplicity to draw the whole created order into union with God, and more a system of subordinate authority that ministers to those outside the hierarchy (the laity, now no longer part of "our hierarchy"). Nikitas keeps the Dionysian definition of hierarchy (indeed, often enough his chapters are composed of lengthy quotations from the Areopagite: cf. *H* 56, 57), but its meaning has been transformed into the provision of a sacramental way of deification, administered by the clergy. The goal of hierarchy now, quite explicitly, lies in the next life (*H* 59): in that life, the ecclesiastical hierarchies will be assimilated to their celestial counterparts. It is odd how, despite his learning and faithful citation of his source, in his hands the

Dionysian cosmic vision dissolves into an all-too-comfortable clerical ecclesi-asticism. We have already noticed the way in which Dionysius' notion of hierarchy was being used to support an understanding of subordinating clerical authority as early as his editor and commentator, John of Scythopolis. Nikitas also shares with John another misreading of Dionysius (minor, if indeed it is a misreading at all) in making the highest of the heavenly beings not seraphim, but thrones (*H* 17, 22 f., 25).

The three *Centuries*[26] conform to a familiar style of Byzantine monastic literature, a threefold century devoted to the three stages of the spiritual life, as described by Evagrius: *praktikē*, ascetic struggle; *physikē*, natural contem-plation; *gnosis*, contemplative knowledge of God. By the time of Nikitas it was already commonplace to assimilate Evagrius' triad to the Dionysian triad of purification, illumination, and union or perfection (it is found, for example, in Symeon the New Theologian), so there is nothing unusual in Nikitas' doing the same. The influence of Dionysius is found in countless details, but also in another broad assimilation, whereby the monastic ideal of the "angelic life", found in Evagrius, but much more widespread, is interpreted in terms of Nikitas' understanding of the purpose of hierarchy: the celestial hierarchies constitute our destiny. A corollary of that might be (though Nikitas does not explicitly draw it) that the monastic destiny is merely "angelic", while patri-archs aspire after thrones! *On Hierarchy* and the three *Centuries* culminate in a vision of the parallel hierarchies united in their song: the highest celestial rank chanting "Blessed is the Glory of the Lord in his place!," corresponding to the chant of the highest earthly rank, "Blessed is the kingdom of the Father and the Son and the Holy Spirit, now and for ever and to the ages of ages!"—the opening acclamation of the Divine Liturgy. The middle rank chants in heaven the angelic song of Isaias' vision (there, specifically the song of the seraphim!), "Holy, holy, holy, Lord of Sabaoth, the whole earth is full of his glory," to which the middle rank on earth replies with the *sanctus* of the Divine Liturgy: "Holy, holy, holy, Lord of Sabaoth, heaven and earth is full of your glory. Hosanna in the highest! Blessed is he who comes in the name of the Lord. Hosanna in the highest!" While the lowest rank, both in heaven and on earth, sings: "Alleluia, alleluia, alleluia." (*H* 31, 48, 55). In the next life, the ecclesiastical hierarchies join in the song of their celestial equivalents (*Century* III. 99).

The influence of Dionysius on Gregory Palamas and the other participants in the hesychast controversy is widely acknowledged, but not thoroughly understood. Both sides appealed to Dionysius (and also to Maximus) with the result that both sides display a broad familiarity with the Dionysian corpus. John Meyendorff, indeed, in his pioneering work on the Palamite controversy maintained that the interpretation of *Corpus Areopagiticum* lay at the very heart of the dispute, Barlaam and Akindynos appealing to Dionysius' apophatic theology, which they interpreted in an intellectualist way, while Palamas himself used the distinction between God's unknowable essence and the energies in which he is made known to safeguard apophatic theology in relation to God's essence, while allowing a genuine experiential knowledge of God through his energies.[27] If, however, we look at the use of Dionysius from the perspective of Gregory Palamas himself (this is clearly not the only way of regarding Dionysius' influence, but it is one easily gleaned from Palamas' *Triads*, the work most studied in relation to the hesychast controversy), it is two aspects of Dionysius that predominate. First, the interpretation of the discussion in *Divine Names* 2 of union and distinction in God; second, the topic of angelic mediation (or strictly speaking the mediation of celestial beings, as Dionysius reserves the term "angel" for the lowest rank of these beings). The first topic relates to the distinction that Palamas found in God between his οὐσία and his ἐνέργεια, his essence and his energies (to use the accepted translation, though the Greek word ἐνέργεια corresponds more accurately to the English "activity", rather than "energy", which rather suggests a potentiality for activity).[28] The doctrine of the Trinity already affirms a distinction within the One God between his οὐσία and his ὑποστάσεις; for Palamas in order to affirm a genuine, deifying participation in God it is necessary to add this further distinction between essence and energy, so that deification may be seen as participation in God's energies. For Gregory Akindynos (Palamas' principal opponent in the strictly hesychast controversy), if the energies are genuinely God, rather than God's operations—created effects of God's activity—then the unity of God is compromised, and we fall into polytheism. In defence of this further distinction within God, that does not compromise the divine unity, Palamas invoked Dionysius' discussion of union and distinction (ἕνωσις and διάκρισις) in *Divine Names* 2. Dionysius develops a fourfold differentiation: of the names with which we praise God some represent "union" and others "distinction", furthermore within the "unified" names, some represent union and others distinction, and similarly within the names that express distinction; there are those that represent union as well and others distinction; so there are unified names expressing both union and distinction, and within names of distinction, too, those expressing both union and distinction. Dionysius's discussion of these names is not entirely clear, but the unified names that express union refer to the attributes of God ascribed to the one divine substance (goodness, justice, mercy, etc.), while the names of union that express distinction are the names of the persons of the Trinity—Father, Son and Holy Spirit. Amongst the names of distinction, those that express distinction seem to refer to the Incarnation *par excellence*, while those that express union seem to refer to "processions and manifestations of the thearchy" (*DN* 2. 4: 640D), that is, perhaps, the manifestations of God as good, wise, just, merciful, etc., among the creatures, which is precisely what Palamas means by "energies". It would seem then that Palamas has some justification for appealing to Dionysius in defence of his notion of energies, as a distinction within the Godhead parallel to the Trinitarian Persons—unified distinctions as opposed to distinct unions—even though Dionysius does not use the word *energeia* in this sense (though he does use it in other senses). But the obscurity of this section of the Areopagite means that it is not difficult for Akindynos to quote against Palamas passages from Dionysius in which he affirms uncompromisingly the unity of God.[29]

The other topic on which Palamas makes reference to Dionysius concerns the question of angelic mediation. Palamas is concerned to refute the idea that angels are necessary intermediaries between humans and God, so that human union with God must take place through angelic mediation. Meyendorff argues that Palamas, following Maximus, "corrects" Dionysius and affirms a more thoroughly Christological understanding of union with God through Christ.[30] It is not clear, however, that this is necessary, for Dionysius' understanding of hierarchy does not interpose the hierarchies between God and humankind, with ascent to God entailing ascent through the hierarchies.[31] It is here that Dionysius, though using their language, breaks away from the Neoplatonic tradition on which he is drawing. Whereas in that tradition, as represented by Proclus, lower beings proceed from higher beings, who proceed from still higher beings, who ultimately proceed from the One—there is a genuine ontological hierarchy—for Dionysius it is only so far as the impartation of illumination, wisdom, is concerned that there is hierarchy; at the level of being all beings proceed immediately from God. The point of hierarchy, for Dionysius, is not to explain how the manifold nature of existence derives from the One, but rather it is the way everything "after God" functions as a theophany, a manifestation of God, drawing all back into union with God.[32]

> When he [Dionysius the Areopagite] reveals to us the origin of the angelic names, he says that many visions appear to us through intermediaries, but not that they are all revealed by [the angels], nor that all union and all enlightenment comes through them. When he speaks of 'that many-hymned doxology of the innumerable heavenly host', which at Christ's nativity was passed on 'to those on earth', when he says that an angel announced the good news to the shepherds because, 'in withdrawal and silence they had been purified', he does not say that the glory of God that enlightened them came through the angels. On the other hand, it was not by the illumination of that glory that the shepherds received the revelation of salvation: because they were afraid, being unused to such visions, the angels announced to them the meaning of the presence of the light.[33]

In this passage, Palamas is not imposing on Dionysius an alien meaning; he is simply demonstrating that he understood the limited purpose of Dionysian hierarchy.

Evidence of a broader, less polemical, influence of the Areopagite is found in hesychast circles in the writings of the supporter of Palamas, Nicholas

Cabasilas, concerned with the Divine Liturgy. Both in his *Commentary on the Divine Liturgy*,[34] and even more evidently in his *Life in Christ*,[35] which takes its understanding of the threefold nature of the "Mysteries", as Baptism, Chrismation and the Eucharist, more or less directly from the *Ecclesiastical Hierarchy*, there is clear evidence that Dionysius' understanding of the sacramental nature of the Christian life was still influential in the Byzantine world.

NOTES

1   The phrase seems to be Vanneste's: see Alexander Golitzin, "Dionysius the Areopagite in the works of Gregory Palamas: On the question of a 'Christological corrective' and related matters", *St Vladimir's Theological Quarterly*, 46 (2002), 163–190, here p. 166, n. 8.

2   And his undoubted influence in the West, especially in the High Middle Ages, can be taken as evidence for the corruption of the Christian tradition in the (Catholic) West.

3   Art historians generally seem confident of a Neoplatonic inspiration for Byzantine aesthetics, mediated or popularized by Dionysius, but rarely seem to explore this: see, *passim*, Gervase Mathew, *Byzantine Aesthetics* (London: John Murray, 1963), and more recently, John Lowden, *Early Christian and Byzantine Art* (London: Phaidon Press, 1997).

4   S. S. Averintsev, *Poetika Rannevizantiyskoy Literatury* (Moscow: Nayka, 1977).

5   So Gerhard Podskalsky, in his *Von Photios zu Bessarion. Der Vorrang humanistisch geprägter Theologie in Byzanz und deren bleibende Bedeutung* (Wiesbaden: Harrassowitz Verlag, 2003).

6   So Andrew Louth in "Photios as a Theologian", in Elizabeth M. Jeffreys (ed), *Byzantine Style, Religion and Civilization: In honour of Sir Steven Runciman* (Cambridge: Cambridge University Press, 2006), pp. 206-223.

7   Steven Runciman, *The Eastern Schism* (Oxford: Clarendon Press, 1955), p. 7.

8   Michael Psellos, *Theologica*, I, ed. P. Gautier (Leipzig: Teubner, 1989).

9   N. G. Wilson, *Photius: The Bibliotheca* (London: Duckworth, 1994), p. 27, n. 2.

10   It might be thought that Leo Magistros Choirosphaktes' *Thousand-line Theology* constitutes an exception, given that the index to Ioannis Vassis' edition gives 59 references to the Areopagite (though this is nothing like the number of references to Gregory the Theologian), but close inspection suggests that a good deal of imagination has been exercised in adducing the references. See Leon Magistros Choirosphaktes, *Chiliostichos Theologia*, ed. Ioannis Vassis, Supplementa Byzantina, Texte und Untersuchungen 6 (Berlin: Walter de Gruyter, 2002), p. 232.

11   The Latin translation divided the work into four books (mirroring the four books of the Lombard's *Sentences*), thus obscuring the fact that it conforms to the monastic genre of the century. The original genre of the work emerges in Kotter's edition: *Die Schriften des Johannes von Damaskos*, II. *Expositio Fidei*, Patristische Texte und Studien 12 (Berlin: Walter de Gruyter, 1973). References are to this edition, abbreviated as *exp. fid.*

12   See Andrew Louth, "St John Damascene as Monastic Theologian", *Downside Review*, 125 (2007), pp. 197-220.

13   See, especially, *imag.* III.26 (and the note in my translation, St John of Damascus, *Three Treatises on the Divine Images* (Crestwood, NY: St Vladimir's Seminary Press, 2003), p. 103, n. 93). For the influence of Dionysius on iconodule theology, see Andrew Louth, " 'Truly Visible Things Are Manifest Images of Invisible Things': Dionysius the Areopagite on Knowing the Invisible", in Giselle de Nie, Karl F. Morrison and Marco Mostert (eds), *Seeing the Invisible in Late Antiquity and the Early Middle Ages* (Turnhout: Brepols, 2005), pp. 15–24.

14   The burden of his article, "Note sur l'influence dionysienne en Orient", *Studia Patristica* 2 (= Texte und Untersuchungen 64, 1957), pp. 547–552, which is really concerned with the influence of Dionysius in Palamas. For a survey of the scholarly treatment of the influence of Dionysius on Maximus and an attempt at a new approach, see Andrew Louth, "St Denys the Areopagite and St Maximus the Confessor: a Question of Influence", *Studia Patristica*, 27 (1993), pp. 166-174. Meyendorff's influence is still detectable in the article by Adolph Ritter, "Gregor Palamas als Leser des Ps.-Dionysius Areopagita", in Ysabel de Andia (ed), *Denys l'Aréopagite et sa postérité en orient et en occident*, Collection des Études Augustiniennes, Série Antiquité 15 (Paris: Institut d'Études Augustiniennes, 1997), pp. 565–579.

15 Maximus, *Mystagogia*, *proœm* (PG 91.660D–661A).
16 For this see the brilliant paper by Ysabel de Andia, "Tranfiguration et théologie négative chez Maxime le Confesseur et Denys l'Aréopagite", in *Denys l'Aréopagite et sa postérité en orient et en occident*, pp. 293-328 (reprinted in *eadem*, *Denys l'Aréopagite. Tradition et Métamorphoses* (Paris: Vrin, 2006), pp. 147–184). My approach is not exactly the same, but I owe a great deal to her treatment. For more detail, see Andrew Louth, "From the Doctrine of Christ to Icon of Christ: St Maximus the Confessor on the Transfiguration of Christ", in Peter W. Martens (ed), *In the Shadow of the Incarnation: Essays on Jesus Christ in the Early Church in Honor of Brian E. Daley, S.J.* (Notre Dame IN: University of Notre Dame Press, 2008 (forthcoming)), pp. 260–275.
17 *Centuries on Theology and the Incarnation* II. 13–16; *Quaestiones et Dubia* 191–2; *Ambiguum* 10. 17, 31.
18 Critical edition by José H. Declerck, CCSG 10, 1982 (abbreviated in references as *QD*).
19 Text in Migne, PG 91:1105C–1205C; Eng. trans. in Andrew Louth, *Maximus the Confessor* (London: Routledge, 1996), pp. 96–154.
20 Critical text by Charalampos G. Soteropoulos, Athens 1993; translation by George C. Berthold in Maximus the Confessor, *Selected Writings* (London: SPCK, 1985), pp. 183–225.
21 See St Germanus of Constantinople, *On the Divine Liturgy*, ed. and trans. Paul Meyendorff (Crestwood, NY: St Vladimir's Seminary Press, 1984).
22 For a more detailed account, see Andrew Louth, "Space, Time and the Liturgy" in *Encounter between Eastern Orthodoxy and Radical Orthodoxy*, ed. Adrian Pabst & Christoph Schneider, Ashgate: Farnham, 2009, pp. 215–31.
23 For this, see my article, "St Maximus' doctrine of the *logoi* of creation" (forthcoming in *Studia Patristica*).
24 Explored in two articles: István Perczel, "Denys l'Aréopagite et Syméon le Nouveau Théologian", in *Denys l'Aréopagite et sa postérité en orient et en occident*, pp. 341–357; Alexander Golitzin, "Anarchy vs. Hierarchy? Dionysius Areopagita, Symeon the New Theologian, Nicetas Stethatos and their Common Roots in Ascetical Tradition", *St Vladimir's Theological Quarterly*, 38 (1994), pp. 131–179 (reprinted in Bradley Nassif (ed), *New Perspectives on Historical Theology, Essays in memory of John Meyendorff* (Grand Rapids, MI: Wm. B. Eerdmans Publishing Company, 1996), pp. 250–276).
25 Critical edition, along with other works by Nicetas, in Nicétas Stéthatos, *Opuscules et Lettres*, ed. J. Darrouzès, *Sources Chrétiennes* 81 (Paris: Le Cerf, 1961), pp. 292–362 (abbreviated in references as *H*).
26 Text in the *Philokalia* (Venice, 1782), pp. 785–851; Eng. trans. in *The Philokalia. The Complete Text*, trans. G. E. H. Palmer, Philip Sherrard, Kallistos Ware, vol. IV (London: Faber & Faber, 1995), pp. 79–174.
27 See Jean Meyendorff, *Introduction à l'étude de Grégoire Palamas*, Patristica Sorbonensia 3 (Paris: Seuil, 1959), pp. 280–285.
28 For a concise account of the appeal to the Areopagite in this connexion, see *150 Chapters* 85–95 (critical edition by Robert E. Sinkewicz: St Gregory Palamas, *The One Hundred and Fifty Chapters*, Studies and Texts 83 (Toronto: Pontifical Institute of Mediaeval Studies, 1988), pp. 182–196).
29 For Akindynos' use of Dionysius, see Juan Nadal, "Denys l'Aréopagite dans les traités de Grégoire Akindynos", in Andia (ed), *Denys l'Aréopagite et sa postérité*, pp. 535–564.
30 See J. Meyendorff, "Notes sur l'influence dionysienne en orient" (cited in n.14, above).
31 See Andrew Louth, *The Origins of the Christian Mystical Tradition: from Plato to Denys* (Oxford: Clarendon Press, 1981), p. 171 f.
32 See Andrew Louth, *Denys the Areopagite* (London: Geoffrey Chapman, 1989), pp. 105–109.
33 Gregory Palamas, *Triads*, II. 3. 28 (ed. J. Meyendorff, *Specilegium Sacrum Lovanense*, 30-31, ed. 2, (Louvain 1973), p. 443).
34 Critical edition by Sévérien Salaville: Nicolas Cabasilas, *Explication de la Divine Liturgie*, Sources Chrétiennes 4bis (Paris: Le Cerf, 1967); Eng. trans. by J. M. Hussey & P. S. McNulty, (London: SPCK, 1966).
35 Critical edition by Marie-Hélène Congourdeau: Sources Chrétiennes 355, 361 (Paris: Le Cerf, 1989–90); Eng. trans. by Carmino J. deCatanzaro (Crestwood, NY: St Vladimir's Seminary Press, 1974).

5

THE EARLY LATIN DIONYSIUS: ERIUGENA AND HUGH OF ST. VICTOR

PAUL ROREM

Dionysius the Areopagite arrived in Latin Europe, specifically in Paris, not as the apostolic missionary destined for beheading and a brief miraculous after-life, but rather as an identifiable Greek manuscript destined for translation and a long life of exposition and appropriation. After the initial reception of the manuscript, the two key contributors to the early Latin Dionysian tradition were John the Scot (Eriugena) in the ninth century and Hugh of St. Victor in the twelfth century, who both wrote commentaries on *The Celestial Hierarchy*. This chapter sketches how they interpreted the Areopagite, emphasizing key passages for each. Eriugena's translation of the *Corpus Dionysiacum* and his *Expositiones* on *The Celestial Hierarchy* exerted a tremendous influence on subsequent Latin readers, including Hugh, and even survived the condemnation of his masterwork, the *Periphyseon*. The Victorine, whose own Augustinian inclinations were largely untouched by his encounter with the Areopagite, nevertheless exerted a distinctive influence by (falsely) attributing to Dionysius the view that in our pursuit of God, "love surpasses knowledge." Together, despite their stark differences, they bequeathed a lively Dionysian tradition to the high medieval authors, scholastics and mystics alike.[1]

Eriugena

In the early ninth century, ambassadors from the Byzantine emperor to the Carolingian court of Louis the Pious were apparently aware of the Parisians' conviction that their patron Saint Denis, the beheaded martyr, was originally

Paul Rorem
Department of History, Princeton Theological Seminary, 22 Tennent Hall, Princeton, NJ 08542, USA
paul.rorem@ptsem.edu

the Athenian Areopagite and author. Among the diplomatic gifts they bore in the 820s was a Greek manuscript of the Dionysian corpus, immediately deposited in the Abbey of Saint Denis in the care of Abbot Hilduin. Earlier versions of the life of Saint Denis/Dionysius were pulled together by Hilduin and amplified with summaries of the Areopagite's writings now literally in hand. Hilduin also directed a translation of the Dionysian corpus, reflecting the specific features of this one Greek manuscript, still extant, including its variant readings, omissions and errors. The Greek Areopagite had become a Latin Parisian, martyred but with a long and influential life yet ahead of him.[2]

Within a short generation of Hilduin's labors, another translation took over, this one by an Irishman named John (Eriugena). Using the same Greek manuscript, paired this time not with a life of the saint but with a full exposition of his thought, Eriugena's translation of the whole corpus and his commentary (*Expositiones*) on *The Celestial Hierarchy*, along with his overall appropriation of Dionysian themes within his own formidable corpus, together constitute the first major Latin reception of the Areopagite.[3] Eriugena never said why he worked out a new translation so soon after Hilduin, by the middle of the ninth century. Modern readers often note John's deeper grasp of some Dionysian concepts, especially the (apophatic) appreciation for the transcendence of God, but Hilduin's translation was not so notably deficient by contemporary standards as to need immediate replacement. Although clearly fallible, it was serviceable enough.[4] The motivation for translating Dionysius anew more likely stems from Eriugena's independent and creative energies and his inclination toward Greek theological categories, including eventually the work of Gregory of Nyssa and Maximus the Confessor, rather than from any compelling problems in Hilduin's version.[5]

Eriugena took up the challenge of not only translating the Areopagite, but also incorporating Dionysian insights into his own philosophical theology, notably in his masterwork, the *Periphyseon*. It was late in his career that he also wrote the line-by-line commentary on the first Dionysian treatise in this manuscript, his *Expositiones* on Dionysius' *Celestial Hierarchy*. Here John immediately goes to the heart of the Areopagite's whole corpus as he sees it and as he incorporated it into his own thought. As often noted, *The Celestial Hierarchy* is not first of all about angels, but rather about God, about revelation, about theological method in the broad sense, specifically including apophatic or negative theology in the opening triad of chapters. To Eriugena, the very first sentence in the Dionysian corpus, that is, in chapter one of *The Celestial Hierarchy*, was the key. He first provides the original text, in translation (as here in capitals):

BUT ALSO EVERY PROCESSION OF THE MANIFESTATION OF THE LIGHTS, MOVED BY THE FATHER, COMING FORTH INTO US EXCELLENTLY AND GENEROUSLY, LIKE A UNIFYING POWER, AGAIN FILLS US AND TURNS US TO THE UNITY AND DEIFYING SIMPLICITY OF THE GATHERING FATHER.[6]

As he does throughout his *Expositiones*, Eriugena adds to his translation some specific comments about Greek words, in this case explanations of "moved by the Father" and "generously" and "fills." Next he gives a paraphrase, the "sense" of the passage:

Thus the sense would be: just as the procession of the divine illumination abundantly multiplies us into infinity, it enfolds and unites and restores us again to the simple unity of the gathering and deifying Father.[7]

After paraphrasing the Areopagite, sometimes more than once, Eriugena usually goes on to add some exposition of his own, revealing his theological interests.

Here he considers the opening Dionysian sentence to reflect the heart of the Areopagite's whole corpus:

Now I say this because almost the entire purpose of the blessed Dionysius through all these books is [first] about the infinite plurality of the multiplication of the highest good, subsisting in itself, into all things, which through themselves would neither exist nor subsist as good things, unless they were to exist and subsist as good things by participation in the one who is essence and goodness in himself, and then [secondly] about the leading-back and return again of this multiform plurality into the highest good itself, in whom the infinite plurality finds its goal and is one.[8]

Keying off the opening of the Dionysian corpus, Eriugena here not only identifies the "entire purpose" of the Areopagite's corpus but also reveals his own deep appropriation of the Platonic tradition of "procession and return." The "Father's lights" are not only revelatory, as in the Dionysian quotation, but also creative, as the source of existence itself proceeding from God, and even salvific, in the return of all back to this unifying source. When Dionysius adds another apostolic testimony, Eriugena paraphrases this central thought yet again:

And he affirms this by apostolic testimony, saying: "ALL THINGS ARE FROM HIM AND TO HIM, AS THE DIVINE WORD SAYS" [Rom. 11:36]. It is as if he said: On this account the divine power collects us and enfolds us toward the unity and deifying simplicity of the gathering Father, since all things proceed from this source and all things return to this same goal, as the holy apostolic saying testifies.[9]

Using the explicit language of proceeding from and returning to the same source and goal, Eriugena here isolates the entire purpose (*intentio*) of the Dionysian corpus. His thorough appropriation of this dynamic of procession and return, *exitus* and *reditus*, descending pluralization and ascending unification, is evident in the structure of his own "summa" of philosophical theology, the *Periphyseon*, as often noted. The world's "macro-history" is there framed as procession from God (creation) and return to God (salvation), explicitly "the procession of the creatures and the return of the same," or "the return of all things into the Cause from which they proceeded."[10]

Further, when Dionysius goes on to specify the enlightenment coming down from the Father as "ANAGOGICALLY ENVEILED BY A VARIETY OF SACRED VEILS," Eriugena's paraphrase applies this image of descending yet anagogical (uplifting) veils to specific Dionysian treatises:

> As if he were to say: the paternal providence and the ineffable concern of the divine love, for our salvation and return toward that which we deserted by sinning, has enveiled the ray, invisible in itself, in various sacred veils, for reasons of uplifting. And it has prepared a certain mode of appearance from these [veils] which are co-natural and proper to us, in order that he who cannot otherwise be comprehended might be comprehensible to us. There is a full treatment of these veils both in this book, which is *On the Celestial Hierarchy*, and in the following one which is entitled *On the Ecclesiastical Hierarchy*, and certainly in the third *On the Divine Names*. But if you ask, we shall preview a few things among the many for the explication of the current sentence.[11]

He then summarizes *The Celestial Hierarchy*, *The Ecclesiastical Hierarchy*, and *The Divine Names* under this general category of "veils," itself part of the larger conceptual framework of (downward) procession and (upward) return. The literary legacy here is enormous, first in the *Periphyseon* itself so evidently structured along these lines. Furthermore, even when the *Periphyseon* was criticized and condemned in the thirteenth century (its version of "procession" was too close to a pantheist emanation, and the "return" of all sounded like universal salvation), Eriugena's translation of Dionysius and his *Expositiones* on *The Celestial Hierarchy* nevertheless continued to circulate freely. When interpreters of Thomas Aquinas' *Summa theologiae* debate its fundamental structure, noting his own use of Romans 11 ("From him and to him and through him are all things"), Eriugena's early Latin appropriation of Dionysius is never far away.[12]

Hugh

David Luscombe and Dominique Poirel have both scoured the historical record for any traces of interest in Dionysius after Eriugena in the ninth century and before Hugh of St. Victor in the twelfth, and have found very little.[13] Between Eriugena and Hugh only a few authors took any notice of Dionysius, but interest picked up in the twelfth century, especially in Chartres and Paris. Hugh's use of "the Fathers" is complex: he completely appropriated the Augustinian tradition, usually without attribution; yet in contrast to his contemporaries he rarely amassed patristic citations.[14] The Areopagite was a special case. When in his *Didascalicon*, Hugh itemized the

Fathers regarding Christian literature, such as Augustine or Eusebius, he largely quoted previous lists and decretals. But he added a sentence of his own on Dionysius: "Dionysius the Areopagite, ordained bishop of the Corinthians, has left many volumes as testimony of his mental ability."[15] Nothing more is said there about these writings, and there is no mention of Paris. In *De vanitate mundi*, however, the long narrative about Christian martyrs starts with St. Peter and then: "Dionysius the Areopagite, accepting his mandate, penetrated Gaul," fought for the truth, and showed the power of life by carrying his head in his hands.[16]

These minimal allusions and the relative absence of Dionysius from Hugh's major works raise questions about his one work that was directly on the Dionysian corpus. Long and thorough, his only non-biblical commentary, the Victorine's exposition of *The Celestial Hierarchy* became a major part of a twelfth-century surge of interest in Dionysius.[17] Yet why he originally took on the project is never fully explained. On the face of it, the work seems to have originated in lectures for novice students, and at their request, he says:

> I said first off and I say again now, lest I lead you on in (false) expectation, that I took up your request regarding the "Hierarchy" of Dionysius not to attempt a full scrutiny of the depths of these subjects but only to uncover the surface of the words and expose them to the light. For this [introduction] is first of all more suited for beginners, especially because we know that what we have undertaken for discussion is too great and beyond our possibilities.[18]

Surely Paris students, whether Victorine novices or external scholars who moved about the area, knew that the Abbey of Saint Denis housed not only the bodily remains but also the literary legacy of its patron saint. It would not be surprising if they asked Master Hugh to introduce them to the local saint who was considered the first of the Fathers. On the other hand, Poirel speculates that Hugh brought with him to Paris a deep familiarity with Dionysius from his own student days, and may have initiated the project himself.[19]

Hugh's *Prologue*, although separable and in fact often separated from the *Commentary* itself, twice confirms that this project was for beginners, literally "for those who should be introduced" to Dionysius,[20] and he there makes a rudimentary introduction. In this complex *Prologue*, Hugh introduces Dionysius in one place as a "theologian and describer of the hierarchies," and elsewhere as a "theologian and narrator of the hierarchies."[21] By itself this duplication would not cause much attention, but the *Prologue* also duplicates quite redundantly both its specification that these "hierarchies" are three (the divine Trinity, the triadic angelic hierarchy, and the human counterpart) and also the explanation for why Dionysius starts with the angelic (*The Celestial Hierarchy*), proceeds to the human (*The Ecclesiastical Hierarchy*) and culminates with the divine (*The Divine Names*).[22] For this and other reasons, the *Prologue* seems to be a composite of introductory remarks by Hugh, perhaps written after the *Commentary* itself, and surely assembled later, probably after Hugh's death. These and other textual questions must await D. Poirel's edition and further studies. For now, however, regarding the purpose of Hugh's *Commentary*, the *Prologue* confirms and amplifies the point that this is for beginners. However deep and difficult the Dionysian concepts may be, Hugh's first task is a "moderate, common, and simple explanation unto understanding. Indeed perhaps this will be an explanation more fitting for those who are to be introduced" to such great material.[23] Hugh's patient way of presenting the entire Dionysian text first, passage by passage, and only then offering his own comments on specific words or word order and overall meaning, supports this view of his pedagogical plan, although such was also the pattern in Eriugena's commentary.[24]

Eriugena's *Expositiones* had already explained many Dionysian words and phrases, in the Latin vocabulary used in his own translation. This Latin Dionysius was supplemented by some further comments on the original Greek text translated by Anastasius the papal librarian.[25] Hugh knows this legacy of the Latin Dionysius, and may even be subtly refuting Eriugena on some points, but does not here mention him or any other commentator.[26] A comprehensive analysis of Hugh's commentary, noting his special emphases and relationship to Eriugena's work, is a separate full-length project. Here only a few general observations can be offered, with limited examples. The work cannot be dated precisely, and may have been revised over time, but seems to stem from the middle portion of Hugh's career, perhaps starting a little before the midpoint, around 1125. As a mature author, Hugh's basic emphases were then already in place, yet this project could still influence his later writings. Such timing allows us to look both for Hugh's own imprint in his comments on Dionysius, and also for a Dionysian imprint on Hugh's other works.

Going through Hugh's entire commentary line-by-line confirms the judgment of previous scholars such as R. Roques and R. Baron, that Hugh is here an objective and faithful expositor of the Dionysian text, sometimes giving it his own spin but not forcing it into his own mold.[27] The whole point is to present the Areopagite's own words (in Eriugena's Latin translation) sentence-by-sentence, usually phrase-by-phrase, so that the students can become acquainted with this Father's text on a basic level. Hugh's own *Didascalicon* insisted on a patient encounter with the "letter" of any text first, before going on to the deeper meanings. Outside of the *Prologue*, Hugh never interjects into the Areopagite's thought, for example, his early and prominent pairing of the works of creation and restoration, even when the Dionysian language of "procession and return" might suggest it as in the first chapter of *The Celestial Hierarchy*. Similarly, when Dionysius interprets the scriptural presentations of the angelic ranks and their activities, Hugh presents this exegesis on its own terms, never importing his own hermeneutical pattern of a three-fold sense, namely, literal-historical, allegorical-doctrinal, and tropological-moral. The result of his fidelity to Dionysius is that the Victorine's commentary is minimally "Hugonian": very little salvation history, only faint traces of *conditio/restauratio*, no eschatology, nothing about Noah's ark, no use of allegory or tropology, very little on pride and humility outside of the (pointed) discussion in the *Prologue*.

There are a few obvious Hugonian touches, such as the brief mention of "the three eyes"[28] and the emphasis on the angels as teachers. Here Hugh appreciated the Dionysian emphasis on angelic mediation, for revelation is basically pedagogical.[29] Further, Hugh consistently interprets the Areopagite's texts about knowing (and unknowing) in terms of knowledge and action or love, including service to the neighbor, beyond the Dionysian warrant.[30] One prominent excursus, pursued below, puts love above knowledge in a decidedly non-Dionysian way. Finally, the Victorine grants the Areopagite's point about apophatic or negative theology, that God transcends our categories and language,[31] yet without ever applying it as rigorously as the Dionysian corpus does. In general, Hugh defers to Dionysius, patiently presenting the Areopagite's text phrase-by-phrase for the students' sake. In the end he even apologizes if his own words have covered up the Dionysian wisdom, like mud on marble.[32] With all this deference to the apostolic authority of the Areopagite, Hugh's *Commentary* is explicitly "Hugonian" only rarely, as in the excursus on love above knowledge, presented below as a case study.

There is another side to the relationship of Hugh to Dionysius, the converse of his commentary not being decisively Hugonian: is the rest of Hugh's corpus somehow Dionysian? That is, how did this deferential encounter with *The Celestial Hierarchy* and the other "apostolic" writings by the Areopagite influence Hugh's thoughts and other works? Briefly, as others have also noted, Hugh's overall corpus does not show many distinctive Dionysian footprints, whether from *The Celestial Hierarchy* or in general.[33] As Poirel concludes, there are no sudden signs of Dionysian influence in Hugh's corpus, no new vocabulary or specific themes or overall theological orientation.[34] True, a portion of this Commentary, specifically on how the communion elements both symbolize and also *are* the body and blood of Christ, was incorporated later into the *De sacramentis*.[35] Yet this isolated example comes from a tangent within Hugh's *Commentary*, perhaps as rebuttal to Eriugena and not a specifically Dionysian point.

Outside of his *Commentary* on *The Celestial Hierarchy*, Hugh shows no definite Dionysian imprint in his presentation of the angels, in *De sacramentis* for example, choosing to draw on Gregory the Great but not using the specific triple triad of angelic ranks distinctive to the Areopagite. Nor does he even use the language of "hierarchy" outside of this work, although the possibility that the *Commentary* itself was dedicated to King Louis VII and was "friendly to secular power and monarchy" is worth exploring further.[36] Grover Zinn has seen the Areopagite's triad of "purification, illumination, and perfection" in the Ark treatises,[37] but the texts do not seem Dionysian enough to argue any real influence. Even someone who comes to Hugh eagerly looking for tracks of the Areopagite will not find hard evidence. The Victorine's descriptions of specific sacraments and orders show no trace of *The Ecclesiastical Hierarchy*; his presentation of Moses and the cloud on Mt. Sinai is completely independent of *The Mystical Theology*; *The Divine Names* makes no real difference in Hugh's doctrine of God, the divine names or attributes. The occasional nod to apophatic theology is more generic than Dionysian, as seen before this Areopagite in Augustine himself. Overall, Hugh reflects the Augustinian appropriation of Platonism, not a Dionysian one. Even with Eriugena's thoroughly Dionysian versions of theophany, "procession and return," and the anagogical thrust of the symbolic (especially the incongruous) in his *Expositiones*, well known to Hugh, the Victorine remains relatively non-Dionysian.

In fact, Eriugena provides the decisive contrast, for his encounter with Dionysius left a deep and broad imprint on his thought and overall corpus. John the Scot became a Dionysian, but Hugh of St. Victor remained an Augustinian, or rather, was his own Victorine. Thus the basic contours of his thought can be understood with minimal reference to Dionysian material.[38] One specific excursus will illustrate how Hugh could take the Dionysian text, as mediated through Eriugena, and make it his own, leaving an enormous legacy for Victorine spirituality and medieval mysticism generally. But in general, Hugh's Dionysian *Commentary* remains largely peripheral to his overall corpus.

A Case Study: "Love Above Knowledge"

Commenting on a passage in the Dionysian *Celestial Hierarchy* regarding the angels, Hugh wrote some influential words: "Love [*dilectio*] surpasses knowledge, and is greater than intelligence. [God] is loved more than understood; and love enters and approaches where knowledge stays outside."[39] The context concerns the etymologies of the angelic designations "Seraphim" and "Cherubim." *The Celestial Hierarchy* had carefully noted that the word "Seraphim" means "fire-makers or carriers of warmth," while "Cherubim" means "fullness of knowledge" or "carriers of wisdom." Dionysius discussed the angels, their names, and various angelic ranks frequently, and not only in *The Celestial Hierarchy*, and he here explicated the symbolism of fire quite fully: mobile, warm, sharp, and so on. But Dionysius never identified the seraphic fire as the fire *of love*. To Hugh, with his pervasive interest in fire, it was plain that the Seraphim's fire was, indeed, the fire of love: the fire of *love* is mobile, warm, sharp, etc.

On this point, Hugh is himself adapting a long tradition in Latin exegesis. The deep background is represented by Jerome, Augustine, and Gregory the Great; the crucial discussion is by Eriugena. In Gregory's gospel homilies, especially on Luke 15 and the lost coin, he discusses the angels, their various ranks and names, and the precedent set by the apostolic Dionysius. Three times he refers to the Seraphim and their fiery love as part of an exegetical commonplace. Yet he never claims that this is the Dionysian understanding of the name Seraphim or of the angelic ranks. As noted already, with many aspects of the medieval appropriation and adaptation of Dionysius, the key is Eriugena. In his translation of *The Celestial Hierarchy*, chapter seven (the chapter and the translation used by Hugh), John accurately presents the various attributes of the seraphic fire—warm, super-burning, inextinguishable, and so forth—and does so without adding any references to charity or love. In his commentary, however, Eriugena poetically explains warmth as the warmth of charity, and fire as the ardor of love:

> Their motion is "warm" because it burns with the inflammation of charity and . . . "super-burning" because the first hierarchy of celestial powers burns above all who come after them in love of the highest good.[40]

Ten times in a single passage, love (*caritas* or *amor*) is associated with fire—warmth, ardor, burning or flaming: "The fire itself of the celestial Seraphim is . . . 'inextinguishable' because the divine love always burns in it."[41]

Eriugena provided Hugh with the linkage between the seraphic fire and love, but he did not argue that the Seraphim and love were thus higher than the Cherubim and knowledge. On the contrary, he discusses the various and apparently conflicting orders used by Dionysius such as that in *The Celestial Hierarchy*, chapter 6, where the thrones are first and the Seraphim last in the supreme triad. But in general, as Hugh pointed out, the Seraphim are the highest in the Dionysian hierarchy, especially in this chapter (7) of *The Celestial Hierarchy* where they are superior to the Cherubim, the bearers of knowledge. Thus armed with Eriugena's linkage of seraphic fire and love, Hugh came to this specific Dionysian text, wrote a long excursus, and left behind the influential conclusion that love is superior to knowledge as the Seraphim are higher than the Cherubim.[42]

Hugh's commentary on *The Celestial Hierarchy* has several other smaller digressions, some of them sounding homiletical and usually on the same issue of love and knowledge,[43] but nothing as extensive as the long excursus at the beginning of chapter seven. A single Dionysian sentence about the name "Seraphim" (CH 7, 205C) received fully nine columns of Hugonian expansion in the familiar Migne edition.[44] Besides the length, this excursus is extraordinary for the way it begins and ends. After quoting the Areopagite's sentence on the Seraphim, Hugh first marvels at these words; they are so profound and divine, he says, that they must have been revealed to the one who penetrated the "third heaven" into the paradise of God. Thus the authority of St. Paul is first invoked for special insights into the celestial heights as then passed on to his disciple Dionysius, who wrote down such amazing words for us.[45] The long discussion of love and knowledge that follows is finally concluded nine columns later by breaking off and starting a new book with an explicit admission: "long intervals require a new beginning."[46] Hugh then re-orients the reader to the Dionysian passage at hand, and finally moves on to the Cherubim and their "fullness of knowledge."

Within this mini-essay on fire and love, on love and knowledge, Hugh employs a complex exegetical strategy, as Grover Zinn has already explored. What is this fire, moving and warm and sharp?

> If we have said that this is love [*dilectio*] perhaps we seem to have said too little, not knowing what love is. Whoever says love never says little, unless perhaps he speaks of a little love. Now this [author] did not wish to speak of a little love, who has said so many things of love. "Mobile," he says, and "unceasing and warm and sharp and superheated."[47]

The fire of love, now applied to human longing, is mobile, warm, and sharp, in that order, as seen in St. Luke's road to Emmaus. "Walking and loving, igniting and fervoring, what were they saying about Jesus, whom they heard and yet did not know along the way?"[48] When the walking disciples felt their hearts burn within them, they had mobility and warmth but did not yet have the sharpness of knowledge. "Because, however, they loved first, then they knew, so that 'sharp' might be in love as also 'warm.' First 'warm,' then 'sharp.' "[49] The sharpness of love penetrates to comprehension. "This love . . . goes through and penetrates all things until it arrives at the beloved, or rather goes into the beloved. For if you do not go into the beloved, you still love externally, and you do not have the 'sharp' of love."[50] With this conjugal imagery we are ready for the *Song of Songs*, with the melting and entrance and embrace:

> Therefore he himself will approach you, so that you will go in to him. You approach him then, when he himself goes in to you. When this love penetrates your heart, when his delight/love reaches as far as the innermost [space] of your heart, then he himself enters into you, and you indeed enter yourself so that you may go in to him.[51]

It is in this context of the bridal couch that Hugh says: "This is not . . . a great love, unless it go through as far as the bridal chamber, and enter the room, and penetrate as far as the interior things, and rest in your innermost [space]."[52] Then comes the well-known passage quoted earlier: "Love [*dilectio*] surpasses knowledge, and is greater than intelligence. He [the beloved of the *Song*] is loved more than understood, and love enters and approaches where knowledge stays outside."[53] Although Hugh was not overly concerned with the apophatic, he perceives from the *Song* that love reaches deeper than knowledge, and that the end of knowledge marks the beginning of *un*knowing. These angels "surround by desire what they do not penetrate by intellect."[54] The bridal chamber of love is beyond the realm of knowing, and thus later authors can associate it with the darkness of unknowing, whether the cloud of Mt. Sinai or the dark night of the lovers' embrace. St. Bonaventure, of course, became the master of these poetic associations, but it is Hugh of Saint Victor's excursus that opened the way for this influential turn of the Dionysian apophatic toward the Franciscan affective.

Yet there is still more in Hugh's mini-treatise, as he waxes rhapsodic on every Dionysian word about the seraphim ("warm, sharp, intimate, etc"):

> Because of this kind of marvelous operation of love, he [Dionysius] has said so many things about it, in which he would perhaps have said everything, if everything could be said. Still, we fear that we may have been negligent or fastidious. It is hard for us regarding something so sweet to leave out anything that we have received, and again it seems reckless to us to add something that we ought not. What is love [*dilectio*], do you think? When will everything be said? Behold we called it itself "mobile and unceasing and warm and sharp and superheated and intent and intimate and unbending and exemplative and re-leading and active and re-heating and reviving." And this seems to be much, and perhaps even enough, except that other marvelous things still follow. I do not know whether they are even more marvelous. "Fiery," he says "from heaven, and purifying like a holocaust." Two things should be noted, because he calls it "fiery," and at the same time "of heaven." For there is also another "fiery" from earth, but it is not similar to that which is "fiery" of heaven.[55]

He goes on to speak of a purifying fire, of a purifying love, and so forth. As a whole, this tangential exposition by Hugh marks the decisive step in a Victorine line for authors such as Thomas Gallus and thus for countless later spiritual writers like the *Cloud* Author, Ruysbroeck and Gerson: not only that love surpasses knowledge in the human approach to union with God, but also that this insight stems from a higher celestial realm and from privileged apostolic revelation through St. Paul to Dionysius, for in the "third heaven" seraphic love is higher than cherubic knowledge.

Conclusion

In sum, the *Commentary* seems peripheral to Hugh's corpus and major concerns. Yet, even if the rest of Hugh's works may have been minimally Dionysian, the attention he brought to the Areopagite's corpus, including his use of Eriugena's translation and the way he interpreted it, left a considerable legacy for Richard of St. Victor, Thomas Gallus, Hugh of Balma, St. Bonaventure, and thus many other medieval spiritual writers taken up elsewhere. In the thirteenth century, the Latin Dionysian corpus circulated as an "annotated Areopagite," in the sense that Eriugena's *Expositiones* and Hugh's *Commentary* were routinely attached to it.[56] The early Latin transmission of the Areopagite was a thin tributary of two main authors, the first under later suspicion and the second never deeply Dionysian, yet through them flowed a translation, two commentaries, and a model for reading diligently the first of the Fathers, especially for spiritual guidance.

NOTES

1   For the Pseudo-Dionysian corpus itself and a sketch of its influence in the Latin Middle Ages, see Paul Rorem, *Pseudo-Dionysius: A Commentary on the Texts and an Introduction to Their Influence* (New York and Oxford: Oxford University Press, 1993), including the authorship question and conflation with Saint Denis on pp. 14–18. To be abbreviated as Rorem, *Pseudo-Dionysius*. For much more on Eriugena's interpretation of Dionysius, see Paul Rorem, *Eriugena's Commentary on the Dionysian Celestial Hierarchy* (Toronto: Pontifical Institute of Mediaeval Studies, 2005), including the fuller context for the texts included in this chapter. To be abbreviated as *Eriugena's Commentary*.

2   On this manuscript and Hilduin's translation, see *Eriugena's Commentary*, pp. 21–46 and the bibliography mentioned there, especially G. Théry, *Études Dionysiennes I: Hilduin, Traducteur de Denys* (Paris: Vrin, 1932). Recently on Hilduin, see Marianne M. Delaporte, "He Darkens Me with Brightness: The Theology of Pseudo-Dionysius in Hilduin's *Vita* of Saint Denis", *Religion and Theology*, 13 (2006), pp. 219–246.

3   The commentary by Eriugena is *Expositiones in Ierarchiam coelestem Iohannis Scoti Eriugenae*, J. Barbet (ed), (*CCCM* 31 [1975]), and will be cited as Exp with chapter and line numbers, followed by page, with translations taken from the appendix to *Eriugena's Commentary*.

4   See Théry, and *Eriugena's Commentary*, p. 73, for an example.

5   Frequently, however, Eriugena's labors are explained by way of critiquing Hilduin. For a recent example, see L. Michael Harrington, *A Thirteenth-Century Textbook of Medieval Theology At the University of Paris* (Paris: Peeters, 2004), p. 1.

6   Exp 1. 144–148, pp. 4–5; *Eriugena's Commentary*, pp. 78 and 184.

7   Exp 1. 202–205, p. 6; *Eriugena's Commentary*, pp. 79 and 185.

8   Exp 1. 205–212, p. 6; *Eriugena's Commentary*, pp. 79 and 185.

9   Exp 1. 212–218, p. 6; *Eriugena's Commentary*, pp. 79 and 185f.

10 *Periphyseon*, PL 122: 528D–529A and 638C; see also 688D and 741C–744A. See the modern edition by É. Jeauneau (*CCCM* 161–165) as used in *Eriugena's Commentary*. On "procession and return" in Eriugena, see Rorem, *Pseudo-Dionysius*, p. 171 and the bibliography cited there, especially the foundational study of M. Cappuyns, *Jean Scot Érigène* (Louvain: Abbaye du Mont César, 1933).

11 Exp 1. 373–384, p. 11; *Eriugena's Commentary*, pp. 80f. and 189.

12 On Thomas, see the chapter in this volume, and Rorem, *Pseudo-Dionysius*, pp. 172–174.

13 David Luscombe, "The Commentary of Hugh of Saint-Victor on the Celestial Hierarchy", in T. Boiadjiev, G. Kapriev and A. Speer (eds), *Die Dionysius-Rezeption im Mittelalter* (Turnholt: Brepols, 2000), pp. 160-164; to be abbreviated as Luscombe, "Commentary." D. Poirel, "Le 'chant dionysien' du IXe au XIIe siècle", in M. Goullet and M. Parisse (eds), *Les historiens et le latin medieval* (Paris: Publications de la Sorbonne, 2001), pp. 151–176.

14 See Dominique Poirel, "'Alter Augustinus der zweite Augustinus': Hugo von Sankt Victor und die Väter der Kirche", in J. Arnold, R. Berndt and R. Stammberger (eds), *Väter der Kirche* (Paderborn: F. Schöningh, 2004), pp. 643–668.

15 *Didascalicon* 4.14 (PL 176: 787A); translation by Jerome Taylor (New York, NY: Columbia University Press, 1961), p. 116.

16 *De vanitate mundi*, PL 176: 737A.

17 A modern edition has been prepared by D. Poirel who kindly supplied a copy of his basic text, to appear as *Hugonis de Sancto Victore Opera III: Super Ierarchiam Dionysii* (Turnhout: Brepols), *CCCM*, vol. 178. Besides the prefatory material in that forthcoming volume, the major study on this entire topic of Dionysius and Hugh will be Poirel's companion volume, *Hugues de Saint-Victor et le réveil dionysien du XIIe siecle: Le "Super Ierarchiam beati Dionisii"* (Paris/Turnhout: Brepols) (Bibliotheca Victorina). All other studies are provisional, awaiting Poirel's two books, although some of his conclusions have been previewed in briefer essays: "L'ange gothique", in A. Bos and X. Dectot (eds), *L'architecture gothique au service de la liturgie* (Turnhout: Brepols, 2003), pp. 115–142; "*Hugo Saxo*: Les origines germaniques de la pensée

d'Hugues de Saint Victor", *Francia: Forschungen zur westeuropäischen Geschichte*, 33/1 (2006), pp. 163–174; Gothic and "Le 'chant dionysien'", mentioned already.

18   PL 175: 960CD.
19   Poirel "*Hugo Saxo*," p. 173f. If the particular variants in Hugh's Dionysian text, or perhaps some marginalia, match the German group of Dionysian manuscripts rather than the Parisian, this speculation would be confirmed, and might even explain how Parisians (including Abelard and Suger) suddenly became interested in Denis in the early 1120s.
20   "introducendis," PL 175: 928B, 931BC.
21   "theologus et hierarchiarum descriptor," chap. 2 PL 175: 927C; "theologus et narrator hierarchiarum," chap. 3 PL 175: 929C.
22   PL 175: 929C/930C and 931C/932B.
23   PL 175: 931B.
24   See Barbet's introductory comments to *Expositiones*, x.
25   See the recent work on Anastasius in Harrington (n. 5 above).
26   See H. Weisweiler, "Die Pseudo-Dionysiuskommentare 'In Coelestem Hierarchiam' des Skotus Eriugena und Hugos von St. Viktor", *Recherches de théologie ancienne et médiévale*, 19 (1952), pp. 26–47; Jean Châtillon, "Hugues de Saint-Victor critique de Jean Scot", in É. Jeauneau, G. Madec, R. Roques (eds), *Jean Scot Érigène et l'histoire de la philosophie* (Paris: CNRS, 1977), pp. 415–431. I am grateful to Ralf M. W. Stammberger for a pre-publication copy of his essay "*Theologus nostri temporis Ioannes Scotus*: Hugh of St. Victor's assessment of John Scotus Eriugena's reception of Pseudo-Dionysius", a paper given at the 2000 Maynooth meeting of the Society for the Promotion of Eriugenian Studies, forthcoming in *Irish Theological Quarterly*.
27   René Roques, "Conaissance de Dieu et théologie symbolique d'après 'In hierarchiam coelestem sancti Dionysii' de Hugues de Saint-Victor", *Structures théologiques de la Gnose à Richard de Saint-Victor* (Paris: Presse Universitaires de France, 1962), pp. 294–364; R. Baron, "Le Commentaire de la 'Hiérarchie céleste' par Hugues de Saint-Victor", *Etudes sur Hugues de Saint-Victor* (Paris: Desclée de Brouwer, 1963), pp. 133–218.
28   PL 175: 975D/976AB.
29   See D. Poirel's contrast of Gregorian and Dionysian angelology in "L'ange gothique," note 17 above.
30   Jong Won Seouh, "Knowledge and Action in Hugh of St. Victor's Commentary on the Dionysian *Celestial Hierarchy*", Ph.D. dissertation, Princeton Theological Seminary, 2007.
31   PL 175: 972C to 978D, esp. 974AB–975A.
32   PL 175: 1154C. On this text, and the other few where Hugh comments on his own commentary, see D. Poirel, "La boue et le marbre: le paradox de l'exegese du Pseudo-Denys par Hugues de Saint-Victor", forthcoming.
33   Luscombe, "Commentary", p. 173.
34   Poirel, "Le 'chant dionysien.'" Curiously, Poirel speculates from this absence of discernable Dionysian influence ("*Hugo Saxo*", p. 173f.) that Hugh must have been a subtle Dionysian all along, already incorporating the Areopagite's thought into his own even before coming to Paris. The alternative argument, suggested here, is that Hugh was never that deeply affected by the encounter with Dionysius.
35   PL 175: 951B–953D in PL 176: 465D–408A, *De Sacramentis* (Two, three, vi–viii). Hugh also gave a compact and influential definition of "symbol" at 941BC.
36   Luscombe, "Commentary", p. 171.
37   Zinn, "*De gradibus ascensionum*: The Stages of Contemplative Ascent in Two Treatises on Noah's Ark by Hugh of St. Victor", in J.R. Sommerfeldt (ed), *Studies in Medieval Culture V* (Kalamazoo, MI: The Medieval Institute, 1975), pp. 61–79.
38   Such as my own forthcoming introductory overview, from Oxford University Press, entitled *Hugh of Saint Victor*, where "Hugh and Dionysius" is an appendix, including some material from this chapter.
39   PL 175: 1038D.
40   Exp 7. 139–43, p. 95.
41   Exp 7. 170–174, p. 95.
42   See also Hugh's terse linkage of love and knowledge in his homilies on Ecclesiastes at PL 175: 175D and 195C.
43   PL 175: 1043D, 1062–1066C, 1118B–1119C, 1130B.

44 PL 175: 1038–1044.
45 PL 175: 1036A; see also 1029C.
46 PL 175: 1045A. This phrase has often been taken to mean a major gap, perhaps several years, in the writing of the Commentary; Baron, "Le Commentaire", p. 134f.; Poirel, *Livre*, p. 110.
47 PL 175: 1037A.
48 PL 175: 1037B; Luke 24, as discussed by Grover Zinn, "Texts Within Texts: The Song of Songs in the Exegesis of Gregory the Great and Hugh of St. Victor", *Studia Patristica XXV* (Leuven: Peeters, 1993), pp. 209–215.
49 PL 175: 1037C.
50 PL 175: 1037D.
51 PL 175: 1038BC.
52 PL 175: 1038C.
53 PL 175: 1038D.
54 PL 175: 1041A.
55 PL 175: 1044AB.
56 H. F. Dondaine, *Le corpus dionysien de l'Université de Paris au XIIIᵉ Siècle* (Rome: Edizioni di Storia e Letteratura, 1953). See now Harrington's work cited above (n. 5). Besides the other studies in this volume, see also the essays by Isabel de Andia, especially on Hugh of Balma and his adaptation of the Victorine Thomas Gallus, in *Denys l'Aréopagite, Tradition et métamorphoses* (Paris: J. Vrin, 2006), pp. 213–256.

6

THE MEDIEVAL AFFECTIVE DIONYSIAN TRADITION

BOYD TAYLOR COOLMAN

This chapter investigates the medieval "affective" interpretation of the CD, an innovation first introduced by Hugh of St. Victor but developed and disseminated by a handful of influential theologians from the thirteenth and fourteenth centuries. Simply put, this tradition, following Hugh but departing from Dionysius, champions love (*amor*, *dilectio*, *affectio*) over knowledge in the pursuit of union with God. The central concern of this chapter, however, is not to police such readings of Dionysius, but to explore this innovative interpretation as reflecting a profound medieval intuition about affect and intellect, an intuition that finds in the Dionysian framework a particularly fruitful vehicle for working out their relationship. While some might legitimately label this "affective" innovation a "misreading" or even a "distortion" of Dionysius' theology, it both reflects and effects profound shifts in the history of western theology, the reverberations of which continue to be felt. In the course of the more than two centuries surveyed below, both the conception of, and relation between, love and knowledge undergo significant changes. Arguably, this medieval interpolation of love over knowledge is produced by the convergence of two theological traditions flowing through the western Middle Ages: the (Augustinian) assumption that God is fully known and loved in a beatific *visio Dei*, which is the goal of human existence, and the (Dionysian) insistence that God is radically and transcendently unknowable. The affective reading of Dionysius is one of several medieval attempts to resolve this contradiction.[1] Furthermore, while the Middle Ages are often thought of in terms of the relation between faith and reason, the love-knowledge question is arguably as important, both for the medievals themselves and for moderns after them, who are often unwittingly

Boyd Taylor Coolman
Department of Theology, Boston College, 21 Campanella Way, Chestnut Hill, MA 02467, USA
coolman@bc.edu

influenced by a relation between intellect and affect that emerged at the end of the Middle Ages.

More precisely, the designation "affective" in the title above refers to a medieval innovation in the interpretation of *The Mystical Theology*. That short treatise, which succinctly encapsulates the Dionysian corpus, depicts Moses' ascent of Mt. Sinai. As he proceeds, Moses leaves behind all sense-perception and intellectual cognition, and at the apex of this ascent, plunges into the "cloud of unknowing," where he is united to God through an absolute negating and utter transcending of all intellectual capacities and cognitive activities. In the affective tributary of Dionysius reception, however, this account of strictly intellectual transcendence was supplemented by the introduction of an affective dimension that posited love (*amor, dilectio, affectio*) as an essential feature of this ascent to and union with God. While *The Mystical Theology* contains no references to charity, love, delight or to the affections generally, for these medieval readers, when Moses finally abandons all intellectual and cognitive activity, he is united to the unknown God *through love*. But that is not all. This affective tradition interpolated love into the Sinai ascent precisely at this point because, in the inaugurating words of Hugh of St. Victor, "love surpasses knowledge and is greater than intelligence."[2] This tradition, accordingly, distinguished with varying degrees of clarity and rigidity a loving power or capacity from a knowing one within the human person, and insisted, moreover, on the superiority of the former over the latter at the highest and most intimate point of the divine-human relationship. At stake, then, in this interpretation of Dionysius is not merely an interpolation of love into *The Mystical Theology*, but also a conviction regarding how human beings are most basically constituted and how they relate most fundamentally to God.

The Affective Trajectory of Medieval Dionysianism

Re-thinking this affective tradition of *Dionysius-rezeption* in the Middle Ages requires a rehearsal of what is currently assumed. The scholarly consensus consists more or less in the following narrative, summarized briefly and in reverse chronological order.

One of the most popular works from the Middle Ages, the fourteenth-century, Middle English *Cloud of Unknowing*,[3] is also the best-known instance of affective medieval interpretation of the Areopagite. Indeed, the anonymous author of this spiritual classic indicates his primary inspiration in the very title of the work, a Middle English adaptation of Mt. Sinai's "darkness of unknowing" in *The Mystical Theology*, Chapter One. Later, he explicitly invokes "the works of Denis" as corroborating his own teaching in the *Cloud*.[4] Throughout this text of spiritual direction, the author assumes a rigid dichotomy between love and knowledge as the soul moves toward God, with a pronounced predilection for the former. Every soul has two powers, "a knowing power" and a "loving power," and "God is always incomprehensible to the first, the knowing power."[5] Or again: "our soul . . . is wholly enabled to comprehend by love the whole of him who is incomprehensible to every created knowing power."[6] "Therefore," the author concludes, "it is my wish to leave every thing that I can think of and choose for my love the thing that I cannot think. Because he can certainly be loved, but not thought."[7]

While in a general way the *Cloud* author locates this priority of love over knowledge in the dark cloud of the Dionysian *Mystical Theology*, he does not explicitly associate this teaching with Dionysius in this work. Yet he does so in another work, a Middle English paraphrase of *The Mystical Theology*, entitled, *Denis's Hidden Theology*.[8] At the end of the opening prayer, the author adds, with no basis in either the original Greek or the later Latin translation of this text,[9] the following sentence: "For since all these things are beyond the reach of mind therefore *with affection above mind*, insofar as I can, I desire to win them to be by this prayer."[10] Similarly, in the first chapter, the paraphrase reads:

> For it is by passing beyond yourself and all other things, and so purifying yourself *of all worldly, carnal, and natural love in your affection*, and of everything that can be known according to its own proper form in your intellect, it is in this way when all things are done away with that you shall be carried up *in your affection*, and *above your understanding* to the substance beyond all substances, the radiance of the divine darkness.[11]

Still in the first chapter, the text exhorts the reader to "enter *by affection* into the darkness" and describes Moses as "exercising *his affection alone*."[12] In all, the author interpolates love or affection into this short treatise no less than five times.

Here, in this fourteenth-century treatise, is the most explicit and extensive "affectivizing" of the Dionysian *Mystical Theology* in the Middle Ages. Among many questions to be asked, a quite basic one is what medieval precedents facilitated this move by the *Cloud* author. Two earlier authors, who also interpreted the Dionysian text in this way, and whose writings may have influenced the *Cloud* author, are the Carthusian, Hugh of Balma (c. 1300), and the well-known Franciscan, Bonaventure (d. 1274). In his *The Roads to Zion Mourn*,[13] the Carthusian organizes his discussion of the ascent to God around the three ways derived from Dionysius: purgation, illumination, perfection/union. Adopting a scholastic genre, Hugh devotes a *"quaestio"* to the "very difficult question" of the love-knowledge relationship in the highest reaches of the ascent. Balma too sides in the end with affection above understanding, though not without some careful nuance.[14] Before Hugh, Bonaventure for his part could say in one of his earliest works that "the most excellent knowledge which Dionysius teaches . . . consists in ecstatic love, and it transcends the knowledge of faith."[15] At the conclusion of his famous *The Soul's Journey into God*,[16] the Franciscan describes the soul's final "passing over" (*transitus*) out of itself and into God as an affective ecstasy of love over knowledge: "In this passing over, if it is to be perfect, all intellectual activities must be left behind, and the height of our affection (*apex affectus totus*) must be transferred and transformed into God."[17] This statement is then followed by an extended quotation from the first chapter of *The Mystical Theology*, which describes the required abandonment of all sense perception and intellectual activity in the approach to the one "who is above all essence and knowledge."[18] The *Cloud* author himself, however, greatly assists the historian's search for precedents. In the Prologue of his *Denis' Hidden Theology*, he explicitly cites his source: "In translating [*The Mystical Theology*], I have given not just the literal meaning of the text, but in order to clarify its difficulties, I have followed to a great extent the renderings of the Abbot of St. Victor, a noted and erudite commentator on this same book."[19] This "abbot of St. Victor" is known today as Thomas Gallus (d. 1246).

Likely born in France, at an unknown date, Thomas Gallus was active on the university scene in Paris in the first two decades of the thirteenth century.[20] Augustinian canon or canon regular at the Abbey of Saint-Victor (over a century old by then)[21] at Paris, Thomas probably became a university master of theology between 1210 and 1218, during which time he likely lectured to the Abbey's students, who ministered in local parishes and priories, especially to the student population.[22] Around 1218-1219, at the request of the papal legate, Thomas (and two other canons) went to Vercelli in Northern Italy to found an abbey and a hospital dedicated to Saint Andrew (where his remains lie today).[23] Apparently chosen for his typically Victorine combination of scholarly rigor and spiritual ardor, Thomas—known in Italy as "Thomas of Paris" (*Thomas Parisiensis*) or "Gallus" ("the Frenchman")—became prior of the new abbey in 1224, and abbot by 1226. After two decades as *abbas Vercellensis*, interrupted only by a year in England in 1238 and a brief period of exile in 1243, Thomas died in 1246.[24]

By all accounts, this last of the great Victorines is the primary architect of, and the fundamental source for later participants in this medieval trajectory of affective Dionysianism.[25] Unfortunately, however, he remains the least studied and understood of all these authors.[26] Gallus' relative contemporary neglect is all the more unfortunate in light of the fact that the wide scholarly recognition of the debt which later authors owe him often gives the impression that these later writers are simply adopting his teaching. The notes for the above-mentioned translation of the *Cloud of Unknowing*, for example, contain numerous citations of Gallus' works, which are intended to demonstrate his influence, both explicit and implicit, on the *Cloud* author. To be sure, the *Cloud* author and others mentioned above are variously indebted to Gallus and frequently adopt certain features of his thought; but what has not received sufficient attention are the *differences* between Gallus' teaching and that of his successors. In fact, crucial dimensions of the Victorine's Dionysianism appear to be lost on his later medieval readers.

The most basic, though for that very reason all the more significant and far-reaching, difference between Gallus and his successors is that to a far greater extent than later thinkers, Gallus entered into and made his own what René Roques has called *"L'Univers Dionysien."*[27] While later thinkers incorporated various Dionysian elements (often mediated by Gallus himself!) into their own teachings, and even made those elements central to them, their interests in and use of the Dionysian corpus were narrower than Gallus', and even what they did appropriate from Dionysius tended to remain distinguishable elements among others in the individual author's own synthesis. By contrast, Gallus' theology is itself a Dionysian world from beginning to end, even as he introduces non-Dionysian elements into it. In light, therefore, both of his importance and his neglect, Thomas Gallus will be the primary focus of this chapter.

Dionysius Among the Victorines: From Hugh to Thomas of St. Victor

An initial appreciation of Thomas Gallus must situate him within the tradition of Victorine interpretation of Dionysius. Although Gallus is the primary architect of this affective tradition, he is not its originator. As noted, that honor belongs to his great Victorine predecessor, Hugh of St. Victor (d. 1141).[28] While the warrants for Hugh's innovation are found in prior authors, he unites them in an original synthesis.

Among Hugh's many works is a commentary on *The Celestial Hierarchy.*[29] Commenting therein on Dionysius' discussion of the etymologies of the various angelic designations, Hugh notes that according to Dionysius "Seraphim" means "fire-makers or carriers of warmth," and connotes mobility, warmth, sharpness, etc., while the word "Cherubim" means "fullness of knowledge" or "carriers of wisdom." For Hugh, most likely drawing on the works of Eriugena and Gregory the Great before him,[30] it is self-evident that Dionysius' seraphic fire was in fact the fire of love, although Dionysius had never suggested this. By itself, this identification of seraphic fire with love was not wholly original to Hugh, and neither was his next move. In this context, Hugh offers the oft-noted statement, quoted above, regarding the superiority of love over knowledge, and then elaborates: "[God] is loved more than understood; and love enters and approaches where knowledge stays outside." This claim for the superiority of love over knowledge is not innovative. A long-standing monastic tradition had said as much, expressed in Gregory the Great's pithy statement: "Love itself is knowledge,"[31] implying thereby the possibility of a "loving knowledge" superior to other kinds of knowing. But, as Paul Rorem has noted, when Hugh attributes to the apostolic Dionysius the teaching that seraphic love of God surpasses cherubic knowledge of God, he made a wholly original claim and so inaugurated a fertile and long-standing trajectory of affective medieval Dionysian reception.[32]

Gallus' Affective Interpretation of Dionysius

Thomas Gallus likely knew Hugh's commentary, since it had become attached to the Dionysian corpus itself as part of the "annotated Areopagite," not just for the Victorines but for all readers, at least in Paris.[33] As a Victorine himself, moreover, Gallus would have had ready access to his predecessor's works while at Saint-Victor. Not surprisingly, in one of his earliest works,[34] Gallus writes in a manner strikingly reminiscent of Hugh: "We are convinced that the affection is ineffably, more profoundly, and more sublimely drawn to God by God himself than is the intellect, because men and angels love more than they have the power to reason or understand."[35] Whether directly influenced by Hugh or not, Gallus pursues and expands a similar line of thought.

Gallus' interest in the Dionysian corpus is part of a surge of interest in the corpus, often described as the "second wave" of medieval Dionysius reception, evident in the early thirteenth century, especially at the University of Paris.[36] Gallus reflects and contributes to this development. Scholars have long noted the massive influence of the Dionysian corpus on Gallus' theology, as he was in the vanguard of the early thirteenth-century revival of interest in the corpus, which by his own admission he studied diligently for twenty years—"with such vigilance! with such labor!"[37] Gallus engaged the Dionysian corpus directly in three different works: the *Exposicio* (1233), an early gloss of *The Mystical Theology;*[38] the *Extractio* (1238), a paraphrase of the entire corpus; and the *Explanatio* (1242),[39] a commentary on each of the treatises in the corpus.[40]

An Affective Reading of The Mystical Theology

Gallus' affective interpretation of the Dionysian corpus is apparent from his first engagement with *The Mystical Theology.*[41] In his *Exposicio* (1233), or "Gloss," the first dateable Latin commentary on *The Mystical Theology,*[42] the Victorine offers several affective glossings to a text that in both its original Greek and subsequent Latin translation remains consistently intellective and apophatic. On Chapter One, for example, he argues that the "peak of the divine secrets . . . is called beyond height, because the intelligence (*intelligencia*) fails at it in virtue of the transcendent uniting of the *affection* (*affeccionis unicionem*)."[43] He exhorts: "rise up . . . in knowing ignorance . . . by means of the principal affection (*principalem affectionem*)" to God, who is "incomprehensibly above all knowing."[44] Similarly, on Chapter Two: "we desire with the whole affection of the mind (*toto mentis affectu*) to be in the darkness beyond brightness, that is, in that state above intellect."[45]

In the *Exposicio*, all of these statements are explicitly Gallus' own exposition of the Dionysian text, which he clearly quotes before adding his own interpretative comments. In his better-known "simplifying paraphrase"[46] of *The Mystical Theology*, the *Extractio* (1238), however, Gallus goes a step further.

Concluding the first chapter, he writes that Moses is "united to the intellectually unknown God through a union of love (*dilectionis*), which is effective of true cognition (*verae cognitionis*), a much better cognition than intellectual cognition."[47] Here, for the first time, the very text of *The Mystical Theology* acquires an affective dimension, which it had lacked heretofore.[48]

In both of these texts, the Abbot of Vercelli has extended Hugh of St. Victor's basic intuition—that Dionysius himself had taught the superiority of love over knowledge in the divine-human encounter—by doing what Hugh (nor, apparently, anyone else) had never done: interpolating that superior love into the very text of *The Mystical Theology*.

The Dionysian Darkness Becomes the Solomonic Lovesick Night

On the basis of his glossings above, Gallus' conception of the relation between love and knowledge (and that of his successors as well) appears rather straightforward: in the soul's ascent, knowledge ultimately fails, while love presses on to union with God. Given his repeated engagement with the Dionysian corpus, moreover, it might be assumed that these are the best sources of his interpretation of it. In fact, it is his multiple engagements with the Song of Songs that contain the fullest expression of his appropriation of Dionysius, and therein Gallus offers a more nuanced view of the knowledge-love relation.

Gallus seems as much preoccupied with the Song as with the Dionysian corpus. Three different commentaries have been attributed to him,[49] the first of which is now deemed spurious.[50] In these, Gallus stood in a long line of medieval thinkers who wed a Neoplatonic metaphysics of *eros* with an allegorical interpretation of the Song of Songs.[51] For Gallus, while Dionysius offered a theoretical account of the soul's ascent to God, in the Song of Songs, "Solomon gives us the practice of this same mystical theology."[52] With this, in Paul Rorem's words, the Dionysian darkness becomes Solomon's lovesick night.[53] Gallus' overall role in the medieval reception of Dionysius is thus well-summarized by Bernard McGinn: "[Gallus] combined Dionysian apophaticism with an affective reading of the Song of Songs to form a potent new mystical theory that had a major influence in the later Middle Ages."[54]

The "Angelized" Mind

Gallus' Song commentaries pose a formidable threat to the most intrepid reader, as the "l'abondance des details et la luxuriance des images"[55] often obscure their organizing principle. As Gallus himself recognized, the crucial interpretive key to the commentaries—and the most distinctive feature of Gallus' appropriation of the Dionysian corpus and the most jarring feature for the modern reader—is his "angelization" of the human mind,[56] modeled on Dionysius' description of the nine angelic orders, subdivided into three triads, each with its own particular name, office, and activity.⁵⁷ In the Prologue to his commentaries, Gallus describes the "angelized" mind as follows. The lowest hierarchy (Angels, Archangels, Principalities) is the basic nature of the soul and its wholly natural activities. The middle hierarchy (Powers, Virtues, Dominions) is the realm of nature assisted by grace, and involves "effort, which incomparably exceeds nature." The highest hierarchy (Thrones, Cherubim, Seraphim) is the realm of grace above nature, and involves "ecstasy" in the literal sense of transcending the mind itself (*excessus mentis*).⁵⁸

While Gallus' angelic "hierarchization" of the human mind and its application to the Song of Songs has been widely noted, its implications both for his affective interpretation of Dionysius generally and for his highly nuanced conception of the relationship between love and knowledge therein, have not been fully appreciated. Perhaps the most insufficient, even distorting, approach to Gallus reads him as narrating a linear itinerary of the soul's ascent to God through the various angelic orders of the soul. Such interpretations delineate the stages along a uni-directional path upwards to union with God. After noting that at the threshold of the final step Gallus explicitly excludes knowledge and allows only love to enter into an "unknowing" union with God, these accounts see him constructing an affective Dionysianism that is basically anti-intellectual.⁵⁹ A sustained reading of Gallus' whole corpus, however, reveals such accounts to be over-simplified and needing both expansion and qualification.

The interpretation offered here differs from this standard account. It argues that Gallus has appropriated first and foremost the Dionysian conception of hierarchy in general—namely, a dynamic ascending-descending structure of inter-related entities that mediates revelation from higher to lower and elevates the lower into the higher. Accordingly, Gallus' angelized mind is most fundamentally and ultimately a dynamic, multivalent, highly-structured state of being, in which love and knowledge are related in reciprocal and mutually reinforcing ways. This can be analyzed in three crucial "moments" or valences: ascending, descending, and, bringing these together, circling/ spiraling.

Ascending

The ascending valence in the soul traverses the path from the lowest to the highest angelic rank in the soul. For Gallus, this ascent involves two forms of *cognitio Dei*. The first kind is "intellectual," "acquired through the consideration of creatures" and "gathered from the prior knowledge of sensible things"; it is a *scientia*, gleaned from the "mirror of creatures," that "ascends from the sensible to the intellectual." This is the realm of philosophical knowledge of God.⁶⁰ The second form is the super-intellectual *cognitio*, described above in his interpretation of *The Mystical Theology*. This is the *sapientia christianorum*, the wisdom that Paul had taught *among the perfect*, which *descends from the Father of lights* (Jas 3:17).[61] It is a "loving and uniting knowledge" (*affectualis cognitio et unitiva*).[62] The first is like "wine" extracted from grapes; the second like milk which flows down from the breast of wisdom itself.[63] The ascent begins with the pursuit of the first, and ends with the reception of the second.

The first triad corresponds to the nature of the soul itself, which consists in "the basic and simple natural modes of apprehension, both of *intellectus* and *affectus*."[64] While Gallus does not linger here, the intimate relation between intellect and affect, whose mutual interaction begins a movement "leading them to the divine"[65] is already evident. This interrelated activity is intensified in the middle hierarchy (Powers, Virtues, Dominions), where, by the "voluntary acts of both *intellectus* and *affectus*" the soul now seeks "the highest good with all the powers of *intellectus* and *affectus*."[66] Here, from the consideration of visible things, the "mirror" of creatures, the middle hierarchy is "led back" and "up" to an intellectual understanding of God as the Artisan and Creator of all things. In the middle triad, this activity reaches its natural limit. Still contained within itself (*enstasis*) and sober (*sobria*), the soul yet desires that which exceeds its capacities and, indeed, even its nature.[67]

The transition from the middle to the highest hierarchy is a crucial "hinge" in the ascent. Having reached the limits of its natural capacities, even as aided by grace, the soul must now be raised "above" and "outside" itself (*ecstasis*). There is also a change in the soul's posture: it now turns from the active derivation of *cognitio Dei* from created things, to a more passive or responsive reception of the supra-intellectual wisdom coming down from above. Despite these radical shifts in the soul, however, there remain important continuities. For Thomas, the enstatic labor in the lower and middle triads is preparatory for ecstatic reception in the highest triad. The "movements . . . of the affect and intellect" are "simplified (*simplificantur*)," contracted or drawn together.[68] They are, moreover, "simplified *in order to be* extended (*ad extendum*) into the super-simple ray"[69] and "exercised" (*exercetur*) for receiving the "divine inpouring" (*divinos superadventus*).[70] Gallus evokes this emerging capacity of the soul with striking images. By this enstatic labor, the soul "hollows out" within itself "cavities" or "receptacles" of the mind (*sinus mentis*). The soul "extends upward (*sursumextendit*) every capacity of the mind (*omnes mentis sinus*) for receiving the divine light."[71] And, as a *rounded bowl* (*crater tornatilis*) or "navel," "the interior hierarchies are stretched out (*porriguntur*) to receive the nourishment of divine knowledge (*scientie*), cognition (*cognitionis*) and devotion . . . because of their most ample capacity."[72] In short, practiced on the "wine" of knowledge extracted from creatures, the soul is now capacitated (stretched, extended, expanded) for receiving the "milk" which flows down from above.

This capacitating effects the transition from the enstatic second hierarchy to the ecstatic third hierarchy (Thrones, Cherubim, Seraphim), for the soul becomes a Throne by being made capable of receiving her divine Spouse: "There are as many thrones as there are interior cavities (*sinus*) or capacities (*capacitates*) of the mind for [receiving] the super-substantial rays."[73] It must be stressed here that this ecstatic drawing up into the highest triad implicates both the *affectus* and the *intellectus*; both are drawn up out of themselves at this point.[74] From here, the soul is now drawn up into the order of the Cherubim. The cherubic rank, accordingly, contains "every kind of cognition," both of "the *intellectus*, which is drawn up by the divine worthiness, though not able to reach it," and "of the *affectus*, similarly drawn up, without exceeding the heights of the drawn up *intellectus*." Here, the "upwardly pulled affect" (*affectus attractus*) and "upwardly pulled intellect" (*intellectus attractus*) "walk hand in hand" (*coambulant*)[75] up to the point where at "the consummation of its cognition and light" the intellect fails (*defectus intellectus*).[76] Then, to the ninth and seraphic rank, only the "principal affection" (*affectus principalis*) is able to proceed, which alone is able to be united to God.[77] Here, finally, are the "embraces of the Bridegroom," and "Mary's portion," which "will not be taken away."[78] Only now does Gallus separate *intellectus* and *affectus*, barring the former from proceeding further into the final darkness of union with the Word: "here is the cutting off of knowledge," after which only the "*scintilla synderesis*," the "spark of the soul," remains.[79] This is Gallus' unique and influential teaching regarding the "high point of affection" (*apex affectionis*), which alone is capable of ecstatic, loving union.[80] This is the ecstatic climax of the entire ascent: the merging of the love-sick night of Solomon and the apophatic darkness of Dionysius' Moses. This merging of the Song's spousal imagery with the Dionysian ascent allows the Victorine to introduce a Christological dimension precisely where it seems absent in the *MT*—at the very highest point of the ascent, where the soul is united to God. At the seraphic rank, the soul-bride is united to the divine-Spouse in loving embrace, and "cognizes God above every existing intellection and cognition."[81]

"Cognizes God above . . . cognition"—this paradox reflects an important feature of Gallus' teaching. Frequently, he uses the language of spiritual sensation to delineate more precisely the soul's encounter with this higher *cognitio Dei*. On the one hand, he attributes "eye-ishness (*oculositas*)" to the cherubic order, due to "the highest perspicacity of the attracted intellect."[82] And it is this cherubic seeing that is blinded in the amorous darkness of seraphic union, where the soul lacks "mental eyes" (*oculos mentes*), that is, reason and understanding (*carentes ratione et intellectu*).[83] Yet, the soul is not completely senseless here. Rather, the *affectus* is still able to smell, and especially to taste and touch the beloved: "love penetrates by touching, smelling, and tasting."[84] Elsewhere, he explicitly suggests that divine unknowability is overcome through this knowledge by taste:

This refreshment does not occur *through a mirror*, but through the experience of divine sweetness (*divine dulcedinis experientiam*), because taste and touch are not accomplished *through a mirror* ... , though vision is, I Cor. 13:12: *now we see through a mirror*. Therefore Job 1:18 [says] *No one ever sees God* and Ex. 33:20 [says] *man will not see me and live*, but it does not say, he will not taste (*gustabit*) or we will not taste (*gustabimus*)."[85]

Thus, this highest experience of loving union is truly wisdom (*sapientia*), a tasted knowledge.[86] What form of knowing this entails is difficult to say. At the least, for Gallus seraphic union involves a genuine *cognitio Dei*, a term which has a far wider connotation for him than the modern English cognate "cognition"—"whom I cognize (*cognosco*) only by the most intimate experience of love (*dilectionis*)."[87]

Descending

It is often assumed that in a straightforward manner this affective seraphic union above intellective cherubic knowledge is the stopping point of Gallus' mystical theology. In fact, however, it is not. In the Prologue, after narrating the ascent through the soul's angelic hierarchies up through the seraphic union, he observes: "It is from this order [the Seraphim] that the torrent of divine light pours down in stages to the lower orders."[88] This remark introduces a conspicuous feature of his Song commentaries, which is consistently present along with the narration of the soul's ascent to union, namely, Gallus' extensive attention to movement in the opposite direction, that is, descent.

One dimension of this descending valence has already been noted. For Gallus, the higher, super-intellectual *cognitio Dei* is divine revelation that *comes down from the Father of lights*: "This mind God waters from the higher *theoria* of eternal wisdom."[89] In another Vercellian innovation, he conceives of this revelation in terms of divine ecstasy, insisting that in the soul's union with God, not only must there be a human *ecstasis mentis*, but a divine one as well. This is not simply the metaphysical divine *eros* described in the fourth chapter of the *Divine Names*, which generates the cosmic *exitus-reditus* dynamic at the heart of all created reality,[90] but a more inter-personal ecstatic and self-revelatory love evoked by the spousal imagery of the Song of Songs. For Gallus, then, there is a mutual and reciprocal divine-human ecstasy in mystical union: The "fullness of my divinity is always ready ... to inflow (*influere*) minds"[91] and "God's love draws itself out to other minds and attracts them back to itself."[92]

This descending valance in the divine nature itself "drives" and produces a parallel descending movement in the soul. More precisely, the soul receives this divine revelation as hierarchically mediated from higher to lower within itself, beginning with the experience of seraphic union: "the order of the seraphim first flows into (*influat*) the [orders of] the cherubim and thrones, and then into the inferior orders."[93] To describe this fecundating descent, Gallus multiplies images: from seraphic union, "every true refreshment of the mind (*vera mentis refectio*) is transmitted into the inferior orders"[94]; from it, "*spikenard*," "the most sweetly fragrant fervent love (*amor fervidus suavissime fragrans*), is distributed to the lower orders, according to their capacities"[95]; from it like breasts (*ubera*) "are the in-flowings (*influitiones*) . . . into the inferior orders"[96]; as a nourishing "light rain," this influx "re-fills (*replete*) and refreshes (*reficit*) every capacity (*sinus*)" of the mind that has been extended to receive it.[97] Addressing the Groom with the Song verse—*your name is oil poured out*—the seraphic bride says that this oil of loving union is now poured out upon her whole soul, "cleansing, illumining, and healing" her "whole hierarchy."[98]

The significance of this descending valence for Gallus' affective Dionysianism, and in particular for the relation between *intellectus* and *affectus*, is not small. For although the seraphic union is exclusively affective, it nonetheless flows down and fecundates not only the *affectus* but also the *intellectus* at the "lower" ranks of the soul.

> This higher garden [of the seraphim] is made into a fountain by the water flowing down from above and from its abundance; and it pours *affectual* and *intellectual* abundance (*copias affectuales et intellectuals*) to the lower orders; but the Groom commends this fountain from the principal inflowing, namely, the *affectual* inflowing (*affectual influitio*), which is like a fountain of *intellectual things* (*intellectualium*), according to which there is an inflowing from the higher watering.[99]

Leaving the garden for the nursery, both "clarity" (*claritatem*) and "sweetness" (*dulcedinem*) flow down from the chest (*pectore*) of the Groom into the breasts (*ubera*) of the bride, and from the seraphim of the bride into the lower orders.[100] From seraphic union, the bride "draws a great abundance of both the love of true goodness [in the *affectus*] and the cognition of eternal truth [in the *intellectus*], from which a copious abundance flows down into the Cherubim and into the inferior orders."[101] In the Song's language of milk and honey, Gallus describes a cascading descent: *honey* refers to "the affectual in-flowings (*affectuales influitiones*) flowing down from the first hierarchy into the lower ones," while the *milk* that "flows out from the breasts" is the "sober intellectual cognition (*intellectiva cognitio sobria*) flowing down from the breast of the first hierarchy into the second."[102] In short, he posits within the hierarchized soul, not only an ascent through knowledge to love, but also a descent from love to knowledge. Seraphic, affective union flows "back down" into and fecundates the lower orders according to their capacities—"made fecund, having been excited by the taste of divine sweetness."[103]

Circling and Spiraling

After introducing the hierarchies of the soul in the Prologue to his Song commentaries, Thomas Gallus observes that through them the soul is led back up (*reducitur*) into God, who in "the holy and unified convolution of the Trinity" (*convolutione sancta et unice Trinitatis*) is an *eternal circle, moving through the Good, from the Good, in the Good, and to the Good.*"[104] Elsewhere, he gives a similar description: "moving and acting through himself . . . God emanates to existing things and is converted back to the good; in which divine love (*divinus amor*) is shown to be a kind of eternal circle (*quidam eternus circulus*) . . . through a kind of unerring circulation (*circulationem non errantem*)."[105] This divine circulation characterizes God's relationship to the soul: "The divine light descends through the higher orders step by step all the way to the lowest, and . . . filling and reviving both the lowest and all the other orders one by one, it leads them back up (*reducit*) into the divine."[106]

Conversely, Gallus' overarching conception of the soul's relationship to God, and in particular the relationship between love and knowledge, mirrors the divine nature. For the ascending and descending valences in the hierarchized soul ultimately generate a perpetual "circulation" within it too. The bride says that she "will not cease to go after him—*I will seek his face always* (Ps. 104)—by rising up in unknowing in imitation of God to *circle around the city* (Sg. 3:2)."[107] For *the city* is "the super-infinite fullness of the deity, around which [human and angelic minds] are said to circulate (*circuire*) . . . by contemplating the invisible divine things with the highest loving, yet not penetrating intimately the divine depths; therefore, [such minds] are said to circle God (*circuire Deum*) or to be *in the circle of God* (*Celestial Hierarchy 7*)."[108] Fittingly, the Victorine compares this circulation to the angels descending and ascending a ladder in Jacob's vision: There is an "inflowing (*influitio*) of his light from the first order all the way to the last and a flowing back (*refluitio*) all the way back to the highest, according to that verse where Jacob saw the *angels ascending and descending* (Gn. 28:12)."[109] In sum, for Gallus, "circular motions" (*motus circulares*)[110] are the signature activity of angelized souls.

In this unending circulation *affectus* and *intellectus* are always interrelated. Walking together hand in hand (*coambulans*), as noted above, knowledge and love ascend to an exclusively affective union with the divine Groom; yet, from the Groom "pours forth as much perspicacity of contemplation as agility of desires"[111] into the lower orders. Receiving these, "the natural affect and intellect (*affectus et intellectus naturales*) are strongly urged to rise up."[112] So, once again, "through its sober industry, intellection (*intelligentia*) gives birth to affection (*affectionem*), in the same way that *cognitio* precedes and begets *amor*, although the former is excelled by the latter."[113] Accordingly, the "circling (*circuitiva*) and embracing (*amplexativa*) contemplation" of the Groom in the highest hierarchy of the bride "produces (*ingignit*) cognition and love in the inferior orders, that is, it circles around him anew (*de novo* circuivit eam)."[114] In short, the experience of loving union flows down to fecundate the lower orders of the mind with new love and knowledge, which only intensifies the movement of ascent again to loving union.

In light, though, of the super-substantial divine nature, which always transcends and exceeds the capacity of the soul's knowing and loving powers,[115] this intra-mental circulation is a never ending, constantly renewed movement around God—"circular turnings" (circulares convolutiones) lacking "beginning and end."[116] The Groom is always drawing the soul to higher things "as if he comes to me from a new place."[117] The experienced bride "always desires to make progress in the taste of sweetness and in being uplifted (sursumactionem)," such that, "through constant ascensions of contemplation . . . new things are continually succeeding one another unto infinity (in infinitum)."[118] The very last word of the Third Commentary ends on this note: the bride is petitioning the Groom to come to her again and draw her back to himself, a posture in which "she perseveres perpetually (perpetuo perseverat)."[119] Ultimately, this circulation of love and knowledge within the soul becomes a "spiraling" movement of the whole around God. For, "however much any angelic or human mind is taken up . . . such a one is always circling (circuibat) those intimate things."[120]

Conclusion

The implications of the foregoing for "re-thinking" Gallus' affective Dionysianism are not far to seek, though they are far-reaching. An interpretation of the knowledge-love relationship in Gallus derived only (or primarily) from his expositions of the Dionysian corpus itself cannot but yield an oversimplified account. For the full extent of his use of Dionysius is only found in his commentaries on the Song of Songs, where he executes his most original and the most significant appropriation of the Areopagite. The most important are these: the fusion of Moses' "cloud of unknowing" on Sinai with the bridal chamber of the Song of Songs; the concomitant re-interpretation of the Dionysian metaphysical eros as the interpersonal, ultimately Christological dilectio of the soul and the Word, wherein both God and the soul meet in a correlated, though divinely initiated, ecstasy; and most importantly, his "angelization" of the human mind with the Dionysian celestial hierarchy.[121] This last affords him a dynamic, highly-structured, though remarkably supple framework for conceiving a multi-dimensional interaction between the soul and God that engages both the intellectus and affectus. Ultimately, this is not merely a heuristic for classifying and arranging the various powers and acts of the soul (though it is that); not a ladder of steps by which the soul simply sheds the encumbrances of knowledge, which are finally "kicked away" so that love may be united to God; not finally a linear, uni-directional itinerarium mentis in Deum that merely departs from point A (the soul) and arrives at point B (God). Rather, within the angelically "hierarchized" soul,

Gallus finds the soul's intellective and affective powers ascending and descending in an unceasing *circulatio circa Deo*.[122] Apparently, Gallus' commentaries on the Song of Songs were either unknown or largely ignored by his medieval successors, for while many of them seem to be influenced by his interpretation of the Dionysian texts themselves, the complex, "angelized" affective Dionysianism of his Song commentaries is not taken up after him.

NOTES

1 See Simon Tugwell, O.P., "Introduction", in *Albert and Thomas: Selected Writings* (New York, NY: Paulist Press, 1988), pp. 39–55.
2 *In hierarchiam caelestem S. Dionysii* (PL 175: 1038D). See Rorem's chapter in this book.
3 *The Cloud of Unknowing*, trans. James Walsh, S.J. (New York, NY: Paulist Press, 1981). Hereafter, *Cloud*, followed by chapter and page number.
4 *Cloud* LXX, p. 256.
5 *Cloud* IV, p. 123.
6 *Cloud* IV, pp. 122–123.
7 *Cloud* VI, p. 130.
8 *Denis's Hidden Theology* in *The Pursuit of Wisdom and Other Works by the Author of the "Cloud of Unknowing"*, trans. James Walsh, S.J. (New York, NY: Paulist Press, 1988).
9 Paul Rorem argues that "the Areopagite's ascent to union with God through knowing and unknowing dominates *The Mystical Theology* so completely that there is no reference whatsoever to the role of love in the ascent" (Paul Rorem, *Pseudo-Dionysius. A Commentary on the Texts and an Introduction to Their Influence* [New York and Oxford: Oxford University Press, 1993], pp. 215–216).
10 *Hidden Theology* (trans., Walsh), ch. 1, p. 75.
11 *Hidden Theology* (trans., Walsh), ch. 1, p. 75.
12 *Hidden Theology* (trans., Walsh), ch. 1, p. 76; p. 77.
13 Hugh of Balma, *The Roads to Zion Mourn*, trans. Dennis Martin (New York, NY: Paulist Press, 1996).
14 *Roads to Zion Mourn*, pp. 155–170.
15 In *III Sent* d. 24, a. 3, q. 2, dub. 4, *Commentaria in quator libros Sententiarum*, in *Opera Omnia* (Quarrachi 1–4).
16 *Bonaventure: The Soul's Journey into God, The Tree of Life, The Life of St. Francis*, trans. Ewert Cousins (New York, NY: Paulist Press, 1978).
17 *Soul's Journey* (trans., Cousins), 7.4.
18 *Soul's Journey* (trans., Cousins), 7.5.
19 *Hidden Theology* (trans., Walsh), Prol. 1, p. 74.
20 See Marshall E. Crossnoe, "Education and the Care of Souls: Pope Gregory IX, the Order of St. Victor and the University of Paris in 1237," *Mediaeval Studies*, 61 (1999), pp. 137–172, p. 165, n. 98.
21 The abbey of Saint-Victor was founded in Paris by William of Champeaux in 1108 and housed an Augustinian order of regular canons.
22 Crossnoe, "Education and the Care of Souls," p. 169.
23 See Mario Capellino, *The abbey of Sant'Andrea in Vercelli* (Turnhout: Brepols, 2006).
24 For a survey of Gallus' life and works, see Jeanne Barbet, "Thomas Gallus", *Dictionnaire de spiritualité ascétique et mystique* 15:800–816 and Gabriel Théry, "Thomas Gallus: aperçu biographique", *Archives d'histoire doctrinale et littéraire du Moyen Âge*, 12 (1939), pp. 141–208.
25 On Gallus' theology, see Mario Capellino, *Tommaso di San Vittore abate vercellese* (Vercelli 1978); Robert Javalet, "Thomas Gallus ou les écritures dans une dialectique mystique", in *L'homme devant Dieu: À Henri de Lubac*, 3 vols. (Paris: Aubier, 1964), 2:99–110; Kurt Ruh, *Frauenmystik und franziskanische Mystik der Frühzeit* in *Geschichte der abendländischen Mystik*, 4 vols. (Munich: Beck, 1990), pp. 402–405; James Walsh, "Thomas Gallus et l'effort contemplatif", *Revue d'histoire de la spiritualité*, 51 (1975), pp. 17–42.

100   *Boyd Taylor Coolman*

26   Only a small portion of Gallus' works have been translated into English and only a small body of secondary literature is devoted to him, very little of which is in English. For recent English-language surveys of Gallus' theology, see James McEvoy, *Mystical Theology: The Glosses by Thomas Gallus and the Commentary of Robert Grosseteste on* De mystica theologia (Paris: Peeters, 2003), pp. 3–54; Bernard McGinn, "Thomas Gallus and Dionysian Mysticism", *Studies in Spirituality*, 8 (Louvain: Peeters, 1994), pp. 81–96, which is a slightly expanded version of his discussion of Gallus in *The Flowering of Mysticism: Men and Women in the New Mysticism (1200–1350)*, volume 3 of *The Presence of God: A History of Western Christian Mysticism* (New York, NY: Crossroad, 1998); and Paul Rorem, *Pseudo-Dionysius*, pp. 218–219.

27   René Roques, *L'Univers Dionysien* (Paris: Aubier, 1954).

28   Hugh arrived at Saint-Victor in Paris in the second decade of the twelfth century and was the dominant theologian there until his death. Regarding Richard of St. Victor, Hugh's successor at the abbey, the consensus is that he used Dionysius "more as an illustration than an inspiration" (Gervais Dumeige, *Dictionnaire de spiritualité* 3:328, quoted in Rorem, *Pseudo-Dionysius*, p. 229, n. 22).

29   *In hierarchiam caelestem S. Dionysii* (PL 175:923A–1154C).

30   Again, see Rorem's chapter in this book.

31   Gregory the Great, *Homily in Evanglica 27: amor ipse notitia est.*

32   Rorem, *Pseudo-Dionysius*, p. 217.

33   Rorem, *Pseudo-Dionysius*, pp. 218–219.

34   J. Châtillon, "De Guillaume de Champeaux à Thomas Gallus", in *Revue du Moyen Âge Latin*, t. 8, 1952/2–3, pp. 268–269. Gallus' first work was a commentary on Isaiah written at Paris before 1218, known otherwise only by a long quotation of it which the author himself gives in his explanation of the *Celestial Hierarchy* (Cf. G. Théry, *Le commentaire sur Isaïe de Thomas de Saint-Victor*, in *La vie spirituelle*, XLVII (1936), Suppl., pp. 146–162).

35   Walsh, *The Cloud of Unknowing*, p. 123, from Gallus' commentary on Isaiah.

36   The first wave occurred in the ninth century through the work of Eriugena. In addition to Thomas Gallus, Robert Grosseteste and Albert the Great were both part of this second wave (James McEvoy, "Thomas Gallus, *Abbas Vercellensis*, and the Commentary on the *De mystica theologia* ascribed to Johannes Scottus Eriugena: with a concluding note on the second Latin reception of the Pseudo-Dionysius (1230–1250)" in John J. Cleary (ed), *Traditions of Platonism: Essays in Honour of John Dillon* [Brookfield: Ashgate 1999], pp. 389–405, pp. 403–404).

37   Cited in Rorem, *Pseudo-Dionysius*, p. 218.

38   The *Exposicio* has been edited and translated by James McEvoy (see n. 25 above).

39   The *Extractio* is edited in *Dionysiaca: Receuil donnant l'ensemble des traditions latines des ouvrages attribués au Denys l'Aréopage*, Philippe Chevalier (ed), 2 vols. (Paris: Desclée, 1937–50).

40   Regarding the *Explanatio*, only Gallus' commentary on *The Mystical Theology* has been edited [*Thomas Gallus: Grand commentaire sur la Théologie Mystique*, ed. G. Thery (Paris: Haloua, 1934)], but it is not readily available.

41   See G. Théry, *Chronologie des œuvres de Thomas Gallus, in Divus Thomas* (Piacenza), XXXVII (1934), pp. 265–277, 365–385, 469–496.

42   McEvoy, "Thomas Gallus", p. 404.

43   *Exposicio* I.1, 20/21.

44   *Exposicio* I.2, 22/23.

45   *Exposicio* II, 32/33.

46   McEvoy, *Mystical Theology*, p. 4.

47   *Extractio* on *The Mystical Theology* 1 in *Dionysiaca*, ed. Chevalier, 710.578.

48   Rorem notes that Gallus' *Extractio* "was immediately and immensely popular as an alternative and easier way to extract the Areopagite's meaning. The semi-official corpus that circulated in the thirteenth century consisted of the translations by Eriugena and Sarracenus, the *Scholia*, the commentaries by Eriugena and Hugh, and the [*Extractio*] by Gallus" (*Pseudo-Dionysius*, pp. 218–219). McEvoy adds that it was "in constant use from a few years after his death down to the times of Jean Gerson and Vincent of Aggsbach" (McEvoy, "Thomas Gallus", p. 404).

49   J. Châtillon, "De Guillaume de Champeaux à Thomas Gallus," in *Revue du Moyen Âge Latin*, t. 8, 1952/2–3, pp. 268–269.

50 See Jeanne Barbet, *Un Commentaire du Cantique attribué a Thomas Gallus* (Paris-Louvain: Béatrice-Nauwelaerts, 1972). The two authentic commentaries have been edited by Barbet, *Thomas Gallus: Commentaires du Cantique des Cantiques* (Paris: Vrin, 1967), pp. 65–104 and 105–232. Hereafter, abbreviated as *Comm. II* and *Comm. III* respectively, followed by chapter, section and page designations. There is a partial English translation of *Comm. II* in: Denys Turner, *Eros and Allegory: Medieval Exegesis of the Song of Songs* (Kalamazoo, MI: Cistercian Publications, 1995), pp. 317–239.
51 See Turner, *Eros and Allegory*, pp. 25–200.
52 *Comm. II*, prol., p. 66.
53 Rorem, *Pseudo-Dionysius*, p. 218.
54 McGinn, "Thomas Gallus," *Studies in Spirituality*, p. 82.
55 Barbet, "Introduction," *Commentaires*, p. 43.
56 Gallus here expands an intuition of his Victorine predecessors, especially Richard of St. Victor's use of angelic modes of being in human contemplation. See Steven Chase, *Angelic Wisdom: The Cherubim and the Grace of Contemplation in Richard of St. Victor* (Notre Dame, IN: University of Notre Dame Press, 1995).
57 *Comm. II*, Prol., p. 66: "In order to understand this explanation of the [Song of Songs], it is necessary to set down first the meaning of the statement in the *Celestial Hierarchy* that: "each intelligent being, heavenly or human, has its own set of primary, middle, and lower orders and powers" . . . "
58 *Comm. II*, Prol., p. 67.
59 G. Théry, "Thomas Gallus et Égide d'Assisi: le traité De septem gradibus contemplationis," *Revue néoscolastique de philosophie*, 36 (1934), pp. 180–190, at 185: "Le de septem gradibus temoigne de la memem tendance nettement anti-intellectualiste que nous avons signalee maintes reprises dans les escrits de Thomas Gallus."
60 *Comm. II*, Prol., p. 65.
61 *Comm. II*, Prol., p. 65–66.
62 *Comm. II*, 1.A, p. 68.
63 *Ibid.*
64 *Comm. II*, Prol., p. 66.
65 *Ibid.*
66 *Comm. II*, Prol., p. 66.
67 *Comm. II*, Prol., p. 67.
68 *Comm. II*, 4.A, p. 91.
69 *Comm. III*, 4.A, p. 177 (emphasis added).
70 *Comm. II*, Prol., p. 67.
71 *Comm. III*, 5.C, p. 194.
72 *Comm. III*, 7.B, p. 216.
73 *Comm. III*, Prol., p. 115.
74 Accordingly, Denys Turner's claim that "there is no *excessus* of intellect in Gallus, as there is in Pseudo-Denys" (*Eros and Allegory*, p. 337, n. 24) is somewhat misleading, since at this level the *intellectus* has already been ecstatically drawn out of itself, albeit *along with* the *affectus* and as ultimately *outstripped by* the *affectus* at the highest point of ecstatic union.
75 This felicitous rendering of Gallus' Latin is Turner's (*Eros and Allegory*, p. 322).
76 *Comm. III*, Prol., p. 115.
77 *Ibid.*
78 *Ibid.*
79 *Comm. III*, 7.D, p. 219.
80 McGinn notes that Gallus was the first to use this term in the mystical sense and that his role in its subsequent medieval deployment is insufficiently investigated (See McGinn, "Thomas Gallus", pp. 88–89, n. 26).
81 *Comm. III*, 1.O, p. 141: "cognoscit eum super omnem existentem intellectum et cognitionem."
82 *Comm. III*, 4.A, p. 176.
83 *Comm. II*, 1.A, p. 68.
84 *Comm. II*, 1.A, p. 69: ". . . affectus qui penetrat tangendo, olfaciendo, gustando."
85 *Comm. III*, 1.C, p. 124.
86 *Comm. II*, 1.A, p. 69.

87   *Comm. III*, 1.H, p. 132.
88   *Comm. II*, Prol., p. 67.
89   *Comm. II*, 1.A, p. 68.
90   "It was not by accident that Gallus cites this passage [*Divine Names*, 4.14] *in extenso* in the third and most detailed of his commentaries on the Song of Songs in order to justify his grafting of the affective eroticism of the Song into the vision of cosmic *eros* described by Dionysius" (McGinn, "Thomas Gallus," p. 88).
91   *Comm. II*, 5.B, p. 102.
92   *Comm. III*, 1.D, p. 125: "amor ipsius est adductivus sui ad mentes et mentium ad se . . . "
93   *Comm. II*, 3.C, p. 87.
94   *Comm. II*, 2.A, p. 78.
95   *Comm. II*, 1.F, p. 75.
96   *Comm. II*, 4.E, p. 95.
97   *Comm. II*, 2.A, p. 78.
98   *Comm. II*, 1.A, p. 69.
99   *Comm. II*, 4.F, p. 98 (emphasis added).
100 *Comm. II*, 4.E, p. 95.
101 *Comm. II*, 4.C, p. 93.
102 *Comm. II*, 5.A, p. 101.
103 *Comm. III*, 1.C, p. 124: ". . . fecundi, gustu divine dulcedinis excitati."
104 *Comm. II*, Prol., p. 67.
105 *Comm. III*, 1.D, p. 126.
106 *Comm. II*, 3.C, p. 87.
107 *Comm. II*, 3.A, p. 85.
108 *Comm. III*, 3.A, p. 166.
109 *Comm. II*, 5.A, p. 101.
110 *Comm. III*, 1.L, p. 137.
111 *Comm. III*, 8.G, p. 232.
112 *Comm. III*, 1.C, p. 124.
113 *Comm. II*, 1.C, p. 72.
114 *Comm. III*, 3.F, p. 175.
115 *Comm. III*, 3.A, p. 167.
116 *Comm. III*, 1.L, p. 137.
117 *Comm. II*, 2.C, p. 79.
118 *Comm. II*, 2.G, p. 82.
119 *Comm. III*, 8.G, p. 232. Barbet notes the theme of "d'incessants progrès" at the end of the third commentary (Barbet, "Introduction," p. 61), though not the larger context of the soul's eternal circling around God stressed here.
120 *Comm. III*, 3.A, p. 167.
121 It is tempting to speculate, given the medieval concern about angelic mediation of divine revelation, which in Dionysius places the mediating angelic hierarchy *above* and *between* the soul and God, that by placing the celestial hierarchy *within* the soul, Gallus is attempting to "solve" the problem of hierarchically mediated revelation. While giving full weight to the angelic activity of mediating revelation in Dionysius, Gallus can still affirm with the Augustinian tradition, transmitted by the Middle Ages by the treatise *De spiritu et anima*, that "between the soul and God there is no intermediary." See McEvoy, *Mystical Theology*, p. 6.
122 Barbet notes only "la double médiation hiérarchique" in Gallus' commentaries where one sees "*les mouvements corrélatifs*" that occur inside the contemplative spirit: *ascensus* of the spirit and *descensus* of the divine light" ("Introduction," p. 44; p. 60).

7

ALBERT, AQUINAS, AND DIONYSIUS

DAVID BURRELL, C.S.C. and ISABELLE MOULIN

Significant thinkers often defy the categories invented by historians to structure their narrative of the development of a subject. In that story, Albert and
Aquinas belong to "Western theology", while Dionysius the Areopagite
epitomizes "Eastern theology." In a similar vein, historians have been prone
to identify Albert as "neo-Platonist", and Aquinas as "Aristotelian." So recov-
ering their thought for our inspiration and further use often requires that we
deconstruct the figures of those thinkers as construed by intervening scholarship, which is often shaped by categories designed to fit them into a larger
historical narrative. This attempt to trace the ways each of these "Western"
thinkers interacted with Dionysius will carry on that deconstruction of each
of them, as needed; and since fewer expositions of Aquinas' teacher, Albert,
are available, juxtaposing the two, as we illustrate the ways in which each of
these "Western" thinkers is beholden to "Eastern" thought as well as to
Jewish and Islamic interlocutors, can help readers to a fresh appreciation of
both. Moreover, in the case of Aquinas, recent work of this sort now allows us
to recognize the neo-Platonic and theological dimensions of this ostensibly
"Aristotelian" figure.[1] In what follows, Albert is discussed by Isabelle
Moulin, and Aquinas by David Burrell, although the two have been in conversation throughout.

David Burrell, C.S.C
Department of Theology, University of Notre Dame, 130 Malloy Hall, Notre Dame, IN 46556,
USA
dburrell@nd.edu
Isabelle Moulin
145 avenue de l'Eygala, 38700 Corenc, FRANCE
isabellemoulin@yahoo.com

Albert the Great and Dionysius

Since a full account of the relationship between Albert the Great and the *CD* is precluded in such a short compass, I shall propose to readers a more synoptic view that will allow them to go to the very heart of Albertinian metaphysics and theology. Albert the Great (1200–1280), who received the title of *magnus* from his contemporaries, is commonly known to us as the Master of Thomas Aquinas.[2] From this purely historical perspective, he is generally thought of as preparing a way for his fabled disciple. There is indeed some truth in this view, as Albert stands at the crossroads of too many different cultural tendencies to be able to offer a full systematic synthesis of his own. Nevertheless, Albert can never be considered as a *mere* precursor of Thomas Aquinas. Put succinctly, Thomas is an axial figure in the Western theological tradition, while Albert stands astride both East and West in a way that makes it difficult to determine the personal philosophy of the Master of Cologne.[3] I would like to give one example of this point: at the beginning of his *Summa Theologiae*, Thomas underlines the fact that there are two ways to penetrate to the inner act of divine creation, by way of the notion of Being or the notion of the Good.[4] In the first case, God is seen as acting on the world; in the second, as its final cause. Surprisingly, Thomas underlines that the Good comes first when one speaks about God; but on account of our limited faculty of understanding, the order of explanation demands that we begin with the notion of Being, only then to reflect upon the axial distinction of existence from essence. I suspect this strategy to be motivated by the fundamental apologetic dimension of Thomas' work. One may have to qualify this statement, however, as will become evident from the second part of this chapter. Is it an historical coincidence that Albert's secretary for his commentary upon the *Divine Names* was precisely Thomas Aquinas, during their common stay in Cologne? Thomas was doubtless the first reader of Albert's commentary, and even if the influence is difficult to estimate, it cannot be ignored.[5]

Albert, in contrast, in considering divine activity metaphysically, emphasizes the notion of the Good, metaphorically expressing God as the original source of all that exists in terms of flow and of light. While remaining absolutely one and untouched, God communicates goodness and bestows divine prodigality on all beings, as far as it is possible for them to receive it, according to a hierarchy whose order is determined by their degree of proximity to the One. God communicates God's own self by way of a superabundant overflowing upon the beings that flow from that action (intelligence, humanity, and the natural world), so producing being, intellection, life, sensation, etc.[6] So God is compared to the supreme light of the Sun that never ceases to produce light so long as it is not restricted by the receptive capacity of the being upon which it is bestowed[7]. Any darkening of the original light is progressive, following its path of recession from the original fount of all goodness as it descends towards matter.[8] At this point, I hope that readers familiar with the *CD* will have noticed how close we are to the original thought of Dionysius.[9]

"Vere, tu es deus absconditus, Deus Israel, salvator"[10]: The Mystical Theology

This opening quotation contains in a nutshell the program of Albert's commentary on Dionysius' *Mystical Theology*, suggesting also its deepest dimensions: the relative status of human intellects, first, compared to the divine, which alone is capable of reaching and producing the truth (*vere*); the hidden character of God, second, who can only be reached by a *via negationis* (the *deus absconditus*); and the necessity to hide from the profane the most sacred truths so as to save them for the people ready to hear them (*Israel*). Together these features reflect the true dimensions of a theology which is primarily neither theoretical nor ethical, but directed to the salvation of humanity.

I would like to insist upon this aspect of salvation, since Albert is usually classified with the "intellectualist" trend of Dionysian reception. Indeed, he can be so understood, but in a way that needs to be clarified. For Albert, *henôsis* (union with God) is attained *via* the intellect.[11] But the intellection of God does not proceed in an affirmative way using syllogisms and deductions,[12] but in a negative or "mystical" way,[13] because our intellect is as powerless to embrace the divine essence as our eye to receive the radiance of the sun.[14] Ultimately, God cannot be the subject of any predication.[15] We can at best reach, and then only in a certain way, the *quia* of God, never the *quid* or essence.[16] At this point, one should properly attend to the proportionality of cause-and-effect that Albert provides in these few dense pages[17], but space forbids doing it here. Yet any medievalist interested in the analogy of being should read these pages in which Albert refuses any community of genus and species between God and his creatures, even ruling out analogy as well.[18]

"Bonum est diffusivum esse": The Divine Names

The divine essence is not knowable, although we may reach it through processions from it, in which all beings partake. In a way that he deems contrary to Dionysius, Albert holds that these processions are not identical with the divine *esse*, for this multiplicity does not introduce any accidents into divinity.[19] Rather, the simpler a substance, the more communicable it is.[20] Albert's definition of participation does therefore follow, after all, a true analogy of *being*, in which proximity to the first substance is interpreted in terms of receiving more of what proceeds from the first (so being less determined in a formal sense), as well as being more similar to it.[21] This *procession*,[22] better called an "emanation," does not compromise the fundamentally free act of the divine creator, since creation is at once an *opus naturae et substantiae*—an activity of the divine being itself.[23] And since *bonum* is the first and most appropriate name of God, divine action itself cannot but be free.[24]

The difficulty for Albert is to hold a position that will allow him to avoid the pre-existence of matter and any pantheistic vision of God, while maintaining both the inner closeness of God towards his creation and preserving His full transcendence. In his commentary upon the *Divine Names*, he clearly rejects the vision of God as a "Giver of Forms," namely, a "Dator Formarum" which he attributes to "Plato and Avicenna,"[25] on the grounds that such a thesis presupposes an *eternal* pre-existing matter (*materiam coaeternam primo*), which is contrary to Faith.[26] The pre-existence of matter is unavoidable in a system that divides forms coming from the intelligence and forms residing in matter.[27] Moreover, such a solution does not provide a sufficient distinction between the original *lux* and its reception (*lumen*) in matter. In *DN*, Albert thus opposes to the Giver of Forms his theory of the so-called "eduction through creation" (*educere per creationem*) that he had already elaborated upon in his commentary on the *Celestial Hierarchy*.[28] Using what he thinks to be the "Aristotelian" principle of "eduction" (or "calling forth") of the forms existing in potency in matter, under the action of the mover acting as an efficient cause in nature (the passage from potency to act), Albert proposes a theory of creation *ex nihilo* as a free voluntary act of God.[29] This solution preserves the exteriority of the divine substance—the form is not the very light of the first cause[30]—while explaining the variety of the reception: the form is a resemblance of the light, and is caused by it.[31] For Albert, this reading is close to Dionysius',[32] but also presents Aristotle's position which is more "catholic" than Plato's.[33] If these were Albert's last words, one would certainly be surprised by such a position. Does not Aristotle hold the world (and therefore matter) to be eternal? Indeed Albert was not reading Aristotle's eternity of the world as it stands, but he at some point would have had to have been aware of this problem while commenting upon Dionysius.[34] Moreover, Albert's Dionysianism would not be complete without reflecting on his *De Causis et processu universitatis a prima causa*. In this book, creation is not presented as a true "eduction"[35] but as an "effusion" and an "emanation". This evolution is not a drastic change in Albert's works but its difference must be underlined. It expresses an authentic maturation of thought about Aristotle's works,[36] as well as a telling meditation upon the *Liber de Causis*, as if Albert unconsciously needed to go back again to Neo-Platonic origins to account for the divine gift. His hesitations invoke the image of our limited faculty of understanding of the *quia* of God, "as far as it is possible".

"All beings desire the Good": The divinization process in the Hierarchies

In Dionysius, the *exitus* from God is followed by the *reditus*, the return to God that endows a "God-like" process. Each created being possesses a measure (*metron*) that determines its order in the hierarchy, its capacity to reach the "divine mysteries".[37] Even if this progressive lack of capacity to reach the Good is interpreted in terms of progressive deprivation,[38] it is each member's own responsibility, in the hierarchy, to divinize itself in order to reach the divine life at the maximum of its capacity. Even if there is no necessity pertaining to the process of *proodos* and *epistrophe*, there is a sort of dialectic of love in the *CD* that implies a "spiral" movement. This circular dynamic of receiving/returning *as far as it is possible* for the being concerned, i.e., according to its *virtus recipiendi*, is a central theme for Albert the Great, not only when commenting upon the *CD* but also in his last works:[39] "All things desire the Good because of their similarity to the Prime Good, and all their motions, all their actions and all their productions, are performed for it".[40] The Good never ceases to flow upon beings as they never cease to desire it.

One should hardly be surprised that the two authors who most influenced Albert the Great are the very two upon whom he produced close commentaries, linked as this strategy is to his proper philosophical method of constructing while he explains, since interpreting and elaborating are closely intertwined. Yet in Albert's mind, Dionysius must have the last word.[41] While his Dionysianism is largely tempered by the *Liber de Causis*, one should hardly be surprised that the discovery of the true Proclean origin of the *Liber* does not necessitate any change in Albert's system. Despite their differences, for an exacting reader of Dionysius the *Liber de Causis* and the *CD* coalesce in Albert's whole system: once God's ineffability has been linked with the inadequacy of calling God a "cause" or a "principle," conventionally speaking, one is free to speak of the supereffusion of the Good, bestowing prodigalities (*energeiai* in Dionysian language) by way of the progressive narrowing of a unique form (the *Liber*) first through the hierarchical order of Intelligences (the *Liber* and Islamic philosophy), and reflected finally in our world.[42] It is not that Albert has adopted a *pure* Dionysian perspective, although he has surely come closer to Dionysius than to Aristotle.[43]

Aquinas and Dionysius

One would search in vain in Thomas' written works for explicit references to his teacher, Albert, yet we can read this situation as Athanasius did when challenged about the use of the non-scriptural term *homoousios* in the wake of the Council of Nicea: "*Verbum non est, sed res ubique*—the very word is not found [in scripture], but the reality is omnipresent." Marie-Dominique Chenu O.P. alerted us some time ago to the *exitus/reditus* structure of Aquinas' *Summa Theologiae*, and we have just seen how this circular dynamic of receiving/returning is central to Albert, as it is to Dionysius.[44] So it could well be that Aquinas' tutelage under Albert prepared him to resonate as clearly as he does with Dionysius, despite the fact that his manifest attraction to Dionysius did not seem directly to serve his self-appointed mandate to show how *theologia* could indeed be a *scientia*—a clearly Aristotelian undertaking.[45] As Andrew Louth puts it: "Denys is being read in the west in the light of presuppositions that are increasingly remote from . . . the heart of

Denys' theology, [namely] the praise of God, . . . [yet] St. Thomas Aquinas read Denys with great care and attention: and whole areas of his theology—the doctrine of divine attributes, angelology, to name but two—are deeply in debt to him."[46] Indeed, Aquinas' commentary on Dionysius' *Divine Names*, on which we shall focus, ends with a humble confession of homage: "May we ask, after having elucidated what blessed Dionysius put forth, though falling far short of his understanding, that we be corrected in what we may have failed properly to express."[47] Moreover, the Marietti edition ends with eight pages of references to Aquinas' use of this book of Dionysius throughout his writings.[48] Anyone engaged in elucidating Aquinas' philosophical theology, notably questions 3–13 in the *Summa Theologiae*, cannot help but read this commentary on Dionysius as a summary of Aquinas' central teachings on the ineffable relation of creator to creatures, thereby helping to elucidate the more austere treatment of the *Summa Theologiae* as itself a paean to the "praise of God", and so effectively diminishing the stereotypical divide between East and West.[49]

We may begin to deconstruct this ostensible "divide" by asking what attracted Aquinas to the writings we call "Neo-Platonic"—notably, Dionysius' *Divine Names* and the Islamic *Liber de Causis*—to clarify key metaphysical issues regarding the creator/creature distinction so axial to his philosophical theology.[50] Edward Booth's magisterial *Aristotelian Aporetic Ontology in Islamic and Christian Thinkers* traces Aquinas' ability to resolve the *aporia* regarding essence/existence, as it perdured through the entire commentary tradition on Aristotle, to the way Aquinas uses Dionysius to elucidate the centrality of *existence* [*esse*].[51] For the way Aristotle had left things in his treatment of substance allowed individual things—his very paradigm for substance—to be absorbed into an account in which they become mere instances of a kind.[52] Let me suggest that Aquinas sensed in these writings a return to Plato's robust insistence on the centrality of "the Good" as drawing our human intellects beyond what we can properly conceive to the very source of our understanding. The Platonic vein is clearly at work as Aristotle opens his *Metaphysics* with the dictum that "all human beings desire to know;" yet philosophers beholden to Aristotle tended to focus more on "know" than on "desire". Dionysius seems to prefer to characterize human beings as "good-seeking animals" (like "heat-seeking missiles") rather than as "rational [or speaking] animals"; and the same can be said for the *Liber de Causis*, despite its refined intellectual cast.[53] Aquinas' appropriation of the Arabic text *Kitâb al-khaîr* [Book of the Pure Good] in its Latin translation [*Liber de Causis*] will prove to be as significant (or more) as the particular re-casting of Proclus by the anonymous Muslim writer. Yet Aquinas did fasten on this work as key to his endeavor to incorporate a free creator into the Hellenic heritage, just as he insisted on employing the term "emanation" for creation, even after removing and gutting the scheme of necessary emanation enthusiastically adopted by the Islamic thinkers al-Farabi and Ibn Sina, ostensibly to articulate the revelation of a unitary creator of the universe. That same scheme, trenchantly attacked by al-Ghazali and Moses Maimonides in the name of revelation as impugning a free creator and so rendering revelation itself incredible, was rejected by Aquinas, ostensibly for mediating the act of creation; yet in the end he came to feel that *emanation* offered the best metaphor for the *sui generis* activity of creation, even of a free creator. My suggestion for this about-face turns on the centrality of *the Good* in his text, as in Dionysius. Indeed, it is part of being intentional beings that the capacities which emanate to us from the One *desire* their perfection, that is (in *Liber de Causis* terms), they are so shaped from within as to strive to return to their proper good, their source. Such is the power of a creation-centered picture of *being*. This picture is completed in fully intentional, or free, agents, whose freedom can be expressed as a "hunger for the Good" and so best seen as a response rather than an initiative.[54]

Moreover, the fullness of the act of existing is displayed in its order, much as the efficacy of any of our actions is assured by the ordering it displays towards its goal. We focus authentically, not by eliminating all but one feature, but by aligning all the relevant features in a proper order, so that the effect is orchestrated. Notice that we cannot escape metaphors here, for there is no given ordering. Revelation assists by allowing us to name "the Good", and also by providing us with some strategies of ordering—the Torah, the example of Jesus, the Qur'an—yet here again, discernment is always needed, and traditions can subvert as well as elaborate a given revelation or way. The Ur-pattern derives from creation, as conceived by the *Liber de Causis*: it is an orderly emanation from the One so that the intentional portion of creation desires to return to its source. Moreover, such an order is not imposed but inherent, since *existing* is not an added feature but an inherent gift. This is seen most fully, according to Aquinas, when we can appreciate this unitary source as freely bestowing what it truly is. For since its manner of being is triune, in creating it freely communicates the manner in which it naturally communicates.[55]

Yet the sober language of "orderly emanation" can fail to make explicit how pervasive is "the good" with its inherent attraction for intentional beings like us. As the *Liber de Causis* puts it, "the first cause infuses all things with a single infusion, for it infuses things under the aspect [*sub rationem*] of the good."[56] Aquinas concurs in commenting how it had already been shown that "the first cause acts through its being, . . . hence it does not act through any additional relation or disposition through which it would be adapted to and mixed with things."[57] Moreover, "because the first cause acts through its being, it must rule things in one manner, for it rules things according to the way it acts."[58] The following Proposition 21 links this "sufficiency of God to rule" with divine *simplicity*: "since God is simple in the first and greatest degree as having his whole goodness in a oneness that is most perfect."[59] Hence Proposition 23 can assert: "what is essentially act and goodness, namely, God, essentially and originally communicates his goodness to things."[60] With such a One there can be no anxiety about "control"; indeed, the metaphor which the proposition on divine rule elicits is that "it is proper for a ruler to lead those that are ruled to their appropriate end, which is the good."[61] For to "infuse things under the aspect of the good" is precisely to bring all things to be in a certain order, inherent in their very existing, so there is nothing "external" about divine providence, no imposition—neither "inasmuch as it establishes things, which is called creation; [nor] inasmuch as it rules things already established."[62] Indeed, the initial diversity comes from the first cause, who "produces the diverse grades of things for the completion of the universe. But in the action of ruling, . . . the diversity of reception is according to the diversity of the recipients" (137 [123]). Yet since the original order comes from the One, the One in ruling will "effortlessly" adapt itself to the order established in creating. Another way of putting all this, and one which should dissolve most conundra regarding "divine action", is to remind oneself that the creator, in acting, acts always as creator; and this proposition elucidates Aquinas' contention that *creating* and *conserving* are the same action, differing only in that conserving presupposes things present.

Since the manner of that action will ever escape us (for its very simplicity belies any *manner* at all—no "relation or disposition"), the best we can do is to remind ourselves that the creator ever acts by constituting the order which inheres in each existing thing, in the measure that it is. (And since essence measures *esse*, it is pointless to oppose essence to existing, in things that are.) Yet since "order" is a consummately analogous term, we can never be sure we have detected the originating divine order in things, though our conviction that there is one, inscribed in their very being and our intentional attitudes towards them, will continue to fuel our inquiry. Crude classifications—inanimate, animate, intentional—can be supplemented by refined mathematical structures and symmetries (as now in DNA); yet each stage of analytic description will be serving our innate desire to unveil the activity present in these infused "goodnesses" which constitute our universe.[63] And to grasp something of that constitutive ordering is to come closer to its source, "because every knowing substance, insofar as it has being more perfectly, knows both the first cause and the infusion of its goodness more perfectly, and the more it receives and knows this the more it takes delight in it, [so] it follows that the closer something is to the first cause the more it takes delight in it."[64] All is not light or delight, of course, because in truth we cannot, ourselves, hope to *know* "the first cause and the infusion of goodness." Indeed, "the most important thing we can know about the first cause is that it surpasses all our knowledge and power of expression", for "our intellect can grasp only that which has a quiddity participating in 'to-be' [while] the quiddity of God is 'to-be itself'".[65] Indeed, that is why Aquinas can concur that "the first cause is above being inasmuch as it is itself infinite 'to-be'".[66] Yet since "what belong to higher things are present in lower things according to some kind of participation", we can be said to share, as beings, in this inaccessible One.[67]

After having shown how cognate are the concerns of the *Liber de Causis* with those of Dionysius, let us return to the *Divine Names* to note how Aquinas employs this text to focus on the axial distinction and connection of creator with creator. We shall review five features of Aquinas' appropriation of the text: the unique status of the creator (the "distinction in itself"); the orderly emanation from this transcendent source; Aquinas's attempt to clarify the meaning of "peace"; Oneness as culminating his attempts to say what one cannot know about the One; and finally, the way he places this entire "discussion" under the rubric of *praise*! In each case, the "he" in question is both Dionysius and Aquinas, as the commentator makes the original text his own, in a way similar to Albert's mode of commenting on texts key to his endeavor.

When it comes to articulating "the distinction" by focusing on "the One, the Superknowable, the Transcendent, Goodness itself," human minds cannot take in its measure:

> Such things can neither be talked about nor grasped except by the angels who in some mysterious fashion have been deemed worthy. Since the union of divinized minds with the Light beyond all deity occurs in the cessation of all intelligent activity, the godlike unified minds who imitate these angels as far as possible praise it most appropriately through the denial of all beings. Truly and supernaturally enlightened after this blessed union, they discover that although it is the cause of everything it is not a thing since it transcends all things in a manner beyond being. . . . Because it is there, the world has come to be and exists. All things long for it.[68]

In commenting on this text, Aquinas makes it his own in ways which are reflected in his other writings. As he opens the *Summa Theologiae* by reminding us how very special a *scientia* is *theologia*, since its principles are known only to "the saints," so his commentary proceeds here:

> the primary mode of "naming God" will be according to the way in which the minds of the saints, that is the prophets and apostles, are conformed to God by being removed from [earthly things] and united with the emanations already mentioned [from the creator to creatures, which keeps them in being], by way of imitation of the angels—not as though they were equal to them, but in so far as is possible in this life, praising God by distancing themselves from all existing things.[69]

Dionysius specifies:

> From him who is comes eternity, essence and being, comes time, genesis, and becoming. He is the being immanent in and underlying the things

which are, however they are. For God is not some kind of being. No. But in a way that is simple and indefinable, he gathers into himself and anticipates every existence.[70]

Aquinas unveils his metaphysical arsenal in an attempt to explicate these gnomic assertions:

> so everything else [that is not the creator] has being [*esse*] that is received and participated, so does not have being [*esse*] according to the fullness of being [*essendi*], which is what he means by saying that God can be the cause of being [*essendi*] for all things [precisely] because God does not exist in some determinate way ["God is not some kind of being"], but infinitely and universally "gathers into himself and anticipates every existence," because [every existent] pre-exists in Him as in its cause, and from Him passes it on to others.[71]

It would be idolatry to think one could speak of the creator bereft of so powerful a metaphysics, for it would then become one being among others, however large or powerful.[72]

When it comes to speaking of the act whereby this One creates all-that-is, one will need to employ similarly recondite strategies:

> The divine Wisdom knows all things by knowing itself. Uniquely it knows and produces all things by its oneness: material things immaterially, divisible things indivisibly, plurality in a single act. If with one casual gesture God bestows being on everything, in that same one act of causation he will know everything by derivation from him and through their pre-existence in him, and therefore, his knowledge of things will not be owed to the things themselves.[73]

This assertion will allow Aquinas to resume his teaching on creation, an act which cannot be a process and so cannot take time nor be susceptible of any description "how" it happens:

> It should be clear that all knowledge is according to the mode of the one by whom something is known, just as all operation takes place according to the mode of the form by which something operates. So since divine wisdom knows all things by the fact that it knows itself, . . . it follows that there cannot be in God one knowledge by which God knows himself and another by which He knows all things in common. For were it the case that, in knowing Himself, God did not know all things, then it would follow that His causality would not extend everywhere, and there would be some things not caused by Him. Yet since it is impossible that there be anything not caused by God, it is impossible that there be something not known by Him.[74]

It is illustrative to note how Aquinas employs the unique creator/creature relation to say something about God's mode of knowing without claiming to have any insight into what that mode is!

Such an exalted doctrine of creation allows Dionysius to offer what some might call a "naturalistic" view of salvation as:

that which preserves all things in their proper places without change, conflict, or collapse towards evil, that it keeps them in peaceful and untroubled obedience to their proper laws, . . . [so that] benevolently operating for the preservation of the world, [it] redeems everything in accordance with the capacity of things to be saved, and it works so that everything may keep within its proper virtue . . . this is why the theologians name it "redemption," because it does not permit the truly real to fall into nothingness . . .[75]

Aquinas responds in the same spirit:

That [Dionysius] defines the primary *ratio* of salvation to be conserving things in good—[the good of creation]—which militates against conflict or gives courage to resist it when it occurs.[76]

Which leads Dionysius into a masterful reflection on peace:

God is the subsistence of absolute peace, . . . the one simple nature of that peaceful unity which joins all things to itself and to each other, preserving them in their distinctiveness and yet linking them together in a universal and unconfused alliance.[77]

Aquinas turns to homely examples to illustrate the contrast with the human condition:

There are things which are in some way one in themselves, but which are not one within themselves, like single human beings who are hardly one since they are at odds within themselves. But God is one within God's own self, because no diversity can be found in God. . . . Even when God proceeds into all things by his similitudes communicated to things, God remains totally God's own self.[78]

So human beings have a model for peaceful coexistence, even if we find ourselves unable to emulate it.

The final chapter of the *DN* begins in this way:

So much, then, for these names, and, if you will, let us proceed to the most enduring of them all . . . The name "One" means that God is uniquely all things through the transcendence of one unity and that he is the cause of all things through the transcendence of one unit and that his is the cause of all without ever departing from that oneness. Nothing in the world lacks its share of the One.[79]

Aquinas links this profound sense of *unity*—cognate to Muslim *tawhid*—to divine providence, offering the example of angels as well as human beings, who, however exalted they may be in their respective ranks, "receive the gifts of God in great simplicity, in as much as whoever possesses simple and uniform God-likeness and goodness is that much more assimilated to God."[80] It is also worth recalling how Aquinas' articulation of the "formal features" of divinity in the *Summa Theologiae* (1. 3–11) culminates in the elucidation of *oneness* as crowning these imperfect human ways of identifying the proper subject of theology in a way that leads away from, rather than concealing, the endemic human penchant for idolatry.

Conclusion

Completing the trajectory from Dionysius through Albert to Aquinas is not unlike rounding out a circle, as we are brought to appreciate how the profound affinities among these thinkers fairly define a "rule of faith", to paraphrase Augustine. For they converge in the impossible task of seeking to know an unknowable God, yet proceed on that path of discovery without flinching. Affinities with other Abrahamic faiths abound, as Roger Arnaldez so ably reminds us in his *Three Messengers for One God*,[81] and even beyond these cognate paths, as Sara Grant has articulated so deftly in her Teape lectures *Towards an Alternative Theology: Confessions of a Non-dualist Christian*:

> In India as in Greece, the ultimate question must always be that of the relation between the supreme unchanging Reality and the world of coming-to-be and passing away, the eternal Self and what appears as non-Self, and no epistemology can stand secure as long as this question remains unanswered. . . . A systematic study of Sankara's use of relational terms made it quite clear to me that he agrees with St. Thomas Aquinas in regarding the relation between creation and the ultimate Source of all being as a *non-reciprocal dependence relation*, i.e., a relation in which subsistent effect or "relative absolute" is *dependent on its cause for its very existence as a subsistent entity*, whereas the cause is *in no way dependent on the effect for its subsistence*, though there is a *necessary logical relation between cause and effect*; i.e., a relation which is *perceived by the mind* when it reflects on the implications of the existence of the cosmos.[82]

So the very existence (*esse*) of a creature is an *esse-ad*, an existing which is itself a relation to its source. As we have noted, nothing could better express the way in which Aquinas' formulation of the essence/existing distinction transforms Aristotle than to point out that what for Aristotle "exists in itself" (substance) is for Aquinas derived from an Other in its very in-itselfness or substantiality. Yet since the Other is the cause of being, each thing which exists-to-the-creator also exists in itself: derived existence is no less substantial when it is derived from the One-who-is, so it would appear that one could succeed in talking of existing things without explicitly referring them to their source. "The distinction", in other words, need not *appear*. But that simply reminds us how unique a non-reciprocal relation of dependence must be: it characterizes one relation only, that of creatures to creator.

If creator and creature were distinct from each other in an ordinary way, the relation—even one of dependence—could not be non-reciprocal; for ordinarily the fact that something depends from an originating agent, as a child from a parent, must mark a difference in that agent itself. Yet the fact that a cause of being, properly speaking, is not affected by causing all-that-is does not imply remoteness or uncaring; indeed, quite the opposite. For such a One must cause in such a way as to be present in each creature as that to which it is oriented in its very existing. In that sense, this One cannot be considered as *other* than what it creates, in an ordinary sense of that term; just as the creature's *esse-ad* assures that it cannot *be* separately from its source.[83] So it will not work simply to contrast creation to emanation, or to picture the creator distinct (in the ordinary sense) from creation by contrast with a more pantheistic image. Indeed, it is to avoid such infelicities of imagination that Sara Grant has recourse to Sankara's sophisticated notion of "non-duality" to call our attention in an arresting way to the utter uniqueness of "the distinction" which must indeed hold between creator and creation, but cannot be pictured in any contrastive manner.[84] Nor does Aquinas feel any compunction in defining creation as the "emanation of all of being from its universal cause (*emanatio totius entis a causa universali*)".[85] While the all-important "distinction" preserves God's freedom in creating, which the emanation scheme invariably finesses, we must nevertheless be wary of picturing that distinction in a fashion which assimilates the creator to another item within the universe. Harm Goris has shown how close attention to the uniqueness of the creator/creature relation, with its attendant corollary of participation as a way of articulating this *sui generis* causal relation, can neutralize many of the conundra which fascinate philosophers of religion.[86]

Although it may seem that we have strayed far from Albert and Aquinas in invoking Sankara's hybrid term of "non-duality", we should have realized by now how Aquinas helps himself to various ways of expressing the inexpressible: the "distinction" as well as the "relation" between creatures and their creator. Both prove to be foundational to any attempt to grasp our transcendent origins as gift. Dionysius offers an object lesson to show how astute metaphysical reflection can conspire with scripture to highlight the creator's freedom, as well as finding ways to think both creature and creator together. And the final reference in this rich smorgasbord is suggested by Andrew Louth, who reminds us how Dante's *Divina Commedia* structures "heaven as light irradiating in splendid multiformity, expressing the outward flow of God's love and the loving response of the cosmos"—all this is close to the Dionysian vision:

The primal light that irradiates them all
Is received by them in as many ways

116   David Burrell and Isabelle Moulin

As are the splendours with which it is joined,
And therefore, since the affections flow the act of conceiving,
Love's sweetness glows variously
In them, more and less.
See how the height and breadth
Of the eternal Goodness, since it has made for itself
So many mirrors in which it is broken,
Remaining in itself one as before (*Paradiso* 29.136–45).[87]

NOTES

1 Wayne Hankey, *God in Himself: Aquinas' Doctrine of God* (Oxford: Oxford University Press, 1987); for a plethora of references, see Matthew Levering, *Scripture and Metaphysics: Aquinas and the Renewal of Trinitarian Theology* (Malden MA: Blackwell, 2004).
2 Cf. the lament of Roger Bacon, *Opus Tertium*, quoted from James A. Weisheipl, "Albertus Magnus and the Oxford Platonists", *Proceedings of the American Catholic Philosophical Association*, (1958), pp. 124–139, at p. 126. Albert received the title of *Magnus* while he was still alive.
3 In this perspective, I think that the "Cologne Tradition" from Ulrich of Strasbourg to Meister Eckhart is more in harmony with the thought of Albert than Thomas Aquinas himself.
4 I-I, q. 5, a. 2. Dionysius is quoted ad. 1.
5 See P. Simon, *Prolegomena, Opera omnia* t. 37/1, pp. VI–VII. Manuscript from Napoli (*Bibl. Naz*. I. B. 54). The same *reportatio* occurs for the Nicomachean Ethics (cf. J-P. Torrell, *Initiation à Saint Thomas d'Aquin* (Fribourg, Editions Universitaires, 1993), p. 38, after Pelzer).
6 *Metaphysica* XI, 2, 12, p. 499, l. 79–82; *De causis et processu universitatis a prima causa* (hereafter *Dcpu*), I, 4, 1, p. 43, l. 1–6. For the progression from being towards sensation, see *Liber de Causis*, 1 (5 [4]); all quotations from the *Liber de Causis* [*Book of Causes*] are from the following edition, citing proposition, page numbers of the English translation, in parentheses, and page numbers from Saffey's Latin edition, in brackets: Vincent Guagliando, O.P., Charles Hess, O.P, and Richard Taylor (trans), *St. Thomas Aquinas: Commentary on the Book of Causes* (Washington, DC, The Catholic University of America Press, 1996).
    The *Liber de Causis* or *Book on Pure Goodness* derives from Proclus' *Elements of Theology* and is suspected of having come from the vicinity of Baghdad around 850 (see *St. Thomas Aquinas: Commentary on the Book of Causes*, p. xiv). It was translated into Latin by Gerard of Cremone at the end of the twelfth century. Belonging to the *ratio studiorum* of the thirteenth century, it has been commentated upon by many Latin scholars who strongly doubted its Aristotelian origin and ascribed it to Ibn Daoud or Alfarabi.
7 *Metaphysica* XI, 2, 11, p. 497, l. 53; 20, p. 508, l. 86–87; *Dcpu* I, 4, 2, p. 44, l. 14–19; 5, p. 48 sq.
8 See *Liber de Causis*, 23 (60–61 [54]).
9 The order of redaction of the commentaries and translation used is: *De Caelesti Hierarchia* (1248), *De Ecclesiastica Hierarchia* (1249, for *CH* and *EH*, trans. Eriugena with quotations from Sarracenus, called *alia translatio*), *De Divinis Nominibus* (1250, trans. John Sarracenus from now on, cf. *DN* 1, p. 3, l. 47–48), *De Mystica Theologia, Epistulae* (1250). All our quotations come from the critical "Edition of Cologne".
10 *Isaïe* 45. *MT*, I, p. 453, l. 1–2.
11 *Oportet per intellectum uniri deo*, *MT*, 2, p. 465, l. 8–9.
12 *MT*, 1, p. 458, l. 60–62.
13 Description of the two ways, *MT*, 1, p. 454, l. 79–455, l. 11. Albert's methodology, as Dionysius himself, notwithstanding the superiority of negation, implies both, and it is not contradictory (*MT*, p. 459, l. 47–49).
14 *MT* 1, p. 457, l. 18–20. Avicenna, *De Anima, Avicenna Latinus*, V, 5, t. II, p. 127, l. 36–39.
15 *MT* 5, p. 474, l. 8–26. Some detractors would say that at this point any theology, namely, *logos* about God, is impossible. But a "negative mystique" produces both a limit and a "warning" against a reason too proud about itself: there is a limit, as at one point one has to receive a

divine Revelation accompanied with a true assent of Faith. This is a warning against our common language and categories (see *DN*, 981B).

16 *MT* 1, p. 456, l. 72–74; *DN*, 1, p. 10, l. 64–72. But see *MT* 2, p. 466, l. 59–69: we do not know, absolutely speaking, even the *quia* of God, as there is no proportionality between our intellect and its cause, God. As Albert puts it in his *Metaphysica*, there is a true equivocity between our knowledge and the divine one (*Metaph*. XI, 2, 23): the divine substance's knowledge is said to be equivocal to ours, for our knowledge is caused by the beings we know, whereas the divine knowledge is the cause of being. If we do reach the *quia* of God, it is through a confused supernatural knowledge (*cognoscimus eum quadam supernaturali cognitione sub quadam confusione, TM* 1, p. 464, l. 1–3, compare with Thomas Aquinas. Note that Thomas produced no commentary upon the *MT*).

17 See also *DN* 1, p. 8, l. 64–65.

18 The analogy between God and his creatures is defined here in terms of the pure analogy of imitation (*analogia imitationis*), in which the distinction *prius/posterius* is preserved (*TM* 1, p. 459, l. 27–31). Compare with *DN* 1, p. 1, l. 27–32. This statement is implied by the methodological difference between *TM* and *DN* (see, *DN*, V, 3, p. 304, l. 51–65).

19 *DN* V, 4, p. 306, l. 10. 20–23.

20 A principle that Albert says comes from Aristotle. Cf. *DN*, V, 4, p. 306, l. 51–64, and compare with *In Metaph*. XI, 2, 6.

21 *DN* V, 9, p. 308, l. 43–62.

22 *Dcpu*, I, 4, 1, p. 43, l. 14–18; 4, 6, p. 49, l. 74–p. 50, l. 5.

23 *De IV coaequaevis*, I, 1, 5, Borgnet 34 p. 314 (quoted from Anzulewicz, p. 260. See n. xliii for the full reference).

24 *DN* 13, p. 449, l. 19–22: *bonum primum est et dignissimum*.

25 *DN* IV, 90, p. 194, l. 56–65.

26 *DN* II, 44, p. 73, l. 39–40.

27 *DN* II, 44, p. 73, l. 30–39.

28 *CH*, p. 60, l. 67–70.

29 *CH*, p. 60, l. 71–80.

30 *DN* I, p. 15, l. 48–49, repeated at l. 58–59.

31 *DN* I, p. 15, l. 59.

32 "And this is how one must understand Dionysius", l. 61. Compare with *CH*, p. 60, l. 59–62.

33 *DN* II, 45, p. 73, l. 41–42: "et ideo sequimur opinionem Aristotelis, quae magis videtur catholica". See also *DN*, I, p. 15, l. 45–47: "Nos autem aliter dicimus convenientius theologiae et philosophiae secundum opinionem Aristotelis", and *DN*, IV, p. 194, l. 72–75.

34 *DN*, VII, p. 352, l. 34–47. The philosophers were unable to explain the real causality of God: neither the first heaven nor the motion of the Sun along the ecliptic suffice to explain the diversity of species found in our world. God is not a "prime mover", as there is no proportionality between God and his creation. He would be a craftsman if he were thought of as creating not only the form of the house but also its matter; see *CH*, p. 60, l. 70–79: the "eduction" through creation must be interpreted in the light of the Good: God not only freely produces the world, but he *desires* to do so.

35 Some scholars would see a discontinuity between the works of the earlier period and particularly the "theological" commentaries and the last ones (Duhem, *Système du monde*, V, p. 440; Alain de Libera, *Albert le Grand et la philosophie*, p. 120); others think that emanation and eduction are "two aspects of one coming-to-be" (Thérèse Bonin, *Creation as Emanation*, p. 16).

36 *Metaphysica* XI, 20: "educere" a form from matter can only apply to material beings. In immaterial beings, causing amounts to providing substance (*substantiare*).

37 *EH*, 400B. "Therefore the founding source of all invisible and visible order quite properly arranges for the rays of divine activity to be granted first to the more godlike beings, since theirs are the more discerning minds, minds with the native ability to receive and to pass on light, and it is through their mediation that this source transmits enlightenment and reveals itself to inferior beings in proportion to capacity", *EH*, 504D. Compare with Albert the Great, *Dcpu* I, 4, 1, p. 42, l. 72–74. See also *Liber de Causis* 23 (131 [117]).

38 "The rays of the sun pass easily through the front line of matter since it is more translucent than all the others. The real light of the sun lights up its own beams more resplendently through that section of matter. But as it encounters more opaque matter, it appears dimmer

118   David Burrell and Isabelle Moulin

and more diffuse, because this matter is less suited to the passage of the outpouring of light. This unsuitability becomes progressively greater until finally it halts completely the journey of light", *CH* 240C. Compare with Albert the Great, again *Metaphysica*, XI, 2, 20, p. 508, l. 23–25, 30–32; XI, 2, 11, p. 497, l. 53; *Dcpu* I, 4, 2, p. 44, l. 14–29; 3, p. 45, l. 31–35; 4, p. 46, l. 72–73.; 5, p. 48, l. 41–42.

39   *DN*, I, p. 16, l. 44–53; *DN*, IV, p. 345, l. 72–79; for the Eucharist, *CH* II, p. 89, l. 10–25.
40   *Metaphysica* XI, 2, 39.
41   This aspect of Albert the Great is not always underlined by the scholars acquainted with his Aristotelian paraphrases.
42   *Dcpu*, I, 4, 1, p. 42, l. 36–74. See *Liber de Causis*, 19 (116 [104–105]).
43   A few references may be supplied for further reading: Henryk Anzulewicz, "Pseudo-Dionysius Areopagita und das Strukturprinzip des Denkens von Albert dem Grossen", in T. Boiadjiev, G. Kapriev, and A. Speer (eds), *Die Dionysius-Rezeption im Mittelalter. Internationales Kolloquium in Sofia vom 8. bis 11. April 1999 unter der Schrimherrschaft der S.I.E.P.M. Rencontres de Philosophie Médiévale 9*, Turnhout: Brepols, 2000, pp. 251–295; Gilles Emery O.P., *La Trinité créatrice* (Paris: Vrin, 1995), esp. pp. 140–158; William J. Hoye, "Mystische Theologie nach Albert dem Grossen", in Walter Senner (ed), *Albertus Magnus: Zum Gedenken nach 800 Jahren: Neue Zugänge, Aspekte und Perspektiven* (Berlin: Akademie, 2001), pp. 587–603; John D. Jones, "An absolutely simple God? Frameworks for Reading Pseudo-Dionysius Areopagite", *The Thomist*, 69/3 (2005), pp. 371–406 (I thank the author for a very helpful discussion concerning the divine *energeiai* in Dionysius); Simon Tugwell (trans.) and Leonard E. Boyle (intro.), *Albert and Thomas: Selected Writings* (New York/Mahwah: Paulist Press, The Classics of Western Spirituality, 1988); Edouard-Henri Weber, "Introduction", *Albert le Grand: Commentaire de la «Théologie mystique» de Denys le pseudo-aréopagite, suivi de celui des épîtres I–V* (Paris: Cerf, 1993), pp. 7–58; Edouard-Henri Weber, "L'interprétation par Albert le Grand de la Théologie mystique de Denys le Ps-Aréopagite", in G. Meyer and A. Zimmermann (eds), *Albertus Magnus: Doctor Universalis 1280/1980* (Mainz: Matthias Grünewald Verlag, 1980), pp. 409–439.
44   Marie-Dominique Chenu, O.P., *Towards Understanding St. Thomas*, trans. A.-M. Landry and D. Hughes (Chicago, IL: Henry Regnery, 1964).
45   Aquinas' task of showing *theologia* to be *scientia* is nicely developed in Eugene F. Rogers, *Thomas Aquinas and Karl Barth* (Notre Dame, IN: University of Notre Dame Press, 1995).
46   Andrew Louth, *Denys the Areopagite* (London: Geoffrey Chapman, 1989), pp. 126, 125.
47   *In librum beati Dionysii de divinis nominibus expositio* (Torino/Rome: Marietti, 1995), #1008. All quotations are from this "Marietti" edition, citing paragraph (#) and page numbers.
48   *Ibid.*, pp. 399–407.
49   Cf. Olivier-Thomas Venard, O.P., *Littérature et Théologie: Une saison en enfer* (Geneve: Ad Solem, 2002); the review by David Burrell is in *The Thomist*, 68:4 (2004).
50   Robert Sokolowski, *God of Faith and Reason* (Washington, DC: Catholic University of America Press, 1995).
51   Edward Booth, O.P., *Aristotelian Aporetic Ontology in Islamic and Christian Thinkers* (Cambridge: Cambridge University Press, 1983).
52   See David Burrell, "Essence and Existence: Avicenna and Greek Philosophy", MIDEO [= *Melanges Institut Dominican d'Etudes Orientales-Cairo*], 17 (1986), pp. 53–66.
53   The presentation of the following three paragraphs is largely taken from David Burrell, "Aquinas' Appropriation of *Liber de Causis* to Articulate the Creator as Cause-of-Being", in Fergus Kerr (ed), *Contemplating Aquinas* (London: SCM Press, 2003), pp. 55–74.
54   See David Burrell, "Freedom and Creation in the Abrahamic Traditions", *International Philosophical Quarterly*, 40 (2000), pp. 161–171; and the development by Eleonore Stump, "Intellect, Will, and the Principle of Alternate Possibilities", in Michael Beatty (ed), *Christian Theism and the Problems of Philosophy* (Notre Dame, IN: University of Notre Dame Press, 1990), pp. 254–285; and later in her *Aquinas* (New York and London: Routledge, 2003).
55   *ST* 1.32.1.3.
56   *Liber de Causis* 20 (123 [110]).
57   *Ibid.* 20 (123–4 [111]).
58   *Ibid.* 24 (134 [111]).
59   *Ibid.* 21 (125 [112]), (126 [113]).
60   *Ibid.* 23 (132 [118]).

61 *Ibid.*
62 *Ibid.* 24 (137 [122]).
63 *Ibid.* 22 (130 [116]).
64 *Ibid.* 24 (138 [123]).
65 *Ibid.* 6 (46 [43]), (52 [17]).
66 *Ibid.* 6 (51 [47]).
67 *Ibid.* 4 (30 [17]).
68 *DN* 1.5 593B-C (53, 54). All quotations from the *DN* cite chapter and section, Migne columns, and, in parentheses, page numbers from the English translation by Colm Lubheid, *Pseudo-Dionysius: the Complete Works* (New York, NY: Paulist Press, 1987).
69 Marietti, #83, p. 28.
70 *DN* 5.4 817C-D (98).
71 Marietti, #629, p. 234.
72 See David Burrell, "Creation, Metaphysics, and Ethics", *Faith and Philosophy*, 18 (2001), pp. 204–221.
73 *DN* 7.2 869B (108).
74 Marietti, #724–725, p. 271.
75 *DN* 8.9 897A-B (114).
76 Marietti, #788–89, p. 295.
77 *DN* 11.2 949C (122).
78 Marietti, #896, p. 335.
79 *DN* 13.1–2 977B, C (127–8).
80 Marietti, #956, p. 357. See David Burrell, *Al-Ghazali on Faith in Divine Unity and Trust in Divine Providence* (translation of Bk. 35 of Ihya' Ulum ad-Din) (Louisville, KY: Fons Vitae, 2000).
81 Roger Arnaldez, *Three Messengers for One God*, trans. David Burrell, Mary Louise Gude, Gerald Schlabach (Notre Dame, IN: University of Notre Dame Press, 1993).
82 Sara Grant, *Towards an Alternative Theology: Confessions of a Non-dualist Christian* (Notre Dame, IN: University of Notre Dame Press, 2001), p. 39.
83 See the exchange between David Burrell and Tom Flint in *Freedom and Creation in Three Traditions* (Notre Dame, IN: University of Notre Dame Press, 1993), p. 112, esp. note 33.
84 Kathryn Tanner develops a sense of transcendence that is expressly "non-contrastive", illustrating that suggestive category though the history of some key questions in philosophical theology, in her *God and Creation in Christian Theology* (Oxford: Basil Blackwell, 1988).
85 *ST*, I, 45, 1.
86 Harm Goris, *Free Creatures of an Eternal God* (Leuven: Peeters, 1996).
87 *Denys the Areopagite* (London: Geoffrey Chapman, 1989), pp. 126–127. For a presentation and analysis of Dante's *Commedia* which elaborates this point to display the affinity with Dionysius, notably in the incorporation of philosophical acuity to elucidate the scriptures as "divine teaching," see Christian Moevs, *The Metaphysics of Dante's Divine Comedy* (Oxford: Oxford University Press, 2005).

8

DIONYSIUS AND SOME LATE MEDIEVAL MYSTICAL THEOLOGIANS OF NORTHERN EUROPE

DENYS TURNER

The influence of Dionysius on the theologies of the late Middle Ages is at once so pervasive and so varied in character that it defies the construction of any summary that might be more illuminating than misleading. Even within the more limited scope of the mystical theologies of northern Europe in the fourteenth and fifteenth centuries, the narrative of that influence is hardly simple. Any brief reconstruction even of its main lineaments is bound to be selective, and no selection can do justice to the way in which Dionysius' thought is woven into the very fabric of the vocabulary, imagery and argument of Marguerite Porete, Meister Eckhart, Jan van Ruusbroec, Jean Gerson, Denys the Carthusian or Nicholas of Cusa, to mention but those I will discuss in this chapter. In the days before the invention of copyright—bringing with it the curious notion that authors *own* ideas and their verbal expressions—it is an anachronism to describe such authors as these as plagiarising their sources. In such terms, in any case, they do not so much plagiarise as shamelessly plunder. In their own terms, however, they are but drawing on a common resource, as we draw breath from the common air; and they no more notice, or feel the need to draw attention to, their theological debts than we do to the presence of oxygen in the atmosphere. Such, at any rate, was the standing of Dionysius in relation to the mystical theologies of the late Middles Ages in northern Europe. He is less what you speak about than he is the air you breathe as you speak.

Denys Turner
Yale Divinity School, Yale University, 409 Prospect Street, New Haven, CT 06511, USA
denys.turner@yale.edu

"Intellectualist" and "Affectivist" Readings of the Mystical Theology

That said, there are particular contexts of controversy in which the standing of Dionysius' mystical theology, and more particularly that of his *Mystical Theology*, becomes a topic of explicit discussion in the late Middle Ages. It is not so much that his theology as such is disputed; on the contrary, that is distinctly *not* an issue. It is rather that some key matters of theological controversy come to be conducted from the early fourteenth century until the end of the fifteenth in terms of a competition for the ownership of Dionysius' undisputed authority. One such issue—which I will not discuss in any detail here[1]—is that over the so-called "affectivist" as against "intellectualist" readings of the soul's ascent to union with God, as it is described in the concluding paragraphs of chapter one of the *Mystical Theology*. There, Dionysius describes the ascent of the mind into the "brilliant darkness" of unknowing in the medium of an allegory of Moses' ascent of Mount Sinai into the cloud in which God is hidden, there to become so "one" with God "as to belong completely to him who is beyond everything":

> [B]eing neither oneself nor someone else, one is supremely united by a completely unknowing inactivity of all knowledge, and knows beyond the mind by knowing nothing.[2]

We will return to this passage later in another connection, but in terms of the "affectivist/intellectualist" controversies of the thirteenth to fifteenth centuries, the issue turned on how to characterise the epistemic character of the "unknowing" Dionysius here describes. Is that "unknowing" itself a cognitive *act*—as Dionysius describes it, "a *knowing* beyond the mind", indeed the supreme act of intellect, which, as it were, fully realises itself in the act of its self-abolition, as you might well read Marguerite Porete as implying, or Meister Eckhart as explicitly saying? Is it, as the mid-fifteenth century Denys the Carthusian says in a similarly "intellectualist" spirit, intellect which is formally united with God in the Dionysian "unknowing", albeit, in concession to "affectivist" priorities, he affirms that it is love that drives the intellect into that "oneness"?[3] Or is it, as the Victorine Thomas Gallus in the earlier thirteenth century interpreted the Dionysian passage, as also the Carthusian Hugh of Balma in the late decades of the same century, to imply that it is not intellect which unites "the mind" to God, but love, and that, correspondingly, his "darkness of unknowing" consisted in intellect's being simply disabled and set aside in the highest stage of the soul's ascent to God? For these latter, in the end you cannot be "supremely united" to "him who is beyond everything" except by finally abandoning all forms of intellectual knowledge, thus clearing the path for a love which alone unites the soul to God. Dionysius' "divine darkness of unknowing" is no longer as for Marguerite, Eckhart, Denys the Carthusian and Nicholas of Cusa, intellect's supreme *act*; it is rather achieved by love only on condition of intellect's *in*action, or, as Dionysius says, "an unknowing *inactivity* of all knowledge".

Now it is unfair to say that the "affectivism" of either Gallus or Hugh of Balma entailed any form of theological *anti*-intellectualism, for, as Gallus put it, "knowing" and "loving" walk "hand-in-hand" nearly but not quite all the way up the hierarchy of ascent to God. For Gallus it is only at the last stage that love "steps out on its own". And for Bonaventure, if it is love which in the highest form of "contemplation" throws the ladder of knowledge away so as to enter alone into the darkness of the *Deus absconditus*, there will be no throwing ladders of intellect away for those who have not climbed them first. More radical, perhaps, and implying a more anti-intellectual form of Dionysianism, was the position of another Carthusian, the anonymous late-fourteenth century Author of *The Cloud of Unknowing*, who in a more unqualified spirit (perhaps because he is less patient than Gallus or Bonaventure with a staged hierarchy of ascent to God) asseverates: "by love he (God) may be held and kept, but by thinking never".[4] Moreover, as with those of Gallus, Bonaventure and Hugh, the *Cloud*'s "affectivism" is explicitly attributed to Dionysius. In his *Dionise Hid Divinite*, a paraphrase of Dionysius' *Mystical Theology*, the *Cloud* Author interpolates the text in an "affectivist" spirit with references not found in Dionysius to the uniting power of love—in this following closely the paraphrase of the same text contained in Gallus' *Extractio*. (As the *Cloud* Author himself says, he has reworked the *Mystical Theology* "according to the sentence of the Abbot of Vercelli".) Neither Gallus nor the *Cloud* Author believes that their "affectivist" interpolations do any sort of violence to the "sentence" of Dionysius himself.[5]

Jean Gerson in the early fifteenth century is, again, perhaps a little more nuanced than the *Cloud* Author—at least he allows intellect a significant role in the articulation of a mystical theology. Worried as we will see him to be about other issues of mystical theology, particularly those of doctrinal orthodoxy, he qualifies a broadly "affectivist" reading of Dionysius' apophaticism—it is love which unites to God, not knowledge—with an insistence on an important regulatory function of intellect. What Gerson fears is too unqualified an affectivism, one which he believes leads inevitably (and has led in fact to exaggerated forms of what we would nowadays call "autotheism") to the doctrine that the soul is so united to God by love as to extinguish all distinction between creature and creator, and so as to lose all created identity of its own. This fear, he believed, had more than just some foundation in the writings of some near contemporaries, more particularly, as we will see, in the theological errors of Jan van Ruusbroec and in what Gerson perceives are the closely associated Beguine and Beghard heresies. The safeguard against such pernicious teachings is a firm grounding of love in orthodox doctrine, in a critical, if not in a substantively unitive, function of intellect: it is indeed love which unites the soul with God, but the theology of that "union" may be articulated only subject to the regulatory regime of critical intellect.

Gerson, Ruusbroec and Denys the Carthusian and the Question of "Autotheism"

Gerson's anxieties about the orthodoxy of some late medieval mystical theologians extends however beyond his doubts about overly "affectivist" interpretations of Dionysius. It extends into what he clearly regards as a much more dangerous extremism in the interpretation of Dionysius' language of "oneness with God" found in the *Mystical Theology*. Here it is Ruusbroec who is the main target. The story of an extended late medieval controversy, one which is in essence a dispute over the rightful inheritance of the Dionysian theological estate, goes, in summary, as follows: Gerson thought Ruusbroec misdescribed the union of the soul with God in a manner which placed him in the company of the "free-spirit" heretics; Denys the Carthusian responded that Gerson had misconstrued what Ruusbroec said, or at least what Ruusbroec plainly meant; I, for my part, think both Gerson and Denys miss the point and that in our plot it takes a fourth character at the beginning of the fourteenth century, Meister Eckhart, and a fifth in the mid-fifteenth, Nicholas of Cusa, to tell us why. Moreover, rumbling on within this dispute there are the reverberations of an early fourteenth-century historical event: the execution of Marguerite Porete in 1310 for her supposed association with the "free-spirit" heresy.

The bare story-line of the disagreements between Ruusbroec, Gerson and Denys the Carthusian is fairly quickly told, although I shall tell it even more briefly than will do full justice to all the nuances. What is more interesting is the "why", and that will occupy me for the greater part of this chapter and lead me to conclude that Gerson and Denys give us opposed misreadings of Ruusbroec for one and the same reason: both have lost grip on the central claim of Dionysius' theological epistemology, that is, of what one might call his "dialectics" of identity and difference. Marguerite Porete and Ruusbroec retained a firm practical grasp on this central feature of Dionysius' thought, and Eckhart and Nicholas of Cusa knew the theory very well. This "dialectic" connects that question of how correctly to describe the nature of the soul's "oneness" with God in "mystical union" with the other issue between the "intellectualist" and the "affectivist" theologians. For the abandonment of Dionysius' "intellectual" apophaticism lies at the root both of the "affectivist" turn in late medieval theology, and of the recurrent late medieval condemnations of those who so emphasized that "oneness" as apparently to deny to the soul any existence independent of God's. These factors lay behind the condemnations of Marguerite Porete in Paris in 1310, of Meister Eckhart in Avignon in 1329, and of Ruusbroec by Gerson in 1426.

Gerson's Critique of The Spiritual Espousals

Though the best known passages of the Gersonian polemic against Ruusbroec are to be found in his *De Mystica Theologia* of 1407[6], the most sustained critique is to be found in two letters Gerson wrote towards the end of his life in 1426 to a Carthusian prior, brother Bartholemew.[7] Apart from the greater comprehensiveness of these later critiques, there are two reasons relating to our story why we should pay more attention to them than to the earlier work. In Ruusbroec's own lifetime and for some time after his death in 1381, Carthusians had on the whole been enthusiastic supporters of his reputation,[8] and Gerson, who liked the Carthusians almost alone among the monastic orders, could not abide Ruusbroec. Gerson was therefore particularly keen to detach Carthusian support from Ruusbroec's reputation—and by and large succeeded. This brings us to the second historical reason for paying attention principally to these polemical letters addressed to Carthusians. By the 1440s, when Denys the Carthusian was writing his central mystical work *De Contemplatione*, Gerson's influence on the Carthusians had already contributed decisively to the anti-speculative bent of Carthusian piety, which, like so many other late medieval spiritualities was now distinctly hostile to the sort of daring speculations which had characterised the fourteenth century Rhineland schools. Denys, an enthusiast for Ruusbroec and an ardent supporter of the "intellectualist" tendencies of Rhineland mystical thought, was already in trouble with his order, vexing his superiors as he did with what they thought of as these inappropriately "intellectualist" priorities.[9] So, in summary, Gerson had an interest in dissuading the Carthusians of support for Ruusbroec; Denys, on the other hand, had an equal personal interest in defending his own intellectual position via the rebuttal of Gerson's critique of Ruusbroec.

What worried Gerson most was the orthodoxy of the first few chapters of the third book of *The Spiritual Espousals*.[10] He had no problem with the first two books, in which, he says, he "found many things said . . . which are safe and sound and offering testimony of sublime matters".[11] Not that Gerson will accept the opinion which he has heard expressed that this work "was written by a simple and unlearned person and . . . that therefore it would seem to have been compiled . . . in a miraculous fashion and by means of divine inspiration",[12] for the work as a whole reveals its author to have been a considerable scholar, the style is sophisticated and, more conclusively, the third book contains material which is at least "uncertain" doctrinally or "even false", and such opinions cannot be attributed to the Holy Spirit.[13] In fact, the third part of *Spiritual Espousals* "must be completely rejected and rescinded, since it is either ill-expressed or else is openly contrary to and discordant with the doctrine of the holy teachers who have spoken about our beatitude".[14] More specifically, the doctrines of this third book are close in spirit and word to those of "the sect of the Beghards, who were condemned some time ago by the decree of the Church"[15]—referring, of course, to the decree *Ad Nostrum* of the Council of Vienne in 1312, condemning the Beguines and Beghards for their espousal of "free-spirit" heresies.[16]

As Lerner[17] and Lambert[18] agree, the so-called "heresy of the free spirit" never actually existed, even in the early fourteenth century, at least in the form of specific doctrines promoted by any organised body, still less by any sect and least of all by the Beguines or Beghards. Lambert even goes so far as to say that "[d]efinitions in *Ad Nostrum* helped create heretics to match the Bull",[19] and our best evidence of what this heresy was thought to amount to is found almost exclusively in the official church documents which condemn it. On the evidence of the decree *Ad Nostrum*, the doctrines which got called by that name were chiefly two: autotheism and antinomianism, the doctrines that the perfected soul and God are indistinguishably one and that the soul thus perfected has no need of, or worse perhaps, has no use for, Christian virtue or devotional practice. The French inquisitor in 1310, William Humbert, considered that both heretical doctrines were to be found in Marguerite Porete's *A Mirror of Simple Souls*[20] and he decreed that this *pseudo-mulier*, this "fake woman", a "certain Beguine",[21] was to be executed for a relapsed heretic, and on June 1 of that year she was duly burned.

Gerson appears to know little of the detail of this history, indeed he appears to confuse these condemnations of supposed Beguine heresy in 1310 and 1312 with a quite different condemnation in 1333 by the University of Paris of the views of Guiral Ot (and indirectly those of Pope John XXII) on the beatific vision.[22] But what mattered was that the mud of free spirit heresy discharged at the Beguines and Beghards in 1312 was still sticking in 1426, and Gerson is determined that some will attach to Ruusbroec. But the mud was first thrown at Marguerite Porete, and however muddled Gerson may have been about the history of her condemnation, there is little doubt that it is the *grounds* on which Marguerite's *Mirror* was condemned, namely almost exactly those on which the Council of Vienne condemned the heresy of the free-spirit, that Gerson has in mind as tainting the third book of Ruusbroec's *Spiritual Espousals*. For everything Gerson finds objectionable in Ruusbroec is found in similar terms in Marguerite. And so Gerson tells us:

> As I think, this author was a near contemporary of (the Beghards) and it could be that it was expressly in order to counter his conceit about the beatific or contemplative vision—which he perhaps shared in common with many others at the time—that the decretal [Gerson does not say which] was issued which laid down that beatitude consists in two acts.[23]

Above all it is the ordure of autotheism that he detects the smell of in Book Three of *Spiritual Espousals*.

> The author asserts in the third part of this work that the soul which contemplates God perfectly not only sees him by means of that light which is the divine essence, but actually *is* that same divine light . . . He adds that the soul of the contemplative person is lost within the abyss of the divine existence so that it is beyond recovery by any creature. It is possible to make use of a metaphor for this—though it is not one employed by him—that a small drop of wine, dropped into the sea is quickly mingled with it and changed into it.[24]

Of course this metaphor of wine losing its identity in water—not, as Gerson admits, Ruusbroec's own, but rather Gerson's gloss—has no less authority behind it than that of another century's chief pursuer of heretics, Bernard of Clairvaux,[25] but this does not stop Gerson from exploiting what he thinks of as its heterodox implications, which are, of course, that, on Ruusbroec's account of it, the soul's union with God is such that its character as created is entirely lost in its absorption into the Creator. And, *prima facie*, Gerson has a point. He quotes Ruusbroec's words—or rather the Latin rendering of them from which I am translating:

> In that emptiness of [God], the spirit loses itself in blissful love and receives the light of God with nothing mediating, and it ceaselessly becomes the very light which it receives.[26]

And

> Our created existence depends on the eternal existence and is one with it according to its essential existence.[27]

And

> All those who are raised up above their created existence into the utmost heights of the contemplative life are one with this God-making light, indeed they are this light itself. Accordingly, through this God-making resplendence, they see and feel and discover themselves to be uncreated in their existence and in their life, and to be one and the same with the simple emptiness of the Godhead.[28]

And even more outrageously, Ruusbroec says:

> There, the spirit is taken up above itself and is united with God, and tastes and sees in the oneness of the brilliant abyss, where in its uncreated existence it takes possession of the immense riches which he himself is, in the manner in which God tastes and sees them.[29]

One can see how Gerson might have observed some sort of connection between Ruusbroec and such as he knew of the "free-spirit" heresy, if, at any rate, Marguerite Porete can be taken as representing the "errors" supposedly contained within that heresy. For she says of the soul who has reached the sixth and penultimate stage of spiritual growth:

> The sixth stage is that the Soul does not see herself on account of such an abyss of humility which she has within her. Nor does she see God on account of the highest goodness which He has. But God sees Himself in her by His divine majesty, who clarifies this Soul with Himself, so that she sees only that there is nothing except God Himself Who is, from whom all things are.[30]

Gerson comments:

You might suppose, from the sound of these words [he is, of course, referring to Ruusbroec], that in that case the soul ceases to exist in that mode of existence which it possessed previously in its own kind, and is changed or transformed and absorbed into the divine existence, and flows back into that ideal existence which it had, from eternity, in the divine nature.[31]

Such an opinion Gerson could very well have supposed further confirmed his association of Ruusbroec with "Beghard and Beguine errors", given what Marguerite goes on to say:

Thus the soul has nothing more to do for God than God does for her. Why? Because He is, and she is not. She retains nothing more of herself in nothingness, because He is sufficient of Himself, that is, because He is and she is not. Thus she is stripped of all things because she is without existence, where she was before she was.[32]

And if these formulae of the soul's union with God appear to negate the distinction between Creator and creature, they must, consequently, obliterate the individual identity of the person. For if matters stood as Ruusbroec (or Marguerite) explains them, then, in the beatific vision in heaven the glorified body would lose its own soul and

would in [its own soul's stead] acquire the divine essence as that which formally gives it life—or else it would have no life at all; but in that case the soul would not be of the same kind as it was before, in fact it would have only that existence and life which it had from eternity, in the divine art; and then the soul's bliss would consist in that manner of existence in which from eternity any soul, including the damned soul, [possessed] the divine life. For the human body in glory would not be able to recover its soul as its formal principle of life; or if it could the soul would not be annihilated in the way he says it is. And innumerable consequences, all absurd, would follow . . .[33]

There is no doubt that Ruusbroec says those things which Gerson believes entail these "absurd consequences", although equally there is no doubt that Ruusbroec did not accept that his words did in fact entail them. But that on the surface Ruusbroec's words were ambiguous to contemporary readers, even to some more kindly disposed than Gerson, is shown by the fact that Ruusbroec composed his later *Little Book of Clarification* in response to anxieties which Carthusian friends had expressed to him about the orthodoxy of *Espousals*, Book Three.[34] And, when Denys the Carthusian wrote his own work on contemplation, it is very probably to the *Book of Clarification* that he appeals in his defence of Ruusbroec against Gerson's polemic.

Denys the Carthusian's Defence of Ruusbroec

"To be united with [God]", Denys says, explaining both his own views and those of Ruusbroec whom he believes he is following,

> is to be lifted above oneself, it is to fall and flow away from oneself, it is to be plunged into God, it is to expire and die in him, it is to be absorbed into him so as to become one and the same with him, it is to possess and draw upon that life which makes the living person to be god-like, it is to be made divine by the most completely free gift of likeness.[35]

For his part, Denys adds, neither he nor Ruusbroec intend anything by this to imply

> the destruction of created existence or its displacement, or that [the person's] being is carried over into or transformed into the divine or "ideal" existence, for it is in the nature of an elevation of the mode of existence, involving a qualitative change, of a very special and exceptional resemblance,[36]

one which, as he puts it, "forges between *two wills* a singleness of yea and nay"[37]—and not between two existences a singleness of identity. Moreover, he insists, this is all John Ruusbroec means when he says "that we are to become one with God, one life, one happiness",[38] clearly, here, paraphrasing the language of the *Spiritual Espousals*. Consequently, "one author" (meaning, of course, Gerson)

> who attends to the surface meaning of [Ruusbroec's] words rather than what he intended, wrote that [Ruusbroec] proposed to revive the error of those who say that the rational creature, by virtue of his being raised up to God, returns to and is changed into his "ideal" and uncreated existence: which was a very vulgar and most crass error. It should not be thought that this John ever intended to make such a claim or revive it: in fact he wrote bitter words against this error. Nonetheless, his manner of speaking was often hyperbolical, as was that of certain other saints, in the excess of their devotion and the fervour of their charity.[39]

The "Modus Loquendi" of the Platonists

Loyal though Denys' defence of Ruusbroec may be, it is, in my view, uncomprehending of the inner logic of Ruusbroec's thought. Ruusbroec's "hyperbole" is not the product merely of pious fervour, and in any case, were it but that, he would still be left open to Gerson's second level of critique that Ruusbroec's intended meaning can be derived only from what he has actually written; so that even if he is let off the hook of explicitly heretical aforethought, his failure still lies in the manner of his expression, which piety cannot be allowed to excuse.[40] There is, in any case, more to it than that; the diagnoses of Gerson and Denys, opposed as they are, are equally superficial. What leads Ruusbroec to his hyperbolical formulae of the soul's oneness with God are pure necessities of thought and language, necessities which derive from the Dionysian soil in which Ruusbroec's theology is rooted. An earlier diagnostician of Neoplatonic thought, Thomas Aquinas, came very much nearer to comprehending this inner logic of this Christianised Platonism than did either Gerson or Denys, though his discussion relates to a different, if not entirely unrelated, issue.

That was the issue raised for him immediately by Peter Lombard's discussion of the status of the charity with which the soul loves God, for Peter, following William of St Thierry before him,[41] took the view that since God, and more specifically, the Holy Spirit, is charity, the love by means of which the Christian soul loves God *is* the Holy Spirit itself.[42] Thomas, in the *Summa Theologiae* as also elsewhere, notes that it is Augustine's authority no less which is commonly appealed to in defence of this view. For Augustine in *On the Trinity* says that "God is said to be charity in the same sense in which he is said to be spirit".[43] Therefore, Peter's argument goes, "charity in the soul is nothing created, but is God himself",[44] to which Thomas replies that of course it is true that the divine essence is charity just as it is wisdom and goodness. For this reason we do say that the good are good by virtue of the divine goodness and that the wise are wise by virtue of the divine wisdom, but this is because the goodness by which we are constituted as good is a kind of participation in the divine goodness, just as the wisdom which makes us wise is a sort of participation in the divine wisdom. It is in the same sense that the charity by which we love our neighbour is a sort of participation in the divine charity. But, he goes on, participation is not the same thing as identity, though "*this way of putting it is customary among the Platonists, by whose teachings Augustine was suffused*". There are, however, those who "are unaware of this and derive cause of error from his words".[45]

Now this does get nearer to the point, which is that it is neither pious exaggeration, nor theological ignorance, which leads to the kind of language of identity which we find in Ruusbroec, for it is rather something endemic within the specific mentality of the Dionysian mystical theology. Thomas, however, is too ready to excuse this language as a mere mode of expression, customary among the Platonists, as if they really meant something their words disguise—understandable though his generosity may be when it is the authority of Augustine which is at stake. But for once, one is inclined to throw Thomas' own words back in his face, *magis amicus veritas*.

It will not do justice to the case to say, as Thomas implies, that Platonists use the predicate of identity in a merely rhetorical fashion when what they really mean is "participation". For Neoplatonists, degree of existence *is* degree of participation. And this means in the first instance that a thing's identity as what it is lies in the degree to which it participates in its form, so that its "isness" as this or that is directly proportional to its participation in "what-it-is-to-be-this" or that. It means in the second instance that the extent to which a thing participates in its form is the extent to which it *is* the form it participates in. Whereas, therefore, for Thomas, a thing's participation in another entails its *non*-identity with what it participates in, for the Neoplatonist total participation in another *is* identity with it. And what holds for Neoplatonism thus roughly characterised in general, holds for Ruusbroec, for this is what his famous "exemplarism" amounts to. This is why Ruusbroec can say so emphatically that thing to which Gerson takes such exception:

> this eternal going forth and this eternal life which we eternally have and are in God apart from ourselves is the cause of our created being in time. *Our created being depends upon this eternal being and is one with it in its essential subsistence.*[46]

Here, then we get to the crux of the matter. "Our created being", says Ruusbroec, ". . . is one with [this eternal being] in its essential subsistence". Well, we may ask, how both? How "created", if one with the creator's being "in its essential subsistence"? Thomas, we may imagine, could resolve the paradox on the assumption that Ruusbroec did not really mean that creature and creator are identical existentially, but only that an exceptional degree of participation is rhetorically misdescribed in those terms. Denys could and does put it down to pious hyperbole. But what if Gerson is right and Ruusbroec means what he says, particularly if what he says is so to be construed neo-platonically as to mean that the soul becomes one existent with God? What are we then to make of the oxymoron: our *created* existence is one existent with the *creator's*? And note that it will not be enough, in Ruusbroec's defence, *merely* to list the innumerable texts in Ruusbroec, whether in *Spiritual Espousals* itself or in the later and more consciously defensive *Little Book of Clarification*,[47] in which he makes clear that nothing he says about oneness with God should be taken as entailing the denial of the created identity of human persons, for that only intensifies the oxymoronic effect of saying both. In any case, the question is not *whether* Ruusbroec wants to say both things, for he constantly does, but *how consistently* he can say both things, for he clearly seems to *think* he can. How, in short, does the Dionysian mystical theologian get away with affirming my "union [with God] without distinction" consistently with affirming my identity as a creature? How, even more simply, can one consistently say: Ruusbroec is one existent with God, Gerson is one existent with God, yet Ruusbroec and Gerson are two distinct created individuals?

Dionysius and the Transcendence of Identity and Distinction

The answer, I believe, lies in an adequate understanding of late medieval dialectics of "identity" and "distinction", an understanding altogether lacking in Gerson, inadequate in Denys, implicit in Marguerite Porete and

Ruusbroec, and fully articulated at least by Meister Eckhart and Nicholas of
Cusa. A paraphrase, I think, goes something like this.

Dionysius himself had said in *Mystical Theology* that "[the cause of all] is
beyond assertion and denial"; and again, "We make assertions and denials of
what is next to it, but never of it, for it is both beyond every assertion . . . [and]
also beyond every denial";[48] and yet again, "[The One is] beyond . . . the
assertion of all things and the denial of all things, [is] that which is beyond
every assertion and denial".[49] For this reason, Dionysius adds, the Cause of
all is "beyond similarity and difference".[50] Now when Eckhart says of creatures that all of them are in one way or another "distinct", but that of God you
can say only that s/he is, if indeed "One", so only by virtue of being "indistinct"; and when Nicholas of Cusa entitles one of his last works *De li non-
Aliud*, "on the (one and only) *not*-other", he is but glossing those concluding
words of Dionysius' *Mystical Theology*. What all three acknowledge is the
highly paradoxical character of our language of the divine transcendence, a
paradoxicality at the level of ontology which *has to* flow into a consequent
paradoxicality in our language of the union of the soul with God.

For "assertion" and "denial" constitute the grounding logic of our speech
about creatures. Every assertion of "this" entails the denial of at least some
"that"; every assertion of a "one" entails the exclusion of an "other". "Sameness" and "difference" hold of creatures. But if, in search of some grounding
for the distinction between God and creatures, you suppose that the same
logic must hold, if, that is to say, you suppose that you can answer the
question: "*How* different is God?", or "*In what* does the divine transcendence
consist?" in terms of some "how" or "what" by which that "difference" is
marked out, then you do but inevitably—it matters not in what terms you do
it—misconstrue the divine transcendence. For by drawing God's difference
into the family circle of construable differences, you have necessarily drawn
the divine existence within the family of creaturely existences. To put it in
another way: if, having resisted the inclination to construe the divine difference in this way or that, you are forced into saying that God is *totally* different,
you have not said anything about what *kind* of difference there is between
God and creatures. For a "total" difference between one thing and another is
not a difference of any *kind*; or again, to put it in the manner of Nicholas of
Cusa, if God is "totally" different from creatures, then God is "not-other"
than them, because we have lost our handle on "sameness" and "otherness"
as such—which is no more than Dionysius affirms when he says that God is
"beyond every denial". For, as he also says, "He does not possess *this* kind of
existence and not *that*. No. He is all things, since he is the Cause of all
things".[51]

But if God is beyond "difference", then God is beyond "sameness", and for
the same reason that "He does not possess this kind of existence and not
that". Eckhart glosses: every creature is "different" in one way or another
from every other such that there is this or that that they differ *as*, there is a

shared background against which they contrast, some "sameness" they commonly possess, such that their differing in respect of it is intelligible. But there is no common category to which God and creatures belong, no common ground occupied by both. Hence, if the language of "difference" is disabled by the divine transcendence, then so is the language of "sameness", for they are the *same* language. To deny that God is "different" from creatures by way of *created* distinction does not entail that God is identical with creatures by way of created identity. For God, as Meister Eckhart says, differs *maximally* from creatures in that whereas every creature is "different" from every other in some respect, God is different from creatures only in this: that God is "one", but not one among many, and is identified precisely by the fact that God is the one and only being who is "indistinct", an *unum indistinctum*. Which is no more than to say, as Dionysius says, that God is "beyond every assertion", or, as he also says, "God is not some kind of being."[52]

It follows from this that statements of the soul's "oneness" with God, such as those of Marguerite, Meister Eckhart, and Ruusbroec can be maximally emphatic—not merely rhetorically hyberbolic—without imperilling the created soul's created identity. In fact, what follows is quite the contrary. For on Dionysius' doctrine of the divine transcendence, the creature's union with God cannot be opposed to the creature's numerical identity. For if Gerson is one with God, and so is Ruusbroec, then Gerson and Ruusbroec remain distinct from one another on all the standard secular criteria for the numerical distinctness of persons. As creatures they are discernibly distinct from one another. On the other hand, neither Gerson nor Ruusbroec are distinct from God by virtue of *God's* numerical distinctness. For as Eckhart knew and said, and both Marguerite and Ruusbroec imply, God is not numerically distinct from anything whatsoever, since, God not being any particular kind of thing ("beyond both assertion and denial"), God is in no way numerable. God, in relation to creation, is not an *additional* anything. Therefore, God is distinct from Gerson and God is distinct from Ruusbroec not as one person is distinct from two others, but only as Gerson and Ruusbroec are distinct from one another. For Gerson and Ruusbroec are distinct from one another numerically, as any two creatures are distinct from one another, whereas, in this following through the logic of Dionysius, Eckhart says, God is distinct from Gerson and Ruusbroec only as *esse indistinctum* is distinct from *entia distincta*. Hence, Gerson and Ruusbroec can both be identical with God yet numerically distinct from one another: of one being, as Ruusbroec says, with God, yet a distinct *created individual*.

It was Gerson's assumption that to say with Ruusbroec that "our created existence depends on the eternal existence and is one with it according to its essential existence" entails the annihilation of creaturely identity; and it was that assumption which reveals his loss of grip on the Dionysian dialectical mystical theology, Gerson's failure being anticipated equally by the Parisian inquisitor of Marguerite in 1310 and Eckhart's Avignon tribunal. None of these could, or would, grasp that it is precisely the distinction between creature and creator which permits the "hyperbolic" language of union characteristic of these mystical theologians of northern Europe in the late Middle Ages, it being the opposite of the truth that that language of union obliterates that distinction. Given their firm grip on this "dialectic", the way is open to their affirming precisely what Gerson took Ruusbroec to be denying, to their saying that it is precisely in my union with God "without distinction" that I can become *most* fully me, that I most fully realise my created identity. And in saying this, and in their better understanding of the logic of transcendence which permits their saying it, it would seem that the theologies of these northern European mystical theologians are at once more faithful to the spirit and letter of Dionysius, and more orthodox than that of their critics.

NOTES

1 I have done so elsewhere. See Denys Turner, *The Darkness of God: Negativity in Christian Mysticism* (Cambridge: Cambridge University Press, 1995), chapters 8 and 9.
2 *MT* 1.3, 1001A; Luibheid, p. 137.
3 Denys the Carthusian, *De contemplatione* III, ii, in *Opera Omnia Divi Dionisii Cartusiensis*, vol. 9 (Tournai-Parkminster, 1912), p. 256.
4 *Cloud of Unknowing*, chapter 6, in Phyllis Hodgson (ed), *The Cloud of Unknowing and other treatises* (Universität Salzburg: Institut für Anglistik und Amerikanistik, 1982), p. 14.
5 See Turner, *The Darkness of God*, chapter 8.
6 Jean Gerson, *De Mystica Theologia*, Andre Combes (ed), (Lucani: In Aedibus Thesauri Mundi, 1958).
7 In Jean Gerson, *Oeuvres Completes*, P. Glorieux (ed), vol. VII, *L'Oeuvre Spirituelle et Pastorelle* (Paris: Desclee et Cie, 1960), pp. 615–635, 791–804. Cited hereafter as Glorieux.
8 Ruusbroec wrote his *Little Book of Clarification* at the request of the Carthusian Brother Gerard, who was anxious about the orthodoxy of some of his earlier writing.
9 In 1446, Denys was subjected to some sort of enquiry by his superiors into what they judged to be his excessively intellectual and scholarly pursuits, on the occasion of which Denys composed a short *Protestatio ad Superiorem Suum*, in *Opera Omnia Divi Dionisii Cartusiensis*, vol. 9, pp. 625–626.
10 Gerson most probably read Ruusbroec in the Latin translation of Geert Groote, from whose text I have translated Gerson's citations. All other citations of Ruusbroec are from the edition by James A. Wiseman, in *Ruusbroec, The Spiritual Espousals and Other Works* (New York, NY: Paulist Press, 1985).
11 Glorieux, pp. 615–616.
12 *Ibid.*, p. 616.
13 *Ibid.*, pp. 617–618.
14 *Ibid.*, p. 618.
15 *Ibid.*, pp. 627–8; see *Letter 2*, Glorieux, 802, but also 796, where Gerson links Ruusbroec's views with those of the earlier heretic Amaury de Bene.
16 Norman P. Tanner (ed), *Decrees of the Ecumenical Councils*, vol. 1, *Nicaea 1—Lateran V* (London: Sheed and Ward, 1990), pp. 383–384.
17 Robert E. Lerner, *The Heresy of the Free Spirit in the Late Middle Ages* (Berkeley, CA: University of California Press, 1972).
18 Malcolm Lambert, *Medieval Heresy*, second edn. (Oxford: Blackwell, 1992).
19 *Ibid.*, p. 187.
20 *Mirouer des simples Ames*, R. Guarnieri and Paul Verdeyen (eds), *Corpus Christianorum, Continuatio Medievalis*, LXIX (Turnholt: Brepols, 1986).
21 These descriptions of Marguerite are those of the so-called "Continuator of Nangis" who chronicled her trial, from a point of view favourable to the inquisitors.

22 For a discussion of the controversies in the period 1330–36 on the issue of the beatific vision, see Simon Tugwell, *Human Immortality and the Redemption of Death* (London: Darton, Longman and Todd, 1990), pp. 133–148.
23 Glorieux, p. 628. The issue here concerns the views of Pope John XXII and others, including Guiral Ot, the Franciscan Minister General, who held that the souls of the dead do not enter immediately into the beatific vision, but only after the general judgment and final resurrection. Hence, on this view, there is only one "act" of enjoying the beatific vision. The Parisian theologians assembled in 1333 insisted on the orthodoxy of the traditional Latin view, maintained by Thomas Aquinas, that these souls enjoy the beatific vision after their particular judgment and before the general judgment, but that after the general judgment they enjoy it more fully. Hence, their beatitude consists in two acts. It is not entirely clear what led Gerson to connect, or confuse, the Vienne condemnation of the Beghards and Beguines with the Parisian decretal on the issue of beatific vision, unless it was that *Ad Nostrum* appears to connect the "autotheism" of the Beghards and Beguines with the view that the perfected soul can achieve the beatific vision fully in this life (see Tanner, *Decrees of the Ecumenical Council*, vol. 1, p. 383); though of course both sides in the controversies of the 1330s would have accepted the condemnation of that view.
24 Glorieux, pp. 618–619.
25 In *De Diligendo Deo*, 28.
26 Glorieux, p. 620.
27 *Ibid.*
28 *Ibid.*, pp. 620–621.
29 *Ibid.*, p. 621.
30 Marguerite Porete, *Mirror of Simple Souls*, chap. 118, translated and introduction by Ellen Babinsky, (New York, NY: Paulist Press, 1993), p. 193.
31 Glorieux, pp. 618–619.
32 *Mirror of Simple Souls*, chap. 135, 218.
33 Glorieux, p. 624.
34 See *Spiritual Espousals*, 3; Wiseman, pp. 251–252.
35 *De Contemplatione*, 3.25, 288C–D.
36 *Ibid.*, 288D–A.
37 *Ibid.*, 288A.
38 *Ibid.*, 288B–C.
39 *Ibid.*, 288C–D.
40 Glorieux, pp. 629–630: "*Ad talium . . . quaestionum determinationem . . . non sufficit quod homo sit devotus*".
41 *Golden Epistle*, 1.169, Theodore Berkeley, OCSO (trans.), *The Works of William of St Thierry*, Cistercian Fathers Series 12 (Kalamazoo, MI: Cistercian Publications, 1980), p. 67.
42 *Sentences*, I, d.17, 1, 1: "*Cum ergo de dilectione diligimus fratrem de Deo diligimus fratrem*".
43 *De Trinitate*, XV, 17.
44 *Summa Theologiae*, 2–2ae, q23 a2 obj.1.
45 *Ibid.*, ad1.
46 *Spiritual Espousals*, 3; Wiseman, p. 149.
47 E.g.: "I have . . . said that no creature can become or be so holy that it loses its creatureliness and becomes God"; *Little Book of Clarification*, Wiseman, p. 252.
48 *MT* 5, 1048B; Luibheid, p. 141.
49 *DN* 2.4, 641A; Luibheid, p. 61.
50 *MT* 5, 1048B; Luibheid, p. 141.
51 *DN* 5.8, 824B; Luibheid, p. 101.
52 *DN* 5.4, 817D; Luibheid, p. 98.

9

CUSANUS ON DIONYSIUS: THE TURN TO SPECULATIVE THEOLOGY[1]

PETER CASARELLA

The work of Nicholas of Cusa (1401–1464)—philosopher, theologian, mystic, and Roman Cardinal—represents a synthesis of ancient, medieval and Renaissance thought. This work has attracted and also baffled those interested in constructing a bridge between the mystical theology of the Middle Ages and our times. Some might discern an anticipation of Hegel in his highlighting of a Dionysian dialectic. His interpretation of Dionysius tempers the "affective" strand of mystical theology of his medieval forebears and explores the heights of speculative thought and a concern for textuality and textual accuracy more commonly associated with his humanist companions. Not surprisingly for this enigmatic figure, one also discovers in his reading deep continuity in areas such as christology and pneumatology with patristic and medieval authorities.

Cusanus, as he is often called, read the writings of Dionysius the Areopagite and touted his knowledge of the *CD*. In the words of Donald Duclow, "Nicholas, ever the book collector and reader, takes pride in his familiarity with Dionysius."[2] Cusanus refers, for example, to a Greek text of Dionysius that he had possessed in Florence and also writes that Pope Nicholas V gave him Ambrogio Traversari's "very recent translation" of Dionysius. What survives of Nicholas's own library in Bernkastel-Kues includes other translations of the works as well as Latin commentaries. Werner Beierwaltes surmises that Cusanus first intensively studied the works through his association with Heymeric of Camp (a fifteenth century follower of Albert the Great), and later read translations and commentaries of Hilduin, John Scotus Eriugena, John Sarracenus, Hugh of St. Victor, Robert Grosseteste, Thomas

Peter Casarella
Catholic Studies Program, LPC SAC 454, DePaul University, Chicago, IL 60604, USA
pcasarel@depaul.edu

Aquinas, and Albert the Great.[3] Cusanus' copy of Albert's commentary is generously annotated, but Cusanus offers that his knowledge of the *corpus* comes from an acquaintance of a more direct source.[4] In addition, Cusanus' works include frequent citations of the works of Dionysius. Thus, Nicholas' debt to the Areopagite was indeed substantial.

Nicholas even presents his understanding of the *CD* as a key to his own thought. He aligns his theology with that of "the theologian" and lauds the Areopagite as *magnus Dionysius* ("the great Dionysius"), *maximus theologorum* ("the greatest of theologians"), and *sapientissimus, maximus ille divinorum scrutator, divinus vir* ("the wisest and greatest investigator of divine realities, a man himself divine"). Beierwaltes rightly notes that these titles are not a formulaic gesture in the mode of hagiography; they correspond to the German Cardinal's high estimation of the theological preeminence of Dionysius.[5]

A deferral to Dionysius on the question of God may not set Nicholas apart from other medieval figures, but the self-presentation of his indebtedness is unique, for it is rooted in Nicholas's own model of learning as learning about one's own ignorance. Nicholas claims the Areopagite as a teacher of learned ignorance who carries the weight of apostolic authority. Nicholas of Cusa intends for his readers to see his works as inspired by "the theologian" and even to see the vision of "the theologian" as a prime inspiration for his works. That Dionysius' writings were thought to derive from the apostolic period no doubt contributes to his being singled out, since the entire oeuvre of Cusanus in some fashion deals with the connection between the Neoplatonic philosophical tradition and the witness of Christ.[6] At the same time, the prevalence and manner of the citations suggest that Cusanus' interest in the works was deeply theological.

In what follows we will consider some key points of reference to the works of Dionysius. We know that Nicholas was aware of the writings of the Areopagite at least seven years before writing *On Learned Ignorance* (1440), but this work is the proper starting point for a study of his theological engagement.[7] His interest in Dionysius only intensifies in the later works, culminating in the late tetralogue *On the Not Other* (1461–62), in which Cusanus himself plays the role of Dionysius's advocate.

From On Learned Ignorance *(1440) to* A Defense of Learned Ignorance *(1449)*

Nicholas's most famous work, *On Learned Ignorance*, was completed on February 12, 1440. On 1 January of that same year, the thirty-nine year old priest gave a sermon in Koblenz, *His Name is Jesus*. Elsewhere I have argued that the third book of *On Learned Ignorance* and the sermon complement one another.[8] Both texts show that Cusanus drank deep at the well of the Areopagite at this early stage of his theological life.

In *Sermo* XX Cusanus preached on the Lukan text in which Mary's infant was circumcised and given the name "Jesus" (Luke 2:21). There are numerous references to Dionysius in the text that Cusanus prepared for the sermon.[9] Remarkably, he included a lengthy citation from chapter fifteen of *The Celestial Hierarchy*, which here seems to be taken from the commentary of Robert Grosseteste.[10] In order to illustrate that the corporeal image of fire represents God's own fire rather closely, Nicholas elaborates no less than twenty-four definitions of fire as reported by Dionysius.

Moreover, the very structure of the sermon reveals his debt to the Areopagite, for it is based on a dialectical ordering of the paths of naming and unnaming.[11] The first part begins with the way of negation. Here Nicholas explains how names are applied to God through denial and eminence, a path which resembles closely the trajectory of *On Learned Ignorance*, Book I. Having established that God is "more unnameable than nameable," Cusanus in the second part draws upon names of God that are drawn from creation and can be applied to God *proportionaliter* (i.e., by analogy). This is the point, for example, at which he inserts the Dionysian theo-taxonomy of fire. The third part of the sermon demonstrates that the name "Jesus" is not like any other name because it contains a saving power that emanates from the One on whom it was imposed. From this early sermon, we see the inheritance from Dionysius of a dialectical way of thinking about the unsaying and saying of the divine names. A Dionysian dialectic of language pervades Cusanus's works.

In the first book of *On Learned Ignorance*, Cusanus assimilates teachings from Dionysius into the central program of the text. After naming Dionysius, "the greatest seeker of God," Nicholas shows how the claim in *The Mystical Theology* that God transcends all created understanding is a confirmation of his own idea based on geometrical analogies that God can be likened to an absolute maximum.[12] He cites, for example, *On Divine Names* 5: "[God] is not *this* thing or is not any *other* thing; He is not *here* and is not *there*." Cusanus then claims that "Dionysius [himself] endeavoured to show in many ways that God can be found only through learned ignorance."[13]

The question of the proper interpretation of the Dionysian path beyond all names lies at the center of *On Learned Ignorance* and of Nicholas's entire oeuvre.[14] Book I, chapter 26 of "Negative Theology" contains only one direct reference to Dionysius works (i.e., to *MT* 5), but the entire discussion is modeled on a Dionysian way of negation. Every religion, Cusanus avers, mounts upwards by means of affirmative theology. The path of learned ignorance to the affirmation of God leads to a vision in faith of Infinite Light. The move from affirmation to negation is necessary, he states, because "Infinite Light always shines within the darkness of our ignorance but . . . the darkness cannot comprehend it."[15] In turning from divine Light to the ineffable God, Nicholas renames the mode of learning as "sacred ignorance." Nicholas states that all the wise (including Moses Maimonides, who is here mistakenly called "Rabbi Solomon" in accordance with a note from Eckhart's *Commentary on Exodus*) follow Dionysius in holding that God is greater than all nameable things.[16] After applying the removal of all names to some expressions that Hilary of Poitiers attributed to the Trinity, Cusanus concludes that according to the theology of negation, there is not found in God anything other than infinity.[17] The Dionysian way of sacred ignorance thus differs from that of learned ignorance in that it clarifies that in matters relating to God negations are true and affirmations are inadequate. Having said this, Cusanus is quick to add (as he did in *Sermo* XX) that the way of negation does not thereby rule out either the way of affirmation or the hierarchical ordering of theological affirmations. He states, in fact, that "it is truer that God is not stone than that He is not life or intelligence; and [it is truer that He] is not drunkenness than that he is not virtue."[18]

Nicholas wrote his *A Defense of Learned Ignorance* in October 9, 1449 in response to an invective written by John Wenck, a theological and ecclesiastical opponent who taught at the University of Heidelberg.[19] Cusanus tells the reader he composed his defense on the feast of St. Dionysius. This day, he says, celebrates "our Dionysius," i.e., the author of *The Mystical Theology*.[20] Wenck apparently was familiar with Dionysius, for he had written a commentary on *The Celestial Hierarchy*.[21] But he nonetheless warned of the corrupt seductiveness of Cusanus's program of learned ignorance, especially as regards its "heinous" treatment of the theology of the incarnation.[22] Cusanus countered by citing many authorities in his defense but accords preeminence to "our Dionysius." Regarding the illumination of learned ignorance he received from God, Cusanus writes:

> I confess, O Friend, that at the time I received [this] thought from on high I had not yet examined Dionysius or any of the true theologians. But with eager steps I betook myself to the writings of the teachers, though I found only a revelation expressed in various symbols. For example, Dionysius says to Gaius that most perfect ignorance is knowledge; and he speaks in many places about one's knowledge of his ignorance.[23]

In his *Defense* the authority of Dionysius is aligned to that of Augustine and others in order to prove the soundness of learned ignorance as a theological program. Nicholas balks at the notion that he sought to dishonor Jesus since "Holy Dionysius" himself led him to assert these truths. Cusanus elsewhere alleges that a commentator on Dionysius named Maximus had put forth similar assertions.[24]

Later sermons offer further testimony to the Dionysian debt. A sermon delivered on September 8, 1456, *Tota Pulchra es* ("You are wholly beautiful"), is illustrative. On that day the liturgy celebrated Mary's birth. The text Cusanus prepared begins with a treatise on philosophical aesthetics taken directly from Albert the Great's commentary on *Divine Names* 4.[25] At the end of the sermon, Cusanus returns to the glorious Virgin, but this occurs only after elaborating a metaphysics of beauty and the good and addressing problems like the relationship of sensible beauty to the beauty of the human soul and to absolute beauty.

The Marian feast becomes a fitting occasion to return to the vision of "the theologian." For example, Cusanus begins the sermon with an invocation of the Dionysian etymology whereby the Greek term for beauty ("*kalos*") is closely related to the verb "to call," thereby linking the attractiveness of beauty to the pursuit of the good.[26] Accordingly, the path opened by Dionysius is also one of discipleship to the call of beauty.[27] This theme plays a decisive role in the later works.

On the "Not Other" (1461–62)

A few years before his death, Nicholas of Cusa composed a remarkable work bearing the title *De li non aliud*, "On the 'Not Other.'" Together with *De venatione sapientiae* ("On the Hunt for Wisdom"), which was written in the fall of 1462, this work represents the mature re-engagement with the theology of the Areopagite. In it Cusanus shows his interlocutors that Dionysius comes the closest to indicating the correct path to knowledge of God. The entire discussion centers on the philosophical and theological import of the phrase "not other than." In adjoining an article to it (which was not in itself unusual in the Latin of the fifteenth century) and treating the phrase also as a substantive, Cusanus intends to pose a question regarding the relationship between identity and difference as that pair relates to God, the world, and the essential definition of reality, including the definition of definition itself. The referent of the substantive is not a determinate thing. The "Not Other" sometimes seems to be identified with God, but here the point is to illustrate a principle whereby "in all things God is all things even though he is none of these things."[28] The "Not Other" is thus a signifier of a transcendent signified that cannot itself be conceptualized by reference to a higher term or concept.[29]

The figure of "Not Other" is introduced in the dialogue as a *secretum* (NA 1). It is said to be the very secret that is revealed by Dionysius at the end of *The Mystical Theology* when he says that the Creator is neither anything nameable nor any other thing. Cusanus owned a copy of Petrarch's *Secretum* and may be using the term *secretum* in Petrarch's sense.[30] In other words, just as Petrarch had to meditate for his whole life upon Augustine's *Confessions* and the classical rhetorical sources of Augustine in order to grasp the interior meaning of these texts, so too Cusanus used the figure of the "Not Other" as a private synthesis of all that he has read in the Areopagite. Cusanus is nonetheless confident that what he attributes to the *aenigma* (symbolism) of the "Not Other" is exhibited by Dionysius everywhere in other ways (*undique per ipsum aliter explicatum*).

The idea that a casual remark about a secret could contain the key to the whole offers an important clue to the "method" of Cusanus. Cusanus is clearly *not* emulating the medieval models of the scholastic commentaries. On the other hand, the choice of a dialogue format combined with Cusanus' personal familiarity with Italian humanists suggests, at least *prima facie*, that he emulates the highly crafted and eloquent style of the dialogues written by Italian humanists. But the point in this work of unfolding the secret behind all the writings is not developed in the manner of Ficino's *De Amore*, and the sources cited by Cusanus (beyond Dionysius) are restricted to Plato's *Parmenides* and several works attributed to Proclus. For this reason, Jasper Hopkins insists upon the lineage of the dialogue as purely Neoplatonic and opines rightly—but with undue vehemence—that "the existential-heroic-romantic interpretation of Cusa's role at the dawn of Renaissance philosophy miscasts the emphasis of his thought."[31] Whatever his intent, Cusanus here and elsewhere is not interested in rivaling *quattrocento* erudition or literary finesse. Rather than impress, he *plays* with the speculative figure of the "Not Other" expressed by Dionysius the Areopagite and says that the writings of this disciple of St. Paul can be summarized by nothing other than the "Not Other" itself.

Beyond the one brief citation from *The Mystical Theology*, Cusanus devotes a whole chapter of the dialogue to the illustration of how the figure of the "Not Other" is found in the Areopagite's works. He cites over seventy passages from the major works and letters, noting that these are taken from the very latest translation prepared by the humanist scholar Ambrogio Traversari. None of these passages uses the prepositional phrase "not other than."[32] Nor does Cusanus provide his interlocutor with an interpretation of any of the individual passages. In general, he maintains that for Dionysius the only thing that can be known about God is that he is the being of all things (*omnium esse*, NA 14). This places God before all understanding. According to Cusanus, the key to the greatness of Dionysius as a theologian, however, lies in the fact that he knows that perceptible forms are the basis for our knowing about spiritual matters (*spiritualium intelligentia*). Just as these intelligibles are prior to the precepts that image them, so too God is prior to all understanding. In other words, intelligibles transcend perceptibles but are not other than them. God, likewise, transcends all understanding but is not other than that which is known by human understanding.

Cusanus begins with a citation from chapter 1 of *The Celestial Hierarchy* that balances the perspectives of transcendence and immanence and recalls the Areopagite's theophanic aesthetics:

> It is impossible for a human being to ascend unto an understanding of spiritual [matters] unless he is led by forms and likenesses of perceptible things, so that, for example, he regards visible beauty as an image of invisible beauty.[33]

The ascent to the origin of all things suggests that the origin exists before that which is manifest without being wholly other than its manifestation. Consequently, Cusanus highlights passages that speak of the ontological priority of the "Not Other:"

> In this [Supreme Ray] all the limits of all the sciences more than ineffably preexist; and we cannot understand, articulate, or in any way at all behold it, because it is unlike all [other] things and is perfectly unknown.[34]

Cusanus likewise highlights the presence in Dionysius of what he himself considers to be a doctrine of "imparticipable participation.[35] For example, he cites from *DN* 2:

> The Ineffable is spoken of by many words: "Ignorance," "What is understood through all things," "the Positing of all things," "the Negating of all things," "What transcends all positing and negating." The divine things are known only by participation.[36]

Accordingly, one cannot know the ineffable "Not Other" except through its participating others. The participating others are in effect the language whereby the otherwise silent "Not Other" is expressed.

Nicholas' interlocutor (an Aristotelian) protests that the cited passages by themselves fail to elucidate the meaning of the "Not Other." One can nonetheless piece together in rough outline the path from the citation of texts to the "secret" revealed therein. By pointing to a transcendent signified as that which transcends all positing and negating, Cusanus finds in the Areopagite the ground for all positing and negating. All things perceptible and intelligible emanate from this source, and the source remains not other than these beautiful rays of being and displaying. The source is "before" all things epistemologically and ontologically, but there is no way to know the source apart from the participation of what is seen and what is known in it and through it. In this sense, the very idea of being "Not Other" plays with the radical, theophanic disclosure of the source of otherness and its opposite *in* all that it engenders.

It may seem that the figure of the "Not Other" broaches pantheism, i.e., the view that God and the world form a single whole. John Wenck had said as much. In fact, there is no question here of a joining of what transcends and what is being transcended into a single whole. Such a fusion of opposites is negated by the radical otherness of the "Not Other." Being not other is *not* a closer approximation to being the same than unmediated otherness. When Cusanus creates theological symbolisms, he never speaks of a measurable quality. Being not other is other than being the same *and* other than being separate.[37] Being not other is therefore a mode of unity that comprises difference without eradicating it.

So far we have approached the theology of the "Not Other" in terms of a dialectic of transcendence and immanence. Werner Beierwaltes compares Dionysius and Cusanus and makes just such a claim for the double perspective that Cusanus introduces in the dialogue.[38] Accordingly, the "Not Other" is different from all other others because it is the absolute negation of otherness. The "Not Other" is also the creative origin of every other *as such*, since according to Cusanus "whatever is seen to be an other is seen to be an other insofar as it is not other" (NA 5, N. 15). This means, according to Beierwaltes, that the otherness of the "Not Other" stands in a fundamental relationship to what is the same.[39] The two perspectives need to be thought in terms of their inner unity.[40] Beierwaltes makes the same point by showing the inner relationship of the two terms. The "Not Other," he says, is the paradigmatic *aenigma* (symbol) for the transcendent *Über-Sein* ("Reality beyond Being") and immanent activity. If one underscores the negative (*non*-aliud), one refers to the negativity of all things (*nihil omnium*). If one underscores otherness (non-*aliud*) in its negation, then one sees the signifier as all things *in* all things. The latter (the "Not *Other*"), Beierwaltes writes, confirms the former (the "*Not* Other") as its very ground. The negation of otherness is an absolute concept, but the positing of that negation still requires that one not sublate the difference between otherness and its negation into a higher conceptual unity. The revelation of the "Not Other" as such cannot be left behind for a higher concept. The relationship between the two aspects of the term is one of a "reflexive unity," which in Beierwaltes's view can be compared to what Meister Eckhart terms the unity of difference (*distinctio*) and in-difference (*indistinctio*). In any case, the self-disclosure of the world stands between otherness and the "Not Other" and cannot be conceived otherwise.

The reflexive approach can lead to the false impression that Cusanus' thinking about the "Not Other" is an incomplete version of what Hegel later accomplished on a far grander scale. Cusanus himself does not follow the path of reflexive philosophy in the dialogue, although it has frequently been attributed to him. But one approach that Cusanus does undertake in chapter 22 of the dialogue is to direct the reader's attention to his mind's vision. *Visio mentis* in Cusanus should not be contrasted altogether with dialectical thought especially since in 1453 he wrote an entire treatise in a highly dialectical mode on *The Vision of God*. Furthermore, the subtitle of *On the "Not Other"* as it appears in many manuscripts is *Directio speculantis*, or "A Guide for the One Who is Speculating."[41]

Nicholas states that the name of the "Not Other" is *not* supposed to be identified with "the name of he who is above every name," i.e., Jesus. Being "not other" is a conceptual move seen by the mind; it cannot be used as a substitute for the revealed name.[42] Confessing the name of Jesus, on the other hand, cannot be replaced by a mental vision of a concept, a problematic that Cusanus had been facing since 1440 when he delivered the sermon *His Name is Jesus*. The concept is prior to naming, which means that even some names applied by Dionysius derive their being from it. Here Cusanus admits for a second time that Dionysius himself refers to God as "Other."[43] Nicholas tries to summarize this admittedly difficult teaching:

> When I see that [God] is neither the sky nor other than the sky and is not at all either other or other than any other, I do not see Him as if I knew what I saw. For the seeing which I direct toward God is not a visible seeing but is a seeing of the invisible in the visible. For example, when I see it to be true that no one has seen God, then I see God, above everything visible, as not other than everything visible. But that actual Infinity, which exceeds all sight, and which is the Quiddity of quiddities I do not at all see as visible—since what is visible, or is an object, is other than the power [of sight], whereas God, who cannot be other than anything, transcends every object.[44]

The directing of the mind to a non-objective vision of the "Not Other" cannot by definition be simply other than the perception of a physical object. The Cusan aesthetics of the "Not Other" is based rather on a worldly theophany.[45] The mind glimpses the Infinite in the finite and can describe the origin of the hidden appearance only as not other than that which has made an appearance.

Beyond dialectic and mental vision, there is at least one other way to present the teaching on the "Not Other." It is found in the last chapter of the work and is usually left unmentioned in the secondary literature. In chapter 24 Nicholas of Cusa introduces the Biblical and liturgical notion of God as Spirit.[46] He later clarifies that he meant "Creator Spirit," as in the Psalm verse: "Send out your Spirit, and they will be created" (Ps. 104:30).

The Spirit of God, he states, also admits of a reading in terms of the "Not Other." At first, the circumscription of pneumatology by the "Not Other" seems to follow the same path as mental vision. A divine spirit, the Cardinal explains, can be likened to the vision of an incorporeality that precedes corporeality, the nonspatiality that precedes spatiality (*illocale ante locale*), the incomposite prior to the composite, and the whole prior to its parts. Here he clarifies the relationship between the spiritually prior "Not Other" and what comes afterwards to the act of signification: "Yet what is seen in the signified except the sign?"[47] This exercise simply establishes that as God's Spirit the "Not Other" is signified by corporeal, spatial, composite, and divisible spirits. The sign that appears in the signified "acts" (*operatur*) and is described "more precisely" as "a not othering power" (*non aliante*).[48]

Cusanus' pneumatology trades on a likeness between a mental power to "see" unities in difference and a divine power to bring them into being. The *Spiritus Creator* of this work is *not* the same as the unifying power that Cusanus ascribes to mental vision. On the other hand, mental vision of the "Not Other" provides insight into the activity of God's Spirit. Cusanus states:

And so, just as [Divine Spirit] is not other than any creatable thing, so neither is the mind other than anything which is understandable by it. And in the case of a mind which is more free of a body I see a creator spirit shining forth more perfectly and creating more precise concepts.[49]

The aesthetics of theophany supplant mere objectification. The mind is a place of disclosure rather than the subjective counterpart to an objective other. To the degree to which we can grasp the truth of the world as disclosure, so too can the disclosure of the "Not Other" illuminate the worldly activity of a Creator Spirit.

Conclusion

Nicholas of Cusa's debt to Dionysius was at least as great as that of those medieval doctors who undertook to write formal commentaries. In this chapter, I have paid particular attention not only to the expressed statements by Nicholas of Cusa on the CD but also to the forms of citation, praise, and dependence. Cusanus repeatedly grants to the Areopagite an authority on a par with any doctor of the Church. At the same time, there is something syncretistic, even hermetic, about Cusanus' free use of Dionysius' authority, especially when one compares a dialogue written by Nicholas with a scholastic commentary. To attribute Cusanus' freedom as an interpreter of texts to the new spirit of Italian humanism fails to capture all the nuances (including the medieval ones) in the Cardinal's synthesis. In the end, Cusanus sees the *corpus* through the lens of his own program of learned ignorance.

On the "Not Other" represents his most intensive engagement with Dionysius' thought, but even here he does not claim to repristinate Dionysian teaching *verbatim*. Cusanus simply states that Dionysius appears to have come the closest to expressing what *he* was intending to say with the figure of the "Not Other."[50] Such nuances in language carry even more weight when one considers they were penned by someone whose training and public life centered on canon law and the politics of church governance. Even the bibliophilic concatenation of passages in *Sermo* XX and *On the Not Other*, chapter 14, begin to make sense if one thinks of them as legal briefs submitted into evidence at a trial for the sake of future reference.

Nicholas of Cusa saw wisdom in the CD that he found nowhere else except in the witness of Christ himself. Other authors—including Hermes Trismegistus, Proclus, Thierry of Chartres, Albert the Great, Bonaventure, Meister Eckhart, and Ramon Llull—shaped his thinking with as much force. But to Dionysius alone is reserved the epithet of "theologian" because like the evangelist John he appeared to Cusanus as someone who had led him to a vision of the Christian faith that refracted in word and image what could only be described as indescribable beauty.

NOTES

1   I would like to dedicate this chapter to Prof. Karsten Harries, who twenty years ago introduced me to *On the Not Other* and through that to the world of Cusanus.
2   Donald Duclow, "Mystical Theology and Intellect in Nicholas of Cusa", *American Catholic Philosophical Quarterly*, 64 (Winter 1990), p. 111.
3   Werner Beierwaltes, *Der verborgene Gott: Cusanus und Dionysius* (Trier: Cusanus-Institut, 1997), p. 9.
4   These annotations are found in Codex Cusanus 96, which lies in the library in Bernkastel-Kues. The transcriptions and commentary are found in Ludwig Baur, *Cusanus-Text. III. Marginalien. 1. Nicolaus Cusanus und Ps. Dionysius im Lichte der Zitate und Randbemerkungen des Cusanus* (Heidelberg: Carl Winter's Universitätsbuchhandlung, 1941).
5   *Ibid.*
6   I have argued this point in Peter Casarella, "Nicholas of Cusa (1401–1464), On Learned Ignorance: Byzantine Light en route to a Distant Shore", in Jorge J. E. Gracia, Gregory M. Reichberg, and Bernard N. Schumacher (eds), *The Classics of Western Philosophy* (Oxford: Basil Blackwell, 2003), pp. 183–189.
7   On the earlier citations, see Ludwig Baur, *Nicolaus Cusanus und Ps. Dionysius*, p. 20.
8   Peter Casarella, "*His Name is Jesus*: Negative Theology and Christology in Two Writings of Nicholas of Cusa from 1440", in Gerald Christianson and Thomas M. Izbicki (eds), *Nicholas of Cusa on Christ and the Church* (Leiden: E. J. Brill, 1996), pp. 283–284.
9   The sermons of Nicholas of Cusa are preserved in the form of the notes that he prepared. A critical edition of these texts can be found in Nicolai de Cusa, *Opera Omnia* (Hamburg: Felix Meiner, 1970ff.), vols. XVI–XIX.
10 *Ibid.*, pp. 301–303.
11 *Ibid.*, pp. 294–296.
12 *On Learned Ignorance*, Book I, chap. 16. Jasper Hopkins, *Nicholas of Cusa on Learned Ignorance* (Minneapolis, MN: The Arthur J. Banning Press, 1985), p. 67.
13 *Ibid.*
14 Cf. Peter Casarella, "*His Name is Jesus*," pp. 284–288.
15 *Ibid.*, Book I, chap. 26, p. 84.
16 On the citation of Maimonides, see *ibid.*, 189 n.87.
17 *Ibid.*, Book I, chap. 26, p. 85.
18 *Ibid.*
19 On the dating, see Jasper Hopkins, *Nicholas of Cusa's Debate with John Wenck* (Minneapolis, MN: Banning Press, 1988), pp. 3–4.
20 *Ibid.*, p. 55.
21 *Ibid.*, p. 3.
22 *Ibid.*, p. 40.
23 *Ibid.*, p. 50. Cusanus is citing Letter 1 to Gaius.
24 Nicholas is referring to Maximus the Confessor, although the writings in question are now known to have been written by John of Scythopolis. It is also not clear that the passage that Cusanus cites from this text actually derives from it. See *ibid.*, 91 n.64.
25 Nicolai de Cusa, *Opera Omnia*, vol. XIX, fascicle 3, Walter Andreas Euler and Harald Schwaetzer (eds), (Hamburg: Felix Meiner, 2002), p. 254. In the critical edition the text is found as *Sermo* CCXLII. The Biblical text Cusanus is explicating is Song of Songs 4:7.
26 *Ibid.*, *Sermo* CCXLIII, N. 2, p. 254: "Primum quidem occurit dictum Dionysii, ubi de pulchritudine agit, notandum scilicet quod bonum Graece ⟨kalos⟩ dicitur, pulchrum vero ⟨kallos⟩, quasi vicina sint bonum et pulchrum. ⟨Kalo⟩ vero Graece ⟨voco⟩ dicitur Latine; vocat enim bonum ad se et allicit, sic et pulchrum."
27 On the question of philosophical aesthetics in Cusanus, see M.-A. Aris, "'Praegnans affirmatio' Gotteserkenntnis als Ästhetik", *Theologische Quartalschrift*, 181 (2002), pp. 97–111 and Karsten Harries, "On the Power and Poverty of Perspective: Cusanus and Albert", in Peter Casarella (ed), *Cusanus: The Legacy of Learned Ignorance* (Washington, D.C.: The Catholic University of America Press, 2006), pp. 105–126.
28 Jasper Hopkins, *Nicholas of Cusa on God as Not-Other* (Minneapolis, MN: Banning Press, 1983), chap. 6, N. 21, p. 51. (Following the conventions of Cusanus scholarship, citations include the chapter and section number taken from the critical edition and reprinted in the translation.)

29   According to Jasper Hopkins, there are some instances in the dialogue in which Nicholas does use "not other than" to signify straightforward identity. In these instances, he uses the phrase *non aliud a* rather than *non aliud quam*. See Jasper Hopkins, *Nicholas of Cusa on God as Not-Other*, p. 172 n.1.

30   Another possible source for the term is chap. 4 of Traversari's translation of *The Celestial Hierarchy*: "Secretum ipsum dei, quodcumque tandem illud est, nemo unquam vidit, neque videbit."

31   Jasper Hopkins, *Nicholas of Cusa on God as Not-Other*, p. 23.

32   Some cited passages, however, stand at odds with the notion of God as the "not other," e.g., "But God is called Other because he is present to all things by virtue of Providence and because for the well-being of all He becomes all in all, while remaining in Himself and [retaining] His own identity" (*ibid.*, chap. 14, N. 68 p. 95).

33   Jasper Hopkins, *Nicholas of Cusa on God as Not-Other* , p. 85, chap. 14, N. 55, citing *CH* 121 CD.

34   Jasper Hopkins, *Nicholas of Cusa on God as Not-Other*, p. 87 (chap. 14, N. 59, citing *DN* 592D).

35   On this general theme in Cusanus, see, for example, Rudolf Haubst, "'Am Nichtteilnehmbaren teilhaben.' Zu einem Leitsatz der cusanischen 'Einheitsmetaphysik' und Geistphilosophie" in idem, *Streifzüge in die cusanische Theologie* (Münster: Aschendorff, 1991), pp. 243–54. The neologistic phrase "imparticipable participation" is based upon Nicholas of Cusa, *De coniecturis*, II, 6.

36   Jasper Hopkins, *Nicholas of Cusa on God as Not-Other*, chap. 14, N. 59, p. 89.

37   See, however, note 29 above.

38   Werner Beierwaltes, *Der verborgene Gott: Cusanus und Dionysius* (Trier: Cusanus-Institut, 1997), pp. 25–26. See also Donald Duclow, "Mystical Theology and Intellect in Nicholas of Cusa", pp. 112ff. for another interpretation that highlights Cusanus's "negative dialectic."

39   In his *De genesi* (March 2, 1447) Nicholas develops a metaphysics of the same (*idem*).

40   Beierwaltes, p. 26: "Beide Perspektiven müssen ineins gedacht werden."

41   See also Jasper Hopkins, *Nicholas of Cusa on God as Not-Other*, chap. 24, N. 113, p. 139: "For we find to be sufficient the guidance (*directio*) by which you have endeavored to guide us to the Beginning, which defines itself and all things."

42   *Ibid.*, chap. 22, N. 99, p. 127.

43   *Ibid.*, chap. 22, N. 100, p. 129. See also *ibid.*, chap. 14, N. 68, p. 95.

44   *Ibid.*, chap. 22, N. 103, pp. 130–131.

45   By worldly theophany, I am indicating that the mode of presentation of the "Not other" is nothing other than the here and now of temporal existence. All knowing is perspectival; there is no view from nowhere in Cusan theological aesthetics. At the same time, the use of the term worldly is not intended to collapse the dialectical negation of the "Not Other" into an immanentist unity. It is fitting that in the sermon *Tota pulchra es*, for example, Cusanus identifies Christ, the Bridegroom, as *pulchritudo absoluta* ("absolute beauty"). These points are all underscored in Karsten Harries, "On the Power and Poverty of Perspective", p. 126.

46   *Ibid.*, chap. 24, N. 109, p. 135.

47   *Ibid.*, chap. 24, N. 109, p. 137.

48   *Ibid.*, chap. 24, N. 111, p. 137.

49   *Ibid.*, chap. 24, N. 113, p. 139.

50   *Ibid.*, chap. 1, N. 5, p. 33: "Although I have read [it in] no one, nevertheless Dionysius (more than others) seems to have come the closest to it."

10

LUTHER AND DIONYSIUS: BEYOND MERE NEGATIONS

PIOTR J. MALYSZ

Luther and Dionysius?

Throughout Protestantism's theological history, the works of Dionysius the Areopagite have, by and large, enjoyed a singularly negative reputation. The roots of this attitude can be traced back to Luther himself. Luther showed deep familiarity with what may be termed "mystical traditions" and, arguably, continued to make use of both mystical imagery and ideas. But this did not prevent him, already in his early career, from holding a particularly harsh opinion of Dionysius.

Interpreters of Luther's thought—taking their cue from his seemingly unqualified rejection of Dionysius—have seen nothing but an untraversable chasm separating the two thinkers and their respective theologies. In his influential study of Luther's approach to mystical theology, Erich Vogelsang grouped the mystical authors apparently known to Luther in three categories, distinguishing between "Dionysian mysticism" (*aeropagistische Mystik*), "Latin mysticism" (*romanische Mystik*) and "German mysticism" (*Deutsche Mystik*).[1] According to Vogelsang, Luther enthusiastically endorsed the third kind, on account of its affirmation of Christ's humanity and the mystic's temptation and self-despair. He gave only a qualified approval to the Latin variety because, while it did stress the experiential importance of Christ's humanity, it both bypassed the mystic's *Anfechtung* and aimed at ecstatic union with the uncreated Word. By contrast, when it came to Dionysian mysticism, says Vogelsang, Luther saw nothing redeeming in it.[2] That the reformer's negative stance underwent little change throughout his career is also the conclusion of Paul Rorem, who in a recent article offers a review of

Piotr J. Malysz
Harvard Divinity School, Harvard University, 45 Francis Avenue, Cambridge, MA 02138, USA
pmalysz@hds.harvard.edu

Luther's extant references to Dionysius. "Luther had sharp criticism early and late for the 'mystical theologians' who advance the Dionysian agenda", writes Rorem.[3]

In this light, searching for commonalities between the thought worlds of Luther and Dionysius may seem rather quixotic. But this need not be the case. In the first place, as Luther scholars seem to agree, his summary dismissal of Dionysius was motivated by what Luther saw as the pervasive Christological deficiency of the corpus: its Neoplatonic bent and its seeming indifference to the impact of the cross. In *The Babylonian Captivity of the Church* (1520), commenting on appeals to Dionysius as an authority on the number of the sacraments, Luther offers this broader critique:

> it greatly displeases me to assign such importance to this Dionysius, whoever he may have been, for he shows hardly any signs of solid learning. I would ask, by what authority and with what arguments does he prove his hodge-podge about the angels in his *Celestial Hierarchy*—a book over which many curious and superstitious spirits have cudgeled their brains? If one were to read and judge without prejudice, is not everything in it his own fancy and very much like a dream? But in his *Theology*, which is rightly called *Mystical*, of which certain very ignorant theologians make so much, he is downright dangerous, for he is more of a Platonist than a Christian. So if I had my way, no believing soul would give the least attention to these books. So far, indeed, from learning Christ in them, you will lose even what you already know of him. I speak from experience. Let us rather hear Paul, that we may learn Jesus Christ and him crucified. He is the way, the life, and the truth; he is the ladder by which we come to the Father.[4]

Luther's all-embracing Christ-centred approach thus constitutes a major difference between his theology and that of Dionysius. But as Rorem demonstrates, Luther was by no means the first to have reacted against this perceived Christological deficiency. John of Scythopolis, one of the very first Dionysian commentators, as well as Maximus the Confessor, Bonaventure, not to mention Aquinas, had all tried to place Dionysius within a more explicitly and consistently Christological framework; in fact, much of the theological history of the CD had revolved around this interpretive task.[5] That Luther, quite early in his career, gave up such attempts was occasioned largely by Lorenzo Valla's challenge to the previously unquestioned authenticity and "importance" of the corpus. Luther had become acquainted with Valla's doubts through a footnote in Erasmus' Greek New Testament of 1516.[6]

Besides the prevalent and, by Luther's day, already millennium-old efforts toward a more Christ-centred reading of Dionysius, another reason why a search for continuities in the thought of Luther and Dionysius need not be doomed to failure is the imbalance of Luther's own interpretation. A closer look at his references to the elusive author of *The Mystical Theology* will reveal that Luther associates Dionysius' name chiefly with idle speculation about celestial hierarchies, arbitrary pronouncements on the sacraments, as well as with a mystical ascent that takes place outside of the cross and aims at union with the divine majesty outside of Christ's flesh. It is, however, questionable whether this is all that there is to Dionysius, that is, whether Dionysius' thought can simply be reduced to speculative mystical theology. Consequently, when one takes the one-sidedness of Luther's interpretation into account and moves beyond the few negative references to Dionysius, it may be possible to uncover in the reformer's writings ideas that not only are suggestive of those of Dionysius but may also be viewed as *Luther's contribution* to a more Christocentric interpretation of the Dionysian heritage. This need not be "little more than an exercise in contrasts" (as Bernard McGinn opines).[7]

Moving—in Dionysian fashion—beyond mere negations and, above all, beyond the "mystical" framework of analysis, this chapter seeks to reclaim such common ground. Specifically, instead of rehearsing the well-known textual evidence as testimony to Luther's negative approach to Dionysius, I will argue that Luther's concept of the hidden God, especially as developed in *The Bondage of the Will* (1525), shares some interesting affinities with Dionysius' "Deity [who] is far beyond every manifestation of being and of life", but who allows himself to be "enticed away from his transcendent dwelling place."[8] In addition, I will also show that Luther's strongly ontological doctrine of justification has a procession-return structure, and, moreover, that within this structure the status of the justified person, *qua* justified, is expressed in terms remarkably similar to the Dionysian *analogia*.

God Who Works All in All

Let us begin with elements of Luther's and Dionysius' understanding of God. My brief exposition will focus on God's relationship to creation, creaturely identity, and, in this light, the possibility of knowing God.

Dionysius is at pains to emphasise the qualitative difference between God and creation. If all that exists is viewed as having being, then God is not.[9] God is not an object, and hence not an object of knowledge, either. In God's self, he is *theos agnostos*, "beyond assertion and denial."[10]

But the Dionysian God does not wish to remain within himself. By knowing his self, which God alone can do, God knows the possibility of otherness.[11] Moved by love for this otherness, God, therefore, "comes to abide within all things", but, interestingly, "does so by virtue of his supernatural and ecstatic capacity to remain, nevertheless, within himself."[12] This creative *self-sharing through rest within Godself* is possible precisely on account of the difference between God and creation. Because he "is not some kind of being", God enables the distinct identity of the world and is the framework for the unfolding of the world's astounding multiplicity: "He is the time within which things happen."[13] More correctly put, God has the world present to God's self, rather than himself being present in it.[14]

Although the Areopagite frequently refers to God as the cause of all, this God is not Aristotle's unmoved mover. For Dionysius divine causality is characterised by both "greatness" and "smallness". In his greatness, God comprises all space and communicates himself as an abundant and undiminished gift.[15] In its smallness, God's self-communication is "the most elementary cause of everything". Everything in the realm of being owes its existence to God's "penetrating unhindered into and through all things, energizing them."[16] Dionysius thus understands causality in terms of sharing in God's self-impartation: having a place in God and being energised by God.

As this all-energising power, God is "known in all things" and, at the same time, necessarily "distinct from all things."[17] This entails two things. First, "we cannot know God in his nature, since this is unknowable and is beyond the reach of mind or of reason. But we [do] know him from the arrangement of everything, because everything is, in a sense, projected out from him, and this order possesses certain images and semblances of his divine paradigms."[18] Second, this must not be taken to mean that God can be known from *any particular thing*. What is known, rather, is that "the power of the Godhead spreads out everywhere, penetrates all things irresistibly and yet remains inapparent to all . . . because it transmits all its providential activities in an ungraspable way."[19] God is recognised as being causally at work, but, as such, the precise character of his activity vis-à-vis creaturely particularity remains beyond our understanding.

Bernard McGinn suggests that Luther's preference for the term *Deus absconditus*, over against the Dionysian *Deus incognoscibilis/incognitos*, is rooted in the reformer's rejection of apophatic mysticism.[20] More, however, seems to be at stake here than a preference for a certain type of mystical theology. It is questionable whether Luther's term, strictly speaking, is meant to refer to the *Deus in se*, God in his inner nature. It is this God that Dionysius describes as "[he] who is beyond everything . . . the completely unknown". To this God one can be united, in a short-lived liturgical ecstasy, only by means of self-renunciation and "an inactivity of all knowledge."[21] Admittedly, Luther does speak of the hidden God as "God in his own nature and majesty (*Deus in maiestate et natura sua*)."[22] But the God he has in mind is God as he is, and as he must be by virtue of being God, in his relationship to creation: "God hidden in his majesty" who "works life, death, and all in all . . . free over all things."[23] Luther's hidden God is thus more closely akin to Dionysius' God "immanent in and underlying the things which are."[24]

It is in *The Bondage of the Will* that Luther offers a sustained elaboration of this divine hiddenness. Though it was penned against Erasmus' defence of free will, published a year earlier, the book's concern is ultimately pastoral. God alone, as opposed to feeble human striving, can infallibly underwrite one's salvation and thus bring peace to a troubled conscience. He can do so, not only because he remains faithful, but, first and foremost, because he is "great and powerful."[25] Luther's insistence on the bondage of the human will flows directly out of his philosophical-theological elucidation of this pastoral conviction. If God is all-powerful and if he foreknows nothing contingently, then, on the one hand, God cannot be a mere first cause or causal ground or first mover, and, on the other hand, neither can human will be free. Rather, what God foresees is that which he also wills and which he infallibly brings to pass: "in what he foreknows . . . the thing foreknown must of necessity take place; otherwise, who could believe his promises?"[26] Consequently, "everything we do, everything that happens, even if it seems to us to happen mutably and contingently, happens in fact . . . necessarily and immutably, if you have regard to the will of God. For the will of God is effectual and cannot be hindered, since it is the power of the divine nature itself; moreover it is wise, so that it cannot be deceived."[27] According to Luther, God—precisely by virtue of being God—is at work in the realm of creation in an immediate manner. God in his majesty is always a *Deus praesens*.

Of necessity, therefore, he works even in Satan and the ungodly, since he cannot on their account suspend his omnipotence. "But he acts in them as they are and as he finds them; that is to say, since they are averse and evil, and caught up in the movement of this divine omnipotence, they do nothing but averse and evil things."[28] The unfolding of God's omnipotent will does not annihilate, coerce, or replace the human, or any other, will. It merely animates it to make the only choices it would make anyway. In other words, the immediacy of divine operation does not preclude the spontaneity of the will. But spontaneity—lack of external coercion—is no freedom. Rather, freedom, as Luther understands it, consists in actual choice, that is, the doing of the good out of one's own powers. This, he insists, cannot be done without the Holy Spirit's assistance. The point to underscore here is epistemological: given the character of God's preservation of creation, the latter, according to Luther, cannot yield any reliable knowledge of God: "God so orders this corporal world in its external affairs that if you respect and follow the judgment of human reason, you are bound to say either that there is no God or that God is unjust."[29]

Eeva Martikainen observes that this immediacy of divine activity is what distinguishes Luther's understanding of divine causality from the entire preceding tradition of Aristotelian scholasticism.[30] Admittedly, Aquinas affirms that humans are in no position to choose their ultimate goal, which is beatitude. But this does not mean that particular situations carry with themselves no real possibility of choice.[31] By contrast, for Luther, God's upholding of the created realm is none other than the unfolding of his *all*-embracing foreknowledge and will. Paradoxically, Luther preserves the identity of everything created by immediately and intimately tying it with God's creation-wide operation, which he regards as a necessary expression of God's nature. From Luther's perspective, the scholastic distancing of God for that same purpose—to preserve the identity of creatures as expressed in *their* choices, however feeble—cannot but compromise God's divinity.

In summary, *pace* McGinn, Luther does not reject divine unknowability but locates it, as does Dionysius, on the level of divine operation *ad extra*. Luther departs from Dionysius in questioning whether God's unknowability can be conceptualised *at all* apart from God's being God in relation to creation. It is fundamentally as *praesens* that God, for Luther, is unknown and unknowable.

In *The Bondage of the Will* Luther characterised the hidden presence of God as an all-embracing active impact—one, however, that does not lead to the erasure of the creaturely but rather preserves and animates it, regardless of how whole or broken its state. Not long after responding to Erasmus' challenge, Luther was again forced to grapple with the presence of God. This time the context was the denial, by Zwingli and his followers, of the presence of Christ's body and blood in the Lord's Supper. In his *Confession Concerning Christ's Supper* (1528), Luther seeks to dispel Zwingli's fear that, were Christ to be bodily present in the Eucharist, he could not at the same time be in heaven; or, if Christ's body were to coincide with divine omnipresence, it would necessarily end up being stretched out throughout the universe, "like an immense straw-sack with God and the heaven and the earth inside."[32]

For Luther the integrity of Christ's person requires that wherever Christ is present as God, he must also be present as a *true* man. To show that this does not destroy Christ's humanity Luther draws attention to the "divine, heavenly mode" of Christ's presence (one of three he discerns in the Scriptures).[33] In this mode, which *directly correlates the presence of Christ's humanity with God's presence*, "all created things are . . . much more permeable and *present to him* than they are in the second mode" (that is, when the risen Christ passed through closed doors, for example). From a localised perspective, the divine mode appears to be dialectical. On the one hand, this presence is "far, far beyond things created, as far as God transcends them; and on the other hand . . . as deep in and as near to all created things as God is in them."[34] In other words, God's being present does not consist in his filling space. Rather, it is space that is present to God (and consequently also to Christ in his theanthropic totality). Luther explains this further by emphasising the opposition between God's simultaneous greatness and smallness:

> God is no such extended, long, broad, thick, high, deep being. He is a supernatural, inscrutable being who exists at the same time in every little seed, whole and entire, and yet also in all and above all and outside all created things. . . . Nothing is so small but God is still smaller, nothing so large but God is still larger . . . He is an inexpressible being, above and beyond all that can be described or imagined.[35]

At bottom, God's ubiquity does not mean that God is localised, let alone occupies space (as did Christ in his creaturely modes). Heaven is not a place to which Christ's body has been removed to sit at God's right hand but is rather the majesty of God, who is, as it were, his own place, and who as such has the world immediately present to himself. On this presence the existence of created things crucially depends. Yet, since this is a presence consisting simultaneously in unparalleled closeness and removal, God cannot be known unambiguously from created objects. He can be known only where *he offers himself* to be known, where he, as it were, concentrates his presence: in Christ during his earthly life, in Baptism, in the Supper, in the proclamation of the Gospel.[36] All in all, as Luther sees it, Christ's body is far from destroyed by virtue of its coincidence with his divinity. And we may conclude that Luther's radically a-spatial construal of God's relationship to the world, with space being a vital element of the human relation to, and perception of, the world, may be seen as indirectly prefiguring Kant. In short, God *is* not in the same manner that objects in the world *are*.

To summarize, Luther conceptualises God's relationship to creation as intimate, direct and dynamic involvement. Nothing short of this can do justice to God's divinity. This leads Luther to break with the consensus of the preceding scholastic tradition on two points. First, it is the unparalleled, unbroken and volitionally active nearness of God to created things that upholds their *particular* existence, "work[ing] life, death, and all in all". Nothing is too small or abhorrent for God. But God exerts his impact in such a way that, although free will properly belongs to God alone, his working does not erase creaturely identity. Second, this is possible because God's presence is, *from a creaturely perspective*, a dialectic of presence and absence, of being and not being. More properly put, in guaranteeing the world's existence, it is God who has the world present to himself. One final thing to add is that the scope and manner of God's *Allwirksamkeit* makes any knowledge of God based on it inherently uncertain. Dionysius' words, quoted above, would not be an inappropriate summary here: "the power of the Godhead . . . penetrates all things irresistibly and yet remains inapparent to all . . . because it transmits all its providential activities in an ungraspable way."

Thus both Luther and Dionysius maintain that God has the world present to himself: he is the time and space of the world. As Creator God, therefore, remains in God's self while simultaneously imparting himself to the world. Thanks to this dialectic of intimate presence and removal, creaturely identity, as distinct from God's, can be preserved. This, however—in addition to the sheer scope of divine operation—makes the possibility of unambiguously locating God or knowing him from his creation-wide impact uncertain.

From Yearning for Being to Sharing (in) Being

Keeping in mind the similarities, we must not ignore the differences, even if they *might* prove to be less significant than expected. Whereas for the Areopagite the hidden-yet-all-embracing activity of God in creation is reassuringly carried out with a view to returning everything to God's self, for

Luther God in his majesty evokes nothing but terror. In the remaining portion of this chapter, I argue that, although Luther's salvific schema is decidedly more complex than that of Dionysius (both in psychological and theological terms), it, too, has a procession-and-return structure and is to be construed relationally as proper placement. Both these elements echo the Dionysian understanding of "analogy" as one's *God-given* capacity to actualize and express the presence of God with one's life.

At first, Luther's God whose *Allwirksamkeit* nothing can escape and, consequently, in whose power lies also human salvation, must appear as not only an arbitrarily predestining but also evil deity. This realization must fill one with dread. Yet the terror is ultimately meant to lead, as in the case of Luther's own anguish over God's justice, to "salutary . . . despair."[37] Although God hidden in his majesty is the God who wields the power of salvation, he is not a different God from the God who veils himself in the weakness of the cross for the sake of the world's salvation. Rather, the purpose of his all-working hiddenness is to bring proud humans down to nothing, at which point they are no longer able to trust in themselves. This is the moment when, ready to clutch at straws, they can finally live out of the grace of God. They now understand the nature of faith, which becomes what it is—faith—precisely through having to rely not on God's power but on God's veils.[38] Thus the despair over God's *majestic* hiddenness gives way to an actual faith-ful appreciation of his *salvific* hiddenness.

In this process, sinners become transformed through faith in the veiled God, Christ. Sin, according to Luther, is a state of compulsive self-justification, a belief that one is powerful enough, or perhaps only that one has no other choice but, to underwrite one's own being and identity. In consequence, all of the sinner's works, however good in appearance, are directed to the inside. Without exception, they are a modality of self-interest.[39] The sinner is a being hopelessly turned in on herself (*homo incurvatus in se ipsum*).[40] Because everything and everyone beyond the sinner becomes a vehicle of self-definition and self-preservation, the sinner's relentless working only adds to her progressing relationlessness. But God, whom the sinner, likewise, seeks to manipulate, will have none of that. The *all-working Deus absconditus* eludes all attempts to be harnessed in the sinner's service and, in so doing, proves to be an insurmountable obstacle. Faced with the work of God's hidden majesty, the sinner's working must eventually come to nothing. The sinner must come to nothing.

The sinner's relationlessness becomes absolute as her last relationship— the self-justificatory relationship to herself—is undercut. The sinner dies. Yet it is precisely in this absolute relationlessness that a relationship is re-established: the hidden God, who has been at work all along, makes known his claim on the sinner. On her part, the sinner acknowledges this claim when, drawn by the gift of faith, she flees from God's majestic hiddenness and takes refuge in the hiddenness of God's revelation, the cross. Only there can the sinner's despair give way to the joy that salvation is in the hands of him who can guarantee it absolutely, apart from works, and who, for its sake, offered himself to humanity in the life and death of Jesus and continues to offer himself in the Church's proclamation and sacraments.

Significantly, this veiled presence of God *sub contrario* cannot be exploited in an instrumental manner, either. On the one hand, it seems too weak and too unlikely. On the other hand, though seemingly dissimilar, these veils are the veils of *God*, who is not negated by them but rather negates *their* frailty. The ubiquitous body of Christ is no more rationally or instrumentally graspable than God in his naked hiddenness.

Rather than being instruments, the locales of God's favour are Christ's testament, which establishes the believer's identity by imparting to her Christ's life, righteousness and salvation.[41] More importantly, they convey God's relationship to humanity by defining this relationship as unquestionably favourable, rooted in God's merciful identity. Luther expresses this Christological disambiguation of God's relationship to the world in his characteristically paradoxical manner: "when God makes alive he does it by killing, when he justifies he does it by making men guilty, when he exalts to heaven he does it by bringing down to hell."[42] It is also worth noting that Luther refers to this disambiguation as "the light of grace", which enables one to understand the purpose of God's hidden work.[43] Still, the light is powerless to comprehend how God can threaten damnation to those who are helplessly entangled in sin. The light of grace calls for faith, and makes one yearn for the light of glory, which will, in turn, reveal the full righteousness of God's justice.

The impact of the light of grace is not only epistemological; it also has far-reaching ontological consequences. By living in an identity-bestowing relationship with God, the believer exists as properly placed. Her status is assured, both in relation to God and, consequently, in relation to fellow humans. Freed from debilitating self-justification, the believer is open to relational living, which no longer treats creation, including other people, in an instrumental and self-serving manner but takes seriously its otherness, its need for recognition. Proper placement means ordered relationships: just as God inscribes the believer into the sphere of his re-creative activity, so also the believer is now empowered meaningfully to inscribe others into her life in all its socio-vocational dimensions. Because divine justification frees a person from the need to justify herself, the person is free to orient her works toward others and so to justify them. Luther's dramatic plea that public offices be filled by Christians must be seen in this context. The transactional nature of civil law, despite its capacity for social order, cannot by itself assure justice, for the law objectifies those under it. It is, therefore, imperative that public officers not lose sight of those under their authority as persons and apply the law with equity.[44] In brief, the Christian, according to Luther, not only "understand[s] the deed of Christ . . . receive[s] and preserve[s] it" but above all "imparts it to others, increases and extends it."[45] Believers are transformed into the likeness of Christ[46] and become Christs to those around. Luther speaks of "giving away one's righteousness" so that it might serve the sinful neighbour.[47] By virtue of having received Christ's life, Christians exhibit in their lives Christ's other-justifying descent.[48] They pass on the light of grace.

Interestingly, the increase of justification—its procession from its source in God—is simultaneously a return to the source. In justifying others through a loving recognition of their personhood, the Christian also justifies God, actualising in her freedom from self-concern the power of God's justification and so his Godhood. As those who have received their identity from God, believers justify God as God indeed and the only giver of an enduring identity. In acknowledging God as the source of every good, faith, insists Luther, "consummates the Deity . . . it is the creator of the Deity, not in the substance of God but in us." What is returned to God is precisely his Godhood, which is thus shown to be not an abstraction but a reality with a creation-wide impact. As Luther explains, "God has none of His majesty or divinity where faith is absent"; and further on, "If you believe . . . You justify and praise God. In short, you attribute divinity and everything to Him."[49]

Dionysius' account may not be as nuanced in its depiction of the divine-human relationship. It is, however, its emphasis on the will's freedom that seems to suggest that any comparison with Luther's understanding of salvation must be doomed to failure. But it would be rather imprudent simply to thrust the Areopagite's corpus into the interpretive framework of the Western concerns over human freedom. Luther's point of departure in his psychologically-elaborated course of salvation is the sinner in need of condemnation. For Dionysius it is the diversity of creation, created in perfect harmony by God's self-effusion and now being returned to its original perfection—"the innate togetherness of everything."[50] If this is recognised, finding soteriological convergences may not be a forlorn hope after all.

As already noted, Dionysius' God preserves creation in a manner that allows for the distinct identities of his creatures. The creature's identity is its proportion (*analogia*) to God as its cause:[51] it is its *capacity* for participating in God's creative self-impartation and the *extent* to which this participation occurs. But this analogical identity is not merely individualistic. In that the divine act of creation is neither arbitrary, corresponding as it does to God himself, nor simply accidentally ecstatic, since it proceeds from God's desire to create—everything in creation has its appointed place,[52] determined by each creature's capacity for appropriating the divine light and for sharing the divine treasures.[53] Identity comprises also the creature's placement within this larger created structure.[54]

Creatures, however, possessing a free will, can act against their analogical predetermination. Externally, this leads to "strife and disorder,"[55] subverting God's creative love and allowing one "stupidly [to glide] away from those good things bestowed on [one] by God". Internally, sin deprives one of true life and plunges one "into the utter mess of passion."[56]

Nonetheless, all of creation both yearns and is actually called to return to God, even and especially that part which, out of ignorance, has plunged itself into almost-non-being and "destructive defilement."[57] But, for creation's yearning not to remain misdirected, God must be known. The question arises: how can "the inscrutable One [who] is out of the reach of every rational process" be known, given that no "words come up to the inexpressible God"?[58] Further, how can God be known by sinful creatures who are "at war with God and with themselves"?[59] Not knowing themselves, they cannot know God, either. And, after all, are we not "told not to busy ourselves with what is beyond us"; are we not warned that to think one sees and understands God is only to mistake something he has created for him?[60] Interestingly, Luther invokes a similar principle, *quae supra nos nihil ad nos*, as a warning against attempts to manipulate the hidden God.[61]

By ourselves we cannot speak of God. To enable our speech, therefore, the "unspeakable Deity"[62] veils himself in the largely dissimilar images of Scripture and in the church's liturgy.[63] Moreover, to reconstitute and preserve our analogy, God has also veiled himself in the humanity of Christ, in whom "the transcendent has put aside its own hiddenness . . . by becoming a human being" and yet remains "hidden even amid the revelation."[64] In response, humans must leave behind their own notions of the divine and call a halt to the activities of their mind.[65]

God's ecstatic and erotic revelation brings with itself not only recognition of gifts already enjoyed but also new gifts whose purpose is specifically that of returning all of creation to its Maker. Among the former are creation itself and life within it.[66] The new gifts help overcome the deadly effects of sin and evil by bringing about "knowledge of God and of beings as they really are".[67]

The above outline of Luther's and Dionysius' understanding of salvation does not presume to be more than a sketch. But before a flood of detail should obscure this general picture and create the impression of the two schemas' insuperable divergence, it may be useful explicitly to underscore their commonalities. Both Dionysius and Luther see creation's harmony as a structure of impartation: Luther, in more ethical terms, as impartation of justification, Dionysius, more epistemologically, as enlightenment. This impartation has the form of procession and doxological return, whereby reception of the imparted gifts returns one to God—it, so to speak, makes visible in creaturely life God's claim on the creature. For Luther, of course, this impartation takes its impetus from Christ. Further, underlying this view of creation's interconnectedness is the insistence of both thinkers on a relational conception of the human person. A person is defined, above all, by her relationship to God. It is through that relationship that all her other relationships are determined. The scope of Dionysius' vision is, of course, more cosmic and hierarchical, whereas Luther's psychological conception of sin restricts him to humanity.

160   Piotr J. Malysz

For Luther sin is not only alienation from one's true self and a (misdirected) yearning for being, as for the Areopagite, but it is also self-justification; both theologians, however, see its impact in the fracturing of bonds. Finally, both share a suspicion of natural reason in theological matters. Dionysius simply dismisses its futile and deceptive attempts to arrive at God; for Luther, by contrast, the futility of reason's quest is an important stage in reducing the sinner to nothingness. Despite this latter difference, however, both Luther and the Areopagite assume a revelatory progression from one's speculative attempts to scale the divine heights to being properly (analogically) placed through God's self-actualizing disclosure *sub contrario*.

Conclusion

This chapter has attempted to uncover continuity between Dionysius and Luther—despite the latter's rhetorical protestations to the contrary. Against the prevalent view of Dionysius as a speculative mystic with no sense of restraint (a view also held by Luther), I have shown that Luther's strongly Christological emphasis did not preclude the reformer from espousing a doctrine of God that, like that of Dionysius, relied on immediacy unfolding itself within a non-spatiotemporal dialectic of distance and nearness.[68] Further, building on this aspect of the divine, both theologians inscribe soteriology into a procession-and-return schema, which gives rise to a relational ontology. It is undoubtedly correct that for Luther the cross plays a *far* more prominent normative role, but his untiring insistence on this point need not be seen as being at odds with the Areopagite's theology but as a contribution to a more Christ-centred reading of Dionysian insights. In the end, putting Dionysius and Luther side by side will perhaps turn out to be not so much "little more than an exercise in contrasts" as *a little bit more* than that.

NOTES

1 Erich Vogelsang, "Luther und die Mystik", *Luther Jahrbuch*, 19 (1937), pp. 32-54. For an overview and critique, see Heiko Oberman, "*Simul Gemitus et Raptus*: Luther and Mysticism", *The Dawn of the Reformation* (Edinburgh: T&T Clark, 1986), esp. p. 130.
2 As Volker Leppin notes, not only is this division of medieval "mysticism" problematic, but also the term "mysticism", while handy, lacks heuristic value. If one were to use it, one can at best speak, preserving some of Vogelsang's insight, of the impact upon Luther of German Dominican "mysticism" and the imagery of Bernard of Clairvaux. But this must be seen, according to Leppin, as little more than Luther's indebtedness to the literary, rather than theological, tradition of Tauler and Bernard. "Mystik", in Albrecht Beutel (ed), *Luther Handbuch* (Tübingen: Mohr Siebeck, 2005), pp. 57-61. Oberman's analysis also shows that Luther's use of mystical vocabulary differs radically from that of his "mystical" predecessors.
3 Paul Rorem, "Martin Luther's Christocentric Critique of Pseudo-Dionysian Spirituality", *Lutheran Quarterly*, 11 (1997), p. 297.
4 *Luther's Works* [LW], Jaroslav Pelikan and Helmut T. Lehmann (eds) (St. Louis, MO: Concordia, and Philadelphia, PA: Fortress Press, 1955-1986), 36:109 = *Dr. Martin Luthers Werke* [WA] (Weimar: Böhlau, 1883-1993), 6:562.

5 Although methodologically different, these efforts continue to this day. Today the argument for a predominantly Christian vs. decidedly Neoplatonic interpretation involves the ordering of Dionysius' treatises and a reconstruction of their ecclesial context. Rorem's edition opens with *DN*, followed by *MT*, *CH*, *EH* and *Ep.*, with *MT* understood as the centre and the interpretive key. This ordering has been challenged on text-critical grounds by Alexander Golitzin ("Dionysius Areopagita: A Christian Mysticism?", *Pro Ecclesia*, 12:2 [2003], p. 170). Placing *CH* and *EH* before *DN* and *MT* allows Golitzin to see the corpus "as at once the explication of and the entry into the one and unique mystery, Christ."

6 Rorem, "Martin Luther's Christocentric Critique of Pseudo-Dionysian Spirituality", p. 298.

7 Bernard McGinn, "*Vere tu es Deus absconditus*: the hidden God in Luther and some mystics", Oliver Davies and Denys Turner (eds), *Silence and the Word: Negative Theology and Incarnation* (Cambridge: Cambridge University Press, 2002), p. 100.

8 *CH* 2.3 (140C); *DN* 4.13 (712B).

9 *DN* 5.4 (817D); 5.10 (825B).

10 *MT* 5 (1048B).

11 *DN* 7.2 (869A-B).

12 *DN* 4.13 (712B).

13 *DN* 5.4 (817C-D); cf. 2.11 (649B).

14 *DN* 5.8 (824A-B).

15 *DN* 9.2 (909C); cf. *DN* 2.11 (649B); *EH* 4.3.3 (476D).

16 *DN* 9.3 (912A).

17 *DN* 7.3 (872A).

18 *DN* 7.3 (869C-D).

19 *CH* 13.2 (301A); *DN* 7.3 (872B).

20 McGinn, "*Vere tu es Deus absconditus*", p. 99.

21 *MT* 3 (1001A).

22 Though Luther's term harks back to Isaiah 45:15 (which McGinn recognises), Luther actually finds justification for it in 2 Thessalonians 2:4 (*Bondage of the Will*, LW 33:139; WA 18:685).

23 *LW* 33:140; *WA* 18:685.

24 *DN* 5.4 (817C-D).

25 *LW* 33:289; *WA* 18:783.

26 *LW* 33:185; *WA* 18:716.

27 *LW* 33:37-8; *WA* 18:615–616.

28 *LW* 33:176; *WA* 18:709.

29 *LW* 33:291; *WA* 18:784.

30 Gabriel Biel, to whom Luther is indebted, is also somewhat of an exception. Eeva Martikainen, "Der Begriff 'Gott' in *De servo arbitrio*", Kari Kopperi (ed), *Widerspruch Luthers Auseinandersetzung mit Erasmus von Rotterdam* (Helsinki: Luther-Agricola-Gesellschaft, 1997), esp. pp. 34-43.

31 Thomas Aquinas, *Summa Theologica*, p. I, q. 83, art. 1.

32 *LW* 37:228; *WA* 26:340.

33 Luther believes that Christ's promise to be bodily present in the Supper is sufficient to guarantee this presence. The systematic-exegetical exposition is for the sake of his opponents.

34 *LW* 37:223; *WA* 26:336.

35 *LW* 37:228; *WA* 26:339-340.

36 Robert Jenson notes that Luther, soon to be followed by some Swabian theologians, breaks here with the medieval tradition, which failed more broadly to conceptualise Christ's Eucharistic presence and, in order to avoid the notion of cosmic travel, was forced to characterise it as "supernatural". Commenting on Johannes Brenz's *Von der Majestät unsers liben Herrn und einigen Heilands Jesu Christi* (1562), Jenson writes: "Since the creation is for God but one place immediately over against the place that he is, his simultaneous presence to the whole creation is unproblematic. And his exercise of that presence will not be modulated by location within the creation, since for God there *are* no plural created locations, but only by ontological context". Unfortunately, Jenson does not quite seem to appreciate the complex dialectical character of this divine presence. Robert W. Jenson, *Systematic Theology*, vol. 1 (Oxford: Oxford University Press, 1997), pp. 201-204.

37 *LW* 33:190; *WA* 18:719.

38 *LW* 33:62; *WA* 18:633.
39 *Heidelberg Disputation* (1518), *LW* 31:43; *WA* 1:356.
40 *Lectures on Romans* (1515–16), *LW* 25:291, 313, 345; *WA* 56:304, 325, 356.
41 *Preface to the New Testament* (1522/46), *LW* 35:359; *WA DB* 6:5. Luther's *Babylonian Captivity* is devoted, in part, to showing that the Lord's Supper is not an act whose efficacy lies in its mere performance but is rather Christ's testament (esp. *LW* 36:37; *WA* 6:513).
42 *LW* 33:62; *WA* 18:633.
43 *LW* 33:292-3; *WA* 18:785.
44 "If we do not make exceptions and strictly follow the law we do the greatest injustice of all" (*Whether Soldiers, Too, Can Be Saved* [1526], *LW* 46:100; *WA* 19:630).
45 *LW* 37:366; *WA* 26:506.
46 *Two Kinds of Righteousness* (1519), *LW* 31:300; *WA* 2:147.
47 "das groest [werck der liebe] ist das, wenn ich mein gerechtigkeit hyn gib und dienen lassz des nechsten sünde" (*Predigt am 3. Sonntag nach Trinitatis* [1522], *WA* 10^III:217).
48 *Freedom of a Christian* (1520), *LW* 31:371; *WA* 7:69.
49 *Lectures on Galatians* (1535), *LW* 26:227, 233; *WA* 40^I:360, 369.
50 *DN* 4.7 (704C).
51 *DN* 7.3 (872A).
52 *DN* 5.8 (824C).
53 *EH* 5.1.2 (501C); *DN* 3.3 (684C).
54 In *EH* 5.7 (513D) Dionysius speaks of "hierarchical analogies"; cf. *DN* 8.7 (896B).
55 *DN* 4.21 (721D).
56 *EH* 3.3.11 (440C, 441A).
57 *EH* 3.3.11 (441B).
58 *DN* 1.1 (588B).
59 *Ep.* 8.5 (1097A).
60 *DN* 3.3 (684C); *Ep.* 1 (1065A).
61 *LW* 33:139; *WA* 18:685.
62 *CH* 15.8 (336D).
63 *CH* 1.2 (121B-C).
64 *Ep.* 3 (1069B).
65 *DN* 1.4 (592C).
66 See 644A, 645A, 593D; 336A.
67 *EH* 4.3.4 (477C); 1.3 (376A).
68 Luther regarded the preaching of God's all-working majesty as a vital part of proclaiming the cross (*LW* 33:71; *WA* 18:639).

11

DIONYSIAN THOUGHT IN SIXTEENTH-CENTURY SPANISH MYSTICAL THEOLOGY

LUIS M. GIRÓN-NEGRÓN

I

In his *Auto de Pasión* (first published in 1514), the Salamancan playwright Lucas Fernández retells the Lord's Passion through vivid exchanges among a few Gospel witnesses—St. Peter, St. Matthew, the "three Maries"—along with two other Biblical interlocutors—the prophet Jeremiah and, most unexpectedly, St. Dionysius. St. Peter barely appears on stage—wandering in penance as he bitterly laments the cowardly negation of his Lord—when he stumbles upon the befuddled saint. Poor Dionysius was trying to no avail to decipher the natural marvels—the solar eclipse, the earthly tremors—accompanying Christ's death, the Savior he had never met. After a brief exchange, Dionysius identifies himself:

Yo soy Dionisio de Atenas	I am Dionysius of Athens
y, en faltarme Astronomía,	and, when Astronomy failed me,
alcancé a sentir las penas	I was able to feel the pain,
de fatigas tanto llenas	overflowing with sorrow,
que aqueste Dios padescía.[1]	that this God had suffered.

Dionysius is thus presented as a sagely man predisposed to conversion, an astronomer whose knowledge falls short, but who grasps nonetheless the mystery of salvation through his affective response to the sufferings of Christ. As a cipher of the first Gentiles receptive to the Gospel, Fernández turns Dionysius from that point onwards into the main co-narrator of his sacred drama.

Luis M. Girón-Negrón
Department of Comparative Literature, Harvard University, Dana Palmer House, Cambridge, MA 02138, USA
giron@fas.harvard.edu

A modern reader may be surprised by the prominent role played in this theatrical piece by a seemingly minor biblical character—Paul's Athenian convert from Acts 17:34. Such amazement is dispelled, however, upon realizing the nature and scope of Dionysius' reputation in sixteenth-century Spain. As with most Western Christians throughout the Middle Ages, Spaniards identified the Pauline convert with the venerable author of the *Corpus Dionysiacum*, the late fifth- early sixth-century Eastern (perhaps Syrian) monastic writer whose theological works were to shape the history of Christian mystical theology so profoundly.[2] In Fernández's play, Dionysius' puzzlement over the astronomical signs of Christ's passing harks back to the seventh letter of his pseudonym addressed to Polycarp.[3] Dionysius' name is reverently invoked by Spanish religious authors in the sixteenth century as the leading patristic authority on mystical theology, including—most notably—the Franciscan exponents of *recogimiento* spirituality (Francisco de Osuna, Bernardino de Laredo) who were, in turn, so deeply influential among the Carmelite *mystici maiori*, John of the Cross and Teresa of Ávila. The so-called "affective Dionysianism" of Thomas Gallus, Hugh of Balma and Hendrik Herp[4] was the main formative cadre for the Franciscan codification of *recogimiento* theology and the latter's interpretation among the Carmelites. It shaped as well Dionysius' interpretation among the other ascetico-mystical writers of the Golden Age pantheon: Luis de Granada, John of Ávila, Luis de León, Peter of Alcántara. As Teodoro Martin-Lunas sharply observes: "tratar de oración en la España del siglo XVI era seguir a Dionisio Areopagita directamente o a través de sus intérpretes Harphius y Hugo de Balma."[5] Even in the heyday of Spanish Erasmism, Valla and Erasmus's devastating critique of the Areopagite's authorship as pseudo-epigraphic could not erode his apostolic authority as the mystical theologian par excellence among Spanish mystics.[6]

Our purpose in what follows is to illustrate just how repercussive Dionysian thought was in Hispano-Christian mystical theology via a succinct overview of his discernible influence in John of the Cross and Teresa of Ávila.[7] Our overview will be framed by a brief excursus on the broader reception of Dionysius in fifteenth- and sixteenth-century Spain, especially among the ascetico-mystical precursors and contemporaries of both Carmelite saints. Such an excursus will allow us to reconnoiter with some historical precision how and to what extent Dionysian themes were interpreted and woven into signature components of their mystical theology: John's taxonomy of dark nights and Teresa's views on the suspension of the faculties as a preamble to *unio mystica*.

II

According to Father José de Jesús María Quiroga, the first historian of the Discalced Carmelites, John of the Cross, "would mix with the scholastic subjects he studied (in Salamanca) what he had learned from mystical authors, especially Dionysius and Gregory."[8] John's explicit references to the Areopagite corroborate his direct access to the *CD*. But what versions of the *CD* did John actually read? His references do not suffice to determine on textual grounds which Latin translations he may have favored,[9] but we are at least in a solid position to surmise the early modern editions to which he had access. Numerous manuscripts and editions of the Areopagite's *oeuvre* have survived in various Spanish libraries, both in the Greek original and in Latin translation, the latter also accompanied by the medieval commentaries.[10] Two of these editions proved absolutely crucial to the reception of Dionysian theology in sixteenth-century Spain. A tripartite anthology of Dionysius' *Opera* in Latin was published in Strasbourg in 1502–1503.[11] This massive encyclopedia, edited by Jacques Lefèvre d'Etaples, contained (1) John Sarrazin's 1165 *Veteris translationis* with the medieval commentaries by Hugh of Saint Victor, Albert the Great, Thomas Aquinas, Thomas Gallus and Robert Grosseteste;[12] (2) Ambrosius Traversari's 1436 commented translation of the entire *CD* (the *Noue translationis*);[13] and (3) Marsilius Ficino's 1492 commented translation of *MT* and *DN* (*Novissime translationis*). Almost a dozen copies of the Strasbourg edition are still extant in various Spanish libraries.[14] The other major compilation, published in Spain, was the 1541 Alcalá edition of the *Scripta Sanctii Dionisii Areopagitae cum D. Ignatii martiris epistolis* with the various Latin versions of Dionysius' works by Sarrazin, Traversari and Ficino. Most Spanish readers in the sixteenth century engaged the Latin Dionysius in these two editions, copies of which are also preserved at the University Library in Salamanca where John of the Cross (then Juan de Santo Matía) pursued his unfinished theological studies between 1564 and 1568.[15] These popular volumes provided John and his learned peers direct access not only to Dionysius' entire corpus in various Latin translations, but to his most repercussive medieval and early modern interpretations, including Gallus' *extractio* and Aquinas' commentary on *DN* (a particularly important source for the future Carmelite).

Of course, direct engagement with the *CD* and its commentators was not the only means of access to Dionysian ideas. Teresa, for one, unlike her beloved John, could not read any of the Latin translations. She barely knew Latin and there seems to be no extant translation either of the *CD* into Spanish. Teresa's efforts to ward off Inquisitorial suspicions and ecclesiastical hostilities as a female reformer and theologian of Jewish descent make the identification of her mystical sources an even dicier affair.[16] Nonetheless, the Carmelite nun had well-documented access to major vernacular sources on Dionysian theology, a cluster of theological treatises and contemporary authorities that Teresa and John both knew in depth. Although scattered references to Dionysius can already be gleaned in fifteenth-century Iberian sources,[17] the *CD* became in the following century an ubiquitous point of reference for ascetico-mystical literature. Three of the great Spanish spiritual masters of the sixteenth century—John of Ávila, Luis de Granada and Peter of Alcántara—three religious authorities whom Teresa either read or even consulted in person and in writing about mystical matters, quoted extensively and appreciatively from the entire Dionysian corpus.[18] Teresa's extensive engagement with her mendicant and Jesuit mentors also gave her access to a wealth of Dionysian ideas and the mystical traditions they helped shape. Most importantly, Teresa and John were both indebted to a particular Spanish tradition of Dionysian affective spirituality: the *recogidos* movement.

Recogimiento broadly designates an ideal of mystical prayer that flourished among the observant Franciscans of new Castile in the immediate aftermath of the late fifteenth-century Cisnerian reforms. The two most eloquent expositions of this contemplative ideal are Francisco de Osuna's *Third Spiritual Alphabet* (1527) and Bernardino de Laredo's *Ascent to Mount Zion* (published for the first time, anonymously, in 1535), two Hispano-Christian classics of spirituality read, studied and admired by the Carmelite reformers.[19] Building upon the spiritual ideals of the *devotio moderna* and the Northern European mystics (Ruysbroeck, Tauler, Gerson) as well as the classic medieval authorities on love mysticism (Richard and Hugh of St. Victor, Bonaventure, Bernard of Clairvaux), these Franciscan *recogidos* envisioned the *summum bonum* of Christian life as the ascent to loving union with God—who dwells in the human soul—through the apophatic path of unknowing. That is, they advocated the casting aside of all discursive thought, all lower forms of intellectual activity, to purify desire and attain in silence and in solitude—intellect, memory and will suspended—the mystic's affective union with the divine darkness: the prayer of orison or prayer of quiet. As expected, one of their primary authorities for this contemplative ideal was Dionysius. Osuna and Laredo explicitly adduce him to support their apophatic understanding of a superessential union with the hidden God beyond knowledge, the *recogimiento* ideal which they identify with Dionysius' "theologia mystica."[20] In fleshing out their theology, they also call upon even more extensively the authority of two major proponents of affective Dionysianism, the contemplative tradition harkening back to Gallus' pioneering conjunction of Dionysius apophatic theology with medieval affective theology: i.e. the Carthusian Hugh of Balma (d. 1340) with his *Mystica Theologia* (known in Spanish as *Sol de contemplativos* [Toledo 1514]),[21] and the Flemish Franciscan Hendrik Herp (d. 1477), famous in Spain for his *Directorium aureum contemplativorum* (also known as the *Speculum perfectionis humanae*), the second part of his own *Theologia mystica*.[22] Gallus, Balma and Herp were the key figures in the *recogidos'* affective reinterpretation of the Areopagite's *via negativa*.

The theological reach of the CD in Spain was not confined to the *recogidos'* tradition, as can be gauged, for example, from Luis de León's indebtedness to DN and its kataphatic theology in his monumental summa *De los nombres de Cristo*.[23] *Recogido* theology is, however, the main conduit for affective

Dionysian spirituality into the ascetico-mystical literature on contemplative prayer of Golden Age Spain. The great Carmelite mystics offer a case in point.

III

The *recogidos* appropriation of the Areopagite's theology allows us to speak with some precision about Dionysian themes in Teresa of Ávila's work. The Carmelite reformer devoted great energies to fleshing out a cohesive phenomenology of mystical prayer. This mystical phenomenology integrated, in turn, her psychological insights and life story into a broader theological frame deftly associated with the *recogido* understanding of Dionysius mystical theology. Early on in *Libro de la Vida* (10.1), Teresa, for example, explicitly identifies an experiential claim to "un sentimiento de la presencia de Dios" as *mística teoloxía*:

> I sometimes experienced, as I said, although very briefly, the beginning of what I will now speak about. It used to happen, when I represented Christ within me in order to place myself in His presence, or even while reading, that a feeling of the presence of God would come upon me unexpectedly so that I could in no way doubt He was within me or I totally immersed in Him. This did not occur after the manner of a vision. I believe they call the experience "mystical theology."[24]

With a rhetorical sleight of hand ("creo lo llaman . . ."), she cautiously invokes the Dionysian sobriquet, a term that was, of course, common currency in her theological readings and conversations with other learned mentors on contemplative spirituality. Similar circumspection is shown in her second promise to elucidate it: "for I shall speak afterward of the other stages I began to mention in regard to mystical theology, which I believe it is called" (*Vida* 11.5).[25]

But what is the core of this "mystical theology"? Right after the first quotation, Teresa shows a more precise appreciation for its Dionysian meaning. She dissects that unequivocal "feeling of the presence of God" in terms of a psychological preamble, redolent of the Areopagite, to the *recogidos'* "prayer of quiet," i.e., *mystical theology* as the suspension of all three faculties of the soul—intellect, will and memory—in a supraessential apprehension of God that transcends all lower forms of knowledge:

> The soul is suspended in such a way that it seems to be completely outside itself. The will loves; the memory, it seems to me, is almost lost; the intellect does not work discursively, in my opinion, but is not lost. For, as I say, the intellect does not work, but it is as though amazed ("espantado") by all it understands because God desires that it understand, with regard to the things His Majesty represents to it, that it understands nothing.[26]

In this key passage, Teresa's introduction to her first literary effort at a phenomenology of contemplative prayer (i.e., *Vida* 10–22, 37–40), the reformer highlights a central element in her theological understanding of union which Osuna, along with his peers, consistently expounded under the authority of the Areopagite: the sleep of the faculties with its apophatic thrust as a preamble to *unio mystica*. The prayer of quiet and the sleep of the faculties, as affective reelaborations of Dionysian apophaticism, are central to her theology: they will become the subject of fuller treatment, not only in the *Vida* but in the fourth and fifth dwellings of the *Moradas*.

Two chapters later in her *Vida*, the Dionysian core of her identification of mystical theology with the prayer of quiet is reasserted and further nuanced:

> What I say about not ascending to God unless He raises one up is language of the spirit. He who has had some experience will understand me, for I don't know how to describe this being raised up if it isn't understood through experience. In mystical theology, which I began to describe, the intellect ceases to work because God suspends it, as I shall explain afterwards if I know how and He gives me His help to do so. Taking it upon oneself to stop and suspend thought is what I mean should not be done; nor should we cease to work with the intellect, because otherwise we would be left like cold simpletons..." (*Vida* 12.5)[27]

Couched by two caveats—the ineffability trope and the inaccessibility of such insights to non-mystics—Teresa now reaffirms that at this pivotal stage in the path to union divine agency is central. The transcendence of all lower forms of knowledge—the Dionysian suspension of the active intellect—is not tantamount to the deliberate effort at suspending one's thoughts, an effort which she criticizes, perhaps in association with the *dejamiento* practices of the *alumbrados*. It rather signifies a purely passive acquiescence to God's singular prerogative. Later on (*Vida* 18:14), even God Himself explains an ecstatic experience to Teresa as a form of Dionysian *cognitio supraintellectualis*, invoking a *conceptista* locution clearly resonant with John of the Cross's epistemological musings: "After having received Communion and been in this very prayer I'm writing about, I was thinking ... of what the soul did during that time. The Lord spoke these words to me: 'It detaches itself from everything, daughter, so as to abide more in me ... Since it cannot comprehend what it understands, there is an understanding by not understanding [*es no entender entendiendo*]' " (cf. the paradoxical antitheses of John's *Entréme* further, below).[28]

It is true, as noted by McGinn,[29] that Teresa's understanding of union evolves in her writings and hence it is not merely reducible to *recogido* formulations. In *Vida*, union is an intermediate state of prayer below ecstasy, whereas in *Moradas*, Teresa distinguishes between the prayer of union in the fifth dwelling and a spiritual union in the seventh. In both cases, her theological account of the prayer resorts to "the language of the union of wills found in the medieval mystics." The affective interpretation of Dionysius makes itself felt in the nature and very centrality to both accounts of the prayer of quiet.

Poetic echoes of its Dionysian lineage also filter into Teresa's treatment of such prayer elsewhere in her writings. A telling example is in her daring *Meditaciones sobre los Cantares*, Teresa's ruminative comments on the biblical epithalamium (a first version was written in San José de Ávila between 1566 and 1567). Reflecting on the second hemistich of *Song of Songs* 2:3 ("I delight to sit in his shade, and His fruit is sweet to my mouth"), Teresa thus glosses her mystical understanding of the Beloved's shade (*Meditaciones* 5.4):

> It seems that while the soul is in this delight that was mentioned it feels itself totally engulfed and protected in this shadow and kind of cloud of Divinity. From it comes inspirations ("influencias") and a delightful dew which indeed rightly takes away the weariness that worldly things have caused the soul. The soul feels there a kind of repose that will even make breathing wearisome to it. And the faculties are so quiet and calm that the will would not want them to admit any thoughts, even good ones, nor does it admit any by way of inquiry or striving after them.[30]

The Beloved's shade here becomes the *nube de Divinidad*, truly a "cloud of unknowing" that envelops the soul in delight with the quieting of its faculties, making it impervious to all lower forms of discursive thinking. The next lines on the shadow analogy provide the Dionysian clincher: "For in this prayer all the soul does is taste, without any work on the part of the faculties; and present in this shadow of Divinity—well does she say 'shadow,' since we cannot see It clearly here below but only under this cloud—is that brilliant Sun."

A woman of the Spanish church under the Inquisition's gaze, Teresa was in no position to flaunt theological learning with as lofty and delicate a subject as Dionysian mystical theology. And yet, her circumspect comments on the subject clearly point to a fundamental understanding of some of its key themes and Dionysian lineage. They were mediated by her readings on *recogido* spirituality and life-long conversations with various mentors, but are nonetheless reflective of a Dionysian inflection in her theological views on the contemplative life. The path of unknowing to God, imaged as supernal darkness, was not a privative theme of her "little Seneca."

IV

John of the Cross only refers to a handful of authorities by name and yet he mentions Dionysius explicitly four times, one in each of his four great commentaries on his own mystical poetry: *S* 2.8.6; *N* 2.5.3; *CB* 14–15.16 and *Ll* 3–3.49. Each quotation adds a small nuance to his selective appropriation of

Dionysius, especially as a constitutive element of his doctrine on the Dark
Night.[31] In *Subida* 2.8.5–6, a pivotal exposition on how the intellect cannot
come in the way of the soul's loving union with God, John explicitly identifies
the highest echelon of contemplation, the unitive apprehension of God's
secret wisdom, as both "mystical theology" and the Dionysian "ray of darkness" (as with Teresa, this Dionysian interlude is framed with a lengthy
disquisition on the soul's suspension of its faculties—the fundamental theme
of the *recogidos*):

> Manifestly, then, none of these ideas can serve the intellect as a proximate
> means leading to God. In order to draw nearer to the divine ray, the
> intellect must advance by unknowing rather than by the desire to know,
> and by blinding itself and remaining in darkness rather than by opening
> its eyes. Contemplation, consequently, by which the intellect has a higher
> knowledge of God ("más alta noticia de Dios") is called mystical theol-
> ogy, meaning the secret wisdom of God. For this wisdom is secret to the
> very intellect that receives it. Dionysius on this account refers to contem-
> plation as a ray of darkness ("rayo de tiniebla"). The prophet Baruch
> (3.23) declares of this wisdom: *There is no one who knows her way or can
> think of her paths.* To reach union with God the intellect must obviously
> blind itself to all the paths along which it can travel.[32]

The following chapter (*S* 2.9) fleshes out his Dionysian exegesis of the biblical
tiniebla both as the darkness of faith and as the very darkness of God, which
is object, in turn, of the soul's union beyond knowledge ("union with God in
this life ... demands that we be *united with the darkness* [*unirse con la tiniebla*]"—*S* 2.9.4). John even glosses the Dionysian reference both to Psalm
18(17):12 and to Moses' hierophanic ascent to Sinai from *MT* 2–3.[33]

The same Dionysian reference to the *rayo de tiniebla* as noetic darkness is
further belabored in his second set of glosses on the dark night symbol (*Noche*
2.5.3—his commentary on the opening heptasyllable "En una noche oscura"):

> Hence when the divine light of contemplation strikes a soul not yet
> entirely illumined, it causes spiritual darkness, for it not only surpasses
> the act of natural understanding but it also deprives the soul of this act
> and darkens it. This is why Dionysius and other mystical theologians call
> this infused contemplation a "ray of darkness"—that is, for the soul not
> yet illumined and purged. For this great supernatural light overwhelms
> the intellect and deprives it of its natural vigor. David also said that
> clouds and darkness are near God and surround him, not because this is
> true in itself, but because it appears thus to our weak intellects, which in
> being unable to attain so bright a light are blinded and darkened. Hence
> he next declared that clouds passed before the great splendor of his
> presence, that is between God and our intellect. As a result, when God
> communicates this bright ray of his secret wisdom to the soul not yet
> transformed, he causes thick darkness in its intellect.[34]

Related discussions in *Noche* include 2.12.15 and, especially, 2.17.2, where John also equates mystical theology, under Aquinas' authority, with that "contemplación tenebrosa" from 2.5.[35]

The *Canticle* passage (14–15.16) suggestively associates the unbearability of God's knowledge to the human intellect with the most dramatic moment in his poetic reelaboration of the Song of Songs, i.e., when the Lover, about to fly towards her Beloved, asks him to cast aside those "ojos deseados" which are at once irresistible and forbidding. This *sanjuanista* passage subtly dovetails the conjunction of theory and practice in the affective Dionysian concept of mystical theology, that is, the conjunction of Dionysian apophasis with the amatory language of Solomon's canticle at the threshold of mystical *unitio*:

> It must not be thought that, because what the soul understands is the naked substance, there is perfect and clear fruition as in heaven. Although knowledge is stripped of accidents, it is not clear because of this, but dark, for it is contemplation, which in this life is a ray of darkness, as Saint Dionysius says. We can say that it is a ray and image of fruition, since it is in the intellect that fruition takes place. This substance understood, which the soul calls "whistling," is equivalent to "the eyes I have desired" of which the soul said when they were being revealed to her, "Withdraw them, Beloved" (¡*Apártalos, Amado!*), because her senses could not endure them."[36]

Finally, the *Llama* reference (3–3.49) further underscores the affective tradition of Dionysian mystical theology, succinctly equating the intellect's benightedness with a "noticia sobrenatural amorosa": *cognitio supraintellectualis* as the high point of mystical love.

> . . . But in the contemplation we are discussing (by which God infuses himself into the soul), particular knowledge as well as acts made by the soul are unnecessary. The reason for this is that God in one act is communicating light and love together, which is loving supernatural knowledge ("noticia sobrenatural amorosa"). We can assert that this knowledge is like light that transmits heat, for that light also enkindles love. This knowledge is general and dark to the intellect because it is contemplative knowledge, which is a ray of darkness for the intellect, as Dionysius teaches.[37]

These passages inscribe at the very heart of *sanjuanista* mystical theology— not only in content but in imagery and language—Dionysius' apophatic theology as tersely summarized in *MT* 1 and buttressed by the medieval commentators, especially Aquinas and Gallus. John equates Dionysius' *via negativa* with the foundational meaning of the *noche oscura* as the intellectual "darkening" of the unpurged soul in contemplation, the soul passively enabled to attain a higher way of knowing God that transcends the human mind and hence metaphorically blinds it with an overpowering radiance. There are other exegetical hooks, besides the ones invoked in *MT*, that allow John to weave in his writings this Dionysian *Leitmotiv*: e.g. his nuanced glosses on the Beloved's *nescivi* in Song of Songs 6:12, and the Psalmist counterpart in Ps. 72:22, as biblical references to mystical unknowing. There are other discussions as well about the absolute transcendence of God laced with Dionysian motifs: his comments on how Beauty, Grace, Goodness and Wisdom are differently applied to God and his creatures (*S* 1.4.4), and the subsequent explanation of the soul's nescient union with divine Wisdom (*S* 1.4.5), or his other kataphatic excursa on divine attributes in the *Cántico* (e.g. Beauty in *CB* 36.5 and *DN* 4.7–9). But the dark night is his poetic cipher *par excellence* for the mystical path of unknowing in a Dionysian key.

Of course, Dionysius' noetic darkness only provides a theological point of departure for his complex phenomenology of contemplative prayer. His gloss on the *rayo de tiniebla* as infused contemplation gives way throughout his commentaries to other competing meanings of the "dark night" symbol— i.e. the fourfold scheme of the active and passive nights of both the senses and the spirit and its tripartite exegesis as mystical unknowing, sensual deprivation and spiritual purgation. As the dark night acquires conceptual density, it goes beyond the Areopagite's views on human finitude and the *divinae tenebrae radius*. The *sanjuanista* phenomenology of spiritual purgation—for example—is not simply coextensive with the patristic darkness of God nor is it limited to Dionysius' acknowledgement of Moses' purification as signifying a prerequisite for mystical ascent (*MT* 1.3 [1000C]: "Etenim non simpliciter divinus Moyses mundari ipse primum precipitur, et rursus a non talibus segregari"). Purgation in John, as Louth (*op. cit.*, 185ff) rightly underscores, encompasses that process begun by a refined awareness of sinfulness *subsequent* to the soul's immersion in the Dionysian dark night and coincident with its affective descent into contemplation.

Still, the Dionysian inspiration of the *sanjuanista* nights was never far from sight in his mystical theology. The Areopagite's theology remained a corner-stone of his mystical theology, as it becomes clear in what is arguably the best lyrical summation of Dionysian apophaticism in sixteenth-century Spain: John's popular "glosa" *Entréme donde no supe*, entitled in the manuscripts *Coplas del mismo hechas sobre un éxtasis de harta contemplación*.[38] *Entréme* may only rank as a minor composition vis-à-vis his three major poems (his most haunting contributions to the Golden Age Spanish canon), but its conceptual economy and emotional intensity has few paragons and could rival in succinctness *MT* itself. This popular poem is built upon a short *estribillo*, a three-line refrain part of which serves as a recursive *Leitmotiv* at the end of each stanza: "Entréme donde no supe / y quedéme no sabiendo / toda sciencia trascendiendo" ("I entered into unknowing / and there I remained unknowing / transcending all knowledge"—all but one of its eight septets end with the third octosyllable).[39] In line with the rhetorical conceits of its fifteenth-century predecessors (the popular amatory verses of the Spanish *cancioneros*), John's Dionysian *manifesto* is carefully woven around a basic thematic antithesis—knowing/not knowing—and its correlate—understanding/not understanding. His very first *copla* dramatizes the biblical *nescivi* ("Yo no supe") as a tacit allegory of mystical unknowing:

Yo no supe dónde entraba	I entered into unknowing
pero, cuando allí me vi,	yet when I saw myself there,
sin saber dónde me estaba	without knowing where I was
grandes cosas entendí;	I understood great things;
no diré lo que sentí,	I will not say what I felt
que me quedé no sabiendo,	for I remained unknowing
toda sciencia trascendiendo.	*transcending all knowledge.*

All lower forms of intellectual activity are subsumed in that *sciencia* inescapably pushed down by a higher form of infused knowledge ("grandes cosas entendí") which is, in turn, identifiable throughout with the titular "ecstasy of high contemplation." The essential unknowability of supernal realities, albeit unequivocally affirmed ("yo no supe," "sin saber" "me quedé no sabiendo"), is paradoxically offset by that ecstatic knowledge beyond the mind that culminates in union (it is not a coincidence that John places its assertion in the very middle of the stanza). Subsequent *coplas* revisit from different angles the Dionysian paradox of knowing by not knowing (e.g. "un entender no entendiendo" [3f]; "y su sciencia tanto cresce / que se queda no sabiendo" [4ef], "que no llega su saber / a no entender entendiendo" [6ef], "con un no saber sabiendo" [7f], etc.). And yet again, in its fifth stanza, the Dionysian provenance of his theological cornerstone is succinctly established by his chosen imagery from *MT* 1.3:

Cuanto más alto se sube	The higher he ascends
tanto menos se entendía	the less he understands
que es la tenebrosa nube	because the cloud is dark
que a la noche esclarecía;	which lit up the night;
por eso quien la sabía	whoever knows it,
queda siempre no sabiendo	remains always in unknowing
toda sciencia trascendiendo.	*transcending all knowledge.*

The loving ascent to an unknowable God is unequivocally ciphered in the Dionysian image of Moses' *tenebrosa nube* and its poetic association with the night of unknowing which the glowing cloud illuminated. The final septet circumvents paradoxical locutions (no polyptoton!) in a more synthetic characterization of that "summa sciencia" as "un subido sentir de la divinal Esencia." Never the direct object of metaphysical knowledge, the divine Essence can only be apprehended via the *principalis affectio* ("un subido sentir") of the Dionysian love mystics.

V

There are other interesting concomitances in John's work with Dionysian theology and imagery, whether as an indirect fruit of the Areopagite's influence in Christian tradition or directly reinforced by the saint's readings of the CD: e.g. the tripartite scheme of the mystical path as purgation, illumination and union (cf. *CH* 7.3 [209C-D]), the popular image of the solar rays traversing different panes of glass (cf. *N* 2.12.3 and *CH* 13.3 [301B]),[40] the attendant theory of the soul's illumination as mediated by the celestial hierarchies (cf. *N* 2.12.4 and *DN* 7.2 [868B-C] and *CH* 13.3 [300C-304B]) or the comparison of God and His attributes to a circular shape without beginning or end (*CB* 37.7 and *DN* 4.14 [712D]). But his primary debt, just like Teresa, is to the Areopagite's apophaticism as a foundational template for the mystical theology of unitive love. They were both steeped in the multi-secular efforts of their medieval predecessors to forge a Dionysian theology of contemplative prayer. Ironically, the acceptance of both mystics in Inquisitorial Spain was comparably well-served by their dissimilar engagement—indirect in her case, explicit in his—with the Areopagite's corpus. Teresa could not be forthright about most of her theological sources, however mediated, but the Dionysian inspiration of her *recogido* mystics lent an unimpeachable theological foundation to her phenomenological synthesis. John's explicit avowal of a Dionysian debt helped forestall, on the other hand, Inquisitorial suspicions about the orthodoxy of his theology, especially after the posthumous publication of his works in 1618. His seventeenth-century advocates (Basilio Ponce de León, Father Quiroga, etc.) adduced again and again the apostolic authority of the Areopagite in defending his mystical doctrines against detractors.[41] This was Dionysius' parting gift to sixteenth-century Spain. The *apologia pro vita contemplativa* of these spiritual giants found refuge from Inquisitorial onslaught in the umbrage of his teachings.

NOTES

1 María Josefa Canellada (ed), Lucas Fernández, *Auto de la Passión* (Madrid: Castalia, 1976), p. 214. English translation mine.
2 Dionysius is the subject of a monumental amount of scholarly literature. See Placid Spearritt, *A Philosophical Enquiry into Dionysian Mysticism* (Bösingen: Rotex-Druckdienst, 1975), pp. 173–282; and the bibliographic repertoires in Colm Lubheid and Paul Rorem (trans), *Pseudo-Dionysius: The Complete Works* (New York, NY: Paulist Press, 1987), p. 291. For an authoritative overview of Dionysius' thought and his place in Christian mystical theology, see David Knowles, "The Influence of Pseudo-Dionysius on Western Mysticism", *Christian Spirituality. Essays in Honour of Gordon Rupp* (London 1975), pp. 79–94; Andrew Louth, *The Origins of the Christian Mystical Tradition: From Plato to Denys* (Oxford: Clarendon Press, 1981), pp. 159–178; and Bernard McGinn, *The Foundations of Mysticism: Origins to the Fifth Century* (New York, NY: Crossroad, 1991), pp. 157–182.
3 Lubheid and Rorem, *op. cit.*, pp. 268–269.
4 On Gallus' pioneering synthesis of this Dionysian tradition, see Bernard McGinn, *The Flowering of Mysticism: Men and Women in the New Mysticism-1200–1350* (New York, NY: Crossroad, 1998), pp. 78–87. For a broad history of this mystical trend, in contra-distinction

to other medieval interpretations of the *CD* (e.g. "affective" versus "speculative"), Paul Rorem, *Pseudo Dionysius: A Commentary on the Texts and an Introduction to Their Influence* (New York and Oxford: Oxford University Press, 1993).

5 *Obras completas del Pseudo Dionisio Areopagita*, second edn. (Madrid: BAC, 1995), p. 35.

6 In his *Enchyridion*, Erasmus still acknowledges Dionysius as one of the Church's mystical doctors—cf. Marcel Bataillon, *Erasmo y España*, second edn. (México: FCE. 1966), p. 199.

7 Although John's indebtedness to the *CD* is acknowledged in the critical literature, monographic studies on the subject are rare: cf. Jean Krynen's dissertation *La théologie du baroque. Denys le Mystique et Saint Jean de la Croix* (La Sorbonne, 1955) and the recent synthesis of his views in *Saint Jean de la Croix et l'aventure de la mystique espagnole* (Toulouse: Presses Universitaires du Mirail/France-Iberie Recherche, 1990), pp. 15–45; also Martin-Lunas, *op. cit.*, pp. 38–44. On the other hand, we have not documented as yet a single scholarly work on Teresa's indirect engagement with Dionysian mystical theology—only a fleeting and, in our estimation, unpersuasive claim that her reflections on God's sufferings are comparable to the Areopagite's (cf. Figura's entry in Peter Dinzelbacher [ed.], *Wörterbuch der Mystik*, second edn. [Stuttgart: Kröner, 1998], pp. 424–425).

8 Cf. his *Historia de la vida y virtudes del venerable Padre Juan de la Cruz* (Brussels 1628), p. 35.

9 It is suggestive, but inconclusive, to note that his rendering of Dionysius' τοῦ θείου σκότους ἀκτῖνα as *rayo de tiniebla* may be closer to Sarrazin's (and Grosseteste's) "divine tenebrae radium" than to Traversari's "caliginis radium" or Ficino's "divinae caliginis radium."

10 For a more comprehensive list, Martin-Lunas, *op. cit.*, pp. 98–102.

11 For descriptive purposes, we have consulted Harvard's copy at the Houghton Library (f*MGC.D623.C502).

12 To be more precise: (1) Sarrazin's translation of *CH* with the commentaries by Hugh and Albert; (2) Sarrazin's version of *EH*; (3) Sarrazin's *DN* with Aquinas' commentary; (4) Sarrazin's *MT*; (5) Grosseteste's *MT* with his commentary; (6) Sarrazin's *Epistles* and (7) Gallus' 1238 *Extractio* on the four main works of the Areopagite, along with the *Epistle to Titus*.

13 Part II is a reprint of a 1498 edition of Traversari's *CD* as prepared by Lefèvre d'Etaples for his compendium of the Apostolic fathers *Theologia Vivificans: Cibus Solidus*.

14 Martin-Lunas (p. 99) identifies at least ten in his catalogue scattered in Madrid, Salamanca, Zaragoza, Barcelona, Sevilla, Zamora and Logroño.

15 Salamanca's University library owns two copies of the Strasbourg edition and one copy of the Alcalá compilation, along with a 1516 edition of the complete works in Greek (Florence, Philippi Iunctae), a 1561–1562 *Opera quae extant in eadem Maximi scholia G. Pachymerae paraphrasis et M. Syngeli* (Paris) and a 1565 *Opera omnia. Ejus vita. Scholia incerti auctoris in librum Ecclesiastica Hierarchia* of Jesuit provenance (cf. Martin-Lunas, pp. 99–101). On John's Salamancan experience, see Luis Enrique Rodríguez-San Pedro Bezares, *La formación universitaria de Juan de la Cruz* (Valladolid: Junta de Castilla y León, 1992).

16 On her gender and Jewish ancestry, Francisco Márquez Villanueva, "Santa Teresa y el linaje", *Espiritualidad y literatura en el siglo XVI* (Madrid: Alfaguara, 1968), pp. 139–205 and Alison Weber, *Teresa of Avila and the Rhetoric of Femininity* (Princeton, NJ: Princeton University Press, 1990). On her sources, influences and cultural formation, see Gaspar Etchegoyen, *L'amour divin. Essai sur les sources de Sainte Thérèse* (Bordeaux-Paris 1923); Víctor García de la Concha, *El arte literario de Santa Teresa* (Barcelona: Ariel, 1978); and María Pilar Manero Sorolla (ed), *Santa Teresa de Jesús, Antología* (Barcelona: PPU, 1992), pp. 53–93.

17 A quick survey of the *CORDE* easily identifies allusions and quotations to the Areopagite in fifteenth-century works by Vicente Ferrer, Alfonso Fernández de Madrigal, Alfonso de Cartagena, Enrique de Villena, etc.

18 John of Ávila read Traversari's translation (Martin-Lunas, p. 37) and often quoted from the entire corpus: cf. Luis Sala Balust and Francisco Martín Hernández (eds), San Juan de Ávila, *Obras completas*, 5 vols. (Madrid: BAC, 2000), pp. 1:688, 3:114, 3:471 and 3:538. The Dominican Luis de Granada also quotes extensively from the *CD*, whether directly or via Balma, especially in his *Introducción del símbolo de la fe* (1583) and even Peter of Alcántara, who did not write as much, invokes his authority in *Tratado de la Oración y Meditación*: cf. Rafael Sanz Valdivieso (ed), *Vida y escritos de San Pedro de Alcántara* (Madrid: BAC, 1996), p. 279.

19 For an authoritative overview of *recogimiento* mystical theology, see Melquiades Andrés, *Los recogidos* (Madrid, 1976); on Osuna in particular, see Saturnino López Santidrián's

176 Luis M. Girón-Negrón

introduction to *Tercer abecedario espiritual* (Madrid: BAC, 1998), pp. 5–82; finally, on Teresa's indebtedness to Osuna and Laredo, see Fidèle de Ros, *Un maître de Sainte Thérèse*. *Le Père François d'Osuna*. *Sa vie, son ouevre, sa doctrine spirituelle* (Paris: Beauchesne, 1936) and *Un inspirateur de Sainte Thérèse, le Frère Bernardin de Laredo* (Paris: Vrin, 1948).

20   Both Osuna and Laredo adduce Dionysius' authority extensively throughout their works: e.g. *Tercer abecedario* 21.5 and 21.7 (pp. 558–559, 565) and *Subida* 3.9 and 3.15 (A. Alonso González et al [eds], *Subida del Monte Sión* [Salamanca: FUE/Universidad Pontificia, 2000] pp. 465, 480).

21   On Balma's influence among the *recogidos*, Andrés, *op. cit.*, pp. 70–76.

22   *Speculum perfectionis* was translated into Latin in Venice in 1524. In 1538, Herp's entire *Theologia mystica* was published. Cf. Juan Martin Kelly's edition of the *Directorio de contemplativos* (Madrid: Universidad Pontificia de Salamanca, 1974), with a substantive study on Herp's mystical theology and formative influence on Spanish spirituality.

23   Cf. Cristóbal Cuevas (ed), Luis de León, *De los nombres de Cristo*, third edn. (Madrid: Cátedra, 1982), pp. 151, n.33; 169, n.82 and 406, n.312.

24   Kieran Kavanaugh and Otilio Rodríguez (trans), *The Collected Works of St. Teresa of Avila*, 2 vols. (Washington, DC: ICS Publications, 1976), p. 1:74. Spanish original in Efrén Madre de Dios and Otger Steggink (eds), *Obras completas*, eighth edn. (Madrid: BAC, 1986), p. 66.

25   English, p. 1:80; Spanish, p. 71.

26   English, p. 1:74; Spanish, p. 66.

27   English, p. 1:87; Spanish, p. 76.

28   English, p. 1:121; Spanish, p. 102. At the end of *Vida* 18.4, Teresa pushes this paradox to its limits with a lengthy polyptoton.

29   Bernard McGinn, "Love, Knowledge and *Unio mystica* in the Western Christian Tradition," Idel and McGinn (eds), *Mystical Union in Judaism, Christianity, and Islam: An Ecumenical Dialogue* (New York, NY: Continuum, 1996), pp. 81–82 (pp. 59–86).

30   English, p. 2:249; Spanish, p. 455.

31   For a compelling analysis of the relationship between John's *noche oscura* and the Dionysian contribution to the patristic theme of the Divine Darkness, see Louth, *op. cit.*, pp. 181–190.

32   Kieran Kavanaugh and Otilio Rodríguez (eds), *The Collected Works of Saint John of the Cross*, revised edition (Washington, DC: ICS Publications, 1991) p. 176; Spanish original in Lucinio Ruano de la Iglesia (ed), San Juan de la Cruz, *Obras completas*, eleventh edn. (Madrid: BAC, 1982) p. 148. The basic intertext is *MT* 1.1 [1000A]. Cf. also *DN* 7 and Aquinas' commentary *ad locum*—another pivotal reference for John.

33   On God's transcendence and absolute dissimilitude with His creatures, see also *S* 3.12: cf. Ruano de la Iglesia, *op. cit.*, pp. 252–253. Cf. as well *MT* 1.3 [1001A] on Moses' entrance into the cloud of unknowing: "Tunc et ab ipsis absolvitur visis et videntibus, et ad caliginem ignorantie intrat, que caligo vere est mystica."

34   *Ibid.*, p. 402, Spanish in Ruano de la Iglesia, *op. cit.*, pp. 361–362.

35   "Primeramente llama *secreta* a esta contemplación tenebrosa, por cuanto, según habemos tocado arriba, ésta es la teología mística, que llaman los teólogos sabiduría [secreta, la] cual dice santo Tomás que se comunica e infunde en el alma por amor; lo cual acaece secretamente a oscuras de la obra del entendimiento y de las demás potencies . . ." (Ruano de la Iglesia, *op. cit.*, pp. 397–398). There are several Thomistic *loci* that may correspond with this *sanjuanista* claim: e.g. *Summa* 2–2, q.45, a.2 and, again, his commentary on *DN* 7.

36   Spanish, p. 629. See also *CB* 39.12.

37   English, p. 693; Spanish, p. 832. See also *Ll* 3–3.48, which Martin-Lunas suggestively juxtaposes with *DN* 7.872AB, as well as *Ll* 3.12–13 on the shadows of the divine *obumbraciones*.

38   *Stanzas concerning an ecstasy experienced in high contemplation*—Spanish, pp. 35–37; English, pp. 53–54. For a literary analysis of this popular *glosa*, Colin Thompson, *St. John of the Cross: Songs in the Night* (Washington, DC: The Catholic University of America Press, 2003) pp. 61–62.

39   John retouches verse 7g to highlight the processual nature of mystical apophasis ("irá siempre trascendiendo").

40   Cf. Herp, *Directorium*, chap. 50 (Martin Kelly 1974), p. 639.

41   Cf. Jean Krynen (ed), *Apología mística en defensa de la contemplación de fray José de Jesús María Quiroga, O.C.D.*, Anejo LII del *BRAE* (Madrid 1992), pp. 13–14 and Martín-Lunas, *op. cit.*, p. 39.

12

THE RECEPTION OF DIONYSIUS IN TWENTIETH-CENTURY EASTERN ORTHODOXY

PAUL L. GAVRILYUK

The *CD* has made an indelible mark on the development of the Byzantine Orthodox tradition and the overall tenor of Orthodox theology. Although much in the *CD* could justifiably provoke controversy, the incorporation of the *CD* into the canon of patristic writings was surprisingly quick and met with relatively little resistance.[1] Commenting on this peculiar development, Jaroslav Pelikan wrote:

> There is both historical significance and theological irony in the chrono-logical coincidence between the condemnation of Origen and the rise of Dionysian mysticism, for most of the doctrines on account of which the Second Council of Constantinople anathematized Origen were far less dangerous to the tradition of catholic orthodoxy than was the Crypto-Origenism canonized in the works of Dionysius the Areopagite.[2]

Admittedly, the characterization of Dionysius as an *Origenes redivivus* should not be accepted without qualifications. Clearly, the Byzantine theologians did not endorse the *CD* out of repressed nostalgia for Origen. Besides, there are just as many differences as there are genetic links between Origen and Dionysius' own versions of Christian Platonism. Nevertheless, there is much truth in Pelikan's provocative remark: Dionysius is in some ways more dangerous "to the tradition of catholic orthodoxy" than Origen. The boldest speculations of the Alexandrian theologian pale in comparison before the linguistic and mystical audacity of the Areopagite.

Paul L. Gavrilyuk
Department of Theology, University of St. Thomas, 2115 Summit Avenue, St. Paul, MN 55105, USA
plgavrilyuk@stthomas.edu

The rediscovery of Dionysius by twentieth-century Orthodox thinkers is a largely untold story, which deserves a book-length exposition. Here I will be able to sketch only the main contours of this story. Most of the influential Orthodox interpreters of Dionysius located the CD within the framework of larger master narratives. Such narratives in turn have helped to forge twentieth-century Orthodox theological identity vis-à-vis Western theology. In the process, Dionysian theology has been used as a historical source as well as a polemical weapon. Ironically, while offering an interpretation of the CD that is non-Western in character, some Orthodox thinkers strongly relied on Western sources.

My survey will proceed in chronological order. I will begin by considering the treatment of the CD in the pre-revolutionary and later works of Sergius Bulgakov (1871–1944), indicating the roots of his sophiological system in the writings of Vladimir Solovyov (1853–1900). Banished from the Soviet Union in the aftermath of the Bolshevik revolution, Bulgakov for the last two decades of his life taught at the newly-founded Orthodox Institute of St. Sergius in Paris. Bulgakov's sophiology was a source of much discord in émigré Russian Orthodox circles and beyond. Hence, it is misleading to speak of a single Paris school of Russian theology, as some scholars do, because neither Nicolas Berdyaev (1874–1948) nor his younger contemporary Vladimir Lossky (1903–1958), whose use of the CD will be considered next, had great affinity with Bulgakov's sophiological speculations, or with each other's work for that matter. Lossky's approach to Dionysius' apophaticism finds a number of parallels in the work of the Greek theologian Christos Yannaras (1935–). I will then consider another Russian émigré theologian, John Meyendorff (1926–1992), who left Western Europe and crossed the Atlantic to play a major role in establishing St. Vladimir's Theological Seminary in New York. Meyendorff's critique of Dionysius' Christology and liturgical theology stimulated further discussion in contemporary Orthodox scholarship.[3]

It is one of the strangest turns of history that most Eastern Orthodox thinkers discussed in this chapter wrote, thought, taught, and spent considerable time, if not all of their lives, in the West. For Sergius Bulgakov, Nicolas Berdyaev, Vladimir Lossky, and Georges Florovsky (1893–1979) the painful experience of dislocation occasioned by the revolution added an existential dimension to the already troublesome question of modern Orthodox Christian identity. Faced with a largely non-Orthodox intellectual world, some of these thinkers came to emphasize more sharply the dividing line between the thought and ethos of the Christian "East" and those of the Christian "West". I deliberately put the categories of the "East" and "West" in quotation marks, since these categories were not used in their primary geopolitical sense, but in a rich and evocative metaphorical sense, reaching into the depth of history and having as their primary reference point the Greek patristic tradition and the culture of Byzantium together with its Slavic expressions.[4]

In light of the quest for a modern Orthodox identity, it is hardly surprising that some Orthodox thinkers conflate—sometimes inadvertently, at other times quite deliberately—the markers of identity with the criteria of truth.[5] In such accounts "Eastern Orthodox" becomes synonymous with "authentic", "correct", and "true." Conversely "Western" comes to be closely associated with "distorted", "misguided", or simply "false". Throughout this chapter I will have several opportunities to comment on this peculiar use, or rather a very telling misuse of the terms.

Vladimir Solovyov, Sergius Bulgakov, and Nicolas Berdyaev

Three main periods may be distinguished in Bulgakov's complex intellectual evolution: (1) a philosophical period, during which he was largely preoccupied with articulating and subsequently overcoming a Marxist political economy; (2) a religious-philosophical period, which will be our main interest here; (3) and finally, a theological period, during which Bulgakov brought to completion his comprehensive sophiological system.[6]

Vladimir Solovyov provided the main impetus for Bulgakov's turn to Christian idealism. In addition to being a metaphysician, Solovyov was a poet and a mystic, who is said to have been visited three times by the mysterious figure of Sophia, the Wisdom of God. Nature mysticism, Spinoza's pantheism, and German idealism, especially Schelling, played a major role in Solovyov's metaphysics of "all-unity" (*vseedinstvo*). The guiding notion of Solovyov's system is the idea of Godmanhood (*Bogochelovechestvo*).[7] The incarnation of the Godman Christ is expanded into a metaphysical principle that provides the paradigm for all instances of divine-human interaction. In this scheme, empirical humanity strives towards ideal humanity, which is eternally inseparable from the being of God. History is interpreted as a process of divine-human cooperation culminating in deification.

Bulgakov drank from the same philosophical wells and made Solovyov's sophiological vision fully his own. In *The Unfading Light* (*Svet Nevechernii*, 1917) Bulgakov makes a foray into religious epistemology, cosmology, and anthropology. He emphasizes that any account of the experience of the divine is fraught with the fundamental antinomy of the transcendent that reveals itself and thus becomes immanent, while also remaining transcendent, a point that will be developed later by Lossky and Meyendorff. Following Pavel Florensky (1882–1937), Bulgakov speaks of the irreducibly paradoxical character of the central Christian dogmas, such as the Trinity and the incarnation.[8]

The Unfading Light is divided into three main sections, the first dedicated to the doctrine of God, the second to creation, and the third to theological anthropology. The first section is provocatively entitled "Divine Nonbeing" (*Bozhestvennoe nichto*), an expression that is Dionysian in inspiration. According to Dionysius, since God does not belong to the order of created beings, all creaturely properties must be denied of God, including existence. Following Plotinus, Dionysius concludes the *Mystical Theology* by observing that God "falls neither within the predicate of nonbeing nor of being".[9] With his characteristic penchant for sweeping generalizations, Bulgakov declares: "religious philosophy knows no more central problem than the meaning of divine nonbeing".[10]

In a drawn-out chapter of about forty pages Bulgakov provides the first sketch of the history of negative theology in Russian philosophy. Without following chronological order consistently, he begins his discussion with Plato, Aristotle, Plotinus, Philo, Clement of Alexandria, Origen, the Cappadocian Fathers and reaches Dionysius, whom he calls "the true father of apophatic theology".[11] According to Bulgakov, the central point of the *Divine Names* lies in upholding the utter transcendence, inexpressibility, and incomprehensibility of God. Bulgakov observes that Dionysius offers a form of apophaticism that is more radical than that of Plotinus: for Dionysius God surpasses even the notion of oneness. In light of recent scholarship it seems clear that Bulgakov has exaggerated the epistemological difference between Plotinian and Dionysian apophaticism, since Plotinus is equally insistent that the One surpasses being, as well as all human categories and powers of expression.[12]

Bulgakov notes in passing a prominent role accorded to *eros* in Dionysius' account of the ecstatic experience of God, aptly characterizing this account as "erotic epistemology" (*eroticheskaia gnoseologiia*).[13] After the *CD*, Bulgakov turns to Maximus the Confessor, John of Damascus, Gregory Palamas, John Scotus Eriugena, Nicholas of Cusa, as well as Jewish, German, and English mystics. Bulgakov closes his overview of the history of negative theology quite surprisingly with Kant. The Russian philosopher sees an unrealized potential for negative theology in Kant's notion of *Ding-an-sich* to which no human categories apply and which remains outside the boundaries of human experience.[14] Kant himself, Bulgakov is quick to point out, was not a mystic, but a rather narrow rationalist, as attested by his *Religion Within the Limits of Reason Alone*, a book that Bulgakov calls "religiously tasteless".[15] Bulgakov, however, finds Schelling and Hegel, while not entirely unmusical to the mystical dimension of theology, nevertheless lacking the apophatic dimension, since for them all transcendent features of reality ultimately become immanent states of self-consciousness.

Thus Bulgakov inserts the *CD* into a metanarrative which begins with Plato and, continuing through select Church Fathers, philosophers, and mystics, ends with Kant. Bulgakov reads Dionysius as a philosopher would, not as a student of *Dogmengeschichte* (in a typical early twentieth-century sense of that term). Unlike other Orthodox theologians discussed below, Bulgakov is not concerned whether and how the *CD* fits into the patristic tradition or Byzantine Orthodoxy. Rather, Bulgakov's consideration of the history of negative theology plays a constructive role in articulating his own theological system.

The approach of Bulgakov's friend and critic, Nicolas Berdyaev, presents several intriguing points of comparison. In *Spirit and Reality: the Foundations of Divine-human Spirituality* (1937) Berdyaev inserts the *CD* into a master narrative similar to Bulgakov's, dedicating even more attention to the German mystics, especially Meister Eckhart and Jacob Boehme. Following the dominant view in the Western scholarship of his time, Berdyaev dismissively treats the *CD* as "mainly a repetition of Plotinus and Neoplatonism".[16] In his earlier work, *Freedom and the Spirit* (1928), Berdyaev criticizes the Church Fathers for sidelining mystical writers.[17] Berdyaev observes that "school theology" has a tendency towards either ostracizing or domesticating mystical theology. For Berdyaev, the purpose of the dogmas is to express the mystical experience of the Church, not to stifle mystical life. He recognizes the possibility of the "approved orthodox mysticism", such as that of Dionysius or Symeon the New Theologian, but insists that the church authorities have often been afraid of the mystics and distrusted them. Berdyaev also points to the potential of the mystical writings for surpassing narrow, confessional boundaries.[18] Bulgakov in contrast does not see a strong tension between the official teaching of the Church and the work of the mystics.

Although what might be called the apophaticism of Dionysian inspiration played a constructive role in Bulgakov's *Unfading Light*, the situation changed during his third, "theological" period. In his great trilogy *On Godmanhood*, comprising *The Lamb of God* (1933), *The Comforter* (1936), and *The Bride of the Lamb* (written in 1939, posthumously published in 1945), the distinctive epistemic concerns of apophatic theology have receded into the background. For example, while covering in *The Bride of the Lamb* many of the same subjects as he had a quarter century earlier in *The Unfading Light*, Bulgakov no longer engages the *CD* or the broader apophatic tradition in any depth. Vladimir Lossky correctly criticizes Bulgakov's sophiological speculations for lacking apophatic reserve.[19] Bulgakov tends to "eternalize" the content of revelation, folding the events of salvation history into the inner life of the Trinity, with the result that the distinction between the divine economy and the immanent Trinity all but disappears.

The points of continuity between Dionysius and the Russian sophiologists (Solovyov and Bulgakov) are, strictly speaking, meager. What unites them is a common trajectory of Christian Platonism. Like Dionysius, they insist upon the foundational significance of mystical theology. However, if for Dionysius the paradigm of this theology is provided by the ecstatic, ineffable union with God, completely imageless and surpassing all powers of perception and intellect, for the Russian philosophers, in contrast, the experiential paradigm is given by the image of the eternal feminine in the figure of Sophia, the Wisdom of God. Perhaps the contrast between apophatic and sophiological mystical theologies should not be drawn too sharply, since one aspect of sophiology is the awareness of the eternal beauty of God in creation, which has some parallels with Dionysius' vision of the cosmos as a complex hierarchy of symbols bespeaking the beauty of God.

Still, the Dionysian version of Christian Platonism sharply differs from that of the Russian sophiologists in another respect. Sophiology baptizes Platonism and "Platonizes" revelation by transforming the divine incarnation into a general metaphysical principle of Godmanhood, the principle by means of which the material cosmos and humanity acquire their ontological link, eternal ground and transformative potential in God. Despite recent attempts to defend Dionysius on this score, it is obvious to most commentators that his cosmology does not account for the centrality of the divine incarnation in a comparably strong way.[20] Russian sophiology is a version of Christian panentheism that in the final analysis does not do justice to the apophatic dimension. Dionysian Platonism is a form of Christian apophaticism that has a tendency to obfuscate the importance of the incarnation. Where Dionysius speaks apophatically about the things revealed,[21] the Russian sophiologists presume to speak cataphatically about the things hidden.

Vladimir Lossky and Christos Yannaras

Bulgakov's younger contemporary, Vladimir Lossky, was also one of his most unwavering critics. When the controversial elements of Bulgakov's sophiology came to the attention of the Russian Orthodox ecclesiastical authorities, it was Lossky who compiled a comprehensive report on the basis of which the head of the Russian Church, Metropolitan Sergius Stragorodskii (1867–1944), and the synod of the Patriarchate of Moscow issued their condemnation of Bulgakov's system.[22] Lossky conceived of the project of modern Orthodox theology very differently from Bulgakov and Berdyaev. Together with Georges Florovsky, Lossky was at the forefront of the "return to the Fathers" in Eastern Orthodox theology, a movement that was coterminous and developed in conversation with the Roman Catholic *ressourcement* movement in Europe, which was particularly influential in France.

Both Florovsky and Lossky saw the post-Palamite Orthodox theology of the last four hundred years as becoming increasingly more captive to the theological categories of the "West".[23] For them, Orthodox theology's liberation hinged on a strongly apologetic re-reading of the Eastern Fathers. This led both authors, on the one hand, to exaggerate the historical continuity of the Eastern Fathers of untainted orthodoxy, overlooking more problematic features of their theologies, and, on the other hand, to tend to establish rigid, sometimes even impenetrable intellectual boundaries between the "East" and the "West". Florovsky's "neopatristic synthesis" aimed at a comprehensive recovery of all aspects of patristic thought, with an emphasis on the contribution of the early Fathers and the Seven Ecumenical Councils. Lossky's work, in contrast, looked to Byzantium, and especially to Gregory Palamas as the theologian who achieved the definitive synthesis. For this reason, Lossky's project, subsequently continued by John Meyendorff and others, has been referred to as Neopalamism. This project may be viewed as the theological antipode to Neothomism.

If one were to name one patristic author who influenced Lossky's theological vision most, it would be Dionysius.[24] Lossky began his scholarly career by publishing an article on the apophaticism of the Areopagite.[25] The study of various forms of *via negativa* and related epistemological issues remained a focal concern throughout his life, and is especially prominent in *The Mystical Theology of the Eastern Church* (1944), the book for which Lossky justly became well-known in the West. In his article "The Elements of 'Negative Theology' in the Thought of Saint Augustine" Lossky distinguishes between apophaticism as a speculative method and as a religious attitude towards the incomprehensibility of God.[26] Lossky criticizes the Thomistic tradition for its tendency to downplay the role of the *via negativa* and to subordinate it to the *via positiva*. For Aquinas, as Lossky interprets him, the method of negation amounts to a qualification that no positive predicates apply to God in a finite, creaturely sense. But the predicates can be applied to God analogically, understood in a more elevated sense, befitting God. Lossky contends that the Thomistic form of apophaticism fails to account for Dionysius' insistence that ultimately all talk about God must be abandoned in the unitive experience beyond all words and beyond knowledge.[27] Apophaticism is "above all, an attitude of mind which refuses to form concepts about God".[28] Elsewhere Lossky also criticizes Aquinas's doctrine of analogy on exegetical grounds, arguing that the Latin translation of the *CD* that Aquinas had at his disposal did not do justice to the conceptual richness of the Greek term *analogia*.[29] According to Lossky, *analogia* refers primarily to the creaturely "capacity" or "aptitude" to participate in God.[30] I concur with Florovsky's judgment that "Lossky dismisses the Thomistic versions of the 'negative theology' probably too easily".[31]

Lossky's understanding of apophaticism has had considerable influence upon many twentieth-century Orthodox thinkers, including the Greek theologian Christos Yannaras. In the introduction to his book *On the Absence and Unknowability of God: Heidegger and the Areopagite* (1967) Yannaras observes that the main purpose of his study is "to clarify the difference between Greek thought and the west".[32] If Lossky allows for different kinds of apophaticism in the West, Yannaras mistakenly, but confidently, reduces all forms of Western apophaticism to the method of correcting the limits of analogical predication in natural theology.[33] Like Lossky, he contrasts this view with Dionysian apophaticism properly understood, which points to the experiential immediacy and relatedness of God.

According to Yannaras, the knowledge acquired in an ineffable personal encounter with God surpasses propositional knowledge. Whether the emphasis upon the non-propositional *personal* knowledge of this sort can be credibly derived from the *CD* is rather dubious, although both Yannaras and

Lossky are convinced that it can be. Yannaras goes so far as to make a distinction between the Greek "apophaticism of person" and the Western "apophaticism of essence". This distinction, historically unsupportable, is at odds with the Palamite insistence that it is the essence (or unnamable "super-essence") of God, not the divine persons, that is absolutely incomprehensible.[34] The distinction with which both Orthodox theologians work looks surprisingly close to Bertrand Russell's "knowledge by acquaintance"/ "knowledge by description" distinction, the "I-Thou" theology of Martin Buber, and similar motifs in French existentialism. According to Rowan Williams, "Lossky is able to develop his emphasis on personal encounter in the knowledge of God in a way which at times seems consciously and deliberately to echo philosophers like Sartre."[35] It appears that the Eastern Orthodox theologians are fighting the misguided "West" with ammunition borrowed from the enemy.

Having defined Dionysian apophaticism as "the abandonment of every conceptual necessity" and "the annihilation of all conceptual idols of God",[36] Yannaras transfers this concept into the context of contemporary European nihilism and agnosticism. Yannaras argues that the Enlightenment and later critique of Christianity applies to the "conceptual idol of God" or to the God of Western European natural theology. When Nietzsche's superman proclaimed the death of God, it was the God of Western rationalism and scholasticism that became defunct. The God of Dionysian apophaticism cannot be conceptually attacked, because this deity cannot be conceptually expressed. It is impossible to prove or disprove the existence of a God who surpasses being, as well as all other categories of human thought. Yannaras resonates with Heidegger's critique of ontotheology, but criticizes the German philosopher for failing to see the connection between his philosophy of being and Dionysius' ontology. Although Yannaras's position has been rightly criticized for being dangerously close to agnosticism, the parallels that he sees between Heidegger and Dionysius are not without foundation. Like Lossky, he believes that Eastern Orthodox theology, when purified of Western influences, can withstand the intellectual onslaughts of post-modernity.

Lossky makes Dionysius the centerpiece of the normative master narrative leading from the early Fathers to the fourteenth-century Byzantine theologians, from Clement of Alexandria to Gregory Palamas.[37] In his lectures read at the Sorbonne in 1945–6, subsequently translated into English and published posthumously under the title *The Vision of God* (1963), Lossky likewise accords the central place to his intellectual hero. He sees in the CD the synthesis of all previous patristic discussion of the possibility of direct, unmediated experience of God.[38] Earlier patristic authors, such as Clement and Origen, are viewed against the norm of Dionysian mystical theology. Clement's account of the vision of God is deemed "intellectualist" on the grounds that such experience allegedly involves exclusively intellectual faculties, exalts the knowledge of God above salvation, and is not quite as radically apophatic as that of Dionysius.[39] Origen is similarly accused of "intellectualism", for he construed divine incomprehensibility as a function of the limitations of created, rational beings.[40] Eunomius represents "intellectualism" of the worst kind, since he taught that even the fallen human mind was able to comprehend the essence of God.

Thus the proponents of what Lossky calls the "subjective unknowability of God", Clement, Origen, and Eunomius, are contrasted with the Cappadocian Fathers, Dionysius, and other patristic writers of unblemished orthodoxy as the advocates of the "objective unknowability of God", that is, the view that God's essence cannot be known in principle, even by the deified intellect.[41] The *CD* becomes, on Lossky's reading, a "dogmatic basis" for the distinction, already inherent in the thought of the Cappadocian Fathers and most fully developed by Gregory Palamas, between the unknowable essence and the uncreated, but cognitively accessible, energies of God.

Lossky's aim is to show the profound continuity between Dionysius and Palamas. For the purpose of this largely apologetic task Lossky makes Dionysius appear more orthodox than he really was. Although dependent upon Proclus (Lossky more often speaks of Plotinus in this context), Dionysius is credited with modifying the Neoplatonic scheme by making both Trinity and oneness equally inapplicable to the superessence of God.[42] Lossky adds that Dionysian apophaticism does not relativize the trinitarian distinctions, which inhere in the divine essence.[43] In defense of this claim, which on the surface appears to be in tension with the *CD*'s radical apophaticism, he points to the Dionysian distinction between the "unified names", such as power and goodness, which apply to the Godhead as a whole, and the "differentiated names" of the Father, Son, and Holy Spirit, which refer to the divine persons. Recent scholarship seems to support the main thrust of Lossky's interpretation.[44]

In Lossky's scheme the term "Western" has a very strong connotation of "doctrinally questionable". (As the reader may recall, for Yannaras, the "West" also stands for everything that is wrong with theology in general). In other words, a complex geopolitical category has been transformed into the criterion of truth. Lossky's Neopalamite synthesis may be represented by the three concentric circles of ever-increasing doctrinal rigidity. The larger circle would contain all patristic and Byzantine authors and would exclude all Western authors after the Great Schism of 1054. The smaller circle would include all Eastern Fathers of unblemished orthodoxy and would exclude all those regarded by the Church as heterodox. Finally, the third circle would encompass select doctrinally acceptable Eastern Christian mystical theologians with Dionysius in the center.

One feature of the Neopalamite synthesis stands out as particularly pertinent for the present study: Dionysian mystical theology, from which the roads have historically led to most daring speculations (for example, those of Meister Eckhart and John Scotus Eriugena), is turned, after much apologetic effort, into the standard of orthodoxy. Dionysian Hellenism is treated as successfully Christianized, whereas Origenism is dismissed as "Platonic intellectualism and spiritualism alien to the spirit of the gospel".[45]

Lossky's apportionment of blame upon the heretics and praise upon the orthodox theologians is not likely to gain him much credibility among contemporary patristic scholars. Lossky alternatively presents the following view as an *a priori* theological assumption and as a result of historical inquiry: "doctrinal tradition—beacons set up by the Church along the channel of the knowledge of God—cannot be separated from or opposed to mystical tradition: acquired experience of the mysteries of the faith. Dogma cannot be understood apart from experience; the fullness of experience cannot be had apart from true doctrine".[46] Lossky took the CD to be a paradigmatic case of how *theosis* can lead to the heights of speculative theology.

For better or for worse, Lossky's impact on the Western understanding of the normative boundaries and experiential character of Eastern Orthodox theology has been significant, although somewhat exaggerated. This is all the more surprising, if one realizes just how novel Lossky's choice of theological friends and enemies was. As Ysabel de Andia observes, "il était devenu banal de dire [. . .] que Denys a plus influence l'Occident que l'Orient, la position se renverse avec Vladimir Lossky qui fait de Denys le modèle de la théologie mystique de l'Église d'Orient".[47] If Dionysius was for Lossky the synthesis of patristic tradition and the "dogmatic basis" of Byzantine theology, another influential Orthodox churchman, Alexander Schmemann (1921–1983) could write *The Historical Road of Eastern Orthodoxy* (1963) without as much as mentioning Dionysius!

John Meyendorff

While working within the same master narrative, John Meyendorff attempts to break free of the confines of Lossky's *Dogmengeschichte*. In his own approach to doctrinal history, Meyendorff follows the main contours of the same historical narrative leading from the early Fathers to Gregory Palamas. In contrast to Lossky, however, Meyendorff moves the focus of the Palamite master narrative from mystical theology to Christology. Dionysian Christology, as is generally admitted, leaves many questions unanswered.[48] Hence, it is to be expected that in Meyendorff's version of Neopalamism, Dionysius loses his status as the "dogmatic basis" of Byzantine theology (Lossky's classification) to take the backstage and at times even to be turned into an anti-hero. In his early work, *Christ in Eastern Christian Thought* (1969), Meyendorff writes: "If [Dionysius] was successful in the area of *theologia*, his success was much more questionable in the realms of cosmology and ecclesiology, in which the absence of common Christological references made illusory his effort to bridge completely the gap between the Gospel and neo-Platonism".[49]

One of the enduring critical questions that Meyendorff pursued throughout all of his works on Byzantine theology is the relationship between the expressions of Christian thought and practice on the one hand and the intellectual structures of Hellenism on the other hand. Meyendorff follows Florovsky in turning the Harnackian thesis on its head: instead of viewing the history of dogma as a sad saga of the pernicious Hellenization of Christianity, both Russian historians describe the same process as the Christianization of Hellenism.[50] In Florovsky's judgment, it is not patristic theology that needs to be de-Hellenized, but it is rather post-Palamite Orthodox theology that needs to rediscover Christian Hellenism through the Fathers. While Florovsky and Lossky at times tend to smooth the rough edges of this development in order to present the orthodox Fathers in the best possible light, Meyendorff is not as invested as they are in apologetics.

Meyendorff recognizes that the struggle between non-Christian and Christian intellectual currents in Hellenism was prolonged and at times acrimonious. Origen's attempt at Christianizing Platonism represents one of the earliest stages of this process. But a historical theologian—and this is Meyendorff's remarkable insight—should not freeze Origen's alleged failures in time, but consider how Origenism was in turn reworked, partially rejected, and more fully Christianized by the later Fathers. Unlike Lossky, Meyendorff does not present Origen as a failure and Dionysius as a success in the story of the gradual Christianization of Platonism. For Meyendorff, both of them in some respects failed and in other respects were successful.

In Meyendorff's view, Dionysius' endorsement of the hierarchical structure of the Neoplatonic universe is problematic, because it tends to obscure the centrality of God's unmediated becoming man in the incarnation. It also leads Dionysius to a somewhat arbitrary taxonomy of the nine angelic orders, which has "no foundation in Scripture".[51] Still Meyendorff credits Dionysius with having initiated the process of baptizing the hierarchical conception of cosmos by making the hierarchy of being a feature of the created order, not an outcome of the noetic fall, as it was for Origen. In this respect, Dionysius moves one step beyond Origen in Christianizing Neoplatonism.

While criticizing Harnack's Hellenization thesis, in his own approach Meyendorff is equally preoccupied with showing the distinctiveness of Christian theology. Following Lossky, Meyendorff unduly emphasizes the differences between Neoplatonic and Dionysian theological epistemologies. The Neoplatonists are (wrongly) credited with the view that it is possible for the purified human intellect to know the essence of God. For Dionysius, as we saw earlier with Bulgakov and Lossky, God is absolutely incomprehensible in his essence, not due to any creaturely limitations.[52] In ecstatic experience God reveals himself to the deified mind as surpassing all knowledge and understanding. Meyendorff holds that these epistemic and ontological differences enable Dionysian apophaticism to point to the reality of the living God of scripture, not the knowable God of the philosophers. In assuming such a sharp dichotomy between the *deus philosophorum*, which can be conceptually grasped, and the "biblical" *deus absconditus*, Meyendorff comes dangerously close to Harnack's methodological dichotomy between the gospel and Hellenism, meanwhile consistently questioning Harnack's historical conclusions. Both scholars start with the presupposition that to be authentically Christian a given doctrine must be dissimilar from anything recognizably Hellenic.

Meyendorff finds Dionysius' theology in need of further correction in the area of ecclesiology. He claims that Dionysius' conception of celestial and ecclesiastical hierarchies is static and artificial. Dionysius' attempt to correlate the three stages of the spiritual progress—purification, illumination, and perfection—with the threefold ministerial orders of deacons, priests, and "hierarchs" (Dionysius' preferred term for bishops) does not correspond well to their liturgical functions in the Church of his time. The most serious problem is that "the relationships between God and man are conceived in a purely individualistic manner and are completely determined by the system of intermediaries".[53]

More damaging is Meyendorff's critique that Dionysius' liturgical theology reduces the material objects used in ritual activity to the symbols of higher, immaterial reality. According to Meyendorff, Dionysius' theology of the Eucharist is insufficiently Christological and incarnational. In his later work Meyendorff became increasingly more critical of the CD and found Dionysius' "static" hierarchical vision and symbolic liturgical theology responsible for what the Russian historian saw as the Byzantine abuses of earlier patristic practices, including clericalism.[54] Along similar lines, Paul Wesche argues that the CD fails to account for the soteriological significance of the transformation of the human body and material creation and, in the final analysis, "renders superfluous the incarnation of Christ".[55]

Similarly negative conclusions have been a part of the Protestant and Roman Catholic readings of the CD for quite some time. Meyendorff's and Wesche's criticism provoked two other Orthodox scholars, Alexander Golitzin and Eric Perl, to attempt to restore Dionysius to the diptychs.[56] Eric Perl aims to meet Wesche's criticism by arguing that Dionysius' symbolic ontology offers a sacramental vision of the world, since the entire cosmos participates in the divine energies. Perl writes:

> Dionysius represents precisely those doctrines which are most typical of Orthodoxy in distinction from the west: creation as theophany; grace as continuous with nature; knowledge as union of knower and known; Incarnation and sacrament as fulfillment, not exception or addition; liturgy as the realization of the cosmos; mysticism as ontological union rather than psychological condition; sin as corruption and loss of being, not legalistic transgression; atonement as physical-ontological

assumption, not justification or juridical satisfaction; hierarchy as service and love, not oppression and envy.[57]

While the precise correlation between the Dionysian participatory metaphysics of symbols and sacramental realism remains debatable, it is clear that the inclusion of the *CD* into the Orthodox tradition has historically required from John of Scythopolis, Maximus the Confessor, Gregory Palamas, and others, and continues to require, much apologetic effort.

Conclusion

The reception of the *CD* into the bosom of Byzantine theology may be compared to the impact that the famous Grecian horse had on Troy: *timeo Danaos et dona ferentes*.[58] If I may be permitted to paraphrase Virgil, *timeo Dionysium et dona ferentem*. Beware of Dionysius, even if he brings gifts! The reception of the Dionysian gifts into Eastern Orthodox theology has been intertwined with an uneasy quest for its modern identity. While both Lossky and Meyendorff are in agreement that Dionysius is better understood if read through the eyes of Palamas, not through the eyes of Aquinas, they come to very different conclusions. For Lossky, Dionysian mystical theology points to the experiential ground of all theological discourse. Dionysian mystical theology is turned into the criterion of earlier patristic thought on the knowledge of God and the "dogmatic ground" of Byzantine theology. Along with the Cappadocian Fathers, Dionysius is also viewed as the mastermind of the foundational distinction between the unknowable essence and the knowable energies of God. To borrow Luther's expression to make an un-Lutheran point, Dionysian apophaticism is, in Lossky's master narrative, *articulus stantis et cadentis ecclesiae*.

Meyendorff agrees with Lossky that Dionysius' religious epistemology does not fall into some of the traps into which earlier Christian Platonists, such as Clement and Origen, fell. The historical signposts of Meyendorff's account are the same: the selective emphasis upon the Greek patristic authorities culminating in the "Palamite synthesis" of the fourteenth century. However, since Meyendorff's organizing theme is the development of Christology, in contrast to Lossky's and Bulgakov's emphasis on mystical theology, Dionysius' role changes from that of "the true father of mysticism" (Bulgakov) and "dogmatic ground" (Lossky) to that of *enfant terrible* in need of baptism with much water. Lossky regards Dionysian Platonism as authentically Christian. For Meyendorff and his followers the matter is more complex: Dionysius' system, while it continues the Christianization of Platonism, requires a "Christological corrective", provided by Maximus the Confessor and Palamas, among others.

Russian sophiology represents a different way of thinking through the metaphysical implications of integrating Neoplatonic idealism and incarnation. Sophiology, while correctly emphasizing the sacramentality of material creation, takes a different form of religious experience as paradigmatic. In sophianic mysticism the images of divine beauty are not superseded by the utterly imageless and ineffable experience of God, a distinguishing feature of Dionysian apophaticism. Nor are Bulgakov and Berdyaev preoccupied with offering a normative metanarrative of Eastern Orthodox theology, purified of Western influences, as are Lossky and Meyendorff. The scope of Bulgakov's and Berdyaev's interests is broader and is less conditioned by the rigid dichotomy between the theologically orthodox East and the heterodox West. Both of them are prepared to admit that mystical theology and doctrinal orthodoxy were sometimes at odds with each other.

In contrast to Berdyaev, Meyendorff claims, following Lossky, that "Byzantium never knew any conflict, not even a polarization between theology and what the West calls 'mysticism'".[59] Both Lossky and Meyendorff turn the normative claim about the ideal relationship between mystical theology and dogmatic theology into a descriptive generalization about the historical development of Byzantine theology. Such a conflation of theological desideratum with what purports to be a historical description is a peculiar temptation of the Orthodox reading of the patristic past.

Lossky, and Yannaras, are deeply invested in "de-Westernizing" Dionysius and presenting his theology as an authentic form of Christian Hellenism. In my judgment, these apologetic preoccupations, on the one hand, make these scholars turn a blind eye to the CD's more problematic features and, on the other hand, allow the quest for historical and theological truth to be driven by the quest for Orthodox theological identity vis-à-vis the Christian West.

Dionysius himself, however, appears to have been more interested in seeking truth, rather than identity labels: "As far as I am concerned I have never spoken out against the Greeks or any others. In my view, good men are satisfied to know and to proclaim as well as they can the truth itself as it really is."[60] For Dionysius truth-seeking was far too important to be subordinated to some other task, even the legitimate quest for one's religious identity in an intellectually fractured world.

NOTES

1 For a discussion of this issue, see Andrew Louth's first contribution to this volume.
2 Jaroslav Pelikan, *The Christian Tradition* (Chicago, IL: University of Chicago Press, 1971), I, p. 348; Cf. John Meyendorff, *Christ in Eastern Christian Thought* (Crestwood, NY: St Vladimir's Seminary Press, 1975; French original published in 1969), p. 92.
3 Considerations of space will not allow treating the important contributions of Paul Wesche, Andrew Louth, Eric Perl, and Alexander Golitzin here.
4 For a similar methodological move, see the study of Aristotle Papanikolaou, *Being with God: Trinity, Apophaticism, and Divine-Human Communion* (Notre Dame, IN: University of Notre Dame Press, 2006), pp. 1, 163.
5 I am aware of the postmodern objections to the legitimacy of the distinction between identity and truth claims. I would argue that these objections are self-referentially and performatively contradictory, but I cannot enter into the details of this argument here.
6 Lev Zander, *Bog i mir* (Paris: YMCA Press, 1948), pp. 29–39.

7   An alternative English rendering of this term is "divine humanity". I prefer "Godman-hood", to keep the term etymologically close to "Godman" (*Bogochelovek*).
8   Pavel Florensky, *The Pillar and Ground of the Truth* (Princeton, NJ: Princeton University Press, 1997), pp. 106–123; Bulgakov, *Svet Nevechernii*, pp. 88–92.
9   *MT* 5, 1048A.
10 *Svet Nevechernii*, p. 130.
11 *Svet Nevechernii*, p. 105.
12 Plotinus, *Enneads*, VI. 9. 3: "strictly speaking, we ought not to apply any terms at all to It [the One]; but we should, so to speak, run round the outside of It trying to interpret our own feelings about It, sometimes drawing near and sometimes falling away in our perplexities about It", trans. A. H. Armstrong, *Plotinus*, LCL 440 (Cambridge, MA: Harvard University Press, 2000), p. xv. Cf. *Enneads*, III. 8. 10; V. 3. 13. See also J. M. Rist, *Plotinus: The Road to Reality* (Cambridge: Cambridge University Press, 1967), p. 25.
13 *Svet Nevechernii*, p. 108. Bulgakov's contemporary, a little known émigré philosopher Boris Vysheslavtsev spoke of Dionysius' vindication of *eros* in the *CH* as "a monumental system of 'sublimation'". See, *Etika preobrazhennogo erosa* [*The Ethics of Transfigured Eros*] (Moskva: Respublika, 1994, first published in Paris in 1931), p. 47. Olivier Clement speaks of Diony-sius as the "poet of erotic love", *The Roots of Christian Mysticism* (London: New City Press, 1995), p. 22.
14 Bulgakov's contemporary Semen Frank developed, in a deeply original way, the idea that every act of cognition is surrounded by a transrational ocean of incomprehensible reality in his *Nepostizhimoe* [*The Incomprehensible*] (Paris, 1939).
15 *Svet Nevechernii*, p. 130.
16 N. Berdyaev, *Filosofiia svobodnogo dukha* (Moskva: Respublika, 1994), p. 431.
17 *Freedom and the Spirit* (New York, NY: Arno Press, 1935/1972), pp. xiv–xix.
18 *Freedom and the Spirit*, p. 258.
19 Vladimir Lossky, *The Mystical Theology of the Eastern Church* (Crestwood, NY: St. Vladimir's Seminary Press, 2002; original published in French in 1944), p. 80.
20 For a more charitable reading of Dionysius on this issue, see the recent work of Alexander Golitzin, "Dionysius Areopagites in the Works of Saint Gregory Palamas: On the Question of a "Christological Corrective" and Related Matters", in B. Lourié and A. Orlov (eds), *The Theophaneia School: Jewish Roots of Eastern Christian Mysticism* (St Petersburg: Vizantino-rossika, 2007), pp. 83–105; " 'Suddenly, Christ': The Place of Negative Theology in the Mystagogy of Dionysius Areopagites", in M. Kessler and C. Sheppard (eds), *Mystics: Presence and Aporia* (Chicago, IL: University of Chicago Press, 2003), pp. 8–37.
21 See *Ep*. 3, 1069B.
22 V. Lossky, *Spor o Sofii* [*The Sophia Debate*] (Moskva: Izdatel'stvo Sviato-Vladimirskovo Brat-stva, 1996; first published in French in 1954), pp. 7–79.
23 The first study that fleshed out this agenda was Florovsky's influential *The Ways of Russian Theology* (1937). Berdyaev aptly dubbed this book "the waywardness (*besput'e*) of Russian theology", since Florovsky's goal was largely negative: to show that Russian theology has abandoned its patristic foundations.
24 For Lossky's interpretation of Dionysius' apophaticism, see A. Papanikolaou, *Being with God*, pp. 12–25.
25 "Otrizatel'noe bogoslovie v uchenii Dionisiia Areopagita", *Seminarium Kondakovianum*, 3 (1929), pp. 133–144.
26 "Elementy otrizatel'nogo bogosloviia v myshlenii blazhennogo Avgustina", in *Spor o Sofii*, p. 128; cf. "The Theology of Light in the Theology of St. Gregory Palamas", in *In the Image and Likeness of God* (Crestwood, NY: St Vladimir's Seminary Press, 2001), p. 51.
27 "Apophasis and Trinitarian Theology", in *In the Image and Likeness of God*, p. 26. See *DN* 1. 1, 588B; 7. 3, 872A.
28 *Mystical Theology*, pp. 38–39.
29 Lossky, "La notion des 'analogies' chez Denys le Pseudo-Aréopagite", *Archives d'Histoire Doctrinale et Littéraire du Moyen-Age*, 5 (1931), pp. 279–309. This interpretation is also accepted by J. Meyendorff, *Christ in Eastern Christian Thought*, p. 95.
30 Lossky's reading has recently been endorsed by Ysabel de Andia, *Henosis: L'union à Dieu chez Denys l'Aréopagite* (Leiden: E. J. Brill, 1996), pp. 101–103 and supported by Raoul Mortley, *From Word to Silence* (Bonn: Hanstein, 1986), II., pp. 226–227.

31   G. Florovsky, "Review of *The Mystical Theology of the Eastern Church*", *Journal of Religion*, 38 (1958), p. 207. For a nuanced treatment of Dionysius' influence on Aquinas, see Wayne J. Hankey, "Dionysian Hierarchy in Thomas Aquinas", in Ysabel de Andia (ed), *Denys l'Aréopagite et sa postérité en Orient et en Occident* (Paris: Institut d'Études Augustiniennes, 1997), pp. 405–438. For a recent attempt to account for the variety of *viae negativae* stemming from Dionysius, see Jan Miernowski, *Le dieu néant: theologies negatives à l'aube des temps modernes* (Leiden: E. J. Brill, 1998).
32   *On the Absence and Unknowability of God: Heidegger and the Areopagite* (New York: T&T Clark International, 2005), p. 15.
33   *On the Absence and Unknowability of God*, p. 28. Dumitrou Staniloae offers a particularly uncompromising version of this position: "If Roman Catholic theology reduces all the knowledge of God to knowledge from a distance, Eastern theology reduces it to a theology of participation in various degrees which are ascended through purification", *The Experience of God*, trans. Ioan Ionita and Robert Barringer (Brookline, MA: Holy Cross Orthodox Press, 1998), p. 112.
34   *On the Absence and Unknowability of God*, pp. 71, 87.
35   "The *Via Negativa* and the Foundations of Theology: An Introduction to the Thought of V. N. Lossky", in Stephen Sykes and Derek Holmes (eds), *New Studies in Theology* (London: Duckworth, 1980), p. 111.
36   *On the Absence and Unknowability of God*, p. 73.
37   A very different trajectory is explored in his dissertation on Meister Eckhart *Théologie negative et connaissance de Dieu chez maître Eckhart* (Paris: Vrin, 1960).
38   *The Vision of God* (Bedfordshire: The Faith Press, 1973), p. 103. Lossky finds in the *CD* a form of the doctrine of the spiritual senses, but does not discuss any specific texts.
39   Lossky quotes Clement's statement that salvation and the knowledge of God are "absolutely identical" and then proceeds to argue against the text: "Whatever Clement may say, the contemplation of God and eternal salvation are actually separate here, if only in thought", *The Vision of God*, p. 45. Lossky's exegetical *faux pas* is followed by John Meyendorff, *Byzantine Theology: Historical Trends and Doctrinal Themes* (New York, NY: Fordham University Press, 1983; first published in 1974), p. 13.
40   Origen's position on divine (in)comprehensibility is complex and not entirely consistent. For a valuable discussion, see J. M. Dillon, "The Knowledge of God in Origen", *Knowledge of God in the Graeco-Roman World* (Leiden: E. J. Brill, 1988), pp. 219–228; H. F. Hägg, *Clement of Alexandria and the Beginnings of Christian Apophaticism* (Oxford: Oxford University Press, 2006), pp. 255–257.
41   *The Image and Likeness of God*, p. 35.
42   *The Vision of God*, p. 101.
43   "Apophaticheskoe bogoslovie v uchenii Dionisiia Areopagita", in *Spor o Sofii*, pp. 101–102; cf. *Mystical Theology*, p. 65. G. Florovsky similarly claims that "Dionysius makes a distinction between general Divine names, which he applies to the entire Holy Trinity, and *hypostatic* names", *The Byzantine Ascetic and Spiritual Fathers* (Belmont, MA: Büchervertriebsanstalt, 1987), X, p. 220.
44   John N. Jones, "The Status of the Trinity in Dionysian Thought", *Journal of Religion*, 80 (2000), pp. 645–657; Jeffrey Fisher, "The Theology of Dis/similarity: Negation in Pseudo-Dionysius", *Journal of Religion*, 81 (2001), pp. 529–548; Ysabel de Andia, *Henosis*, pp. 29–49.
45   *The Vision of God*, p. 55. Cf. Meyendorff, *Byzantine Theology*, p. 13.
46   *Mystical Theology*, p. 236.
47   Y. de Andia, *Henosis*, p. 452.
48   G. Florovsky, *The Byzantine Ascetic and Spiritual Fathers*, p. 225.
49   *Christ in Eastern Christian Thought*, p. 100.
50   G. Florovsky, "Faith and Culture", *St. Vladimir's [Theological] Quarterly* 4, (1955–6), p. 40; J. Meyendorff, *Byzantine Theology*, pp. 1–31.
51   *Christ in Eastern Christian Thought*, p. 102; *Byzantine Theology*, p. 28.
52   *Christ in Eastern Christian Thought*, pp. 93–95; *Byzantine Theology: Historical Trends and Doctrinal Themes* (New York, NY: Fordham University Press, 1983; first published in 1974), p. 12. Meyendorff follows Lossky's questionable distinction between the One of Plotinus and the God of Dionysius, who transcends all concepts, including the concept of oneness. See *Christ in Eastern Christian Thought*, p. 101.

53 *Christ in Eastern Christian Thought*, 104. The charge of individualism was later addressed by Andrew Louth in his monograph *Denys the Areopagite* (Wilton, CT: Morehouse-Barlow, 1989), pp. 18, 131–133. Louth reconstructs the social and liturgical context of the *CD*'s theology and argues that the concept of the hierarchy presupposes the interdependence and harmonious connection of lower and higher orders. The hierarchy is constituted by the members of the church and, more broadly conceived, comprises the whole cosmos. Hence, the claim that Dionysian mystical theology is individualistic is without serious foundation.
54 Meyendorff, *Vvedenie v sviatootecheskoe bogoslovie* [*Introduction to Patristic Theology*], second edn. (Moskva: VIMO, 1985), pp. 292–295; *Byzantine Theology*, p. 28.
55 K. P. Wesche, "Christological Doctrine and Liturgical Interpretation in Pseudo-Dionysius", *Saint Vladimir's Theological Quarterly*, 33 (1989), pp. 63–64.
56 Eric J. D. Perl, "Symbol, Sacrament, and Hierarchy in Saint Dionysios the Areopagite", *Greek Orthodox Theological Review*, 39 (1994), pp. 311–356; Alexander Golitzin, :"'On the Other Hand' [A Response to Fr Paul Wesche's Recent Article on Dionysius," *Saint Vladimir's Theological Quarterly*, 34 (1990), pp. 305–323. Considerations of space do not allow doing justice to Perl's important article "The Metaphysics of Love in Dionysius the Areopagite", *The Journal of Neoplatonic Studies*, 6 (1998), pp. 45–73, and to Golitzin's extensive work on Dionysius here.
57 Perl, "Symbol, Sacrament, and Hierarchy in Saint Dionysios the Areopagite", p. 356.
58 Virgil, *Aeneid* II. 49.
59 Meyendorff, *Byzantine Theology*, p. 13.
60 *Ep.* 7. 1, 1077C.

13

DIONYSIUS, DERRIDA, AND THE CRITIQUE OF "ONTOTHEOLOGY"

MARY-JANE RUBENSTEIN

A Warm(ish) Welcome

The question of Jacques Derrida's reception of Pseudo-Dionysius—and more broadly, of the hospitality deconstruction offers to or withholds from negative theology of the Dionysian tradition—can be traced back to Derrida's 1968 lecture, *"Différance,"* in which he first sketched the contours of this notoriously slippery pseudo-concept. Marked by an inaudible "a," *différance* encodes equiprimordial processes of spatial differentiation and temporal delay. "In a conceptuality adhering to classical strictures," Derrida explains, " *'différance'* would be said to designate a constitutive, productive, and originary causality, the process of scission and division which would produce or constitute different things or differences."[1] Derrida claims, however, that "classical conceptuality" can never quite get a grip on this aboriginal *mouvance*, because *différance* gives rise to conceptuality in the first place. Neither a word nor an idea, *différance* opens the possibility of representations themselves, thereby exceeding and preceding all of them. This movement of difference and delay can therefore be said to be neither present nor absent, neither passive nor active; before darkness and light, beyond good and evil.

Particularly in the context of this particular collection of chapters, Derrida's twentieth-century address to the *Société français de philosophie* seems positively haunted by Dionysius' sixth-century address (by way of Timothy) to the Trinity that dwells "considerably prior" to all oppositions, "beyond privations, beyond every denial, beyond every assertion."[2] Like *différance*, the Trinity is "higher than any being, any divinity, any goodness."[3] Like *différance*, it exceeds the metaphysical distinctions of which it is the transcendent Cause. And indeed, Derrida acknowledges in the opening minutes of

Mary-Jane Rubenstein
Department of Religion, Wesleyan University, Middletown, CT 06459, USA
mrubenstein@wesleyan.edu

this lecture that *différance* does tend to collide strategically with apophatic discourse: "already we have had to delineate *that différance is not*, does not exist, is not a present-being (*on*) in any form; and we will be led to delineate also everything *that* it *is not*, that is, *everything*; and consequently that it has neither existence nor essence. It derives from no category of being, whether present or absent." At one level, then, *différance* seems at times to be "indistinguishable from negative theology."[4]

"And yet," he goes on to say, "those aspects of *différance* which are thereby delineated are not theological, not even in the order of the most negative of negative theologies." The reason Derrida is so intent upon making this distinction is that, as he understands it, negative theologies "are always concerned with disengaging a superessentiality beyond the finite categories of essence and existence, that is, of presence, and always hastening to recall that God is refused the predicate of existence, only in order to acknowledge his superior, inconceivable, and ineffable mode of being."[5] Negative theology, in other words, ultimately services an ultra-positive theology. At the end of the day, even "the most negative of negative theologies" knows where it comes from, where it is going, and how to get there. *Différance*, by contrast, neither is nor has any arche-teleological anchor: no being above being, good beyond being, or God without being to govern the play of signs it unleashes. The clarity of this distinction notwithstanding, the first scholar to respond from the floor in 1968 insisted that *différance* could not be disentangled from the apophatic Creator: "It is the source of everything and one cannot know it," he argued; "it is the God of negative theology." Derrida's infamous response: "It is and it is not. It is above all not."[6]

As Derrida will acknowledge eighteen years later, however, such a disavowal gets him into a bit of a bind. If negative theology operates by means of denial, how exactly is one meant to go about denying that one is doing negative theology? If "the most negative of negative theologies" leads the apophatic voyager to God, then how is one meant to say, "no, I'm not heading for God"? Underscoring this difficulty, Derrida calls his most thorough treatment of the work of Dionysius in relation to his own, "How to Avoid Speaking: Denials [*Dénégations*]." On the one hand, he explains, deconstruction and Dionysius (and Eckhart, who is woven into the analysis) share a certain strategy of denial. Both assert that "predicative language is inadequate" to that which sets it in motion; both are marked by a series of neither/nors that provoke the collapse of binary language; and both can be named by nearly every name, but encompassed by none.[7] Recalling the initial reception of *différance*, Derrida reminds his audience that "very early, I was accused of . . . resifting the procedures of negative theology,"[8] and of falling prey to the same errors to which apophaticism is purportedly inclined: atheism; nihilism; speaking without really saying anything; and worst of all, creating a "secret society"—a brooding "Mafia" of followers who speak a language no one else understands, as if possessed of some private revelation.[9]

Having given voice to all these strategic and accusative alliances, however, Derrida goes on to say—without footnote, qualification, or parenthetical remark—"No, what I write is not negative theology."[10] Of course, it is tempting to recuperate even this denial under the apophatic tent, and Derrida concedes that "this reading will always be possible. Who could prohibit it? In the name of what?"[11] That having been said, the reason Derrida keeps trying to deny what might, in the end, be undeniable is twofold: first, he is attempting to shed the unfortunate image of Theoretical Mafioso. Deconstruction does not—or ought not to—gather a "secret society" around itself because, as John Caputo emphasizes, "the secret is there is no secret."[12] There is no arcane language, practice, or revelation; no decoder ring; no need to purify oneself from the crowds before approaching the unspeakable A of *différance*.[13] By comparison, the Neoplatonic politics and rigid ecclesiology of Dionysius seems—from this perspective—unregenerately exclusivist and hierarchical.[14] Secondly, Derrida maintains that Dionysius, like Eckhart, only denies the predicates of God in order to attribute them to him even more strongly, so that for all its darkness and unknowing, the apophatic voyage retains a determinate *telos*, and is guided "unerringly"[15] by "the promise of a presence."[16] For these reasons, while deconstruction has everything to do with negative theology, it also "has nothing to do with negative theology."[17] In other words, "it is and it is not."

Because this disavowal of apophaticism remains persistently—almost comically—apophatic, it has prompted an outpouring of scholarship. There is an uncanny relationship, these studies suggest, between the deconstruction opened by the death of God and the *via negativa* guided by the living one.[18] Ranking among "the most negative of negative" theologians, Dionysius has been the focal point of many of these variously theological, post-theological, and a/theological perspectives projects. Unsurprisingly, critical theorists with an interest in keeping the *saeculum* secular have tended to overemphasize the prodigious differences between Derrida and Dionysius. Conversely, theologians with an interest in remaining relevant (and employed) in the midst of the ever-imminent ontotheological collapse tend to overemphasize the compelling similarities. It is with this latter "half" of the conversation that I will be most concerned here, mainly because its stakes are so high. If only the gap between these post- and pre-modern negativities could be closed, contemporary theology seems to say wistfully, then we could be assured once and for all that the Trinity is not a transcendental signified; that the God of revelation is not "the God of the philosophers"; that the dead God was never God to begin with. And yet, the sheer proliferation of these studies indicates that neither Derrida nor Dionysius provides such assurance. Is God really a hyper-essence? Is apophaticism really deconstructive? Is deconstruction really apophatic? After all the monographs, edited volumes, articles, lectures, and international conferences, the bottom line seems genuinely to be: "it is and it is not."

At this juncture, it seems important to note that the peri-theological conversation between deconstruction and apophaticism has been almost entirely *linguistic*; that is to say, it has never quite entered the terrain of the ethico-political. This is striking, considering that in Derrida's later work, the political implications of deconstruction become clearer: by provoking the collapse of every totalizing pretension, deconstruction welcomes the emergence of that which totalities exclude. In this chapter, I hope therefore to accomplish two things: first, to set out the critique of ontotheology as groundwork for the conversation at hand, and secondly, to re-examine Dionysius through a more political Derridean lens. Ultimately, I will suggest that establishing a lasting consonance between these thinkers will depend on the relations to otherness in Dionysius; in particular, those grounded by hierarchy and teleology. Does hierarchy for Dionysius function strictly "vertically," bringing a few chosen souls into union with God, or does it also establish ethical relations between and among creatures? And whatever its vectorial specifics, does the *via negativa* draw the soul along a pre-determined path from hyperessence to hyperessence, or might it remain sufficiently indeterminate to welcome the unimaginable?

How Did We Get Here?

Although the term "ontotheology" was brought into common philosophical usage through the work of Martin Heidegger, it first appeared in Immanuel Kant's *Critique of Pure Reason*. For Kant, "ontotheology" designates the philosophical effort to prove God's existence *a priori*, as distinct from "cosmotheology," which endeavors to prove God's existence *a posteriori*.[19] As is well known, Kant accepted the validity of neither approach, dismantling the ontological, cosmological, and teleological proofs of God in fairly rapid succession.[20] This feat, for which Kant earned the title *Der Allzermalmende* (the All-Destroyer), relied on his conviction that reason can know things as they appear (*phenomena*), but can never know things in themselves (*noumena*). God, the archetypal "in itself," fell decidedly for Kant within the realm of the noumenal, and therefore could not be demonstrated through "pure," that is to say, speculative, reason. Justifying pre-emptively his refutation of every proof of God's existence, Kant wrote, "I had to deny knowledge in order to make room for faith."[21] What Kant did *not* write in the first Critique was that faith would not actually get all that much room; he had a different kind of knowledge, and a different kind of proof, waiting in the wings.

In the second Critique, Kant makes what might be called a controlled incursion into the noumenal by designating three "necessary postulates": human freedom, personal immortality, and God.[22] While inaccessible to pure reason, these three are indispensable to practical reason because, in Kant's view, it is impossible to behave morally unless one believes one has: 1) the capacity to choose a moral existence, 2) an infinite amount of time in which to strive after it, and 3) a God who oversees the whole process. In his *Religion within the Limits of Reason Alone*, Kant parlays this final postulate into a "moral proof" of God's existence. To adhere to the moral law, he argues, any ethical subject needs an ethical commonwealth. Any ethical commonwealth needs a common law-giver. And any *moral* law-giver must be able to discern the intentions behind deeds and dispense rewards or punishments accordingly. "But this is the concept of God as moral ruler of the world,"[23] writes Kant, triumphant, having demonstrated that the basic requirements of morality open onto an absolutely necessary (if thoroughly circumscribed) God. With this "moral proof," Kant effectively fills in the space he had carved out for faith, gathering God, religion, and the noumenal itself under the confines of "reason alone." Unwilling to let the unknowable remain unknowable, Kant attempts instead to overcome it by reinstalling God as a (morally helpful) presupposition *a priori*. In short, he resorts to an ontotheological concept of God in order to guarantee the integrity of practical reason.

Over a century later, Martin Heidegger will argue that it is not only Kant who capitulates to ontotheology; rather, the whole history of western metaphysics has refused to abide the unknowable. For Heidegger, metaphysics is *constituted* onto-theologically, by which he means two things: first, that the philosophical concept of "being" has meant nothing more than a property common to all beings, and second, that this fuzzily-conceived property is equated with a presumed "highest being" [*summum ens*], which metaphysics calls God.[24] Conflating being, ordinary beings, and a highest being in this manner, metaphysics has never actually managed to think being at all. Metaphysics thinks it represents being when it represents beings, but fails to realize that being conditions, and therefore eludes, representation itself. As Heidegger explains it, metaphysics represents beings in a certain light, without being able to see the light that allows beings to be in the first place.[25] Or, as he says elsewhere (and here we begin to sense a transition into Derrida), metaphysics calculates the differences between beings, but cannot calculate the incalculable difference that brings differences into being.[26]

What Heidegger argues less often, but no less insistently, is that by equating being with the general run of beings and then identifying this whole ontic mess with God, ontotheology does as much disservice to God as it does to being. Unlike the God who delivers his people from slavery or proclaims good news to the poor, the "God" of metaphysics is merely the first being in a causal chain, the *causa sui* that prevents some dreaded infinite regress. All told, this is a bloodless and boring God, before whom "man" can neither pray nor dance, to whom he would never feel compelled to make a sacrifice.[27] The reason that "man" would not be inclined to give anything over to the *causa sui* is that this "God" is nothing more than a narcissistic projection of "man" in the first place. The thinking self creates him, gives him his lines, and pushes him on stage at the right time: "the deity can come into philosophy only insofar as philosophy, of its own accord and by its own nature, requires and determines that and how the deity enters into it."[28] Ontotheology, in sum, is bad ontology *and* bad theology.

Now Heidegger, at least if we take him at his word, is strictly concerned with rehabilitating the ontological component of thinking. As he insists numerous times in lectures and essays, being is not God; God is not being; and so he is not writing a theology; he has not written a theology; and, as he told an audience in 1951, if he ever *were* to write a theology, "the word 'being' ought not to appear there."[29] Heidegger's lifelong project, despite shifting emphases and fresh neologisms, was rather to recall the truth of being. To the extent that being remains metaphysically unthinkable, Heidegger was thus calling for a thinking of the unthinkable itself, a thinking that would open onto "another beginning" for thought. It is this call to which deconstruction can perhaps best be heard as a response. Like Heidegger, Derrida consistently looks toward a thinking of the unthinkable, in service of the possibility of the impossible.

Where Are We Going?

Although Derrida (and probably Heidegger) would protest vociferously at the comparison, it is perhaps helpful to note the structural similarity between Heideggerian "being" and Derridean *"différance."*[30] In short, both bring into play that which *is*, thereby eluding is-ness itself. Neither can be grasped by the calculations and representations they enable. Both go by many names, but can be encompassed by none of them. And so both of these efforts to unhinge ontotheology lead thinking, once again, toward and away from the Dionysian *via negativa*, with its unknowable, unnameable God.

"I will speak, therefore, of a letter." Thus begins Derrida's lecture on *différance*. This letter, the object of his inaugural promise, is "the first letter": the letter that will set *différance* apart graphically but not phonetically: the letter "A."[31] In the beginning, then, we have an aleph, an alpha; the shadow of the biblical God instantaneously cast over *différance*. Perhaps preferring not to speak of this aleph,[32] Derrida notes instead the resemblance between the A and the shape of the pyramid (managing not to mention it also looks like a mountain). The pyramid is of particular relevance because *différance*, Derrida tells us, proclaims "the death of the tyrant."[33] *Différance*, in other words, sounds the death-knell of the ontotheological God, who nevertheless haunts its every move. This is the reason deconstruction has nothing to do with negative theology, and everything to do with negative theology.

Sympathetic readers of Dionysius—myself included—have been inclined to argue that the Dionysian thearchy bears very little resemblance to Derrida's dead tyrant; that is, to the ontotheological moral guarantor, *summum ens*, *causa sui*, or "transcendental signified" installed as a regulative *punctum* beyond the play of differences.[34] For while it is undoubtedly the case that

Dionysius calls God "being," a "supra-essential subsistence," and "totally undifferentiated," it is also the case that he unsays all of these attributes.[35] Granted, *all* names of God must eventually be unsaid, but good Neoplatonic terms like "being," "essence," and "undifferentiation" can be particularly misleading because the Dionysian God is triune; that is, self-identical only by means of differentiation and relation. Moreover, Dionysius tells us that this internally dynamic thearchy constantly pours itself into the created hierarchies, "carried outside of himself in the loving care he has for everything."[36] Far from remaining transcendentally *in se* like a highest being should, "He is, as it were, beguiled by goodness, by love, and by yearning and is enticed away from his transcendent dwelling place and comes to abide within all things, and he does so by virtue of his supernatural and ecstatic capacity to remain, nevertheless, within himself."[37] Dionysius' God, in other words, refuses to stand still like a good metaphysical lodestone; in fact, it defies the logic of rest and motion, internality and externality. This is the reason the soul must abandon itself as a knowing self before it can be lifted to union with God. As Dionysius advises Timothy, "leave behind you everything perceived and understood, everything perceptible and understandable, all that is not and all that is, and . . . by an undivided and absolute abandonment of yourself and everything, shedding all and freed from all, you will be uplifted to the ray of the divine shadow which is above everything that is."[38]

It is clear, then, that there is a significant conceptual difference between the God to whom Dionysius leads Timothy and the God of modern ontotheology; namely, the Dionysian God refuses to be conceptualized. Rather than securing knowledge, he disables it; rather than affirming human subjectivity, he dismantles it. Rather than performing the role of Archimedean Point, "the Trinity is not in any one location in such a manner as to be 'away from' one place or moving from 'one spot to another.'"[39] Nevertheless, while it is safe to say that Dionysius (at his most negative) stubbornly resists ontotheology, I would submit that he cannot so quickly be called *deconstructive* because of the persistent questions the kind of relations to otherness that Dionysian hierarchy and teleology seem to condone.

As I have mentioned, scholarship on Dionysius and Derrida tends to focus on the "early," "linguistic" period of Derrida's work, rather than on the "later," more explicitly political period. In the *"Différance"* lecture, Derrida had already explained that insofar as deconstruction reveals the inherent instability of all concepts and identities, it unsettles all configurations of domination.[40] What he begins to suggest in his later work is that this structural dismantling opens up possibilities that are, within the reigning structure of things, unthinkable. By revealing the irreducible ambivalence of everyday words, such as hospitality, democracy, and decision, deconstruction pushes ever outward toward a more hospitable hospitality, a more democratic democracy, and a decision that actually decides—all in service of "the undeconstructible" promise of justice.[41] To the extent that justice is never *done*, but always still to-come (*à-venir*), deconstruction functions as "the very experience of the (impossible) possibility of the impossible,"[42] welcoming the coming of the "wholly other" that "the possible" excludes. In this light, deconstruction takes on what Derrida comes to call a "messianic" quality, but "without messianism"; that is to say, without knowing in advance who or what the *à venir* might be, where or when it might come, or for whom.[43]

The relevance of this deconstructive "messianism" to a broadly conceived "religion" has been treated most notably by John Caputo in his *Prayers and Tears of Jacques Derrida*. The relevance of Derrida's later work to *apophaticism*, by contrast, has been all but completely neglected—and perhaps partly owing to Caputo's own strategic fission of the two. "Derrida's religion," Caputo suggests, "is more prophetic than apophatic, more in touch with the Jewish prophets than with Christian Neoplatonists, more messianic and more eschatological than mystical. His writing is more inscribed by the promise, by circumcision, and by the mark of father Abraham than by mystical transports, more like Amos and Isaiah than Pseudo-Dionysius, moved more by prophetico-ethico-political aspiration than by aspiring to be with the One."[44] This separation of the mystical from the political echoes a common enough perception of the apophatic voyager. Traditionally, the "mystical subject" has been construed as individualistic at best and elitist at worst, dragging itself (and a few worthy disciples) up the celestial ranks only to disappear into the divine darkness and leave the rest of the world to its own pathetic devices. Given this set of concerns—seemingly justified by the irreducibly hierarchical constitution of Dionysius' world—it could be the case that any anti-ontotheological retrieval of the Areopagite's work might have the unfortunate side-effect of compromising the sort of justice to which the Algerian calls thinking. This is especially threatening considering Dionysius' instruction to an unruly monk that "justice is pursued when each wishes to give every one his due. And this must always be pursued justly by all, *not beyond their worth and order*."[45]

This irreducibly hierarchical nature of Dionysian justice forms the basis of Derrida's attempt to distance himself from apophasis. *Différance*, he argues, neither establishes nor rules any ontological order; to the contrary, it unsettles all structures of domination, however benevolent they might be. "[*Différance*] governs nothing, reigns over nothing, and nowhere exercises any authority . . . Not only is there no kingdom of *différance*, but *différance* instigates the subversion of every kingdom."[46] Because there is neither king nor kingdom, there is furthermore no "way" to get there. For while Derrida admits that the *via negativa* is a dark and unsettling path, he maintains it is nevertheless a *path* (down the hierarchy and then back up), "leading to union with God."[47] In work on the messianic, Derrida explains that the problem with any such "calculable programme" is that it closes off any opening to something new and unexpected. "Paradoxically," Derrida claims, "the absence of horizon conditions the future itself."[48] For this reason, deconstruction moves without a destination, functioning as a "strategy without finality," or a "blind tactics."[49] And it is precisely this indeterminacy that awaits the coming of the unexpected. The question to be addressed, then, is whether or not these are exhaustive readings of Dionysius. Is it the case that hierarchy can *only* buttress the vertical dominion of certain creatures over others, and of God over all? Does the world-in-the-image-of-the-triune-God simply reaffirm elitist configurations of power? Or might it, in a different light, condition the possibility of unimagined horizontal alliances? Does the cosmic hierarchy invariably serve as a fixed horizon, obstructing the emergence of something genuinely new? Or might the total *agnosia* of the apophatic voyage prepare the way of the *tout autre*?

Hierarchy, Teleology, and the Problem of the Political

It was Dionysius who coined the term "hierarchy," positing it as "a sacred order, a state of understanding, and an activity approximating as closely as possible to the divine."[50] Perhaps for this reason, the Dionysian hierarchies are always articulated in threes: the cosmos is differentiated into spiritual, ecclesiastical, and material orders, themselves triune.[51] So the nine ranks of angels are classed in three groups of three;[52] the Church is arranged into deacons, priests, and bishops; the sacraments into baptism, Eucharist, and chrism; the life of prayer into purification (*katharsis*), contemplation (*theoria*), and union (*henosis*);[53] and the individual soul into appetite, emotion, and reason.[54]

In order to consider the kind of "justice" these hierarchies establish, it is important to note that the Dionysian cosmic order is different from Neoplatonic emanation schemes in two fundamental ways. First, in the same way that God does not rest in himself ontotheologically but rather *is in-ecstasis*, the triune orders in God's image do not simply sit "below" him. Rather, like the Trinity itself,[55] they move in loving relation to one another, both within and between different ranks. For this reason, Dionysius describes the divine intelligences as circling around the Good, diving into creation, and spiraling through all realms, "providing for those beneath them [as] they continue to remain what they are."[56] Similarly, bishops only serve and circle around the Good insofar as they offer guidance to the priests and deacons below them. Likewise all the clergy with respect to the sponsors and catechumens. And so, this constitutive movement and relation within and among striations opens classic emanation onto a different dimension entirely, where motion and rest, identity and difference are non-exclusive.

The other major distinction between Dionysian and Neoplatonic hierarchies is that God does not "trickle down" from seraphim to thrones, from angels to bishops, monks to charging bears, and worms to stones. Rather, as Eric Perl has argued, each creature is, by virtue of the hierarchies, related *directly* to God, who "dwells wholly and immediately in every creature, but in the undifferentiated way which is proper to and constitutive of each one."[57] At the same time, the triune movements within the hierarchies prevent this relation between God and "each one" from collapsing into spiritual solipsism. "There is no opposition between 'direct' and 'mediated' participation in God," Perl explains. "It's one and the same light, that is God himself, which is directly present in the appropriate way at every level."[58] For this reason, each creature becomes fully itself in relation to other creatures *and* to God, "participat[ing] directly in God precisely by occupying . . . its own proper position in the cosmic hierarchy."[59] Or, as Alexander Golitzin puts it, "one does not so much climb *up* our hierarchy, the Church, as enter more fully *into* it."[60] And insofar as the hierarchy images and participates in the thearchy, "entering more fully into hierarchy" amounts to entering more fully into God.

In the language of *The Divine Names* and *The Celestial Hierarchy*, God draws the soul into fuller participation in the hierarchy through love. "Beguiled by goodness,"[61] God pours Godself excessively into creation (*proodos*), which, in turn, is drawn erotically back into God (*epistrophe*). The souls that are drawn into this love become "clear and spotless mirrors reflecting the glow of primordial light and indeed of God himself."[62] Loving divine love by means of divine love, such souls participate in the primordial *generosity* of God: "when its members have received this full and divine splendor they can then pass on this light generously and in accordance with God's will to beings farther down the scale."[63] Granted, this final phrase seems to reinscribe a unidirectional account of relation, "down" the stratified cosmos. But here we should recall the three interwoven movements of all beings, by virtue of which "down" is at the same time up, out, around, and through. "Hence the interrelationship of all things in accordance with capacity. Hence, the harmony and the love which are formed between them but which do not obliterate identity. Hence, the innate togetherness of everything. Hence, too, the intermingling of everything, the persistence of things, the unceasing emergence of things."[64]

Taken on its own, this radical interconnectedness of God and all things might seem to put to rest any concerns about the apophatic subject's purported elitism; to dismantle forever the familiar image of the mystic as "self-absorbed, solitary, narcissistic, and world-renouncing."[65] With his account of the "intermingling of everything" Dionysius clearly indicates that, as Thomas Carlson writes, "proximity to the other and proximity to others" are "inextricably bound."[66] Along this interpretation, there could be no question of the self's abandonment of the wretched world for God, for the wretched world is the means by which we are related to God. Moving more deeply into this possibility, one might even be inclined to draw Dionysian theology into the register of Levinasian ethics, according to which "God" names the infinitely Desirable, who continually redirects our love to the infinitely *un*desirable: the poor, huddled masses around us. This is what "transcendence" means for Levinas: not merely a stubborn inaccessibility to ontology, but more importantly, "A turning around by which the Desirable escapes Desire. The goodness of the Good . . . inclines the movement it calls forth to turn it away from the Good and orient it toward the other, and only thus toward the Good."[67] Might such an "inextricability" of the other and the Other be the ethical outcome of Dionysius' spotless mirrors?

It might and it might not. But Derrida at least entertains the idea. Noting that the apophatic voice "multiplies itself: it says one thing and its contrary,"[68] Derrida writes "Sauf le nom: Post-Scriptum" as a dialogue between two of him. One voice begins by saying that *The Mystical Theology* has a double-addressee: "Dionysius the Areopagite . . . articulates a certain prayer, turned toward God; he links it with an address to the disciple, more precisely to the becoming-disciple of him who is thus called to hear." What this means is that the apophatic address binds the soul to God through other people—specifically, through Timothy and Dionysius' (properly initiated) readers. The first voice continues, "An apostrophe (to God) is turned toward another apostrophe in the direction of him . . . ," at which point his alter-ego interrupts, "—Never of her."[69] No; never of her. As the *Ecclesiastical Hierarchy* warns, "Let your sharing of the sacred befit the sacred things: Let it be by way of sacred enlightenment for sacred men only."[70] This is a significant delimitation. It is nevertheless important to note that Derrida locates in the apophatic apostrophe a relation that is at once vertical and horizontal. Much like the redirection of the Levinasian Good, "This conversation turns (itself) toward the other in order to turn (it) toward God, without there being an order to these two movements that are in truth the same, without one or the other being circumvented or diverted."[71] And so, even in the seemingly churchless, unchristological *Mystical Theology*,[72] there is no way up to God except out through (male) others. Levinasians and social gospelers alike might be tempted at this point to overlook the misogyny as an unavoidable cultural remnant, open the sphere of addressees across lines of sex and gender, and proclaim the thoroughly ethical nature of Dionysius' theology. Except—and this is where Derrida always pulls back from Dionysius—except for the repeated insistence that divine things only be shared within an exceedingly limited circle of friends.

"But see to it that none of this comes to the hearing of the uninitiated," Dionysius admonishes Timothy.[73] In *The Mystical Theology*, this unworthy throng is divided into just two types of people: ontotheologians ("those . . . who imagine there is nothing beyond instances of individual being and who think that by their own intellectual resources they can have direct knowledge of him who has made the shadows his hiding place") and idolators ("those others . . . who describe the transcendent Cause of all things in terms derived from the lowest orders of being").[74] In *The Ecclesiastical Hierarchy*, however, the ranks of the undesirable multiply considerably. During the mass, it is the unfortunate lot of the deacons to rid the church of those who are not suited for Holy Communion, including the possessed, the uninitiated, the incompletely initiated, the previously-initiated-but-now-degenerate, the intemperate, the intemperate-yet-resolved-not-to-be-intemperate, and finally, "those who . . . are neither completely unblemished nor completely unstained."[75] (One wonders if there would be anyone left!) There are similar warnings in *The Divine Names* and *The Celestial Hierarchy*, where half of the function of Scriptural imagery is to ensure "that the sacred and hidden truth about the celestial intelligences . . . be inaccessible to the *hoi polloi*. Not everyone is sacred and, as scripture says, knowledge is not for everyone."[76]

But surely, one might ask, mindful of Matthew 25, surely the things of God *ought* to be for everyone? In particular, for the lowest and hungriest and poorest of all?[77] Did the Nazarene reject the possessed and blemished? Did the Sermon on the Mount not suggest that the *hoi polloi* are beloved of God? I imagine that Dionysius would respond by suggesting that the possessed and blemished masses be initiated and purified. I should clarify: this would be Dionysius in a particularly expansive mood; for while the bulk of his writing is not nearly so universalizing, he does make a few significant gestures toward such a possibility. For example, he attributes to bishops the Pauline desire for "all men to be saved and to come to the knowledge of the truth."[78] Because the bishop images the divine so clearly, he "pours out on everyone the shining beams of his inspired teaching . . . ready to give light to whoever approaches . . . He displays neither a grudge nor profane anger over previous apostasy and transgressions."[79] While it is clear, then, that different people occupy different stages along the Dionysian way, it seems at times that that way is open to all. The deacons purify the catechumens so that the priests might illuminate them and the bishop might perfect them. Every man, it seems, can *eventually* be led "to embark upon the illuminated contemplation of and communion with the most lustrous sacramental rites."[80] Most democratically of all, despite Dionysius' repeated attempts to ward off the *hoi polloi* through spoken warnings, he is, after all, *writing*—disseminating the holiest of holies utterly indiscriminately to God knows who.

On the one hand, then, Dionysius is almost obsessively worried about contamination; on the other hand, he opens the door to "whoever approaches." "Two concurrent desires divide apophatic theology," Derrida explains: "The desire to be inclusive of all, thus understood by all (community, *koine*) and the desire to keep or entrust the secret within the very strict limits of those who hear/understand it right, as secret, and are then capable or worthy of keeping it."[81] So the political vision that emerges from the work of Dionysius is either radically elitist or radically welcoming, which means it becomes important to choose one's interpretations carefully.

Yet even if one were inclined to follow the "whoever approaches" line as far as it goes in Dionysius, one would run up against the problem of the *approach*. To the extent that any and every other is welcome in Dionysius, he is welcome not only insofar as he is a he, but also insofar as he undertakes a specific—one might say prefabricated—journey: from purification to illumination to perfection; from baptism to Eucharist to chrism. At the risk of stating the obvious, those who would prefer not to follow the Christian *via* are therefore excluded from the outset; the welcome is significantly qualified. But the problem of the path is broader than the concerns of liberal ecumenism. As Derrida teaches us, a determinate path, by definition, closes off any relation to the indeterminate. This is a significant concern, considering the apophatic God's transcendence of all determinations. If the *via negativa* knows where it is going and how to get there, is its unknown God truly unknown?

By now, it should be clear that Derrida's critique of teleology stems neither from intellectual snobbery nor from a "postmodern" commitment to "play." Rather, it is attuned to the violent and exclusionary politics of certainty. The moment I know who the Messiah is and when he is coming, I know who is in the kingdom and who is out—and will behave accordingly. This is the reason Derrida tries to imagine a messianic opening "with no way out or any assured path, without itinerary or point of arrival, without an exterior with a predictable map and a *calculable* programme . . . The emergence of the event ought to puncture every horizon of expectation."[82]

Is there a "horizon of expectation" in Dionysius? Well . . . there is and there is not. On the one hand, there is an incontrovertible order to the sacraments (and the clergy and the laity), mirroring the incontrovertible order of the cosmos. On the other hand, this cosmos refuses to stand still—circling, diving down, and spiraling in all directions. On the one hand, the *via negativa* begins with assertions (from first to last) and then moves onto denials (from last to first): "So this is what we say," Dionysius instructs us, as if it were a formula.[83] On the other hand, this determinate path down and up the hierarchies culminates in a negation of the path itself: in silence. On the one hand, the apophatic subject knows it comes from God and knows it is headed to God. On the other hand, the road to God leaves it emptied of any idea of what or where it or God might "be." On the one hand, the highest things most fully image God, while the lowest do so with limitations.[84] On the other hand, the most "inadequate and ridiculous" names are "more suitable for lifting our minds up into the domain of the spiritual than similarities are."[85] So although a man is hierarchically "nearer" to God than a worm (or a woman), this "lowliest and most incongruous of all" is more likely to point the soul to God.[86] And so even hierarchy, determinacy, and certainty unsay themselves.

A popular joke in Derridean circles is set in a temple on the highest of holy days. "On Yom Kippur," the story goes, "the rabbi stops in the middle of the service, prostrates himself beside the bema, and cries out, 'Oh, God. Before You, I am nothing!' Saul Rosenberg, president of the temple, is so moved by this demonstration of piety that he immediately throws himself to the floor beside the rabbi and cries, 'Oh, God! Before You, I am nothing!' Then Chaim

Pitkin, a tailor, jumps from his seat, prostrates himself in the aisle and cries, 'Oh God! Before You, I am nothing!' Rosenberg nudges the rabbi and whispers, 'So look who thinks he's nothing.'"[87]

It is a profound contradiction in the works of Dionysius that the soul must prove itself worthy of realizing it is nothing. Not just anybody can know nothing, and not just anybody can become nobody. To the extent that deconstruction can be said to "receive" Dionysius, then, it receives him with the most respectful kind of critique: by reading him through, and against, himself. For if it is the case that the order of things is a creative disorder, that the path obliterates the path, and that the lowest is most highly reflective of God, then we have in Dionysius a theo-ethic that unsettles the very hierarchy and teleology it posits. It would therefore be the task of any anti-ontotheological retrieval of Dionysius to hold him to his own word(s). "Knowing beyond the mind by knowing nothing," apophatic voyagers could not distinguish worthy from unworthy; high from low; or pure from impure. Or, for that matter, the Messiah herself from the hungry we feed, the naked we clothe, and the stranger we welcome.

NOTES

1   Jacques Derrida, "Différance," trans. Alan Bass, in Margins of Philosophy (Chicago, IL: University of Chicago Press, 1982), pp. 8–9.
2   MT, 1.2, 100B.
3   MT, 1.1, 997A.
4   Derrida, "Différance," p. 6.
5   Ibid.
6   "The Original Discussion of Différance," in David Wood and Robert Bernasconi (eds), Derrida and Différance (Evanston, IL: Northwestern University Press, 1985), p. 84.
7   Derrida, "How to Avoid Speaking: Denials," trans. Ken Frieden, in Harold Coward and Toby Foshay (eds), Derrida and Negative Theology (Albany, NY: State University of New York Press, 1992), p. 74.
8   Ibid., p. 74.
9   Ibid., p. 88.
10 Ibid., p. 77.
11 Ibid.
12 John Caputo, The Prayers and Tears of Jacques Derrida: Religion without Religion (Bloomington, IN: Indiana University Press, 1997), p. 34.
13 Cf. Moses's ascent in MT, 1.3, 1000C-D.
14 Derrida acknowledges Jean-Luc Marion's claim that it is "vulgar" to align ecclesiastical hierarchies with modern political hierarchies, but adds that at the same time, "it is also necessary to see ... the historic, essential, undeniable, and irreducible possibility of the aforementioned perversity which is perhaps only considerable by first having been observable, as one says, 'in fact'" (Derrida, "How to Avoid Speaking," p. 134, n. 9).
15 DN, 4.14, 712D.
16 Derrida, "How to Avoid Speaking," p. 79.
17 Ibid., p. 108.
18 Derrida's most thorough (non-)discussion of his own work in relation to Dionysius' can be found in "How to Avoid Speaking." See also his reconsideration of this question in relation to the work of Angelus Silesius in "Sauf le nom: Post-Scriptum," trans. John P. Leavey, Jr., in Thomas Dutoit (ed), On the Name (Stanford, CA: Stanford University Press, 1993), pp. 35–85.
     Secondary studies of Derrida in conversation with Dionysius include: Kevin Hart, The

Trespass of the Sign: Deconstruction, Theology, and Philosophy (Cambridge: Cambridge University Press, 1989); John Caputo, *The Prayers and Tears of Jacques Derrida* (Bloomington, IN: Indiana University Press, 1997); Denys Turner, "The Art of Unknowing: Negative Theology in Late Medieval Mysticism," *Modern Theology*, 14/4 (October 1998), pp. 473–488; Thomas A. Carlson, *Indiscretion: Finitude and the Naming of God* (Chicago, IL: University of Chicago Press, 1999); Jean-Luc Marion, "In the Name: How to Avoid Speaking of 'Negative Theology,'" in John D. Caputo and Michael J. Scanlon (eds), *God, the Gift, and Postmodernism* (Indianapolis, IN: Indiana University Press, 1999), pp. 20–42; idem., *The Idol and Distance: Five Studies*, trans. Thomas A. Carlson (New York, NY: Fordham University Press, 2001); and Mary-Jane Rubenstein, "Unknow Thyself: Apophaticism, Deconstruction, and Theology after Ontotheology," *Modern Theology*, 19/3 (July 2003), pp. 387–417.

Broader studies of deconstruction, the anti-ontotheological gesture, and negative theology include Thomas J. J. Altizer, et al. (eds), *Deconstruction and Theology* (New York, NY: Crossroad Publishing Company, 1982); John Dominic Crossan, "Difference and Divinity," *Semeia*, 23 (1982), pp. 29–41; Mark C. Taylor, *Erring: A Postmodern A/theology* (Chicago, IL: University of Chicago Press, 1983); Harold Coward and Toby Foshay (eds), *Derrida and Negative Theology* (Albany, NY: State University of New York Press, 1992); John Milbank, *The Word Made Strange* (London: Blackwell, 1997), pp. 36–52; Ian Almond, "How *Not* To Deconstruct a Dominican: Derrida on God and 'Hypertruth,'" *Journal of the American Academy of Religion*, 68/2 (2000), pp. 329–44; Arthur Bradley, "God *Sans* Being: Derrida, Marion, and 'A Paradoxical Writing of the Word Without,'" *Literature and Theology*, 14/3 (2000), pp. 299–312; Ilse N. Bulhof and Laurens ten Kate (eds), *Flight of the Gods: Philosophical Perspectives on Negative Theology* (New York, NY: Fordham University Press, 2000); Merold Westphal, *Overcoming Onto-theology: Toward a Postmodern Christian Faith* (New York, NY: Fordham University Press, 2001); Jeffrey W. Robbins, "The Problem of Ontotheology: Complicating the Divide Between Philosophy and Theology," *Heythrop Journal*, 43 (2002), pp. 139–151; Björn Thorsteinsson, "Possibilities of the Impossible: Derrida's Idea of Justice and Negative Theology," *Svensk teologisk kvartalskrift*, 78/3 (2002), pp. 121–31; Jeffrey Bloechl (ed), *Religious Experience and the End of Metaphysics* (Bloomington, IN: Indiana University Press, 2003); Denys Turner, "Atheism, Apophaticism and 'Différance,'" in J. Haers and P. De Mey (eds), *Theology and Conversation: Toward a Relational Theology* (Leuven: Leuven University Press, 2003), pp. 689–708; Martin Laird, "The 'Open Country Whose Name is Prayer': Apophasis, Deconstruction, and Contemplative Practice," *Modern Theology*, 21/1 (January 2005), pp 141–155.

19 Immanuel Kant, *The Critique of Pure Reason*, trans. Paul Guyer and Allen W. Wood (Cambridge: Cambridge University Press, 1998), A632/B660, p. 584.
20 See *Ibid.*, A583/B661-A642-B670, pp. 559–589.
21 *Ibid.*, BXXX, p. 117.
22 Immanuel Kant, *Critique of Practical Reason*, trans. Werner S. Pluhar (Indianapolis, IN: Hackett Publishing Company, 2002), esp. 2.2.4-2.2.5, pp. 155–170.
23 Immanuel Kant, *Religion within the Limits of Reason Alone*, trans. Theodore M. Greene and Hoyt H. Hudson (New York, NY: Harper & Row, 1960), 3.1.3, p. 90.
24 See Martin Heidegger, "The Way Back into the Ground of Metaphysics," trans. Walter Kaufmann in Kaufmann (ed), *Existentialism from Dostoevsky to Sartre* (New York, NY: Meridian Books, 1956), p. 218.
25 See Heidegger, "Way Back," p. 207.
26 Martin Heidegger, *Identity and Difference*, trans. Joan Stambaugh (Chicago, IL: University of Chicago Press, 2002), pp. 62ff.
27 *Ibid.*, p. 72.
28 *Ibid.*, p. 56.
29 Cited in Derrida, "How to Avoid Speaking," pp. 126–127. By insisting upon the non-identity between being and God, Derrida wonders, is Heidegger perhaps un-saying a particularly calcified name of God, in apophatic service of a more authentic revelation of God? Yes. No. "With and without the word *being*, he wrote a theology with and without God" (p. 128).
30 See Derrida's attempt to dissociate *khora* from being and the *es gibt* in "How to Avoid Speaking," pp. 106–107.
31 Derrida, "*Différance*," p. 3.

210   Mary-Jane Rubenstein

32   See Derrida's discussion of Abrahamic secrecy in relation to Bartleby the Scrivener's "I would prefer not to" in Derrida, *The Gift of Death*, trans. David Wills (Chicago, IL: University of Chicago Press, 1995), pp. 74–75.
33   Derrida, *"Différance,"* p. 4.
34   See Rubenstein, "Unknow Thyself," p. 403.
35   *DN*, 2.10, 648C; 2.4, 641A; *MT*, 5, 1048A.
36   *DN*, 4.13, 712A-B.
37   *Ibid.*
38   *MT*, 1.1, 997B-1000A.
39   *DN*, 3.1, 680B.
40   Derrida, *"Différance,"* p. 21.
41   On hospitality, see Derrida, *Of Hospitality: Anne Dufourmantelle Invites Jacques Derrida to Respond*, trans. Rachel Bowlby (Stanford, CA: Stanford University Press, 2000); on democracy, see idem., *Specters of Marx: The State of the Debt, the Work of Mourning, and the New International*, trans. Peggy Kamuf (New York and London: Routledge, 1994), p. 87; on the undecidable decision, see idem., "Afterword: Toward an Ethic of Discussion," trans. Samuel Weber, in *Limited Inc.* (Evanston, IL: Northwestern University Press, 1997), p. 116; and on the "undeconstructability" of justice, see idem., "Force of Law: The 'Mystical Foundation of Authority,'" trans. Mary Quaintance, in Gil Anidjar (ed), *Acts of Religion* (New York and London: Routledge, 2002), p. 243.
42   Derrida, "Sauf le nom," p. 43.
43   See Derrida, "Faith and Knowledge: The Two Sources of 'Religion' at the Limits of Reason Alone," trans. Samuel Weber, in Anidjar (ed), *Acts of Religion*, p. 56.
44   Caputo, *Prayers and Tears*, p. xxiv. Later on in the book, despite numerous reiterations of this separation (pp. xxvii, 28, 336–337), Caputo articulates deconstruction as "a certain negative propheticism, a negative or apophatic messianic, whose most vivid and perfect illustration or exemplification (or repetition) is to be found in the biblical, prophetic notion of justice, so long as we add the little proviso which throws everything into undecidability" (p. 196). This project is deeply indebted to his insight.
45   *Letter 8*, p. 3, 1092C-D; emphasis added.
46   Derrida, *"Différance,"* p. 22.
47   Derrida, "How to Avoid Speaking," p. 79.
48   Derrida, "Faith and Knowledge," p. 47.
49   Derrida, *"Différance,"* p. 7.
50   *CH*, 3.1, 164D.
51   See Bernard McGinn, *The Foundations of Mysticism: Origins to the Fifth Century* (New York, NY: Crossroad Publishing Company, 1994), p. 164. It should be emphasized that although the hierarchies "approximate," and even "reflect," "image," and "mirror" the triune God (*CH* 3.1-2, 164D-165D), this does not mean that the three persons of the Trinity exist in hierarchical relationship to one another; Dionysius held the full equality and equiprimordiality of the Father, Son, and Holy Spirit. This means, furthermore, that the persons cannot be mapped onto created hierarchies (it is *not* the case, for example, that bishops are like the Father, while clergy imitate the Son, and deacons serve as created functionaries of the Spirit).
52   These are: Seraphim, Cherubim, Thrones; Dominions, Virtues, Powers; Principalities, Archangels, and Angels (*CH*, 160-1).
53   See McGinn, *Foundations*, p. 174.
54   *Letter 8*, 4, 1093C.
55   See note 51.
56   *DN*, 4.8, 704D.
57   Eric Perl, "Hierarchy and Participation in Dionysius the Areopagite and Greek Neoplatonism," *American Catholic Philosophical Quarterly*, 68 (1994), p. 19.
58   *Ibid.*, p. 23.
59   *Ibid.*, p. 19.
60   Hieromonk Alexander Golitzin, "The Mysticism of Dionysius Areopagita: Platonist or Christian?" *Mystics Quarterly*, 19 (1993), pp. 98–114.
61   *DN*, 4.13, 712B.
62   *CH*, 3.2, 165A.
63   *Ibid.*

64 *DN*, 4.7, 704C.
65 Kevin Corrigan, " 'Solitary' Mysticism in Plotinus, Proclus, Gregory of Nyssa, and Pseudo-Dionysius," *The Journal of Religion*, 76/1 (1996), p. 28. In this essay, Corrigan argues that, insofar as the relationship between the apophatic self and its God is constituted by *mutual* desire, it disrupts the presumed inviolability of the apophatic subject. He goes on to argue the same of the Plotinian "Alone to the Alone" (p. 32). Corrigan does not, however, mention relations between and among creatures.
66 Thomas Carlson, *Indiscretion: Finitude and the Naming of God* (Chicago, IL: University of Chicago Press, 1999), p. 167.
67 Emmanuel Levinas, "God and Philosophy," trans. Bettina Bergo, in *Of God Who Comes to Mind* (Stanford, CA: Stanford University Press, 1998), p. 69.
68 Derrida, "Sauf," p. 35.
69 *Ibid.*, p. 38.
70 *EH*, 1.1, 372A.
71 Derrida, "Sauf," p. 38.
72 For an account of these views, as well as a careful interarticulation of the mystical, ecclesiastical, and Christological throughout the works of Dionysius, see Bernard McGinn, *Foundations*, especially pp. 170–181.
73 *MT*, 1.2, 1000A.
74 *Ibid.*, 1000A-B.
75 *EH*, 3.3.7, 436A-B.
76 *CH*, 2.2, 140B; Cf. *EH*, 1.4, 376C. The other half, of course, is to raise souls up to God.
77 "Truly I say to you, as you did it to one of the least of these my brethren, you did it to me" (Matthew 25:40).
78 *EH*, 2.2.1, 393A; cf. 1 Timothy 2:4.
79 *EH*, 2.3.3, 400B.
80 *Ibid.*, 6.1.1, 532A-B.
81 Derrida, "Sauf," p. 83.
82 Derrida, "Faith and Knowledge," p. 47.
83 *MT*, 4.1, 1040D.
84 See *Letter 8*, p. 2, 1092B.
85 *CH*, 2.3, 141A.
86 *Ibid.*, 2.5, 145A.
87 This joke, illustrating the irony of "Derridean circles" themselves, was told at a memorial service for Derrida at Columbia University in the fall of 2004. The version cited here can be found at: http://www.jewishsightseeing.com/jewish_humor/punchlines_and_their_jokes/2006-06-01-Number%2054.htm.

14

DIONYSIUS IN HANS URS VON BALTHASAR AND JEAN-LUC MARION

TAMSIN JONES

Amidst the debate surrounding the incontestable "turn to religion" in recent French philosophy, negative theology is, in the words of Arthur Bradley, "one of the key sites of engagement—in the double sense of *both* commitment *and* confrontation".[1] The engagement with this tradition usually gets further refined into a debate over different readings of the "negative theology" of Dionysius in relation to various understandings of the "deconstruction" of Jacques Derrida. Much ink has been spilled in this confrontation: is deconstruction simply the latest incarnation of negative theology and Dionysius an early sixth-century "Derridean,"[2] or must a stark line be drawn between the two in order to safeguard the originality of the postmodern shibboleth?[3] Despite the wealth of writing on the subject, this debate remains curiously stunted. Concerns about "ontotheology" and "metaphysics of presence" operate as the arbitrating standards by which Dionysius must be evaluated. In other words, advocates from either side start from the same set of premises, those of Derrida. Consequently, the retrieval of Dionysius functions rhetorically as a whetstone against which Derridean deconstruction can sharpen itself while analysis of the pseudonymous texts is inevitably dulled.[4]

Jean-Luc Marion casts a broader net, retrieving more than merely the linguistic or epistemological implications of Dionysius' thought. He draws upon several central themes in the *CD*: the simultaneity of divine "manifestation and concealment"; the notion of "distance" as that which is sustaining of, and sustained in, the relationship between God and creation; and the *eros* which drives this relationship. Further, Marion properly situates Dionysius

Tamsin Jones
Committee on the Study of Religion, Harvard University, Barker Center, Cambridge, MA 02138, USA
tamsin_jones@harvard.edu

within a liturgical context and clarifies the anthropological implications of his apophaticism in order to emphasize that it entails an existential stance of the human person vis-à-vis the divine.

Thus, Marion advances the contemporary conversation with Dionysius significantly. I shall argue, however, that his retrieval does not remain free from the complications of certain rhetorical or apologetic interests. Before evaluating Marion's interpretation of Dionysian thought, I will examine one of its primary influences, that of Hans Urs von Balthasar. By comparing the retrieval of Dionysius by both Marion and Balthasar, certain allegiances (philosophical and theological) and assumed audiences (phenomenological and ecclesial) emerge as unspoken influences that determine which elements of the *CD* are retrieved and which are overlooked.

Hans Urs von Balthasar and the patristic revival in France

The 1930s (and onward) witnessed a revival in interest in patristic literature and theology in France. Led by Henri de Lubac and his students, most notably Jean Daniélou, intensive textual study and historical research was given over to a general retrieval of the "Fathers"[5] for twentieth-century French Catholicism. This included the formation of a collection of the *Sources chrétiennes* by de Lubac and Daniélou in 1940 as well as more "interpretative translation" projects which sought to render the Fathers accessible to a general Christian public.[6] Though Swiss himself, Balthasar was influenced by this patristic resurgence in France and became a significant contributor to it.

After wrestling for a time against the turgid rigours of neo-Scholasticism, Balthasar found "an *entirely new* style of theological thinking" opened up for him through de Lubac's work on the Fathers. Balthasar found in the Fathers, not a series of doctrinal points to be defended, but rather "models for carrying on the work of theology in his own world".[7] Balthasar's interest in Dionysius, specifically, stems from an attraction to his "clerical style" in which the rich gifts of creation and of liturgy might be treated as *icons* of deeper spiritual truths.

This reading emerges out of Balthasar's desire to distinguish early "Christian" thought from its neo-platonic counterpart in the ancient world. In "A Résumé of my Thought" Balthasar clarifies his understanding of the essential difference between the "God of the philosophers" and the "God of the Bible": only in the latter does "God appear". Only "Being himself, revealing himself from himself" could give the "true response" to philosophy.[8] This is the basis of the theological aesthetic that he finds articulated first in Dionysius. Balthasar takes the entire theology of the *CD* to be "a single, sacred liturgical act" which "seeks to echo the form of the divine revelation".[9]

This theological aesthetic is grounded in a play of "manifestation and concealment"; its basis is the possibility that "the radiance of God's glory penetrate[s] the darkness of the world".[10] Balthasar summarizes: "This whole spiritual and yet visible order is, as is said eloquently and ever again, the cosmic beauty, in which the thearchic, surpassing beauty is manifest".[11] The world in its entirety is taken as a sacrament: it reveals God while remaining other than God. From this Balthasar arrives at "the key for unlocking the treasury of the Fathers . . . the tool for all his interpretative analysis": the *analogia entis*.[12] The use of this concept by Balthasar (so significant also for Marion) needs clarification; the *analogia entis* gives as much weight to the dis-similarity between the world and its creator as it does to its relation. Only the *analogia* can guarantee both the transcendence of God and the autonomy of the world, whilst ensuring a saturation of divine presence throughout the cosmos. Balthasar locates this idea in Dionysius' treatise on *The Divine Names* in which the creation of the world is identical to God's self-communication. Balthasar glosses the main thesis of *Divine Names* thus: "God's 'becoming the world' can be described only if it is understood that the immutable one, exalted and transcendent over all, is the one who, in different degrees of intensity, gives to the realms of creation a share in himself while safeguarding the immanent order of all things".[13] As such God is (and is seen) in every thing and in no thing (*The Divine Names* 596C).

From this dialectic of "manifestation and concealment" there emerges the necessary dialectic between affirmative and negative theologies in Dionysius. Both *kataphasis* and *apophasis* speak of God's presence in and, simultaneous transcendence of, God's creation. However, Balthasar makes the claim (crucial for Marion) that Dionysius needs to go beyond a strict dualistic movement between affirmation and negation to a "third step", to the "hymn" as a response of praise.

The mode of praise, the "hymnic," is not merely a third moment in Dionysius' thought. Instead, it functions as the fundamental "methodology of theological thinking and speaking". Indeed, since theology "is exhausted in the act of wondering adoration before the unsearchable beauty in every manifestation," its most proper mode of speech is praise.[14] Thus Balthasar writes that in Dionysian theology "where it is a matter of God and the divine, the word *hymnein* almost replaces the word 'to say'".[15] By claiming the hymnic to be a "methodological" choice for Dionysius, Balthasar argues that the form of the *CD* is just as important, if not more so, than its content. The poetic, "hymnic" resonance to the corpus is not about predicating or defining God. Rather it is the most *appropriate* mode of speech to approach the divine and its self-manifestation because the language reflects the beauty of the manifestation: "Such language . . . is meant to reveal the symmetry, the appropriateness to its object; it is in its way a much more exact expression of the vision of the divinity of God than most of what a theology that works by definitions can say about God".[16]

As we have seen, Balthasar finds in Dionysius a whole new approach to theology, a theological aesthetics more fitting to reflect its subject, the glory of revelation. There are two different backdrops to this retrieval. The first is

Balthasar's desire to articulate a method of doing theology that escapes the dry logic of neo-Scholasticism. The second is a more specific debate on the relation between nature and grace in Catholic thought. Balthasar agrees with his teacher, de Lubac, that between the natural and supernatural there can be no strict delineation. By Balthasar's time, this discussion gets posed around his debate with Karl Barth over the status of the *analogia entis*.[17] Again, Balthasar will stress a continuity between God and the world as a result of God's own creation and self-communication; thus one cannot cleanly separate "nature" from "grace". Both of these debates influence his reading of Dionysius and his emphasis on a "theological aesthetics" which reflects God's glory without threatening its transcendence.

How has Balthasar's reading of Dionysius been received? "Balthasar read the Fathers as he read a stunningly broad range of literature, from ancient Greece to modern Europe: avidly, intelligently, selectively, with deep intuition, and with his own distinctive sense of what was significant".[18] The mixture of admiration and uneasiness in Brian Daley's appraisal is representative of the ambivalence with which many patristic scholars and theologians respond to Balthasar. Balthasar's interpretation of Dionysius, as sketched above, fits into an overall pattern of his apologetic retrieval and use of the Fathers. That is to say, it represents close textual work which, nevertheless, always occurs against the backdrop of contemporary conversations in which Balthasar is engaged. In this vein, Balthasar's primary motive in "listening to the Fathers" is to learn how to *translate* (and not simply *replicate*) them into something of value for his own intellectual context.[19] Those unsatisfied with his approach most often accuse Balthasar of "eclecticism" and also a certain "ahistoricism".[20] Regardless of how one appraises this approach, it is indisputable that Balthasar interprets and utilizes the Fathers, including Dionysius, as authoritative resources for his own time to respond to contemporary concerns.

Balthasar's Influence on Marion

Less a patristic specialist than an avid patristic apologist, Marion is far more Balthasar's heir and student than Daniélou's.[21] This inheritance is duly noted by Marion on more than one occasion.[22] He explicitly credits Balthasar as the inspiration of his own approach to retrieving the Fathers.[23] Indeed, this connection is made in the context of Marion's own defence of his method of retrieval which, he readily admits, some might accuse of being irresponsible because not "authorized" by the reigning secondary sources. Marion defends the strength of this approach without much apology: "Perhaps the most direct possible approach to them—I do not mean the most naïve—alone allows me not to lower them to the level of a text to be explicated or of a thesis to be decided".[24] In other words, Marion shares the conviction with Balthasar that one can (and should) "listen" to these historically distant sources. Marion's purpose is not to "explicate" Dionysius, but to allow him "to instruct us".[25]

Aside from this basic methodological approach, Marion adopts (and adapts) certain specific points of Balthasar's interpretation of Dionysius: specifically, a) the starting point of revelation and the dynamic of a theological aesthetics, b) the replacement of predicative discourse with the pragmatic speech of "hymning", and c) a notion of "distance" which ensures relationality.

First, like Balthasar, Marion insists that one must always start from "God's unconditional *self*-revelation" and turns to Dionysius for an authoritative exemplar of this approach.[26] This self-revelation results in the paradox that God both appears and remains invisible simultaneously. Again this is a notion which Marion takes directly from Balthasar's analysis of Dionysius and adapts to suit his phenomenology. For instance, in the following passage from Balthasar, one can unearth an important seed of Marion's distinction between the idol and the icon:

> If the beholder is blinded, the fault lies not with the light, which gives itself in a bounty innocent of envy, but with the beholder, who has not kept to the proper relation set down for him. The divine light raises to contemplation of itself and to contact with it all those 'who eagerly desire it in a way permitted, suitable to such sacred things, and do not insolently presume to something more exalted than the divine manifestation thus harmoniously offered them, nor because of a weakness for what is worse slip downwards' [DN 1.2, 588D-589A].[27]

Marion's distinction between an "idol," the visibility of which is measured by the capacity of the viewer, and an "icon" which measures "us," and in so doing, invites us into its gaze, resonates with Balthasar's interpretation of Dionysius.[28] Both stress the danger of grasping at more than one can hope to attain and warn against such "insolent presumptions".

Secondly, both Marion and Balthasar cull from Dionysius an emphasis on the "hymn" as a form of theological discourse superior to predication. There is a necessary "third step" (Balthasar) or "third way" (Marion) which, both agree, is "not a cognitive method". Rather, the "hymnic," as a mode of praise, more closely reflects and responds to the beauty of revelation. According to Balthasar, the "hymnic" functions as the fundamental "methodology of theological thinking and speaking" because all of theology is nothing more than a "glorious celebration of the divine mysteries" following the archetype of "liturgical songs of heaven".[29] Such a methodological approach offers Balthasar an attractive alternative to that of neo-Scholasticism. A few years later, involved in a very different debate, Marion also finds the notion of the "third way" helpful.

By presenting Dionysius as offering a "*third* way," Marion negotiates a path outside of the endless discussion over whether or not Dionysius' "negation of negation" is finally positive or negative, whether the term "hyper-essential" designates a positive or negative reality,[30] and finally whether or not Dionysius holds out a "promise" of some super-union or super-knowledge of God attained through the *via negativa*. *Dénomination*—Marion's neologism for the "third way"—overcomes the duel between affirmation and negation by transgressing both together. Marion writes,

> the third way is played out beyond the oppositions between affirmation and negation, synthesis and separation in short between the true and the false. Strictly speaking, if thesis and negation have in common that they speak the truth (and spurn the false), the way which transcends them should also transcend the true and the false. The third way would transgress nothing less than the two truth values, between which the entire logic of metaphysics is carried out.[31]

The implied accusation here is that by insisting upon this duality—the either/or choice between affirmation and negation (or a negation of negation which "really" equals a super-affirmation)—Derrida also remains stuck in "the logic of metaphysics".

Although both Balthasar and Marion agree that the "hymnic" as the "third way" escapes the static dualism of kataphatic and apophatic approaches to theology, they will, nevertheless, disagree on what they think the hymnic can achieve theologically. Balthasar describes this third step as constituting a "proof that there is, beyond anything that a creature can either affirm or deny, only the objective superabundance of God".[32] Marion, on the other hand, distances himself from any language of "proof". The "hymn" serves the purely pragmatic function of addressing the divine or referring oneself to the divine without saying anything about the divine. The significant difference reflects the two different audiences addressed by either writer.[33]

A final notion which Marion takes from Balthasar and applies to his own interpretation of Dionysius is the concept of "distance". Distance is a complex and shifting idea in Marion. Its primary purpose, however, is to conceptualise the possibility of an infinite and eternal gap between God and God's creation which nonetheless enables relation between the two. As a "distance that safeguards" it is necessary to all relationships; as "alterity beyond opposition," it allows reference while resisting *absolute* reference.[34] One should resist conceptualising distance spatially; rather, as the spacing of creation and the spacing with enables relation, distance, in some sense *is* God—God's gracious gift of God's self.[35] Marion often configures distance as the *kenosis* of God—the withdrawal of God at the very heart of God's self-revelation.[36] The very withdrawal evokes a response of love and relationality: "If love reveals itself hermetically as distance (which is glossed by cause and goodness) in order to give itself, only love will be able to welcome it".[37] Again he is explicit about the Balthasarian influence.[38]

Given this overview and comparison of the similar and yet distinct inter-pretations of Dionysius by Balthasar and Marion, certain questions remain. How are these interpretations operating in contemporary conversations? What "politics of retrieval" undergird such deployments? We have already seen the way in which Balthasar's use of Dionysius is motivated by his desire to present a theological "style" which avoids, in his words, "the grumpy, super-organized, super-scholasticised Catholicism and the humourless, anguished Protestantism" of his day.[39] Balthasar takes the entire theology of the *CD* to be "a single, sacred liturgical act". Thus, to "the extent that liturgy is a human, ecclesial act which, as a response of praise and thanksgiving, seeks to echo the form of the divine revelation, the categories of the aesthetic and of art will play a decisive role in it".[40] Dionysius' theological aesthetic is, according to Balthasar, both "Christ-centred" and "Church-centred"—even an "aesthetic of Eucharistic adoration"—and, not unsurprisingly, prefigures precisely the theological vision which Balthasar is attempting to articulate in his multi-volume *Herrlichkeit*.

Similarly, in all of Marion's interpretations of Dionysius certain polemical postures lie barely beneath the surface. In *The Idol and Distance* Marion is explicitly attempting to articulate a notion of "distance" which is conceptu-ally distinct from Heidegger's notion of "ontological difference," Levinas' "other/Other," and Derrida's *"différance"*. In *God Without Being* his aim is to find an instance within the history of Christian thought which is *not* suscep-tible to Heidegger's critique of "ontotheology". To do so, Marion champions Dionysius over Thomas Aquinas.[41] Thus, in both works Marion is responding to a particular current in continental philosophy in which the "death of God" and the "end of metaphysics" are taken for granted.[42] Finally, in his essay, "In the Name: How to Avoid Speaking of Negative Theology," he is most con-sciously and publicly engaged in a debate with Jacques Derrida.[43] This polemical context—both of the original conference debate and Marion's subsequent reworking of the essay—leads Marion to emphasize the purely "pragmatic" quality of Dionysian discourse and seek to cleanse it of any "predicative" stain. In each case, polemic not only fuels Marion's particular reading of Dionysius, but also serves as explanation for the way in which Dionysius functions specifically as an authoritative resource with which Marion can respond.

One of the reasons I opened this chapter with the debate surrounding the relationship between negative theology and Derrida is that the politics of retrieving Dionysius are most starkly highlighted there. Where Derrida is heralded as introducing a freestanding linguistic strategy unallied (and thus unalloyed) with any particular religious tradition, Marion is accused of needing to "police the theological space around negative theology" in a way already determined by certain dogmatic presuppositions.[44] Specifically the charge against Marion is that he approaches "negative theology" assuming from the start a politically conservative "eucharistic hermeneutic" by whose standard all claims must be evaluated.

One might question the simplicity of this distinction. At the very least one must distinguish between an "early" and a "later" Marion. The latter, under the influence of his debate with Derrida, emphasizes the performative and pragmatic functions of discourse which refuse any *a priori* predetermination. There is, however, a more fundamental anomaly to this opposition: it presupposes that "negative theology" not only breaks through all dogmatic boundaries but also begins in a theologically non-determinate locus. Such a "negative theology," however, bears only the faintest resemblance to that of Dionysius. One cannot ignore the liturgical echoes throughout the corpus. Even if it is not ultimate, the liturgy reflects the divine glory in the present. The liturgy is understood, further, in relation to the ecclesial and celestial hierarchies. Dionysius' critique of the limits of language occurs within this context.

While Dionysius refuses to appoint *a* proper name to God, he still offers a vision of the role and use of language in relation to God's gift of creation and self-revelation. As Denys Turner argues in "Atheism, Apophaticism and 'Différance'," the guidelines for appropriate theological speech are determined by the order of creation: "God is equally 'other' than all these names, though they are not equally 'other' than God".[45] In other words, there is a hierarchical differentiation within negativity, and one cannot simply detach the cosmological and ecclesial hierarchies from Dionysius' understanding of language.

Balthasar highlights this paradoxical relationship. He argues that the relation between apophaticism and hierarchy is absolutely necessary to Dionysius' entire theological vision.

> If no one has emphasized so strongly as Denys the transcendence of God, nor has anyone upheld so decisively the givenness of the essential boundaries and hierarchical ordering of creation (because no one has thought through or applied so consistently the consequences of this apophaticism . . . The objective, hierarchical *taxis* (already we are moving towards the Byzantine and Carolingian world-order!) is the form of God's self-manifestation; the Church is the heart of the world and the earthly representation of the heavenly court; and any flight from the world is unthinkable, even for the most exalted mysticism.[46]

This relation between the apophatic and a hierarchical cosmology, moreover, has ecclesial consequences, according to Balthasar. Specifically, there is a "hierarchy of seeing" wherein priests and contemplatives "penetrate more deeply" than do "ordinary people" into the vision of God.[47] For this reason, in the earthly liturgy, perfection is demanded of the bishop "in his contemplation of the divine" just as his movements reflect the divine movement of procession and return.[48]

One might well be reminded, in these latter ecclesial pronouncements, of Marion's controversial remarks in *God Without Being*—that "only the bishop merits, in the full sense, the title of theologian".[49] However, perhaps in the face of the slew of challenges he received, Marion drops this suggestive argument. Indeed, by the time of Marion's debate with Derrida in Villanova he had abandoned almost all mention of both the ontological foundations and the ecclesial consequences of Dionysius' apophaticism. Such a relationship would likely be viewed not merely with suspicion but with explicit hostility in a postmodern context.[50] Marion's recognition of this fact causes him, precisely, to veer away from these implications in his later writings on Dionysius. Balthasar was decidedly less concerned with such implications. This difference between Balthasar and Marion reflects their different audiences. Balthasar is writing for the church within a decidedly Catholic context, whereas Marion is writing, at least explicitly, to scholars of phenomenology.

Conclusion

By drawing attention to some of the polemical and apologetic backdrops of Balthasar's and Marion's interpretations of Dionysius, I do not intend to denigrate their respective retrievals. Between the extremes of attempting to excavate an ancient text in its pristine entirety, on the one hand, and hijacking words from one context to another with total philological abandon, on the other, there are many levels of intervening possibility.

Marion, like Balthasar before him, is translating Dionysius once again for a new audience. The leap in translation that Marion attempts—not simply between far-removed historical contexts, but also between disciplinary and religious worlds—is one fraught with challenges and risk. Marion has a greater onus of responsibility to delineate consciously between his "explication" of Dionysius and his "translation" of him. Thus far, Marion has shown little interest in making such delineations. Nevertheless, he still gives us a richer, broader, and more complex confrontation with Dionysius than has previously been offered within the contemporary discussions of "negative theology".

If the "third way" is located in Dionysius in the verb "to hymn," then "praise" becomes a discursive alternative to predication in which one does not speak *about* the divine, but rather, orients oneself towards the divine. It indicates, thus, an existential place from which one stands and speaks vis-à-vis the divine, rather than providing information about the divine. In this way, Marion does not merely take from Dionysius an understanding of language and the inability of the signifier to ever signify more than other signifiers; more than this, he retrieves from Dionysius a sense of the boundaries of human existence in relation to a "distant" and yet "self-giving" God.

Marion is right, therefore, to insist that one ought not to talk about the "negative theology" of Dionysius, but of "mystical theology" instead. The

222   Tamsin Jones

mystical employs both apophatic and kataphatic strategies in its yearning for
the divine. Far from remaining bogged down in purely epistemological linguistic debates, Dionysius' mystical theology demands a far more multi-
layered view of reality and of the place of the human within it. For surely,
only such a fecund and complex vision could continue to give birth to this
amount of transformative debate.

NOTES

1 Arthur Bradley, *Negative Theology and Modern French Philosophy* (London: Routledge, 2004),
   p. 1.
2 See for instance, Bert Blans, "Cloud of Unknowing: An Orientation in Negative Theology
   from Dionysius the Areopagite, Eckhart, and John of the Cross to Modernity" in Ilse N.
   Bulhof and Laurens ten Kate (eds) *Flight of the Gods: Philosophical Perspectives on Negative
   Theology* (New York, NY: Fordham University Press, 2000), especially, p. 75; Daniel Bulzan,
   "Apophaticism, Postmodernism and Language: Two Similar Cases of Theological Imbalance," *Scottish Journal of Theology*, 50/3 (1997), pp. 261–287; Luke Ferreter, "How to Avoid
   Speaking of the Other: Derrida, Dionysius and the Problem of Negative Theology," *Para-
   graph*, 24/1 (2001), p. 50; Jeffrey Fischer, "The Theology of Dis/similarity: Negation in
   Pseudo-Dionysius," *The Journal of Religion*, 81/4 (2001), especially p. 530; Kevin Hart, *The
   Trespass of the Sign: Deconstruction, Theology and Philosophy* (New York, NY: Fordham Uni-
   versity Press, 2000), p. 183; Eric Perl, "Signifying Nothing: Being as Sign in Neoplatonism
   and Derrida" in R. Baine Harris (ed) *Neoplatonism and Contemporary Thought* Part Two
   (Albany, NY: State University of New York Press, 2002).
3 See for instance, John D. Caputo, *The Prayers and Tears of Jacques Derrida: Religion without
   Religion* (Bloomington, IN: Indiana University Press, 1997), pp. 1–19; David E. Klemm,
   "Open Secrets: Derrida and Negative Theology" in Robert Scharlemann (ed) *Derrida and
   Negative Theology* (Charlottesville, VA: University Press of Virginia, 1992), pp. 8–22, see
   especially, pp. 8–9; Mark C. Taylor, *nOTs* (Chicago, IL: Chicago University Press, 1993), pp.
   47–49; idem., "nO nOt nO" in *Derrida and Negative Theology*, pp. 188–189; Hent de Vries,
   "The Theology of the Sign and the Sign of Theology: The Apophatics of Deconstruction" in
   Flight of the Gods, especially, pp. 184–194.
4 Mary-Jane Rubenstein's chapter in this volume provides a remarkable exception to this
   general prejudice. See also Rubenstein, "Unknow Thyself: Apophaticism, Deconstruction,
   and Theology after Ontotheology" *Modern Theology*, 19/3 (2003), pp. 387–417. Similarly, one
   would do well to distinguish between "Derridean deconstruction" and Derrida himself, who
   offers a more complex relationship to Dionysius than his acolytes and critics often represent.
5 While aware of some of the problematic overtones in referring to some of the writers of the
   early Christian period as the "Fathers," for the purposes of this chapter I shall continue to
   do so primarily because these figures are very much the "Fathers of the Church"—authoritative figures of Catholic tradition central to the proper interpretation of the Gospel—for
   both Marion and Balthasar.
6 See Brian Daley, "Balthasar's Reading of the Church Fathers" in Edward T Oakes, S.J. and
   David Moss (eds) *The Cambridge Companion to Hans Urs von Balthasar* (Cambridge: Cambridge University Press, 2004), p. 193.
7 *Ibid.*, pp. 188–189.
8 Hans Urs von Balthasar, "A Résumé of my Thought" in David L Schindler (ed) *Hans Urs von
   Balthasar: His Life and Work* (San Francisco, CA: Ignatius Press, 1991), p. 2.
9 Hans Urs von Balthasar, *The Glory of the Lord: A Theological Aesthetics. Volume I: Seeing the
   Form*, trans. Erasmo Leiva-Merikakis (Edinburgh: T&T Clark, 1982), pp. 153–154.
10 See Deirdre Carabine, "The Fathers: The Church's Intimate, Youthful Diary" in Bede
   McGregor, O.P. and Thomas Norris (eds) *The Beauty of Christ: An Introduction to the Theology
   of Hans Urs von Balthasar* (Edinburgh: T&T Clark, 1994), p. 90.
11 Balthasar, *The Glory of the Lord: A Theological Aesthetics. Volume II: Studies in Theological Style:
   Clerical Styles*, (hereafter, *Glory of the Lord* II) trans. Erasmo Leiva-Merikakis (Edinburgh:
   T&T Clark, 1982), p. 202.

12 Edward T. Oakes, *Pattern of Redemption: The Theology of Hans Urs von Balthasar* (New York: Continuum, 1994), p. 114.
13 Balthasar, *Glory of the Lord* II, p. 158.
14 *Ibid.*, pp. 160, 170.
15 *Ibid.*, p. 173. Balthasar provides a footnote citing 108 occurrences of *hymnein* and its derivatives in the *CD*. He gives no further textual evidence and makes no further argument to this effect, however (as Marion will go on to do). Nevertheless, this statement underlies his entire interpretation of Dionysius as the quintessential, Christian aesthete.
16 *Ibid.*, p. 177.
17 Balthasar, *The Theology of Karl Barth* (New York, NY: Holt, Rinehart and Winston 1972), pp. 191–260.
18 Daley, "Balthasar's Reading of the Church Fathers," p. 201.
19 See Charles Kannengiesser, "Listening to the Fathers" in David L. Schindler (ed) *Hans Urs von Balthasar: His Life and Work* (San Francisco, CA: Ignatius Press, 1991); Louis Roberts, *The Theological Aesthetics of Hans Urs von Balthasar* (Washington, DC: Catholic University Press, 1987), p. 16.
20 Daley, "Balthasar's Reading of the Church Fathers," p. 202. Daley cites Dom Polycarp Sherwood's appraisal of Balthasar in this context as "audaciously creative," "disconcerting" and "transgressive" of normal bounds of scholarship (pp. 187, 188). Others, however, see this very apologetic quality as one of the strengths of Balthasar's use of the Fathers. For instance, Oakes evaluates the strength of Balthasar's approach which is aimed neither as high or as low as mere "historical clarification," but which issues from the perspective of contemporary questions in Christian life (Oakes, *Pattern of Redemption*, p. 127).
21 The relationship between Balthasar and Marion occupies a particular historical moment within an internal debate in twentieth-century Catholicism: the French journal, *Résurrection*, in which Marion published most of his early theological essays, was incorporated into the *Révue catholique internationale Communio*—the conservative counterpart to the Catholic journal, *Concilium*. Marion was to become one of the founding editors of the French edition of this journal at the behest of none other than Balthasar. For further discussion, see Robyn Horner, *Jean-Luc Marion: A Theo-logical Introduction* (Burlington, VT: Ashgate Publishing Company, 2005), p. 4; idem, *Rethinking God as God: Marion, Derrida and the Limits of Phenomenology* (New York, NY: Fordham University Press, 2001), pp. 175–176, 237.
22 This influence is found foremost in Marion's early theology work, *The Idol and Distance: Five Studies* (New York, NY: Fordham University Press, 2001). Marion offers his gratitude and indebtedness to Balthasar in the opening of the work: "To H. Urs von Balthasar my approach owes much, save the weaknesses in its implementation; the proportion of what is involved here nevertheless forbid me from transforming a dependency into an affiliation" (p. xxxviii).
23 See Marion, *The Idol and Distance*, p. 22, note 19: "The right that one can claim to have to submit certain thinkers to a theological approach escapes the danger of a trivial recuperation only if it goes hand in hand with *the conviction that a theological contribution can come to us from those same thinkers. That these two movements are not contradictory is certainly what I have learned from H. Urs von Balthasar . . .*" (emphasis added).
24 *Ibid.*, p. 22.
25 *Ibid.*, p. 23.
26 *Ibid.*, p. xv.
27 Balthasar, *Glory of the Lord* II, p. 171.
28 Marion, *God Without Being: Hors-Texte*, trans. Thomas A. Carlson (Chicago, IL: University of Chicago Press, 1991); originally published as *Dieu sans l'être: Hors-texte* (Paris: Librairie Arthème Fayard, 1982), pp. 17–22.
29 Balthasar, *Glory of the Lord* II, p. 160.
30 In *The Trespass of the Sign*, Kevin Hart argues that *"hyper"* is an essentially *negative* modifier (and Marion will agree with him), whereas Derrida will argue it is positive. See Hart, pp. 200–202.
31 Marion, *In Excess: Studies of Saturated Phenomena*, trans. Robyn Horner and Vincent Berraud (New York, NY: Fordham University Press, 2002), pp. 137–138.
32 Balthasar, *Glory of the Lord* II, p. 206.
33 In this connection, Marion cites Balthasar's observation that the verb *hymnein* replaces the verb "to say" in Dionysius. Marion provides more of an argument for the justification of this

observation than does Balthasar, providing further textual evidence as well as precedence within the *scholia* of Dionysius (*The Idol and Distance*, p. 184). Marion's provision of further evidence is, perhaps, in response to Derrida's critique of this move which makes much of the qualifier "almost" in Balthasar's observation: ". . . the word almost replaces the word 'to say'," (Derrida, "How to Avoid Speaking . . .", p. 111).

34 Horner, *A Theo-logical Introduction*, pp. 54, 56.
35 *Ibid.*, p. 57.
36 Marion, *The Idol and Distance*, p. 89. See also, p. xxxvii: "distance places the gift of Being at a distance from itself, as its icon".
37 *Ibid.*, p. 155.
38 *Ibid.*
39 Balthasar, cited in Carabine, p. 73.
40 Balthasar, *Glory of the Lord* II, pp. 153–154.
41 Marion has since revised this scapegoating of Thomas Aquinas in the face of a host of criticisms. See, "Saint Thomas d'Aquin et onto-théo-logie" in *Revue Thomiste* (1995); English translation in Michael Kessler and Christian Sheppard (eds) *Mystics: Presence and Aporia* (Chicago, IL: Chicago University Press, 2001). Interestingly, this article also appears as a sort of postscript in the second French edition of *Dieu sans l'être* (Paris: Presses Universitaires de France, 2002).
42 Jean-Luc Marion, *Being Given: Toward a Phenomenology of Givenness* trans. Jeffrey L. Kosky (Stanford, CA: Stanford University Press, 2002), p. x.
43 This debate culminates at the "Religion and Postmodernism" conference held at Villanova University in 1997 but began well in advance of this. Both *The Idol and Distance* and *God Without Being* were already written partly in response to Derrida's statements about "negative theology" in his seminal article, "*Différance*". Derrida then responded to Marion's critique in "Comment ne pas parler: Dénégations," in *Psyché: Inventions de l'autre* (Paris: Galilée, 1987) and also in *Sauf le nom* (Paris: Galilée, 1999), trans. John P. Leavey in (ed) Thomas Dutoit, *On the Name* (Stanford, CA: Stanford University Press, 1995), pp. 35–85. Marion's essay at the Villanova conference presupposes these previous written exchanges. See John D. Caputo and Michael J. Scanlon (eds) *God, the Gift and Postmodernism* (Bloomington, IN: Indiana University Press, 1999).
44 See Bradley, *Negative Theology and Modern French Philosophy*, p. 3.
45 Denys Turner, "Atheism, Apophaticism and 'Différance'" in J. Haers and P. De Mey (ed) *Theology and Conversation: Towards a Relational Theology* (Leuven: Leuven University Press, 2003), p. 692.
46 Balthasar, *Glory of the Lord* II, 166; see also, *ibid.*, p.173.
47 *Ibid.*, p. 169.
48 *Ibid.*, pp. 174–175.
49 Marion, *God Without Being*, p. 153.
50 Toby Foshay characterizes postmodernity's renewed interest in negative theology as a desire to explode limits and, specifically, negate hierarchies: "Formerly trapped within a statically hierarchial vision of the world and having won a costly freedom from a transcendentally determined world structure, our autonomy is most characteristically expressed in its capacity to exceed all centrally defined and anticipatable limits and boundaries" (*Derrida and Negative Theology*, p. 1). One might note the strong "Enlightenment" prejudices in this quotation. Derrida, himself, takes a more nuanced view of hierarchy (see, "How to Avoid Speaking . . .", p. 91).

INDEX

Printed and bound by CPI Group (UK) Ltd, Croydon, CR0 4YY

09/06/2025

14686120-0003